Praise for The Happy Agent

"In his remarkably ingenious book, Ross shares a collection of lessons that will sharpen your skills and set you on the right path in your real estate career. It is an impressive resource that helps you execute your career goals while not losing your sense of self. Highly recommended as a beneficial learning tool for all those who are looking to balance their careers and personal lives."

Fedele Colucci, Broker of Record

"An inspiring and candid tale of one man's journey to success as a real estate agent and achieving inner freedom. This book is sure to ignite the passion and holds the key to unlocking the power that lies within us all."

Gina Ceci, Real Estate Lawyer

"Very smooth and therapeutic read. I found myself reflecting on how the philosophies shared in this book could be applied to enhance my own business and personal life. Great way to give your career a check-up from the neck up. A must read for new and experienced agents alike!"

Rui Alves, Broker/Manager

"Be careful; reading this book could change how you do business and how you live your life! It's an extraordinary resource that's easy to pick up but incredibly hard to put down. The author's knowledge is invaluable and his humour is lovely. Though written for agents, it's also designed to help anyone wishing to live a more peaceful, meaningful and fulfilled life."

Helen McLean, Sales Representative since 2004

"I truly enjoyed every page, every topic and especially the quotes on almost every page. I want to confess that when I started to read "The Happy Agent", I got so pumped and motivated that I didn't sleep that night. I planned my year ahead and entire career. I made some very important decisions after reading this book and I am well on my path to achieving them. Thank you for writing such an amazingly simple yet exponentially motivating "business manual". Making real estate sound so interesting in itself is a huge achievement. Thank you once again for writing such inspiring book."

Naveed Ahmed, Sales Representative since 2006
and Associate Director Commercial Division

The *Happy* Agent

Finding Harmony
with a Thriving **Realty** Career
and an Enriched Personal Life

ROSS WILSON
Real Estate Broker

Edited by Therese Taylor, Writer/Editor,
MA (Journalism), BA (Hon English)

Cover design by Derek Murphy, CreativIndieCovers
Interior design by Jake Muelle

ISBN: 978-0-9936009-0-6

Second Edition

Disclaimer
While every attempt has been made to provide accurate and current information, due to the constantly changing nature of our industry, I cannot guarantee the accuracy, completeness or timeliness of any information provided. Further, a detailed explanation of certain proceedings such as power-of-sale, foreclosure and others is beyond the scope of this book. All information offered is not to be construed as legal, financial, medical or psychological advice. Seek skilled guidance from an appropriate professional since all editorial comments herein are merely my personal opinion. I mean no offence to any particular person, group or association and apologize if they happen to find any of my comments offensive.

Table of Contents

SECTION II – NUTS and BOLTS

SECTION III – REALTY REALITY: MANIFESTING SUCCESS

"Strange is our situation here upon earth. Each of us comes for a short visit,
not knowing why, yet sometimes seeming to a divine purpose.
From the standpoint of daily life, however, there is one thing we do know:
That we are here for the sake of others, for the countless unknown souls with
whose fate we are connected by a bond of sympathy. Many times a day,
I realize how much my outer and inner life is built upon the labors of people,
both living and dead, and how earnestly I must exert myself
in order to give in return as much as I have received."
Albert Einstein

~ Gratitude ~

This book is dedicated to all the sales people, brokers, managers and trainers who, wittingly or otherwise, helped throughout my career by showing me both the better way and the worse way of practicing real estate and living life.

I especially wish to express my gratitude to all those agents with whom I've shared a warm, cordial and mutually respectful relationship over the years; you know who you are. I shall be forever grateful for your kind friendship;

and to

Rui Alves and Fedele Colucci, broker/owners of the success story that is iPro Realty Ltd, who prior to my rough manuscript being edited and revised, patiently and painstakingly peer-reviewed it and offered much valued advice;

and to

Melanie and Joanna Wilson, both successful realty agents in Toronto, Ontario, and Gina Ceci, a highly sought real estate lawyer whom I call friend, as early beta-readers who provided timely and enthusiastic encouragement. To them, I am indebted;

and to

Therese Taylor, my dear editor. A writer's words are like children spawned and not easily abandoned. However, with red pen poised, she skilfully corrected several technical issues, as editors are wont to do, and convinced me to jettison extraneous verbiage, thereby improving clarity and readability. With her considerate assistance, I became a better writer;

and to

Marian Irene Lucy Therese Gain, a warm-hearted former realty agent who magically transformed into my best friend and love of my life, with whose support and guidance I have achieved much joy and happiness.

~ Preface ~

"If you want to be successful, it's just this simple; know what you are doing, love what you are doing and believe in what you are doing." Will Rogers

Convergence and Emergence

The idea of writing this book was unconsciously birthed decades ago. And since that first breath, it continued to gestate. While plying my trade, when I happened to cross paths with another agent who I felt could have performed better professionally, as their closet mentor, I wrote a guest column addressing the topic for our national trade newspaper, *Real Estate Monthly (REM)*. Response from across the country was always swift and encouraging. In recent years, it dawned on me that I possessed the rudiments of a self-help guide for new agents and anyone generally interested in real estate. Even veteran agents keen to move their practice in a new direction might find inspiration within these pages. Thus, I decided to commence the Herculean effort to consolidate these still applicable articles with numerous other business and life experiences into a composition which I hope, dear reader, you'll find informative, inspirational and entertaining. It's my way of giving back to an industry that has richly rewarded me and my family for over 40 years.

Now that my golden years have arrived on schedule, I can honestly say that for the most part, I've enjoyed the voyage. And for the times I didn't, I'm grateful to and have forgiven those who contributed to the adverse circumstances under which I learned a few tough lessons. Not only has creating this digest made me feel good in the knowing that others may benefit from my experiences, it has also proven highly cathartic for me. The necessary introspection has helped further crystallize my own genuine identity, and I trust it will help you do the same. It has also provided me with a platform to briefly express some controversial opinions on the current state of our industry and the world in general, with the occasional political, sociological or economic rant thrown into the mix. And to emphasize certain elements of my narrative, I also sprinkled in some mythical tales and personal life stories.

Conceived to be a convergence of two streams of thought – material and spiritual – the business information and personal anecdotes herein are the compilation of a lifetime of experience, study, observation, discernment and critical independent thought. The subtle merging of these streams has richly contributed to my life in ways I never fully anticipated when more than two score years ago, I obtained my government real estate registration. And from this merging has emerged a lovely pool of accomplishments in both areas of my life.

The first and largest stream, elaborated in the first two sections of the book, encompasses a pragmatic approach to our business. Thankfully, my peers have taught me – advertently and inadvertently – various techniques, skills and business philosophies that resonated with me, which I eagerly adopted and adapted into my professional tool kit. I've learned what I perceived to be the best practices – and the worst – and have grown to understand why a small minority of my fellow registrants do a majority of the business. The reasons for our industry's extremely high attrition rate have been clearly evident.

You'll discover a collection of ethical sales techniques, step-by-step methodologies and principled smart tools, written in an easily digested style, which are immediately implementable into your daily business operation to take your practice to a higher level. Along with valuable and commonly misunderstood industry information, you'll also find practical advice on how to confidently communicate with your clients and help more effectively with their decisions – at the appropriate moment during the home transition process. Throughout my career, from which I usually generated a comfortable six figure gross annual income, I've practiced and polished these techniques, and without being enslaved by the business or spending a king's ransom in promotion.

The second smaller, but no less significant stream described in the third section, introduces a more esoteric approach to our industry. The ideas touched upon – supported by popular, highly credible forward-thinking leaders in their respective fields – may shake your world a little and nudge you down a new path of self-discovery. By providing this information, I hope to help you harmonize the two chief components of your life – professional *and* personal – and to understand the source of true happiness. Think of it as a "build it and they will come" sort of thing; find personal happiness and watch your business thrive. Since it's not an exhaustive treatise on any theoretical aspects of life, I'm not promising the ultimate answers to *all* your life dreams. It's designed simply as an overture, a whetting of your appetite, if you will, to delve further into the examination of self and to appreciate the wonderful mysteries of life.

"Faced with the choice between changing one's mind and proving that there is no need to do so, almost everyone gets busy on the proof."
John Kenneth Galbraith

If success remains elusive, and if your mind's door is ajar, get ready for at least a sliver of light to penetrate that crack. To change your life, to improve your business, you must think, feel and behave differently. You possess the power of choice to go beyond the self-imposed and perpetually rationalized limiting boundaries of your personal no-grow comfort zone. I invite you to empower yourself to attract more positive people into your network, hence improve and enlarge your sphere of influence – along with your income. Unbolt your mind and open your heart, for if you glean just one new idea – just one – then I respectfully suggest that your choice to invest both a pittance of your money and time will have been a judicious one. If you're not a seeker of knowledge while in the stream of life, you're just treading water. And we all know what eventually happens with no or slow progress – exhaustion and unhappiness. What's the solution? Learn how to swim in your life stream and float happily down Victory River with a long and rewarding career.

"When love and skill work together, expect a masterpiece." John Ruskin

We work to live – not live to work. Actually, we live to love, but I'll get to that later. By being the best you can be, the most skilful in your endeavour and by loving yourself, your life and what you do with it, you'll happily begin every new day with a spring in your step. It's my hope that you undergo a life paradigm shift, a delicate and gradual metamorphosis wherein your attitude about life in general – and business in particular – rallies to the point where you become a "people magnet". I pray you join the ranks of an exponentially growing body of happy people who share the belief in a more kind, loving and compassionate world.

Do you believe in serendipity? Was finding this book purely coincidental? They say the appropriate teacher arrives when the student is ready. Are you ready for change? It's my sincere wish that our quality time together brings something good and loving into your life and the lives of those around you. May you live long and prosper!

"In dwelling, live close to the ground. In thinking, keep to the simple.
In conflict, be fair and generous. In governing, don't try to control.
In work, do what you enjoy. In family life, be completely present."
Lao Tzu

SECTION I

CLUES and VIEWS

"It is not the critic who counts;
not the man who points out how the strong man stumbles,
or where the doer of deeds could have done them better.
The credit belongs to the man who is actually in the arena,
whose face is marred by dust and sweat and blood,
who strives valiantly; who errs and comes short again and again;
because there is not effort without error and shortcomings;
but who does actually strive to do the deed; who knows the great enthusiasm,
the great devotion, who spends himself in a worthy cause who at the best
knows in the end the triumph of high achievement and who at the worst,
if he fails, least he fails while daring greatly. So that his place shall never be
with those cold and timid souls who know neither victory nor defeat."
Theodore Roosevelt

Chapter One

The Way We Were

"Until the great mass of people shall be filled with the sense of responsibility for each other's welfare, social justice can never be attained." Helen Keller

Evolution or Devolution?

Once upon a time, in a land not so far away, wealthy principal brokers ruled supreme. Friendly salespeople toiled in homogenous, brightly illuminated bullpens painted utilitarian beige, and diligently plied their trade while sitting on spartan chairs at rudimentary tin desks equipped with black dial telephones. Sounds like a description of a museum exhibit. Well, that's where it all began for me.

Patiently prospecting for listings and answering ad calls generated by company-paid newspaper advertisements and lawn signs were a pleasant part of my daily routine. Most homeowners courteously answered my discreet inquiries since, unlike today, their privacy wasn't annoyingly invaded by every Thomas, Richard and Harriet telemarketer with aggressive approaches as bold as their billboard faces. And the bane of homeowners – automated telemarketing – had yet to be spawned in the swampy brain of some Machiavellian mind. Salesmen and associate brokers, as we were generically registered in those days, regardless of gender, didn't advertise 24/7 availability, but many still earned a decent living, a few more than most, while providing personal, attentive service. As is mostly now the case, incomes were usually directly related to attitude and the number of honest effort hours invested.

Maybe I'm deluding myself, but I seem to recall our business being gentler in those olden days when we shared respectful friendship with others of our ilk. Then again, nostalgia isn't quite what it used to be. I recollect occasionally happening upon consumers already happily established with an agent of my own or even a competing firm. Out of respect for my peer, I ordinarily extricated myself from the situation while endorsing the service of their chosen representative and wishing the prospects well. This attitude appears to have gone the same way as electric typewriters, carbon paper and voice pagers.

Over the past decade or so, I've personally and disappointingly lost valuable prospects to competing agents because, I later learned, those agents dishonestly and unethically misspoke of me and my practice.

Then along came a major categorical transition. Employees transformed into independent contractors and formerly obscure and autonomous brokerages signed up with national or international franchises with associated annual and monthly fees. Accompanying the onslaught of this revolutionary new model was the maximum commission concept. Our industry morphed virtually overnight. With this change came greater stress levels for the now non-coddled agents. Many traditional full service independent brokerages and multi-branch corporations began to experience shrinking market share as their sales reps joined the evolution. Commission plans became increasingly more generous for agents as companies commenced competing more for each other's agents than for sellers and buyers. For all practical purposes, salespeople had essentially become the clients to the emerging agent service-provider companies. Agents began to aggressively compete directly with each other – within and without their own office – and that practice continues to this day, maybe even more aggressively. Times have certainly changed.

> *"It has become appallingly obvious that our technology*
> *has exceeded our humanity."* Albert Einstein

In the old days, all we needed was a desk, phone, secretarial support, a serviceable car, MLS® book (or tear sheets, dare I regress further) and the steadfast will to perform an honest day's work. Nowadays, instead of agents diligently working together as a team, autonomous independent contractors indemnify their companies, manage and pay their own expenses and work their personal businesses, essentially self-employed. They acquire the newest technology (which soon follows the 8-track stereo into the re-cycle bins of the world) and some have licensed and unlicensed personal assistants. Large overheads and small fortunes invested in sophisticated office and communication equipment in their private home offices doesn't do much for cost leveraging. Now, understand this; I'm not saying we were totally better off in those days, for today's technologies offer advantages we hadn't even dreamed about. In some respects, though, I believe we were indeed happier. But then again, don't we tend to look back through rose-coloured glasses?

Technology has integrated itself so thoroughly into everyday life that we seem to have developed a desperate dependence on gizmos. We demand more sophisticated software, superior hardware with greater random access memory, faster Internet speed and super-gigabyte storage capabilities. Mobile connectivity now assures constant and immediate access to the world or unfortunately, to your friend across the table. Where's it headed? Once defined as physically joining actual social clubs and associations for personal human interaction, mutual entertainment and camaraderie, the term "social networking" has assumed an entirely new meaning. Even the word "friend" now carries a different connotation. How much technology is enough?

"Men have become the tools of their tools." Henry David Thoreau

Belly to Belly

"Skill is fine and genius is splendid, but the right contacts are more valuable than either." Sir Archibald McIndoe

Many real estate sales people seem to have lost sight of the fact that they work in a belly-to-belly business. Consumers may be impressed by the apparent benefits of technological wonders, and they no doubt appreciate the improved service it supports. But I believe that personal, trustful relationships still form the cornerstone of our industry – and your business. In the past, I've enjoyed private pleasurable moments when I've accepted a listing and noticed their mailbox stuffed with environmentally-unfriendly, resource-depleting junk mail of competitors who probably rarely took the initiative for personal contact. Apparently having overlooked the fact that it's often the follow-up call that gets the business, some industrious agents simply continue to play the numbers game by delivering a deluge of flyers or fridge magnets, blanketing the entire town, and expecting homeowners to actually read and respond before the over-flowing blue box beckons. Our bulging landfill sites can attest to the ultimate destination of the vast majority of such junk. (Our species is by far the worst offender when it comes to destroying a natural resource – trees – to manufacture another resource – paper – only to quickly waste it.) Many agents seem to have forgotten (or never knew) that personal relationships, regular courteous contact, competent timely advice and skilled, dependable, honest guidance are still the industry's gold standards. Yes, all the technological wonders enhance our efficiency, but it's merely background support for our true purpose.

"When restraint and courtesy are added to strength, the latter becomes irresistible." Mahatma Gandhi

What has happened to professional courtesy and friendly, mutually respectful competition? It appears that s/he who has the most money wins. Get more listings. Win more ludicrous awards. Have bigger advertising campaigns. Get more information onto already busy business cards. Race through the neighbourhood and burn up the streets to beat a competitor to the prospect. And even though your expenses are sky-rocketing, when you arrive, agree to work for a lower fee. Make whatever concessions at whatever the cost and however many toes are crunched in the process; just get your sign on the lawn. Is there something wrong with this picture? Rules and codes of ethics dictate that we refrain from making disparaging remarks about our competitors. I wonder how often this fundamental "golden rule" is violated – naively or with guile. For our industry to sustain a professional reputation into the future, we must maintain a respectable level of professional courtesy with each other and no less vitally, with the public. After all, if we don't exhibit mutual respect, why should we expect different treatment from consumers?

Technology will certainly continue to grow exponentially, hopefully fulfilling its continuing purpose of increasing efficiency while decreasing labour. After all, you want to continue to grow and improve. But remember that it's simply a support tool to enhance your ability to effectively serve and care for your clients. Don't hide behind it. Your mandate is to fulfill, with fiduciary responsibility, the dreams and expectations of those who place their trust in you, and commit to doing an honest day's work.

We are each allotted just so much time on this Earth. Each moment is irreplaceable. Spend each wisely. Personal growth and family time are essential, for a life devoid of love and laughter is a life wasted. Get out there in your community, talk to people and build trusting relationships. And plan to leave the world a better place.

"Intelligence and courtesy not always are combined; often in a wooden house, a golden room we find." Henry Wadsworth Longfellow

Chapter Two

People or Pecuniary?

"A man wrapped up in himself makes a very small bundle."
Benjamin Franklin

Cloaked in Confusion

"Life is really simple, but we insist on making it complicated." Confucius

The real estate business is simple; you help people. It's that straightforward. And you enjoy the work by keeping it simple, or you don't by making it unnecessarily complex. Business life can certainly be stressful, otherwise you'd be subsisting under a rock, but it shouldn't be unpleasant. By keeping it uncomplicated, if you haven't already attained a decent level of achievement, if you stick with it, you probably will eventually. Aside from possessing and polishing the skills described later in this book, all you really need for a long and successful career are patience, persistence, integrity and critically – to identify your core values – and to comport yourself according to those inherent beliefs. (More later on this topic.)

If you're already in the realty business, and full of entrepreneurial spirit, you made a wise career choice. I know of no other industry that permits the launching of a new business with so little capital, yet with such delightful time freedom and high income potential. To build a successful referral-based practice, though, you mustn't take to heart the official label of sales person. Rather, think of yourself as an expert service provider, compensated befitting your level of ambition, vigour and expertise. It's that simple. You're here in this fleeting incarnation, not to live cloaked in confusion, but to learn, advance and enjoy every moment in gratitude and conscious awareness. You're here to be happy while serving mankind. And don't fool yourself; a life of quality service is a life well lived.

"I slept and dreamt that life was joy. I awoke and saw that life was service.

I acted and behold, service was joy." Rabindranath Tagore

Consistency and Persistency

In your attempts to stimulate new business, do you indulge in bombastic self-promotion with colossal photos and boastful, self-congratulatory slogans plastered everywhere? Or to encourage referrals and repeat clients, do you regularly personally network your warm sphere of influence, including former clients, and farm a neighbourhood? Your style clearly depends on your belief system and personality type. If effectively organized and executed, *both* methods – mass advertising and personal prospecting – can be highly productive. However, the former demands a substantial financial commitment combined with a coordinated, long term complementary strategy. And the latter sometimes translates into delayed gratification and initially at least, an unspectacular income. In other words, the personal networking method may not shoot you to superstar status in the short term. Your career, nevertheless, could last considerably longer than average without the need for ongoing promotional expenses. I personally chose the referral generation approach over big budget promo and did quite well. And in an industry characterized by low average income and high failure rate, after 40 years, I'm still around – by choice.

Once you start down the road of expensive self-promotion, during a very busy period or when you need a short sabbatical, you might suspend your advertising. But without personal relationships reinforced with periodic direct contact, people may forget you. Any noted absence of your regular advertising – no matter how brief – could be misconstrued as failure or retirement. Be relentless in your effort – and expense. On the other hand, regular grooming of personal relationships can not only be far less expensive than continuing promotional campaigns, but contacts won't assume you've quit the business during that break. And because you work with friends – both old and new – it can be emotionally rewarding too. Familiarity and trust are common companions. And trust breeds referrals.

"Trust is the glue of life. It's the most essential ingredient in effective communication. It's the foundational principle that holds all relationships."
Stephen Covey

Many mature career agents regularly neglect the basics of prospecting. With the possible exception of placing the occasional ad, they passively rely on referrals and returning clients. Now that I find myself in the autumn of my career, I must admit that I'm guilty of allowing my active prospecting to diminish somewhat, but it was a conscious choice. After so many years of keeping in touch, when they need real estate service, most still remember me. And I'm as busy as I want to be. There's nothing wrong with this less aggressive style, however, provided the resulting non-stellar income is enough. Not everyone cares to earn the big bucks or at least, make the commitment to the extraordinary time and effort needed to do so. Over the years, if senior agents have maintained regular caring contact with past clients, their extensive database should provide at least a comfortable living. It's very gratifying when a former client contacts you. And if you're around long enough, you'll enjoy the benefits of second generation business. What a fantastic feeling when parents recommend you to their adult progeny! It's often a fun "my, how you've grown" moment.

"Make yourself necessary to somebody." Ralph Waldo Emerson

Terms of Enslavement

Homeowners who choose an agent who spends more money promoting themselves than their listings sometimes learn that huge self-promo budgets guarantee neither individual attention nor personal compatibility, nor for that matter, even a successful outcome. Industry giants usually can't afford the time necessary to establish personal direct relationships with each of their numerous clients. It's not part of their success formula. Once the deal is done, unless the self-proclaimed celebrity agent is a shackled slave to the business, they're often onward and upward, leaving their assistant or team member to manage the details and follow-up. It works, but at the price of missing the opportunity to build a deeper relationship with the client. And remember – warm, respectful relationships can lead to referrals and future business.

A superstar's voluminous business is certainly a commendable goal. But after extending an expensive effort, if fame remains elusive, your resources were wasted. I suggest that the placement of your image on a few park benches or bus shelters or a small weekly display ad in the local paper equates to possibly making a personal phone contact every few years to people in your network. In other words, it's not very effective promotion. However, a skilled agent who carefully orchestrates a continuing strategic campaign, with one medium consistently complementing and reinforcing another, thereby generating a repetitive public perception of success, should achieve excellent results. Your name and logo – your personal brand – must appear virtually everywhere. But don't stop until you're ready for retirement. Otherwise, you may lose that highly desired real estate referred to as "front of mind". Memories fade.

While we're on the topic of big budget promotion, allow me to digress a little with a point to ponder. As stated earlier, most agents work autonomously as independent contractors, no matter the size of the brokerage, whether franchised or independent. The single biggest advantage to being linked to a franchise is the benefit derived *from* that association and the institutional promotion of its widely recognized brand. That's the reason for the franchise's very existence! So, why pay expensive monthly and annual franchise fees, only to minimize the popular brand? I've seen thematic lawn signs and print ads that almost make the sales rep appear as a sole proprietor. In my mind, they're wasting their money and might as well be working with a solid independent brokerage and save the franchise fees. My advice? Capitalize on the franchise brand, or build your own brand at an independent and spend the fee savings promoting you and your listings.

When it's time to do some realty trading, a homeowner will usually turn to a trusted friend in the business, someone who always puts their client's interests first. They're more moved by amiable association and regular personal contact than by all the pomp and pageantry found in their mailbox. Ideally, mass advertising should not be your only method of generating business. If you've enjoyed a personable, friendly relationship with your past clients, a periodic follow-up program can be highly productive. But if you choose to not invest your own time, then your old clients may just call a neighbourhood realty megastar or a new friend in the business.

"If you work just for money, you'll never make it. But if you love what you're doing and you always put the customer first, success will be yours." Ray Kroc

To passively influence a small portion of the multitude, you could spend *more* money and *less* time. Or to enjoy active influence, you could spend *less* money and *more* time – possibly achieving the same *net* income. Now, in my view, time is the more valuable commodity and its expenditure produces superior sustainable results. But leverage is the key ingredient in either method. Out of curiosity, I once crunched the numbers of a top producing duo in my employ. I calculated their net income before taxes by deducting their joint promotional expenses from their combined total personal generated commissions, and because they were a partnership, halved the result. Each of their taxable incomes was less than I expected. And they often laboured seven days a week. Having said this, they're still in the business – with huge overhead – and appear to be doing exceptionally well. There's no doubt that if done right, their style can be highly effective. It's your choice, but whatever style you choose, do it consistently.

Is your goal to obtain as many listings as possible, expecting a particular percentage to sell, with the expired listings as acceptable losses? Or is it to increase your sales-to-listings ratio thereby providing each of your clients with superior, hands-on service? If living for your work with huge expenses and trained assistants – with minimal time for personal growth – fails to excite you, try building your business on direct personal contact. Creating trusting relationships can be far less stressful, highly productive and much fun.

Is your business about the money or is it about the people? Where are your priorities? It's been said that it's better to know a few people well than many people a little. Think about this; would you prefer to seek business in a crowd of 1000 strangers where you're forced to sell yourself? Or would you prefer to prospect in a group of 100 who all know your first name? I'd rather have one great friend than an endless list of fair-weather friends. I suggest that most people prefer to associate with someone they trust over another with a great sales pitch and deep promotional pockets. How about you?

"The man who will use his skill and constructive imagination to see how much he can give for a dollar, instead of how little he can give for a dollar, is bound to succeed." Henry Ford

Real Real Estate Agents

Imagine this hypothetical scenario; you're a homeowner and not a real estate agent. Your growing family forces you to seriously consider relocating to a more spacious home. You begin your quest by opening the paper's real estate section. Or you start the tedious process of diligently surfing the dizzying array of realty websites. Dozens, if not hundreds of hungry smiling faces in the newspaper and on a mind-numbing number of websites stare out at you over bold headings: "Number One Agent," "I Never Sleep," "Member of President's Club", "I'm the Best", "Voted Most Popular" or "Awarded Reader's Choice". Do you really believe all those brashly immodest claims? Do you even care? As a consumer, does it really matter how many sales someone had last year? Do you care if they're number one in the country? After all, you're interested in only one neighbourhood. How many number ones are possible – or believable for that matter? Don't all the witty watchwords start to blend together into a flat frieze?

Would you find it more pleasant – not to mention more effective – if all that paper and ink, or the digital version, offered images and information on available properties instead of legions of slick slogans and unfamiliar faces? To a certain degree, self-promotion can be productive, but don't you feel it has reached a saturation point or beyond? How can a full page of little agent photos or a newspaper chock full of screaming headlines and inane catchphrases or hundreds of thousands of realty websites accomplish anything tangible? Maybe all those agents are regularly blowing their advertising budget simply because their competitors are doing it too. Or maybe it's just ego. Instead of passively promoting themselves in print, how about focusing on the important errand of building human connections and growing a personal referral base?

"True happiness, we are told, consists of getting out of one's self.
But the point is not only to get out, you must stay out. And to stay out,
you must have some absorbing errand." Henry James

According to The Canadian Real Estate Association (CREA), there are over 100,000 registered sales representatives and brokers in Canada, working through more than 100 boards and associations. The number of registrants in Ontario alone exceeds 55,000. The American National Association of Realtors (NAR) consists of over a million members! Is this an extremely competitive situation? You bet! And during the past few years, registrations have increased considerably. However, while numerous optimistic beginners join the ranks every year, a deluge of the disappointed regularly surrender their licenses and abandon their brief careers.

In spite of the belief held by many consumers that we're all over-paid with fat bank accounts, according to independent statistical analysis, the vast majority of registrants earn a meagre living, with a sizable percentage of our ranks generating little to no business whatsoever. Unfortunately, such low production often results in personal and family misfortune. Marital conflict, failing health, poor credit, bankruptcy and resignation from the industry are all too common conclusions to a once invigorating adventure. Competition is tough, but everyone leaping onto the same propaganda wagon is ultimately self-defeating too. The sole and biggest beneficiaries of our advertising largesse are the newspaper and web-hosting/design industries.

"One thing I know; the only ones among you who will be really happy are those
who will have sought and found how to serve." Albert Schweitzer

Career professionals interested in personal growth and happiness may wish to consider abstaining from hype, hyperbole and unabashed boasting and retreat from the trough of self adulation. It's time to behave, not like super machines prostituting 24 hours a day, seven days a week, but like real people with real values. When in business mode, focus on your clients. Carefully listen to and earnestly, honestly and dutifully fulfill their wants and needs, manage your expenses and advertise your listings. Realty agents conducted business quite successfully for many years before the Internet, full-page spreads and gigantic billboard faces.

Novel ideas abound that claim to turn a low achiever into a multimillion-dollar producer as surely as the sun will rise in the morning. Announcements arrive regularly in your email inbox of new and improved sales seminars by hugely successful speakers guaranteeing increased income. Attitude engineers make fortunes indoctrinating would-be superstars in the ways of positive thinking. But here's the thing; the vast majority of seminar participants rarely persevere with their newly "learned" skills because as they exit the auditorium, they begin to forget. Those new techniques don't feel right, so they fall back into the same old patterns – the old comfort zone – and grow frustrated again with the same lacklustre results. And then they wonder why nothing ever seems to change for them.

You just might find the wearing of someone else's shoes proves unsustainable. Those fascinating techniques may have been effective for the seminar lecturer, but may not reflect *your* personal values and abilities. Since humans are basically change-averse, in fairly short order, you'll likely return to your own comfortable old slippers. Thankfully, we don't live in a homogenous world. We're all unique. Please don't get me wrong; I encourage personal growth through on-going education, and there's a lot of excellent training available, but don't be anyone but you. Be genuine. Change comes from within – not without.

"The authentic self is the soul made visible." Sarah Ban Breathnach

Presenting your natural self and not some illusory top producer clone is far less stressful. A job well done – without focusing on commissions – will bring financial and emotional rewards. A satisfied client that trusts you and is comfortable with your attentive service will recommend you. Is there a better way to obtain new business? The guy perusing the morning newspaper probably won't find you in that vast sea of ink. And the Internet is an even bigger sea.

To be happily successful and self-fulfilled over the long haul, stop portraying a translucent role as exhorted by the image makers. Good communicators who care about their clients, who develop and polish technical and interpersonal skills, are diligent in their efforts, behave ethically and maintain current market knowledge, commit to regular personal client contact – and enjoy a personally fulfilling life apart from the business – can be happy, contented, confident, successful and more interesting individuals with durable and rewarding careers. And with a critical mass of such self-respecting agents, public respect for our industry will increase. Shakespeare wrote, "To thine own self be true." Try it. Get real. It works.

"When you are content to be simply yourself and don't compare or compete, everybody will respect you." Lao Tzu

Chapter Three

R-E-S-P-E-C-T

"Without feelings of respect, what is there to distinguish men from beasts?"
Confucius

Call Me Disappointed

She refused to return my call. For several years, we'd enjoyed a friendly respectful relationship. But her failure to return my calls after I'd left two courteous messages on as many days had left me disappointed. Not only did her behaviour clearly demonstrate a lack of professional courtesy, but at the time, it precluded me from providing my seller with her and her buyer's valuable comments regarding the property I'd listed and she'd just shown. My seller was not impressed.

My clients have become accustomed to attentive, personal service. It's been my gold standard from day one. Regular and frequent marketing activity reports are an essential part of a listing agent's job description. Nobody enters any of my listings without a follow-up feedback request, usually the next day. Such indispensable information could help my seller. Armed with an accumulation of such comments, I'm better equipped to recommend a repair or renovation, price adjustment or home staging to hopefully increase activity. Another impartial price opinion is always warmly welcomed.

Such a request may not be important to a disrespectful unprofessional who has no time to care. But someone's deliberate effort to contact them should certainly indicate some level of importance to the caller. Return the call or complete the brief on-line request for feedback! It's a basic courtesy that takes a few moments of your time. To be rude or kind to a fellow member is a personal choice. Consider what goes around comes around.

"Self-command is the main elegance."
Ralph Waldo Emerson

Another contentious issue is that of missed showing appointments. Anticipating your arrival for a scheduled appointment, a conscientious homeowner often meticulously prepares their home and inconveniently vacates to facilitate your viewing privacy. When your buyer cancels or neglects to show up on time, promptly contact the listing brokerage to cancel or reschedule. It's not only common courtesy, which sadly seems less common these days, but you can also avoid a fine for unprofessional conduct. On each occasion when you fail to cancel, not only is *your* professional standing tarnished, a tiny sliver of respectability is sliced from our collective professional reputation. And we must all work a tiny bit harder to re-earn that fragment. Think about the rather substantial advertising dollars being spent by your real estate board or association for the sole purpose of instilling a sense of trustworthiness in our industry and its members. It takes many years to build a respectable professional reputation – and only moments to destroy it.

Never underestimate the importance of public perception and just as significantly, how you're perceived by your peers. Nurture a respectful relationship with your colleagues. For all practical purposes, consider them your partners because one day, you might find yourselves working closely to facilitate a transaction between respective clients. With the same ultimate goal, you could be sitting opposite at the negotiation table. A friendly relationship could ease the proceedings toward a mutually rewarding conclusion.

Your level of integrity, ethical behaviour and sense of fairness will contribute to your success – or lack of it – over the long term. So, start building a credit account. The public is poorly served when you treat your colleagues irreverently. Why? Because it's so easy for buyer reps to "mistakenly" overlook your listings when assembling properties to show. Don't grant them any emotional justification to be neglectful of their responsibility to consider *all* appropriate listings. Both you and your sellers could suffer the consequences.

Be a courteous consummate professional, and maybe – just maybe – we might witness a reversal of seemingly declining public respect. It might stem a growing trend toward discounting, and allow our industry to survive relatively unscathed. Respect others as much as you respect yourself and remember the Golden Rule: do unto others as you would have them do unto you. Public perception of our profession is up to each of us – every day.

"If once you forfeit the confidence of your fellow citizens,
you can never regain their respect and esteem."
Abraham Lincoln

Self-Respect = Power

"Self-respect knows no considerations." Mahatma Gandhi

Along with being likable, if not lovable, to be successful in our industry for the long-term, it helps to love and respect yourself as a sovereign power. If you find your own personal company repugnant, why would anyone else feel any differently toward you? To be able to professionally influence people, you need honest, ethical power over them. And that power begins with self-respect.

As the late Blain Lee, BA (Psychology), MA (Educational Psychology), Ph.D. (Instructional Design), co-founder and former senior consultant with the Covey Leadership Centre Inc., wrote in his illuminating book, *The Power Principle,* three types of power exist. "As fear is the source of coercive power, and fairness is the source of utility power, so respect, honor and even love constitute the base of principle-centered power." He believed that "there is a universal principle for being effective with others, maintaining power with others, and sustaining influence with others. Honor is power. The more we are honored, respected, and genuinely regarded by others, the more power we will have with them."

What can you and your client accomplish from working in concert? How much stronger are you working together and amicably – and mutually respectfully – toward a common goal? Consider that you are working *with* them – not just *for* them. You're a team with a shared objective. Isn't honest and caring influence with others our underlying goal? If it isn't part of your intention, you may wish to make it so. Try relating respectfully with your prospects. Help them understand that you're partners. The results may amaze you. Mutual trust may blossom.

Do you measure success by your annual income, the number of homes you've sold – or by how many families you help achieve home ownership? We work in a people-oriented business, not a house-selling business. Media advertising doesn't directly sell real estate; people do. Honest, respectful and honourable word of mouth does. Therefore, get to know a lot of people – with a lot of mouths – honour them with respect and measure your new success with smiles. Now, let's talk about the simple yardstick of our business life – money.

"Getting people to like you is merely the other side of liking them."
Norman Vincent Peale

Chapter Four

Your Money

"A man in debt is so far a slave." Ralph Waldo Emerson

As an efficient conscious controller of your personal economy, the following information may not apply to you. But if a few of these ideas ring true, you may have to shift into another philosophical paradigm because your cultural programming could trigger a habitual reaction because "that's just the way I've always been". Whilst reading, be in the quiet space between stimulus and response, for that's where wisdom is found. Let it simmer. Disengage your ego. After some thoughtful introspection, instead of *reacting* spontaneously, *respond* from a carefully considered and purely pragmatic perspective. Unlike a reaction, which is emotional, a response is rooted in good solid judgment and clear, calculated foresight.

Are you a big hitter, or a medium producer living a big lifestyle and always short of cash? In spite of doing well, are you unable to regularly reduce your debt load and escape creditors? Are you consistently building net worth or carelessly spending? Money in – money out. More money in – more money out. Less money in – the usual money out. It's really easy to spend the bucks while disregarding the inescapable fact that there will be lean times. Hindsight is usually 20/20, but in business, it's foresight that really matters and is the true measure of a shrewd, insightful business person capable of building – and retaining – wealth.

"Business, more than any other occupation, is a continual dealing with the future;
it is a continual calculation, an instinctive exercise in foresight."
Henry R. Luce

Rich Man – Poor Man

Our tumultuous industry is prone to cyclical market peaks and valleys, with commission income correspondingly rising and falling. If it's your intention to at least maintain some financial equilibrium, if not accumulate significant wealth, since you can't directly control your income, you should make every effort to control your lifestyle choices to reflect a realistically attainable and sustainable "regular" income. Now, it's practically impossible to continually adjust your everyday standard of living by temporarily curtailing normal monthly expenses to reflect an ever-fluctuating revenue stream. Live rich one month and as a pauper the next? Tall order. Once you begin to live upscale, when your income drops, you'll be reluctant to abandon the cushy life – even for a short term. So, with no savings to cover the shortfall, debt is created and over time, easily accumulates. Plus it's impossible to accurately predict an upcoming need to conserve. It would be like trying to time stock market fluctuations.

To build wealth, it's fiscally prudent to establish a baseline lifestyle derived from studying *your* income history, commission-generating capability and sensible economic expectations. Don't borrow for the lean times. And avoid making large, long-term financial commitments, such as car leases and home mortgages, in an up cycle because your income may be lower halfway through the lease or mortgage term. Living on a deficit is a formula for financial disaster. Live within realistic means. When you have a bonus month, use the surplus to discharge debt and/or build savings to cover regular overhead during the inevitable down cycles.

> *"To be satisfied with what one has; that is wealth. As long as one sorely needs an additional amount, that man isn't rich."* Mark Twain

Familial Bails

> *"It is not fair to ask of others what you are not willing to do yourself."*
> *Eleanor Roosevelt*

When you're feeling the pinch, borrowing from generous well-intentioned friends and family may seem like a nice notion, but it doesn't usually work very well. As a matter of fact, it can prove disastrous. Sure, it gets you over the hump, but seeking a financial bailout is still a bad idea. Besides, even with the best of intentions, loving family members may ill afford to lose that money and too proud or fearful to admit it. They may be ill-equipped to ignore your desperate pleading and succumb to your beseeching from a misguided sense of responsibility. That's not a high quality living, nor is it conducive to a healthy familial relationship. Besides, aren't you just borrowing from Peter to pay Paul, just kicking the proverbial can down the road? The gloomy truth is that you may just be innocently delaying your inevitable crash, thereby creating a much bigger problem later when the damage from a fall over the fiscal cliff might more significantly break your financial bones.

If you're bent on petitioning family for charity, before proceeding, at least invest the time to prepare a budgetary analysis. Full financial disclosure should include details of all assets and liabilities, including investments, family income and expenses. Unless it's a gift, include repayment terms with interest rate, monthly payment and when it'll be fully paid. Pretend you're applying to a bank. You love your family – not the bank. Right? So, why treat your family with any less consideration? Actually, your well-intentioned family may be doing you and themselves a disservice by inadvertently enabling your irresponsible lifestyle choices, which regrettably have contributed to your current dire straits.

"Blessed are the young for they shall inherit the national debt." Herbert Hoover

Grooming Consuming

"Rather go to bed without dinner than to rise in debt." Benjamin Franklin

If you're ever to extricate yourself from the murky depths of your financial fiasco and maintain your proverbial nose above the surface, unless you have enormous willpower, you must abandon all your beloved credit cards. Or leave them for safe-keeping with your family financier or more economically responsible spouse. Habitual impulse purchases are probably what landed you in the Debt Sea in the first place. For a different result, stop floating through life with no hand on the tiller by creating and committing to a budget. If you lack the willpower to curb your spending, it's imperative you relinquish helm control to someone more familiar with the Rules of the Sea. (How's that for an extended metaphor?)

When preparing a household budget, in addition to all regular financial responsibilities, factor in that life sometimes throws an unexpected curve. Unforeseen things happen. If you're unprepared, you'll be smacked in the head. Savings are important, especially if you've cancelled your credit cards and/or closed your personal credit line. A good rule of thumb is to have an emergency stash of at least six months carrying costs. And when I say emergency, I mean a real money crisis. Mama needing a new pair of shoes or papa wanting a new putter doesn't qualify.

What about your family's combined maxed out cards and credit lines? How much interest are you paying on accumulated debts? In case you hadn't noticed, interest rates levied on outstanding balances are usurious, especially considering our current low-rate environment. And by just making the minimum monthly payment, have you calculated when it will be paid in full? It's measured in years. The actual cost of those fancy new shoes could very well be double or triple the original price tag. Thanks to your blind generosity, bank officers and shareholders are dancing in their cash vaults. Curb excessive spending.

If you find yourself behind the proverbial eight ball and suddenly come into funds, maybe from a series of closings, do you first pay off credit card balances and then go shopping? Hurray! I'm rich. There's credit available. Or do you make a debt payment along with a practical lifestyle adjustment so as to avoid being mired in the money muck again? Do you spend because you absolutely can't live without that trinket or just to feel good all over? Love those endorphins (more later on this honey of a hormone). Reminder – the high you get from buying the latest smart phone passes swiftly. Excepting the obvious big ticket items like a home or car, resist buying stuff until the money is in the bank.

The word "consumer" is a label introduced by manufacturers, mass marketers and advertising agencies to designate target customers. These companies collectively spend fortunes to convince you that your life is meaningless without their "trendy" product or service. As wars destroy weapons for the military-industrial complex, earning them massive profits from ongoing replacements, consumers devour manufactured goods which, once devoured, quickly become obsolete, unfashionable or worn out. The result is that which forms the foundation of our current disposable society – perpetual consuming. Don't think of yourself as a mass consumer. Don't fall for their hype. I mean, how much stuff do you really need anyway? Landfill sites are over-flowing with superfluous discarded junk. Think before you spend.

> *"Too many people spend money they haven't earned, to buy things they don't want, to impress people they don't like." Will Smith*

Falling Down

> *"Some people use one half their ingenuity to get into debt and the other half to avoid paying it." George Dennison Prentice*

If you crunch your numbers, you may actually be insolvent. By definition, if your liabilities exceed your assets, particularly if your income is not consistently sufficient to carry those liabilities, then guess what? Your goose could be cooked. Oh, wait – you may not be able to afford a goose. Without a resolution, particularly if things get economically worse, bankruptcy could be in your future. You could lose your home, vehicles, credit rating, real estate registration and no less important, your self-confidence. Your professional reputation may also take a bruising.

Without a budget and plan, how will you cope financially when the worse case scenario arrives on your doorstep and the market slows and values fall (if they haven't already in your area), as has been boldly forecast in media headlines? Don't fool yourself; at some point, it'll definitely happen. It's merely a matter of time. If it wasn't fated to occur for a while because of "sound" economic reasons, it could happen sooner due to the concept of self-fulfilling prophesy. Whatever is published by the manipulated and monopolistic mainstream media may manifest into reality, particularly if enough people believe it, which many undoubtedly do.

What if your spouse, who has a "real job", is unexpectedly disemployed? With the world's current economic uncertainty, it's entirely possible. What if an anticipated commission fails to materialize? What if, God forbid, your life path leads to illness or a handicap and you're unable to work? What if interest rates increase on your massive mortgage or maxed-out credit cards? Count on it because they definitely will; it's what banks do. And as they have for decades, energy and food prices will almost certainly continue to rise. What if all these scenarios occur simultaneously? Will you be able to carry everything, or would your self-built house of cards collapse in flames? To be prudent and prepared, you absolutely must consider the "what ifs".

If you have insufficient regular income to support your present lifestyle – and build capital savings – you must lower your regular expenses or raise your income or both. It's that simple. If you fail to build a nest egg during peak earning years, your retirement, if even possible, will be meagre at best. Be relatively frugal now so you can have a relatively secure dotage. Now, don't get me wrong; I'm not saying you should live like a pauper. Just exercise restraint by living within your practical financial means. Sadly, without spousal support, many agents will never be sufficiently financially secure to fully retire because they failed to effectively manage their money. Will you be a Willy Loman and pass away while driving yet another for sale sign into another lawn?

Before the healing can begin, as an alcoholic is required to do, you must recognize and admit you have a problem. Hello; my name is (blank) and I am a spend addict. Someone just handing you a bunch of money with no strings attached is synonymous with giving a confessed alcoholic a truck-load of liquor and then expecting them to exercise the strength of will to resist it. You may believe you're completely competent in the money management department, but remember that certainty comes only with a closed mind. Look at your track record. If you have a spouse and s/he is better equipped to handle the family finances, relinquish responsibility to them. Or ask a parent, financial adviser or accountant for guidance. Create a realistic budget and commit to living strictly within it. And start today. It's far better to be prepared a year in advance than to be a day late.

Cache of Cash

"Hope for the best, but prepare for the worst." Old English Proverb

Our industry busyness is inherently up and down like a toilet seat at a stag and doe party. Like the general economy, it's naturally cyclical, with some years and seasons busier than others. Therefore, in order to professionally survive the slack periods, it's prudent for novice and experienced agents alike to plan for both regular and sporadic as well as surprise business expenses.

Just as a wise little squirrel instinctively scurries about gathering and storing its winter food supply, maintaining a business funds reserve for that inevitable snowy day is a wise precaution. You probably don't usually have revenue arriving every month. So, maintaining a stash of cash to cover expenses during lean times, and for quarterly income or "valued added" tax remittances is imperative. Don't rely on commission advance companies with their exorbitant fees and usurious interest rates. Hopefully, you have a reliable second income in the family or you're blessed with financial independence. If not, consider opening a designated business bank account into which you deposit a certain portion of each commission. And be frugal with your business operating line. One must spend money to make money, but just like your personal expenses, do not – I repeat – do not spend beyond your realistic business financial means.

When planning your business budget, anticipate which months are typically busiest and quietist. You may experience lower expenses in the busy times because you're busy serving buyer clients and may not need to spend much lead generation money. Or you may prefer to maintain a constant visual presence with consistent marketplace advertising. Or promotional expenses may vary directly with listing volume, or because your practice is built on referrals. You could budget based upon a previous year. In any case, to establish a minimum cash reserve, your monthly expenditure estimates should be planned in advance as accurately as possible.

At publishing time, many national economies seem to be experiencing a recovery of sorts. However, some experts believe these upturns may be just blips on the radar. If the doom-and-gloom predictions prove true, the many financially destitute and heavily indebted nations may resume their deteriorating spiral. We simply don't know for sure how the real estate market will be affected next month, let alone next year. Be forewarned; only properly prepared agents will survive the inevitable downturns. When agents become discouraged and unable to afford to remain in the business because they refused to budget and failed to squirrel money away for the lean times, they quit in droves. Every major slump generates an exodus of the unprepared.

However, no matter the state of the economy, there'll always be a relative demand for realty service. Just like what happens in the precious metals market, when the spot price of gold suddenly falls, to cut their losses, many worried investors rush to sell. But there's usually another more optimistic investor who, anticipating a rising market just around the corner, sees a bargain opportunity. When one panics and sells, another eagerly buys. Falling realty prices attract various fore-thinking buyers who foresee a recovery on the horizon. Families may choose to transition into a larger home when the market value differential is narrower between their modest home and a more upscale property. Job seekers and transferees often need realty service. And of course, we mustn't forget those who, due to misfortune, are forced to sell. As I said, there's *always* opportunity for market savvy, financially prepared, persevering, insightful and industrious agents.

Prepared agents are not normally forced to hibernate or resign. Cash reserves permit the professionals to survive slower markets. During lean times, they maintain community visibility, hence lay the groundwork for future business. When the market returns, they're still around to reap the fruits of their labour and bitter-sweet as it may be, with fewer competitors. By budgeting and wisely managing your expenses, by smart spending, you'll have increased your chances of being one of the few still standing when many others have fallen.

"Thousands upon thousands are yearly brought into a state of real poverty by their great anxiety not to be thought poor." William Cobbett

Analyse and Channelize

For continued success, generating revenue is clearly important. Also vital, though, is the careful management of regular business expenses. This involves planning, which is addressed in the next chapter, but allow me to address a few issues here.

Having a nice gross income is great, but it's what you actually bring home that's crucial. Review last year's cost of doing business. Was it reasonable? Which outlays produced the best results? Could some promotional money have been directed elsewhere for a better return? Are any other less expensive income-producing activities available? Could you reduce or even eliminate certain expenses? Could the less effective promo fat be cut to allow for a leaner operation? Analyse for areas where money was effectively misspent.

For example, did you lose any lawn signs and lockboxes due to a relaxed retrieval policy, necessitating the purchase of replacements? Or are you throwing away business cards in a futile passive advertising attempt? Small expenses add up. Can you generate new clients in some way that doesn't necessitate spending money on newspaper advertising? Obviously, print ads in a daily paper can be useful for advertising your listings. But for personal promotion, remember that the ad is around for only a day or so. Maybe park benches or bus shelters might be more productive. How about a reallocation of advertising dollars to door hangers in your farm area? Did that door-stuffer campaign produce any positive results?

Does your website generate prospects? Is it worth the regular monthly fee? Or do you have a personal site, one of gazillions, just because everyone else does, to stroke your ego? Is it optimized to maximize traffic? Maybe your company-supplied corporate site would be adequate. Are you sharing too much commission with your brokerage due to an inequitable split or unreasonable service fees and funds? Ask your manager if they'd either pay for a regular ad for you, negotiate your commission split or waive the extraneous monthly fund contributions to allow you to invest that savings into self-promotion. Both you and your brokerage could benefit from the resulting higher business volume.

Do you know the source of each of your trades during the past year? For planning and budgeting purposes, it's a good idea to record the origin of each listing and sale contract. Did they originate from newspaper advertising, flyer distribution, lawn sign, open house, Internet inquiry, personal or company website or the public domain of your MLS® system? Was it a returning former client, from your farm area or a door-knocking escapade? Or were they a referral from another client, friend or family member? Was it a company referral or a walk-in or call-in during office duty? Was it a referral from a member of your agent network? Or from a personal networking contact? How much business did you develop from your golf club membership? How many of your sellers became buyers? What was the ratio of your business between listings sold and sales? To maximize the bang from each business buck – and minute – perform a careful analysis to help designate where to spend money, time and effort in the coming year.

Without sacrificing your preferred quality of life, both professionally and personally, it's wise to maintain a vigil on what and where you spend. To save fuel, finance or lease interest and insurance premiums, could your ego manage with a more economical method of transport? Do you really need all those business lunches? Are you wall-papering your bedroom with illegal parking tickets? Are you benefiting from your telecommunication package or could it be shaved? If your wireless bill is extraordinarily rich, would a land-line with voicemail help reduce costs? Maybe a Voice-Over-Internet-Protocol (VOIP) phone might be more cost effective. It's called micro-managing your expenses. Since it's more important to invest your time and energy on building your practice, I suggest not dwelling obsessively on this aspect of business. Nevertheless, with a few adjustments, you might be surprised at the savings.

"Adapt or perish, now as ever, is nature's inexorable imperative."
H. G. Wells

Instead of spending money to make money, have you considered spending your time? Maybe, networking with your social and referral base would be more productive. Be creative. What are your personal interests? Do you enjoy hiking, cooking, photography or whatever? How about joining a club where you'll have the opportunity to play and network with people with shared interests? Take a course at the local college. Fellow students may appreciate the opportunity to get to know you. You might even have some fun. Participation could be cheap and the tuition or membership fee tax-deductible. Commonality can lead to trust, friendship – and business.

Improved skills can contribute to lower expenses. If every business minute is more effectively spent, it's like money in the bank. How can you improve your business or interpersonal skills? First, you need to identify your strengths and weaknesses. Ask a close friend or colleague to honestly describe you. Or seek a service report card from a trusted client and have a heart-felt dialogue with them. What strengths do they feel you possess? What did they like or dislike about your service? And if you're brave enough (and they are too), ask if they'd honestly opine on your weaknesses. Be vulnerable and really listen to their responses. Maybe you habitually fail to capitalize on your personal skills because you're unaware of them. Maybe you need to focus your efforts on a different aspect of the business. Anyway, accept their constructive criticism with grace. In exchange, they may ask you to return the favour, and an already strong bond may strengthen even further.

Did you suffer a loss of a client's business last year that if handled differently, might have been avoided? What exactly happened? To reduce the chances of repeating history, can you identify a behaviour that could be modified? Is there a professional or personal skill you need to acquire? Do you need to tweak your standard methodology or perform radical surgery? What about adding another business tool or a personal human relation skill? Set an intention to attend courses and seminars that will address any deficiencies. Seek out ideas on how to enhance your skill set. To enjoy an increase in production, make a considered effort to grow beyond your present capabilities. Stretch yourself.

You're not an employee, but an entrepreneur running a business on a budget. Manage your expenses with forethought. And while you're at it, don't forget to have fun connecting with others; you'll benefit both personally and professionally. Think about your priorities, about what's truly important in life. Plan ahead for success and watch your wealth grow.

Sinning and Losing

"Don't go through life; grow through life." Eric Butterworth

On the other hand, life isn't all about money. In his best-selling book, *A New Earth: Awakening to Your Life's Purpose,* Eckhart Tolle, the popular contemporary spiritual sage, wrote; "Literally translated from the ancient Greek in which the New Testament was written, to sin means to miss the mark, as an archer who misses the target, so to sin means to miss the point of human existence. It means to live unskilfully, blindly, and thus to suffer and cause suffering. Again, the term, stripped of its cultural baggage and misinterpretation, points to the dysfunction inherent in the human condition."

I feel that many miss the mark in this life. Innumerable people spend their entire adult lives in the near-obsessive pursuit of wealth, power and fame because they're convinced – or have been so conditioned by their tribe – that such achievements bring happiness. Yes, a fancy new car, lovely clothes or luxury home can certainly induce an ephemeral illusion of happiness, a brief breath of bliss, but it's all transitory. Dedicated happiness hunters, however, mustn't dupe themselves into believing that fulfillment lies outside of them since it can only be found within. To devote one's life to the pursuit of more money than one can plausibly spend, along with more and more consumer paraphernalia destined for the storage locker or landfill, is undeniably sinning – or missing the point of life. And since many people fearfully focus on moving *away from* scarcity and unhappiness instead of growing *toward* abundance and happiness, the chances of ever achieving lasting happiness are doubtful.

If your focus is solely on acquiring monetary riches, beware that money shouldn't be the end, but the means to an end. Money – a simple yardstick that reflects what you did yesterday – certainly won't buy you happiness; many toys, yes, but no lasting joy. And so far, nobody has learned how to take it with them when, after their finale, they make their grand exit from the world's stage. Defrocked kings and homeless paupers look the same on a cold stone slab.

> *"Both abundance and lack exist simultaneously in our lives as parallel realities.*
> *It is always our conscious choice which secret garden we will tend, when we*
> *choose not to focus on what is missing from our lives, but are grateful for the*
> *abundance that's present – love, health, family, friends, work, the joys of*
> *nature and personal pursuits that bring us pleasure – the wasteland*
> *of illusion falls away and we experience heaven on earth."*
> Sarah Ban Breathnach

Chapter Five

Plans and Intentions

"If you don't design your own life plan, chances are you'll fall into someone else's plan. And guess what they have planned for you? Not much." Jim Rohn

Plan Your Work - Work Your Plan

As the end of a calendar year draws near and the frantic festivities of the holiday season are just a pleasant (or unpleasant) memory, it's normal to reflect on the preceding year. When you last partook of this annual retrospection, did you commend yourself for having completed another fantastic business cycle? Bravo if you did! Or did you whip yourself for not having taken more aggressive action? Did you realize everything on your wish list? Any regrets? Did the year go according to plan? Did you even *have* a written plan and specific goals, or just a faint glimmer of what you hoped to accomplish? Regardless, was it a joyful year for you? If you were happy and you didn't achieve your financial goal, if truth be told, maybe earning the big bucks isn't a top priority. Perhaps the price to build a large business is too steep. If this is true, don't knock yourself out. Adjust your goals for the upcoming year to a more liveable level and love your life.

To my knowledge, no one can foretell the future (well, some can through contact with Source, but that's a story for later), so I know no way to know with any certainty what a new year will bring. I'm confident, though, that apart from a cataclysmic event like an extraterrestrial landing, the abolishment of the income tax system or politicians voluntarily cutting their pensions, January will arrive as expected. To improve your productivity over the next year, it's best to have a written realistic business plan. In other words, set your intentions to do what is necessary to improve yourself *and* your financial circumstances. Make a commitment and write it down – in blood (just kidding).

"Our goals can only be reached through a vehicle of a plan, in which we must fervently believe, and upon which we must vigorously act. There is no other route to success." Pablo Picasso

For your practice to be lucrative, you must have a clear entrepreneurial vision and definable goals, complete with calendar deadlines. And since business should support your personal life and not the other way around, to be more inspired, determine your *personal* goals first and then build your business goals around them. Always keep your special heart-felt inspiration in mind, and of course, incorporate personal time for yourself and family into your plan. All work and no play makes for a dull boy or girl – and not many people enjoy dull. Just for the sheer enjoyment of life, it's important to regularly schedule time for yourself. To paraphrase a line from John Lennon's song, *Beautiful Boy,* life is what happens to you while you're busy making other plans. Though the best part of your life is the present "happening" unplanned moment, if you want a comfortable business volume in this time-measured 3-dimensional reality, planning is paramount.

To begin, ask yourself some important questions, for without them, there'd be no answers. And ultimately, it's the answers that will move your business in the desired direction at the appropriate velocity, and provide the needed inspirational impetus to create a dynamic written plan – and the incentive to implement it. The "why" is the primary motivation for achieving any tangible accomplishment.

➢ What inspires you? Hopefully, it's not all about work or money.
➢ What do you want to achieve from life?
➢ Where do you want to be a year from now or in ten years?
➢ What type of lifestyle do you prefer?
➢ What type of practice, full or part-time, would make you feel good?
➢ Do you prefer to work exclusively with buyers, sellers or both?
➢ Would you prefer to work alone or in a partnership or team?
➢ Would a small practice with friends and referrals ring your bell?
➢ Want to be a steady, service-oriented agent or a big hitter?
➢ What sales volume do you need to reach your net income objective?
➢ What expenses will you incur along the way?
➢ What activities are needed to create leads to hopefully turn into sales?
➢ What must be changed to improve your performance and results?

"Create a definite plan for carrying out your desire, and begin at once, whether you are ready or not to put this plan into action." Napoleon Hill

No two styles are necessarily mutually exclusive and there's no wrong way or wrong type, provided your projection is genuine. It's up to you. Once you've determined the life you prefer to live along with short and long term objectives, calculate the volume of business income necessary to achieve those personal goals or to live that lifestyle. Then decide what tools and skills you'll need to build that business. Be deliberate and conscious – and then make it so.

Work doesn't have to be difficult or exhausting. Actually, it should be challenging, but still fun and exhilarating. After all, much of your life is devoted to earning a living. (Is earning a dying the opposite? I've always disliked this phrase, as if to be worthy of living, we must work.) So, doesn't it make sense to be happy with your work? Consistent happy producers often have a savvy, well-considered business plan, if not written, at least intentions based on clear ideas of what they want to accomplish and how they intend to get there. They work smart by planning their business activities, faithfully following their plan and working strategically. And they don't usually depend on just luck and happenstance. Nor do they claim it's merely hard work, or as the old axiom goes, burning the candle at both ends. But no matter how you proceed, your chances of thriving – and enjoying your business – are dramatically greater if you *intend* to shoot for your *own* personal star. But you must *see* it first.

"He turns not back who is bound to a star." Leonardo da Vinci

When are you at your most resourceful, in other words, your most creative or energetic? Are you an animated night owl, and when the alarm sounds reveille in the morning, a lethargic slug? Then, evening is the time to concentrate on creative planning work. On the contrary, if your energy levels plummet with the sun and arise again at daybreak, schedule the planning process and other challenging tasks in the morning. Obviously, in today's digital world, while everyone else slumbers, you can accomplish lots. In order to increase productivity, take advantage of natural biorhythms by working while at your peak, when all cylinders are firing on full power.

Obviously, a solid plan must be created in advance. Unless you operate on a fiscal instead of a calendar year, this timely task is traditionally performed at the end of a calendar year. When most people are partying their way through the holiday season, take some time in a quiet room where you'll not be distracted or interrupted by phones, kids, spouse or the dog. It's imperative that your plan be yours alone. It must reflect *your* personal wants and wishes and not those demanded or insinuated by anybody else.

Mull over the past 12 months and think about what you wish to accomplish during the upcoming year. Consider how you prefer to conduct business, what activities you want to include in your practice and those you dreaded performing last year and would rather eliminate. If you decide to include those objectionable activities again, will you actually do them? And if you do, will you be effective? Unless you can improve your attitude, you'll make last minute excuses to avoid them. Don't try to fool yourself. If you're unable to delegate them, exclude them from the equation and invest that time and energy into activities that will make you smile.

"Perform without fail what you resolve." Benjamin Franklin

Goals and Roles

"If you cry 'forward', you must make plain in what direction to go."
Anton Chekhov

Will you be happy only when you reach a goal? That's called conditional happiness. It means that you perpetually kick your personal happiness ahead of you and risk never quite achieving it. Playing an artificial role will definitely be a problem. Many disillusioned, exhausted and stressed out agents quit because they don't know where they're going, and as a result, fail to enjoy the trip. Or they obsessively deprive themselves of an enjoyable personal life because they guilt themselves into working all the time. They often don't have a solid plan to follow and neglect to set realistic goals. They wander aimlessly and then wonder why they failed.

In the fantastical story of *Alice in Wonderland*, after she fell down the rabbit hole, Alice asked Cheshire Cat, "What road should I take?" He replied with the question, "Well, where are you going?" She said, "I don't know." His witty response was, "Then it doesn't matter. If you don't know where you are going, then any road will get you there." That succinctly sums up the entire concept of goals. When you set out on a road trip, you normally have a destination in mind, unless, paraphrasing a line from a classic Chuck Berry tune, you're riding along in your automobile with no particular place to go. On arrival, you've obviously reached your destination. But if you didn't know in advance where you were headed, how will you know when you get there? Well, setting goals works the same way. How will you know when you've achieved your goal if you fail to set one in the first place? How much satisfaction will you feel just cruising along with no hands on the wheel and no roadmap? You might just end up in the ditch – or lost. Having said this, you may enjoy the ride, but what sense of accomplishment will you achieve? Where's the thrill? Reaching a goal, even a modest one, can be a great attitude booster which in turn, can increase productivity and future goals.

"Follow effective action with quiet reflection. From the quiet reflection
will come even more effective action." Peter Drucker

SWAMIE

Goals are not necessarily money-related and can be anything under the sun – business or personal. They could be a planned participation in certain activities or events, self-improvement, the acquisition of a significant asset, the discharge of a major debt, finding a soul mate, losing body fat – virtually any tangible or intangible noteworthy accomplishment. But business goals should be specific, written, attainable, measurable, inspired and require significant effort. Let's address these one at a time:

> ➢ Specific goals are more motivating since general objectives could be just a wish. If not specific, how will you know when you achieve it?
> ➢ Written is important since a secret goal is easily changed, plus memories are notoriously undependable. In the long term, cheaters never prosper, especially if you're cheating yourself. Also, written goals can be readily affirmed anytime you're feeling off course.
> ➢ Attainable is important because even though your preference is to aim high, you may be setting yourself up for failure. It must be possible.
> ➢ Measurable goals are more motivating. Without a way to measure, how will you mark your progress and know when you've reached the goal?
> ➢ Inspiration is critical because goals are personal. If there's no passion involved, the path could be a boring, bumpy dead-end road.
> ➢ Effort is absolutely necessary, otherwise it's unworthy. If it takes little energy to achieve, the goal isn't ambitious enough. Shoot higher.

"Your goal should be out of reach, but not out of sight." Anita DeFrantz

Here's a simplistic example. Let's say you want to change a burnt light bulb in a high ceiling. You briefly ponder how to accomplish it. You're not tall enough to simply reach up and unscrew it, so you strategize a little. Hmm – I need something to stand on. Okay, I need a ladder and a new bulb. Maybe a quick trip to the local hardware is in order. If you're afraid of heights or aren't physically capable, you think about hiring an able-bodied person. Will you need to learn a skill? In reality, you're oblivious to the entire instantaneous thought process. Anyway, you get the point. Obviously it's not written, but it is specific, attainable and measurable and you're inspired to change the bulb, plus it requires effort.

You set a realistic goal and deduce the steps and necessary tools, skills, guidance or assistance needed to achieve it. Without a deadline or fixed time-frame, a goal is not a goal – it's a wish, a mere dream. If you don't commit to changing that bulb today, it becomes just another item on your "honey-do" list to be accomplished *sometime*. Without a plan and clear goals, your dream for a steady, lucrative practice based on returning clients and referrals will probably remain just that – a dream.

Because it's clearly measurable, let's now use money as a yard stick. If you set your annual or monthly income objective too high and you fail to achieve it, you may become despondent. The opposite holds true too. But if you easily reach your income goal, you'll be strangled by boredom. It was too easy. And boredom can lead to failure. Set your monetary goal at an attainable level that necessitates significant effort. When exerting effort toward something about which you're truly passionate, you'll naturally enjoy the ride.

Lazy people rarely succeed. Well, I suppose that's debatable since if their goal was to do nothing, then one could argue that by doing nothing as planned, they achieved their goal. They do as well as they choose to believe they're capable. There's a joke about a wife asking her sedentary husband what he planned to do that day. When he said "Nothing", she said, "That's what you did yesterday." His clever reply was, "Yes, but I didn't get finished." Now, there's a man with a clear personal goal. You can share your goals with your manager, spouse or best friend, but they're yours – not those assigned to you.

"Goals are dreams with deadlines." Diana Scharf Hunt

When I operated my own brokerage, during private year-end sessions with my sales staff, I'd ask each of them three questions; how much commission do they want to generate next year? After they replied, I'd ask how much they *think* they'll earn. I'd then ask the final question; what's the minimum total commission they absolutely must generate? Almost invariably, each subsequent answer would be a lower amount, sometimes radically lower. Sure enough, at the next year-end review, guess what goal they usually attained? Yup – the lowest amount – the minimum income. Most of them worked as hard as was necessary to earn enough to cover their basic living expenses. The exceptions were those who truly applied themselves, the bigger producers. They usually had business plans with specific goals.

To be able to measure your progress, it's prudent to establish both short and long term objectives. Weekly, monthly, quarterly, semi-annual, annual and even five and ten year goals are common. If you plan to generate the same amount of commission, year after year, because of inflation, you'll be earning a relatively lower net income every successive year. Slightly increase your goals each year because if your business isn't growing, it's shrinking.

"Efficiency is doing things right; effectiveness is doing the right things."
Peter Drucker

Now that you've determined your financial goals, how will you get there? What road will you take? What actions are necessary and in what quantity and frequency? Set your activity goals on a daily, weekly and monthly basis for the New Year and hold yourself accountable by faithfully keeping meticulous records. You can refer back to them in following years to help in your annual planning process.

Setting monthly activity goals allows you to adjust for each season. For example, in many market areas, spring is normally a busy period. Thus, activities such as door-knocking, door-stuffing and hand-shaking may be more fruitful in the warmer weather than during the bitter cold winter, not to mention a whole lot more pleasant. Traditionally, a good time to connect with people in your sphere of influence is in December. You'll probably have the spare time because during the festive season, business activity is normally lower. Also, quieter markets are an ideal time to organize marketing campaigns for the upcoming busy season. When in business mode, keep busy.

"I never worry about action, but only about inaction."
Winston Churchill

How many of your former clients will you commit to contacting during the quiet season or for that matter, each business day? With how many people will you speak daily, in person or on the phone, both familiar and stranger? To achieve a certain number of listings, for example, you may feel it necessary to contact a specific number of homeowners. Asking 20 may lead to a listing or that number might be 50. Much depends on your marketplace, the economy as well as your experience, skill level and determination. How many listings do you intend to have each month? How many sales? How many new clients and prospects do you want to add monthly to your network database? How many doors will you knock daily? How many open houses will you hold each month? How many referrals do you hope to generate? Once you answer such questions, it's just a matter of extrapolation to calculate the corresponding monthly, annual or longer term measurable numbers.

Newsletters are a great way to keep your name out there. However, my preference was the phone because it's more personal, yet still more efficient than knocking on doors, plus it's less invasive. But thanks to national privacy legislation, be careful who you call. After you've set appropriate activity goals – and committed to them – you'll have a solid action plan.

"When it is obvious that the goals cannot be reached,
don't adjust the goals; adjust the action steps." Confucius

Toward – Not Away

"The poor man is not he who is without a cent, but he who is without a dream."
Harry Kemp

Now let's examine goals from a different angle. To be truly effective, a goal should reflect an intention to manifest a dream. Hopefully, you don't dream about what you fear or want to escape from, but about what you want and where you want to go. Thus, a goal should not be to move *away* from something, to escape some adversity, be it poverty or emotional pain, a bad neighbourhood or loneliness. That's focusing on what you *don't* want. Instead, a goal must be to move *toward* something positive, to get somewhere or some thing and most importantly, to embody the person capable of creating that result. It's all about perspective. Positive beats negative every time. Think about what you *do* want – not about what you *don't* want. It's an energetically positive way to live.

Even though most tangible goals can be measured in concrete terms such as dollars, listings and sales, goals are spiritual in nature. I touch on this again later, but big lottery winners often lack the essential skills and beliefs to personally create, manage and retain sudden unexpected wealth, and for the same reason, often lose it within a short time. By actually – and genuinely – being the person who's capable of achieving a certain goal, you'll behave in accordance with your true nature. Your authentic self will unfold and manifest your heart-felt intention. And you'll be better equipped to begin to do whatever is legally and ethically necessary to create your heart's desire.

"The best way to predict the future is to create it." Peter Drucker

Intention Attention

"Nothing stops the man who desires to achieve.
Every obstacle is simply a course to develop his achievement muscle.
It's a strengthening of his powers of accomplishment." Eric Butterworth

Before you retire for the night and again first thing in the morning, when your subconscious mind is most receptive, visualize a clear intention to achieve your goals. Focus your *attention* on your *intention*. Imagine – with feeling – that you've already reached your goal. See yourself already owning that spiffy new car or gorgeous home. Visualize yourself in that wonderful romantic relationship, having perfect body weight or whatever floats your boat. Imagine yourself dressed beautifully in form-fitting attire as you and your loving partner turn your sparkling upscale automobile into the laneway of your very own luxury home. Do you see it? Do you feel it? Emotionalize about it. Get pumped! Get adrenalized! (Well, if you ever want to fall asleep, you might postpone the pumping 'til morning.)

Stick a written goal affirmation on the bathroom mirror and laminate a copy for your wallet. Clip one to your car's sun-visor. It could be something as simple as "I love my new country home" or "I am very grateful for my perfect health and weight" or "I truly appreciate that my phone is ringing every week with new prospects" or "I accept my own power" or "I love and approve of myself"; whatever sincerely inspires you. Repeat it to yourself frequently every day. Sing it in the shower when nobody's listening. Say it out loud (unless, of course, you're with a client; they might not appreciate hearing it). Create a colourful and fun vision board with your goals depicted by magazine photos and written affirmations. Attach shots of a beautiful home, your dream car or a travel brochure to an exotic locale. Post an inspiring quotation or a photo of an attractive business suit on a fit model's body, but with your face. Install it on the wall of your home office, bedroom closet door, the refrigerator or wherever you'll see it frequently. Hang a copy of your mortgage document or car loan, marked paid in full. Such reminders will regularly trigger appropriate thoughts and intentions. Allow your imagination to soar. The amazing results will reinforce a strengthening belief in the effectiveness of the process.

Feelings are vibrations that send out powerful attractive forces to the Universe. Since your subconscious mind doesn't differentiate between vivid visualization and physically experiencing something, visualizing is the key to attracting whatever you want into your reality. With startling results, some athletes and musicians systematically practice their performances this way. They can be reclining on their couch while visualizing their route to victory or hearing the complete musical performance. If you commit to regularly envision the realization of your goals, if you're consistent, persistent and focused on your intention, your subconscious will diligently operate in the background toward their achievement. Awakening each new day, you'll optimistically be ready to take the actions necessary to bring your goals into reality. This is how the Universal Law of Attraction works (more on this later). Live the life you want – first in your mind. Look at everything you want as if you've already got it. Treat apparent obstacles as interesting challenges to get past. Your victory will be much sweeter and so will everyday life. Be grateful for your blessings and the Universe will provide. Plan on it. Energy flows where attention goes.

*"Obstacles are those frightful things you see
when you take your eyes off the goal." Hannah More*

Attitude and Gratitude

"Joy is the simplest form of gratitude." Karl Barth

In your perpetual hunt for happiness, are you driven to acquire ever more stuff? Do you often think about what you don't have? Are you envious of someone who seems to have it all? Do you covet another's lifestyle? Such thoughts and behaviour not only demonstrate a life of ingratitude, but attract more scarcity. Is it wise to believe you'll be happy *after* you finally acquire them? If you consider that we're temporary custodians of our possessions, is it wise to connect your happiness to owning things that can disappear anytime – along with your happiness? Since true wealth is what you have left after all your material possessions have disappeared, would it not be more prudent to be *in* the world and not *of* the world, to adopt the belief that less is more? Wouldn't this lead to feelings of gratitude for whatever you have in every moment – all the time? An attitude of appreciation for all your blessings, as meagre as they may be, can manifest in you a sense of innate happiness. When you show appreciation, you'll attract positive energy. Why? Because you're in higher spirits.

"Acknowledging the good that is already in your life
is the foundation for all abundance." Eckhart Tolle

Setting professional and personal goals – and feeling grateful for the freedom and opportunity to work toward realizing them – will help you achieve not only the income level you wish, but also help reduce your stress. You'll find yourself worrying less and rejoicing more. Since your life will be more harmonious, you'll feel healthier – physically, emotionally and spiritually – and others will enjoy your company. You'll relate more effectively, which in turn will generate even more business. Mid-way through the year, you might reach a point where you have to increase your goals, or create new ones.

Around every corner are sales trainers who rightly profess that business productivity is directly related to attitude. Here's a small popular exercise with a big message. Apply a numerical value to each letter of the alphabet with "A" equalling one, "B" equalling two, etcetera. Then, apply the resulting numerical values to each letter in the term "hard work", thence the word "knowledge" and finally to the word "attitude" with "A" as one, "T" as 20 and so on. Go ahead; do it now and express the result as a percentage. It's those percentages that apply to life in general when it comes to the importance of attitude about anything and everything. Whereas hard work and knowledge will certainly contribute in a big way, it's attitude that will drive you to the finish line.

Life is short. You never know when your time is about to expire. If you were told you had only a week to live, what would you change about your life? What would you do differently? I submit that you'd not likely spend your final days sitting in your new sports car. If you have good health, a loving family, a warm hearth and secure roof, food on the table and a serviceable car in the driveway, then you have much more than the vast majority of our fellow Earthlings. Be grateful for everything in your life – and your attitude will soar.

"Attitude is a little thing that makes a big difference." Winston Churchill

Mission Statement

"We make a living by what we get, but we make a life by what we give."
Winston Churchill

Why are you or want to be a real estate sales representative? What's your aim? What do you hope to accomplish in our industry? Who are your target clients and how do you prefer to contribute to their lives? What services do you provide and how are they rendered? What sets you apart from the hoards of other registrants? How are you and your services unique? Why should a prospective client choose to hire you over someone else?

Once you answer these and other fundamental questions, create a written mission statement for your promotional material. It's not a mere slogan, but an operations manual that will aid you in convincing prospects to hire you. Your statement will serve as an explanatory action guide, determine your business path and help in the planning and goal-setting process. It'll detail your general goals for service and assist when policy and directional decisions must be made with respect to your practice. Consider the following example:

To enthusiastically render competent and dependable realty services to discriminating consumers of Wherever Town who seek personal, competent, considerate, attentive and friendly service at competitive rates.
Why do I do this? Because I love helping people.

Ask yourself what you must do to successfully fulfill the commitments made in such a statement. Do you personally attend to each and every realty need of your clients, or do you delegate responsibilities to assistants? Are you selective when accepting new clients? Are your rates competitive or do you only accept clients who appreciate your highly qualified service and are prepared to pay for it? Do you possess all requisite knowledge and skills to provide competent service? Are you systematic and dependable? Do your friends consider you considerate? And where would others find you on the friendliness scale? Do you love to serve? Know yourself, because this knowing will drive your business.

All business decisions, activities and goals will be guided by your mission statement because it spells out the reasons for your business existence. If you find this sample attractive, improving your education through courses and seminars to increase your knowledge would be relatively easy. Changing your personality, however, would involve a little more effort and commitment; not impossible, but certainly more challenging. Take some time to consider who you are and what excites you. (You may be surprised to learn that you're not who you've been programmed to think you are. Section III will provide you with more tools that may help you self-identify.) Ponder it all. Then create a unique mission statement that reflects who you authentically feel yourself to be. Your business will flourish and you'll live in joy because you'll be completely genuine. Now, let's discuss a very timely subject.

"Success or failure depends more upon attitude than upon capacity.
Successful men act as though they have accomplished or are enjoying something.
Soon it becomes a reality. Act, look, feel successful, conduct yourself accordingly
and you will be amazed at the positive results."
William James

Chapter Six

A Peace of Time

"Opportunity is missed by most people because
it is dressed in overalls and looks like work." Thomas A. Edison

Managing Time

As in any industry, success requires certain specialized skills. Obviously, a direct relationship exists between how highly honed they are and the level of success achieved. Many skills, such as social, interpersonal and communication, are instinctively learned and polished throughout a lifetime. On the other hand, specialized technical skills are learned, adapted and cultivated in the working field by way of hands-on experience, formal training or personal mentoring.

This chapter will address a skill which underlies *all* aspects of life and what is arguably the most important aptitude of all – managing your limited human time. It's practically impossible to manage every minute of every day, and frankly, who'd want to anyway. But by being more conscious of the passage of time – making every *business* minute count – while in your current incarnation, you can become a better agent – and a happier person.

Forgive my tangential thinking, but let's look at time from a lighter philosophical perspective. What is it anyway? Whatever it is, it's definitely fleeting. Is it possible for us to be out of time? Can we turn back the hands of time? Can one actually spend, make, save or waste time? Does time actually fly? Apparently so, since I hear it has wings. Is it possible to arrive somewhere in the nick of time? What exactly is a nick anyway? Is time money?

Apparently, linear or clock time isn't the constant once believed and actually may not be linear anyway. It's been theorized that past, present and future all occur in the same instant. Thus, the relentless progression of time may simply be a figment of our vivid imagination. Further, time may be accelerating as the Universe continues to expand from the Big Bang, that original pea-sized singularity from which the limitless Universe sprang. Some suggest this bang never occurred, that it was more of a fizzle. But if nobody was hanging around the water cooler at the time to hear it, was there really a bang? Anyway, to function in this manifested reality without losing our minds, we've conceptualized time as linear.

I've never met anyone who was technically capable of managing time. Nevertheless, with philosophical and theoretical physics aside, here are my thoughts on the subject from a more down-to-earth time-honoured perspective.

I'm sure that in your business life, you've experienced someone sticking their head through your office doorway or impeding your passage in the hall with innocuous chatter, innocently oblivious to the interruption of your busy schedule. Hey, we're social creatures with an inherent urge to connect. Frankly, I feel that people who need people are the luckiest people in the world. (Oh, wait, I feel a song coming.) You don't wish to be rude, so you politely permit them to steal your time. You enjoy social connections, but you also have a business to run and a schedule to keep. While your mind moves on to other pressing business matters, you politely listen to them drone on and on. The clock is ticking (now there's an old-fashioned concept), your eyes are glazing, you're trying to suppress a yawn reflex or your stress is building to a magnificent crescendo. Maybe after several subtle attempts, you finally succeed in extricating yourself from their verbal embrace, perhaps excusing yourself because you have an appointment or a need to pee. They apologize (maybe) and consume only a few more minutes of your precious time before, as you silently exhale a secret sigh of relief, they reluctantly exit your private space.

This was such a frequent occurrence for me that I finally decided to reverse my open-door policy. I really didn't want to shut people out, but the invasions were becoming far too common. I guess they were drawn to my radiating positive energy. The closed door helped somewhat, but unfortunately, didn't stop everyone. Persistent lurkers would still press their noses against my office window like anxious puppies, and boldly open my door and ask, "Gotta minute?" Of course, it was never just a minute. So, I finally loaded up the trunk and began working at home. That turned out to be a great change, with the added benefit of lower expenses. But when my dear mother, an adorable relic of a bygone era when people left for work in the morning, called to chat, I was never able to convince her that I was working. Sometimes, she thought I was sick and offered to bring over chicken soup. Hey – she was my mother! Anyway, a great deal of valuable energy is wasted due to the inefficient use of our limited amount of clock time.

"Time is the coin of your life. It is the only coin you have, and only you can determine how it will be spent. Be careful lest you let other people spend it for you." Carl Sandburg

Balance Bogosity

"He who lives in harmony with himself lives in harmony with the universe."
Marcus Aurelius

This idea may seem contradictory to common belief, but don't let anyone convince you to seek balance between your business, personal and family time. Why? If your life is balanced, you're spreading yourself thin to maintain that precious delusion of equilibrium – and not excelling at *anything*. Consequently, you're not investing sufficient time and effort into any particular leg of life to make a difference. Other than preserving a possibly mediocre status quo, you're staying afloat by treading water, but not progressing down-stream toward any significant goal. You're not succeeding big at home, at work or even with your "me time". What you really want is harmony.

To give everyone an equal opportunity to play their instrument, an average high school band can sound like the onslaught of a horrible headache. It has balance. Conversely, a professional symphonic orchestra flawlessly blends moments when the string section sings, the brass shines smartly, the melodic sound of the wood-winds flutter, the horns honk at centre stage or the percussion section thunders its presence. With the expert guidance of a skilled conductor following a musical score, orchestrated together, they collectively cooperate to create beautiful harmonious music. Well, your life should be the same, with you as conductor and a written life and business plan as score.

There are days when your business schedule is packed and you arrive home for a quick dinner (maybe) before heading out again for an evening appointment. When you're called out unexpectedly, your family may be disappointedly deprived of your loving company. Or you may miss a scheduled golf game or theatre date with friends; welcome to the real estate business. Hopefully, everyone will understand. With time, they likely will, provided you're consistent in your efforts to seek overall harmony by periodically arranging not only to enjoy private time, but also to have your family and friends regularly dominate centre stage.

When you're not business busy, your family will be the beneficiary of your time largesse. On family days and vacations, direct your attention toward them – and do so guilt-free. Don't be thinking business when you want and need to be in family mode. If you're unable to keep your mind off business, you might as well be working. If you fail to focus, you'll have lost your harmony, your spouse will divorce you and your kids will grow up while you weren't looking. By thinking business all the time, you may end up having lots of money and a great real estate practice. But by paying attention solely to building financial wealth, you'll have sacrificed something far more valuable – your loving family, not to mention your own physical health and soul.

"With an eye made quiet by the power of harmony and the deep power of joy, we see into the life of things." William Wordsworth

Life Supports

Every life is supported by five essential pillars – mental, physical, financial, relational and spiritual. If any of these pillars are unstable or inflexible or if you're devoting an excessive amount of time and energy to one or two, your life's structure could collapse. For example, due to excessively long work hours, if your physical health is suffering, how much energy will you have for yourself or your family? If you burn out mentally, how will you continue to operate a successful business? If there's torment on the home front, how could your business escape damage? If you're not behaving authentically – according to your true spiritual self – or your bank account is over-drawn, how do you think such emotional or financial stress could affect other pillars of your life? In addition to having solid finances and strong relationships, you need personal time for your own mental, physical and spiritual wellbeing. All pillars are inextricably linked.

By ensuring all five are functioning harmoniously like a finely-tuned orchestra, flexing when needed, when you're devoting necessary time and effort to any particular pillar, you'll not feel guilty. And guilt – a manifestation of fear and the opposite of love – attracts more negative energy into your life. In other words, fear spawns *disharmony*, whereas love emanates from *harmony*.

To achieve a healthy, blissful loving life of undulating harmony, of beautiful life music, focus periodic attention on each of these pillars in turn. By careful and conscious planning – with serious intent – and by avoiding rigid balance, you can be successful in all areas of your life. Sometimes it may not seem that way. But from a broad perspective, you'll achieve overall equilibrium. But I don't have time for a personal life, you say? Well, if your overall wellness is important enough, you'll become aware of where you spend your precious irreplaceable time and consciously re-order priorities.

"Happiness is when what you think, what you say and what you do are in harmony." Mahatma Gandhi

Priority Clarity

Many people don't know how to prioritize. Or if they do, because it won't take long, the easy tasks get done first. And once done, they feel they've actually been productive. Well, this may be technically true, but why are you in business? Yes, it's good to enjoy your work; as a matter of fact, for tangible, sustainable success, it's vital. However, isn't the primary purpose of business to earn a living, if not a fortune? Top priority items on your "to do" list should be those activities that will most directly create revenue. The rest is mere window dressing that can be postponed or delegated.

Here's a simple method of prioritizing activities. List everything to be accomplished on a particular day in your business schedule – keeping in mind revenue production – and record a number beside each item from one to four, with one being the highest, absolutely *must* accomplish activity. Two's *should* be done and threes *may* be done if there's time. All the fours, if not completed, can be bumped into the next business cycle. Then proceed to complete the highest priority activities first, followed by the two's and so on.

For overall time planning, divide each week into seven days and each day into three parts – morning, afternoon and evening. Then, block out five business and two family and/or personal days. Typically, to break up the week, you could schedule Sundays and Wednesdays off, with the former for a full family day and the latter as a "me" day when the kids are in school. Don't forget to nurture yourself too. On each of these five days, work two of the three segments. For example, work Monday morning and afternoon with the evening off duty. Work Tuesday afternoon and evening and keep the morning for personal stuff. Thursday, go golfing in the morning and work the rest of the day and evening. Friday could be a full business day with the evening for leisure and social events, and the same again on Saturday. That translates into a reasonable 40-hour work week. And as I said earlier, when scheduled to be off duty, your business mind should be off duty too – guilt free.

"There is nothing constant in this world but inconsistency." Jonathan Swift

As is life, our business is consistently inconsistent. Almost invariably, particularly when the market is hectic, somebody will need your expertise on an off-duty evening or you may have to present an offer on your golf day. Of course when duty calls, you're obligated to make yourself or a delegate available. If that responsibility demands that you work your planned personal evening, simply swap it with an alternate evening. Not too complicated.

However, as anyone in our business will appreciate, occasions will arise that will knock you off your planned schedule. You'll get really busy. Remember my comments about harmony? Well, this exemplifies when you'll be compelled to spend more time away from your familial and personal life pillars and toward business and financial pillars. The opposite will occur too. A client may cancel and unexpectedly gift you with an evening off. Surprise your family with an out-of-the-blue trip to the ice cream parlour or enjoy a personal run along the lakeshore or a hike through the forest. Take heart; if you'll allow the mixed metaphor, the door between pillars swings both ways.

Having said this, if I was unavailable for a client for personal reasons, unless it was absolutely unavoidable, I told them so. When my girls were little, my clients got to know that Sundays were routinely my family day. Use your discretion whether or not to succumb to frivolous demands on your time. Maintain your power by refusing or postponing appointments. You'd be surprised how many people will respect your choice. A request to list a property was fairly easy to schedule since time was usually not of the essence. Offers are a different matter though. And sometimes, a buyer was available on Sunday and not Saturday. No problem; I just switched my day off to Saturday. Or if I was really busy, I'd work both days and take a double day break mid-week. The key is to limit the number of hours devoted to business.

If you're scheduled to work, then that's what you do – work. Conversely, if you're on a family day, be present with your family, without thinking about business. If you're unable to focus, then you might as well be at work. Make a commitment to you because you're worth it. Develop healthy habits, new ways of thinking and behaving that will help you successfully fulfill your intentions. Think consistent harmony – not balance. But whatever you do, make a promise – and keep it.

> *"Words may show a man's wit, but actions his meaning."*
> *Benjamin Franklin*

About Choice

> *"Every man builds his world in his own image. He has the power to choose,*
> *but no power to escape the necessity of choice." Ayn Rand*

We each have 24 hours every day to choose how to spend. Many agents have a tendency to waste time on relatively mundane activities such as checking email, whiling away their time on social media websites or gabbing with friends during extended lunches. Many mistakenly believe they're working toward their goals, but are wasting a lot of time on daily minutiae. Not you? Keep a daily activity log for awhile and you'll see what I mean.

Is your work fun for you? If you're not enjoying your business, then maybe you're in the wrong business. I don't have enough time to do all this stuff? How about hauling your butt out of bed an hour earlier each morning? An hour of extra work time for every day of a five day work-week results in six extra 40-hour business weeks annually! What do you think you could accomplish with an extra six weeks?

"Waste your money and you're only out of money,
but waste your time and you've lost a part of your life." Michael LeBoeuf

Before participating in an unscheduled social event, ask yourself if it will contribute in a constructive way to the attainment of your goal. Your old employee time-killing self might leap at it, but your new entrepreneurial self, the one who'll make your business plans a reality, might decide otherwise. Which self you listen to will determine your path. Either way, your strength of conviction regarding the achievability of your goals will determine the priority of that activity.

As an agent, you're no longer trading time for money. In this context, time *is* money! When you're scheduled to work, don't waste it; leverage it. If a social opportunity arises, that's fine; go for it. But do this too often and you'll jeopardize your business, unless, of course, it's an opportunity to generate leads. Financial wealth is normally created and accumulated by anyone whose disposable income permits them to increase their assets well beyond their personal liabilities. Aside from inheritors and lottery winners, people such as entrepreneurs and successful business people, professionals, investors and upper-echelon bankers fit into this group. Salaried employees rarely accumulate any significant wealth, not only due to limited incomes, but because of limiting beliefs and dependant – sometimes victim – mentality. They often can't even imagine being unemployed. If you still hold the irresponsible employee mentality of trading time for money from when you were a drone in the labour force, or you habitually goof off, you'll never accumulate any significant wealth and will likely remain a debt slave for life.

Where do you fit in? Obviously, to be successful, you must be an entrepreneur. By assuming responsibility for your own success, by choosing calculated risks, by skilfully selling yourself with empathy and by having and respecting your own priorities, you'll undoubtedly create wealth. And the choice to diligently apply yourself to this endeavour by serving a growing clientele, future business will be lining up for you. Now that's leverage.

"Lost time is never found again." Benjamin Franklin

Highest and Best Use

Time is undeniably valuable. Do you consider your time to be more valuable in a monetary sense than that of someone who cleans houses, pools or mows lawns for a living? I'm not saying the people who perform those important tasks are inferior, for they require special skills too. And if they're happy, that's great. Here's my point though. If you're earning, say, an average of $100 per hour, why invest time into labouring on the more mundane aspects of life when you could hire someone else to do it at an hourly rate of $20? Why do your own repairs – and poorly – when you can hire an expert to do it well at $35? Don't waste your time during your peak earning years trying to be an expert at everything and doing it all yourself. If you really enjoy an activity as a hobby, save it for your personal days or retirement years when you have ample puttering time and are enjoying multiple income streams from numerous capital investments.

If you're thinking you can't afford to hire help, then you're right. It's certainly smart to live within your financial means. But you should also realistically consider the element of calculated risk. Just don't get crazy about it. You'll never be able to afford to hire help with an attitude of scarcity. Ask yourself what's the highest and best use of your time; cleaning your own house or prospecting for new clients? Hmm? If you think you'd better wait until you can afford it, you probably won't. But if you do it now, you'll have dramatically increased the odds of achieving fantastic wealth and more importantly, becoming the type of person who possesses the ability to not only create, maintain and enjoy it, but also to sustain the business necessary to continue building it. Let's now talk about talking.

"Time you enjoy wasting, was not wasted." John Lennon

Chapter Seven

Communication and Obfuscation

*"Whatever your grade position, if you know how and when to speak
and when to remain silent, your chances of real success
are proportionately increased." Ralph C. Smedley*

Clarity or Ambiguity

Marvellous technological advances have certainly had a dramatic impact on how realty agents operate. Wireless digital access to virtually infinite reams of data – and each other – has revolutionized the fundamentals of how we live life. But real estate is still all about people – not sticks and bricks and computer chips. It's still and always will be a personal service industry, with the emphasis on personal. Using technology, we've become adept at instantaneous interaction with colleagues, clients and customers. However, to build trusting, respectful relationships and create a durable practice, it's critical to communicate accurately. Any errors or misinterpretations can easily be amplified and harm relationships or worse.

In North America and beyond, a solid understanding of the English language (the current international language of industry and commerce; soon to be replaced by Mandarin?) as well as the language of your ethnic group is fundamental to achievement. For reasons that should be obvious, since major decisions are made based on your professional advice, it's extremely important that you and your clients understand each other. Accordingly, that advice should be unambiguous. When you realize you're repeating yourself, or your electronic message garnered an inappropriate response, maybe you were misunderstood. Don't blame them for their lack of understanding since it's common protocol for the communicator to ensure they're clearly understood. And the communication is not successful until the communicatee understands the verbal or written message.

*"Communication is a skill that you can learn. It's like riding
a bicycle or typing. If you're willing to work at it, you can
rapidly improve the quality of every part of your life." Brian Tracy*

For more general language help, especially if English is not your native tongue, consider registering for a communications or language course at your local community college. To clearly express your thoughts, make the effort to learn how to speak and write English intelligibly. Expand your vocabulary. Don't mumble; learn to enunciate. Speak up and be heard. If you're a *Seinfeld* fan, you may recall the trouble Jerry got into in the *Puffy Shirt* episode when he pretended to correctly hear a "low talker". Life got really crazy for him. And aside from potential misunderstandings, a low volume voice could be interpreted as a lack of confidence, which could damage business credibility. Speak up and not only will you exude more confidence, but it could pay dividends. Be bold. Be clear. Be an articulate professional.

The Art of Conversation

> *"Let's make a special effort to stop communicating with each other so we can have some conversation."* Mark Twain

When it comes to human relationships, smart phones are quite stupid. Actually, contrary to the common perception that we're living in a hyper-connected society, I think wireless communication is partly responsible for the growing sense of separation, of disconnectedness and the "dumbing down" of the world. It's redefining the meaning of community.

In this age of clipped messages, mysterious acronyms, bastardized language and easily misinterpreted tweets, texts and emails, to avoid misunderstandings, encourage prospects to *verbally* express themselves. Given the chance, they'll clearly tell you what you need to know to satisfy their wants and needs. To do this, you may have to initiate and participate in the underused and increasingly defunct art of conversation. Remember that method of exchanging thoughts and words using the human voice? It was the first wireless communication, and has been around considerably longer than trading artificial bytes of digital data over the airwaves. A conversation is defined as a spoken exchange of thoughts, opinions and feelings; key word – exchange. It's not an opportunity for talking heads to jabber at each other or trade digitized gobbledegook, but to converse *with* each other. A sensitive and sensible dialogue will not only help your clients, but also contribute to building a firm relationship for future business.

Communication isn't all verbal; it's also visual or physical. Your body can speak volumes and doesn't naturally lie. Therefore, grasp every opportunity to *personally* converse with your clients – with ears *and* eyes. Here are a few ideas to improve the visual element.

Kinesics

"Don't fake it till you make it. Fake it 'til you become it." Amy Cuddy

The study of body movement and expression, commonly referred to as body language or non-verbal communication, is technically known as kinesics. We move our bodies, as all animals do, in certain ways when communicating to enhance the effectiveness of the message, particularly when it's an emotionally or intellectually difficult one. When strolling through the jungle, have you ever come across a family of gorillas? Perhaps not, but visualize a mighty male silver-back standing daringly erect and thumping his massage fists against his barrel chest; there's a clear message there. Right? He's warning you to keep your distance because he's definitely in charge. And without being instructed otherwise, unless you're an idiot, intoxicated or have a death wish, you humbly and hastily exit his turf. That's non-verbal communication. Effective, right?

Non-verbal expressions can reveal a lot about both the sender and receiver. For example, hand, arm or even one of many timeless international finger gestures (let your imagination soar) can emphasize a point or relay an unequivocal message. Posture can reveal boredom or interest, and depending on the type and circumstance, touch can convey encouragement or caution. Waving and pointing are also commonly used for emphasis.

According to Amy Cuddy, social psychologist, associate professor and researcher at *Harvard Business School*, your body language contributes to who you are, how others see you and how you perceive yourself. Nonverbal behaviour, including body position, can influence others, even your own brain, and a few simple conscious body language adjustments can help increase your personal power. For example, slouching can reduce self-confidence and manipulate hormones that mess with your mind. Dr. Cuddy led a *Harvard* study in which participants were asked to appear smaller for two minutes by slouching while sitting or standing. Not only did they look more insecure, but they reportedly actually felt that way too. The results concluded a 10 per cent decrease in testosterone and a 15 per cent increase in cortisol, the stress hormone. Conversely, when participants were asked to hold a confident posture for another two minutes, standing tall with open arms and shoulders back, thereby making them feel larger, their hormones responded accordingly with a 20 per cent increase in testosterone and a 25 per cent decrease in cortisol. The conclusion? Sit and stand tall to not only radiate confidence and increase self-confidence, but also to decrease your stress level.

"We are what we pretend to be, so we must be careful
what we pretend to be." Kurt Vonnegut

This is a bit off-topic, but it fits into the discussion of hormones and your body's health. Unless you live in a cave, you probably know that testosterone is somewhat responsible for aggressiveness and assertiveness. But you may be unaware that cortisol, an important hormone secreted by the adrenal glands, is important for several bodily functions. It's commonly referred to as the stress hormone because it's also secreted in higher levels during the body's fight or flight response and is responsible for several stress-related bodily changes. Small increases of cortisol have some positive effects. But unfortunately, in our high-octane world, your automatic stress response is activated so frequently that your body doesn't always have a chance to return to normal. Result – chronic stress and adverse health effects.

Compare stress and worry in your life to a glass of water. Hold a full glass in your hand and raise that straightened arm. Easy, right? The actual weight doesn't matter since it's quite light, plus the difficulty depends on duration of the exercise. Raising it for a minute is easy, but elevate it for an hour; you'll likely have an unpleasant arm ache (and people will wonder about you). Raise it for a day and your arm will be exhausted or in pain. In each example, the weight of the glass doesn't change, but the longer you hold it up, and the more water, the heavier it seems to become. Just ask any parent who has carried a child around for awhile.

Now, consider the water in that glass as a negative life issue. If you touch briefly on that issue, say, the loss of a prospect, just long enough to deal with it, nothing much happens with your wellbeing. However, keep that issue on your plate a bit longer by holding a grudge, or regretting some action or inaction that might have contributed to that loss, it begins to cause damage. Dwell on it all day or harbour such thoughts and self-recriminating emotions for weeks on end and you'll feel exhausted and in spiritual pain.

Imagine what an excessive level of life-long stress can do to your wellbeing. Stress is considered a major contributor to the development of many chronic diseases. I'll address this subject later, but suffice it to say for now that thoughts are energy. Whenever you find yourself physically slouching or thinking negative thoughts such as regret, anger or frustration, to release your stress, consciously change your thoughts and posture. And definitely don't go to sleep at night in this condition. Put down all your burdens! Make it a habit to be in the *present* moment and not the past (regret) or future (worry). Feeling better, you'll send out a very clear message.

"We don't change what we are, we change
what we think what we are." Eric Butterworth

Here are a few ideas to help you feel and look more powerful and to communicate better with others:

- > **Fist Pump:** Before entering the negotiating room, calm your nerves by quietly shouting (I guess that's an oxymoron) to yourself, "Yes, yes, yes!" while slowly raising and rapidly lowering your forearm and closed fist. Have a *Rocky Balboa* moment. Hear the trumpets from the top of the staircase? Ensure you're alone, though, since others mightn't perceive you in a complimentary light.
- > **Head Up:** Except when contemplating an answer or referring to notes, looking down when speaking can indicate insecurity or lack of enthusiasm. Look them in the eyes, with occasional glances away to avoid appearing overtly aggressive. If your client or other party is sitting slouched with head down, they may lack confidence in their position.
- > **Open Palms:** While at the table, a palm up with fingertips toward the other person signifies openness to discussion. Conversely, palms down suggest no interest in hearing what is being said. You may be dealing with a flexible seller or an immovable force.
- > **Smile:** Smiling, laughing, frowning and crying are universal signs of happiness and sadness. Laughing is a (second best) stress reliever and consumes less energy than frowning. Only stop smiling to laugh. Unlike phoney smiles, the blatant destroyers of trust, sincere smiles can demolish defence barriers.
- > **Mirroring:** Natural subtle mirroring of a rival's or a client's body language can show understanding and put them at ease. For example, if they lean against the counter-top with hands relaxed in front, or lean sideways against a wall with one leg bent at the knee, casually mimic their stance. If you enjoy a good connection with your client, you may already instinctively exhibit this type of behaviour. When your seller is leaning into the table, copy it to show shared interest. Conversely, when presenting a buyer offer, particularly when the seller or their agent are leaning into the table while attempting to convince you of the merits of their counter-offer proposal, lean back in your chair. They may be consciously unaware, but your subtle, non-verbal message of low interest could change the direction of the negotiations. But be forewarned – you must be absolutely natural with this technique. If your client or counter-part detects artificiality, it could backfire.
- > **Eye Contact:** Maintaining regular eye contact with your client and nodding occasionally can show you're listening, which encourages them to continue. Consistent or extended eye contact can signal that

the client is respectfully open to what you're saying. On the flip-side, it can also mean they don't trust you enough to take their eyes off you; it depends on circumstances. On the other hand, a lack of eye contact can show negativity. If your client suffers from anxiety disorders or a cultural taboo, they may be unable to make comfortable eye contact. If they have arms crossed while making eye contact, something you've said may be bothering them and needs to be discussed more. If they're fiddling with something while looking directly into your eyes, they're probably thinking about tomorrow. You've lost their interest.

➢ **Eye to Eye:** There are three particular areas where a person will cast their eyes that relate to different states of mind. If they alternate their focus from eye to eye, followed by a look to your forehead, they may be assuming an authoritative position. If the same gesture is to the nose instead, they're engaging in what they believe is a neutral conversation wherein nobody is boss. The third is when the eye to eye look is followed by a glance to the lips. If you've ever viewed a romantic flick, this is a strong indication of sexual feelings. They may want you, baby! Be prepared to dash – or not. When your client is unconvinced, their eyes will look away for an extended period. An averted gaze, an ear touch or a chin scratch could show disbelief.

➢ **Head Tilt:** Slightly unfocused eyes looking straight at you or a head tilt to one side implies you've lost their attention – or they're too stoned to do business. Be careful though, because a head tilt may also indicate a sore neck or a lack of trust or physical safety. Unfocused eyes may also indicate ocular problems.

➢ **Forward Lean:** If they're leaning into the table, particularly if holding a pen in their hand, that's a fairly good sign of interest. At that point, trial close them (see the chapter on closing).

➢ **Blinking:** Deceit or withholding information can sometimes be denoted by touching the face or excessive (or no) blinking.

➢ **Yawning:** This is a clear indicator of zero interest or that somebody's exhausted. Attempts to change the subject could also signify you've lost them. To wake things up, have a tea and pee break. If they fall asleep, that's an even clearer sign their interest has vanished into the void and it's time to tuck them in for the night.

➢ **Folded Arms:** When a party's arms are folded across their chest, they're building an unconscious barrier between you. Prepare yourself because your work is definitely cut out for you. However, it could also mean they're cold. Or if the mood is amicable, they may want time to think about things and erect a temporary obstruction. But in a confrontation, particularly if leaning away and/or while speaking, it could mean they're expressing opposition. If their facial expression is harsh or blank at the same time, watch out – they're hostile. Get ready to run. If they're facing the door, they may be ready to bolt.

With non-verbal language, nothing is absolute. As a spoken word used in varied contexts can have multiple meanings, body language depends on circumstances. It's not unlike a phrase having different meanings in different locales. For example, "knocking someone up" in England means something quite different in America (an awakening occurs in either scenario). Since it's not totally dependable, don't rely on it completely, only as an adjunct to verbal communication. When listening to someone speaking their native tongue, and you possess a rudimentary comprehension of their language, physical gestures can improve accuracy. However, the risk of misunderstanding remains. Use it wisely and in context.

Understanding your client isn't solely about listening to what they say. A big part of comprehension includes your innate ability to intuit what is spoken *between* the lines. This is where non-verbal communication enters the picture. Having the capability to "read" your client is a critical skill. Anything you can do to enhance this skill, including taking appropriate courses or reading self-help books would be a good idea. And while you're in the studious mood, learn a second or third language, even if it's purely conversational. In our world's growing cultural melting pot, having additional languages at your disposal would be a great advantage.

It takes years to build a solid reputation of integrity and confidence, and during a miscommunication, mere minutes to destroy it. Think butterfly effect. As the miniscule effect of the flap of a butterfly's wings can theoretically be felt around the world, a misspoken or misunderstood word or gesture can have a devastating long term effect on your career.

"The more you trust your intuition, the more empowered you become, the stronger you become and the happier you become." Gisele Bundchen

Ear to Hear

"Never fail to know that if you are doing all the talking, you are boring somebody." Helen Gurley Brown

The other side of speaking is listening, which arguably is the more vital half of effective communication. Actually, when you think about it, poor listening renders speaking superfluous. In today's hyper world of instantaneous digital communication, you might even say listening is becoming a lost art. Anyway, it's something people take for granted. You've got ears, so it's automatic. Right? Nope. You might think you're listening to someone, but may be hearing your inner voice, remaining alert only enough to recognize the moment to respond. By failing to pay sincere attention, thus misinterpreting a speaker's message, reactive and emotionally inappropriate responses are definitely within the realm of a possibility. And whether personal or business situation, a price could be paid for such inattentiveness.

Have you ever met someone who had what is commonly referred to as the gift of gab? They may have been told they'd make a great salesperson. Why? Because the stereotypical perception of a sales person is one who can blather on and on and talk anyone into doing anything. Well in reality, this definition couldn't be further from the truth. There's little doubt, though, that some sales people fit this description. I've never met anyone who enjoys being coerced to buy something by an aggressive, high-pressure yakker spewing verbal diarrhoea. To escape the barrage, I suppose a pathetic prospect might surrender. However, just like a teacher can't teach someone who refuses to learn, a salesman can't normally sell someone who doesn't want to buy. If they don't run away, the victim may sign the contract, later regret succumbing to the pressure and exercise their right to rescind. The buyer cool-off period for new condominium and vacation timeshare purchases exists for good reason. Also, if a high-pressure agent closes a hapless buyer, they shouldn't count on that buyer ever referring anyone or returning for future service.

"We have two ears and one mouth so that
we can listen twice as much as we speak." Epictetus

Given the chance, a client will deliver their hot buttons to you on how to sell them. The trick? Listen carefully. A gabber can miss important, sometimes subtle closing signals. While awaiting cues, they talk right past the clues. My theory is that they may be so fearfully insecure and desperately in need of a sale, they'd rather not hear what they believe their client might say if given the chance to speak. Therefore, they yammer away in the hope of offering so many good reasons to sign that the overwhelmed prospect finally surrenders.

How can you successfully satisfy a client's wants and needs without knowing what they are? Sometimes, *they* don't even have a clear picture of what they want. If you don't know what makes them tick, what motivates them, how can you serve effectively? Thoughtful, considerate listening by a trustworthy agent facilitates a clear response to a client's questions and the gentle orchestration of a more pleasant sale – without the trusting buyer even realizing they were sold. To enjoy a fruitful career, build a trusting client base by starting in the present listening moment, one client at a time.

"Trust is the glue of life. It's the most essential ingredient in effective communication. It's the foundational principle that holds all relationships."
Stephen Covey

Wandering, Catching and Engaging

"I like to listen. I have learned a great deal from listening carefully. Most people never listen." Ernest Hemingway

There are 2 types of passive listener – reverent and irreverent. The former respectful, non-reactive hearing is acceptable at a cinema, lecture or theatre where, beyond participating in collective applause, a personal response is not expected. The latter more common type is subdivided into 2 subcategories – the Wandering Mind and the Noise Catcher.

When listening with a passive Wandering Mind, you're paying only sporadic, unfocused attention to the speaker and allowing your mind to meander away on mental errands. Where are you going to have lunch? Your back is aching. How can you escape this talking head? While the speaker drones on, you're distracted by your cell phone or eavesdropping on a nearby conversation. While impatiently awaiting the first opportunity to break away or break into what is essentially a monologue, you're already composing a response to your fragmented understanding of what's being said *before* they even finish.

Noise Catchers, even worse passive listeners, absently hear few of the words spoken and aren't even close to comprehending the underlying meaning. In such case, you're not present. There's no connection whatsoever. Because you fail to focus on the continuity of the communication, you miss the real or implied message. You respond with general comments, if at all, and gamble that your replies make sense. You smile, nod and more or less tune out. You're disrespectfully disengaged.

If you want to encourage someone to honestly express themselves, to be absorbed in the buying or selling process, to truly get to the heart of a matter (and you enjoy a good conversation), being an Active Engager is far more productive. While your client is talking, pay undivided attention with appropriate eye contact and body gestures. Put down your pen or personal communication device and quietly focus exclusively on them. Listen to *what* they're saying and *how* they're saying it. Sense the nuance, the feeling behind the words. Observe their body language, their gestures. Don't let their quirks, mannerisms, speech patterns, personality or physical appearance interfere with listening. Listen for the true intent of the message. Nod occasionally and maintain a body posture to show interest and understanding.

Resist judging prematurely and mentally formulating a reply or interjecting until they've finished articulating their thoughts. Why? Because your response may change. Certainly, be aware of your thoughts and feelings as they manifest, but resist the urge to interrupt to express them. When you detect a pause in their monologue, and not merely when they break briefly to breathe, seek necessary clarification. Sensitive questions bespeak sincere respect and caring interest. After they're finished making their point – and you might have to ask repeatedly if they are – for further clarification, summarize what they said and paraphrase it back to them.

To be an effective listener, you must concentrate. Respectful, considerate, focused, active engagement tends to increase rapport. You might even learn something of value about them. What they say is obviously important to *them*. If you care, it should be to *you* too. After you've answered their questions and provided the information they need to make a decision – be quiet. Stop talking and listen to their replies. And when you get the cue, when the time is right, trial close them. Now, that's salesmanship.

> *"Wisdom is the reward you get for a lifetime of listening*
> *when you'd have preferred to talk." Doug Larson*

For obvious reasons, this technique won't be as effective with email or texting. On the phone is slightly better, but it's still not as powerful as face to face. With recurrent and persistent practice, this valuable skill will eventually become habit. Remember that giving appropriate feedback, including sending both verbal and non-verbal signals, is a large part of the process. Whether your client consciously realizes it, if you're a Wandering Mind or Noise Catcher, the usual consequence is they'll feel unimportant because you're essentially ignoring them. Passive listening does not demonstrate the respect they deserve. As no doubt you can imagine, an Active Engager usually generates quite a different feeling – one of trust and respect.

I guess it's obvious that I equate a good sales person with being a good listener. Hear what people say and don't say and you'll be better equipped to present acceptable solutions, handle objections, present logical arguments and fulfill your fiducial responsibility. When the dust settles, they'll be grateful for your thoughtful guidance. Provided their decision was in *their* best interests, they won't feel they've been pressured. With professional attention to detail and sensitivity to their feelings, it will be obvious you honourably put their interests ahead of your own. And since you courageously, considerately and attentively listened to them, you become a hero.

"Courage is what it takes to stand up and speak;
courage is also what it takes to sit down and listen." Winston Churchill

Realty Fealty

It's common knowledge that you are what you eat. But you're also what you breathe, read, hear, watch, think, do and believe. How you take care of your body, mind and spirit reflects on how you live your life. And a large part of your life is your business practice. Thus it follows; to have a great, sustainable business, it helps to have a great personal life; they're not mutually exclusive. Take good care of every aspect of your being. As discussed earlier, manage your time harmoniously with clear priorities for all the pillars of your life because they're interdependent.

We all appreciate the opportunity to express our thoughts and feelings and to have someone hear them. That's why great agents encourage their clients to speak openly. If you want your client's respect and loyalty, actively listen to them. Buying and selling a home is an emotionally charged event for everyone. You're technically creating a sale, but at the same time, have an ideal opportunity to connect and bond with your client. If they're highly satisfied, they'll become the town crier and tell everyone about how wonderful you were throughout the home transition journey. You have the chance to earn their realty fealty for life.

Here's a final thought; the words "listen" and "silent" share exactly the same letters. Coincidence? I think not.

"Find a need and fill it." Ruth Stafford Peale

Chapter Eight

One Agent: Commanding Loyalty

"Unless commitment is made, there are only promises
and hopes, but no plans." Peter Drucker

Human Doing or Human Being?

"Everyone lives by selling something." Robert Louis Stevenson

What do you do? It's a common inquiry. You could say you're a human *being* that lives, loves and grows, or a human *doing* that subsists and struggles for survival. However, to elicit such an esoteric response isn't the usual reason for such an innocuous enquiry. From a more pragmatic perspective, how would you reply? You're registered as a sales person or broker, but what exactly is a sales person? Actually, as a species, since we're always selling ourselves to survive and procreate, to meld into society, it could be said that with varying degrees of success, absolutely everyone on the planet is involved in sales.

Now, here's something else to ponder; who actually sells real estate? If you believe you do, then technically, you'd be wrong because only owners can sell their property (unless forced by government under some Draconian law). You don't have the legal right to sell another's property. A seller sells and a buyer buys. Notwithstanding government legislated designations, you undertake the responsibility to *represent* those needing skilled disposition and acquisition services.

Clearly, just like a building contractor, lawyer, doctor or auto mechanic, you're paid to perform a service. And rather than guaranteed compensation based on an hourly rate or flat association-established fee schedule, you're normally paid a percentage commission on the successful completion of service. So, what exactly are you – a sales person or a service provider? As inferred earlier, I submit that you're the latter. If a lawyer or doctor were compensated only on successful completion of their undertaken task (as some American litigators are paid), could they also be considered sales people? This would normally not be the case, but not because they're paid by the hour or by a flat fee. Doctors are service providers and presume they're correct in their diagnosis, but nowadays, increasingly must convince – or sell – their patient on the accuracy of their medical assessment. Lawyers must argue – or sell – a judge or jury to prove their postulations are correct. Because we provide a valuable service, maybe the norm for our industry should be to offer clients a flat fee or hourly rate in lieu of a percentage commission fee.

Purely Prognosticating

"Skill is the unified force of experience,
intellect and passion in their operation." John Ruskin

Merriam-Webster defines a salesperson (paraphrased) as one who "sells merchandise or services, either in a shop or by canvassing in a designated area." It defines selling as "delivering or giving up property to another in violation of duty, trust or loyalty and especially for personal gain, for something of value, especially foolishly or dishonourably, to exact a price for, to give into the power of another, to deliver the personal services of for money, to dispose of or manage for profit instead of in accordance with conscience, justice or duty, to impose on or cheat, to cause or promote the sale of something or to influence or induce to make a purchase". Well, I don't know how you feel about this definition, but little of it fits with my self-image. If for no other reason than self-respect, you must not think of yourself as such. I'm repulsed by the preconception of the stereotypical deceptive, aggressive, greedy manipulator as commonly depicted in the media.

Think about how you felt when you were last gently persuaded to buy. How did you feel? If the sales rep was pushy, you probably quickly took your leave. To accurately determine your wants and needs, did they ask sensitive questions? Did they patiently listen, or in an attempt to coerce you, simply talk *at* you while extolling the many virtues of their product? Did they honestly explain things, offering valuable information and alternatives? If they showed sincere interest in fulfilling your needs and presented the right product or service, you bought. Right? However briefly, they became a trusted fulfillment specialist.

Maybe the official designation of "salesperson" is a misnomer. Perhaps our industry's regulators should amend the act to more accurately designate a real estate practitioner as a "property transition facilitator", "realty service specialist" or "home marketing consultant"; maybe even the more generic "realty agent". With the gradual implementation of higher educational requirements and increased focus on professionalism, maybe we need a more professional handle. A realty agent is a consultant who usually performs the role of agent in the field of real estate marketing, negotiation, acquisition and disposition. Expert knowledge, experience and various related skills, not to mention expensive tools and overhead, all contribute toward efficiently calming the potentially challenging waters of real estate trading. Thus, you deserve better and more accurate recognition. Though unlikely to occur anytime soon, it's time that our realty designation matched reality. Having said this, redefining the term might be easier, but how do you alter prejudicial public perception? One client at a time.

Regardless of your official designation, you know instinctively what makes a good salesperson, and it's not pressure tactics. To build a solid, sustainable career, a good agent doesn't resort to the more ignoble characteristics as depicted in the current definition. So, how do you develop a lasting business consisting of loyal returning and referring clients? By setting out on the path to be the best you can be, by mastering the skills necessary to assertively and ethically assist consumers achieve their goals – by making yourself indispensable. And a major part of that path is the ability to inspire trust in and win commitment from your prospects. You want to be "The One".

Trust and Commitment

"Commitment is an act, not a word." Jean-Paul Sartre

Many people distrust any and all salespeople because they fear being coerced into committing to do something they'd prefer not to do. Their defences are often immediately raised and sometimes indefinitely remain there. How do you respond when approached by a sales clerk in a home electronics store? Just looking, you say, because you automatically distrust anything they offer in their sometimes poorly veiled attempt to sell you something. They're definitely salespeople loyal to the seller – or to themselves – and not agent intermediaries. Unlike an electronics salesman, your mission is not to pressure someone into a decision. Your task is to determine your client's needs, establish their realistic affordability and patiently and persistently endeavour to fulfill them. And the best way to accomplish that mission, as I continue to say, is to gain their trust.

It's wonderful when you can enjoy the benefits of having your professional advice not fall upon deaf ears or stone-cold hearts. People traditionally and automatically trust their doctor, lawyer or pharmacist (not always justifiably), but you must *earn* your client's trust. Do you not dream about having unquestioned client loyalty? Not to take advantage of them, but for the comfort in knowing that not only will you satisfy them, but when all is said and done, you'll be compensated for your efforts. After all, you often invest considerable resources and don't always receive a return on that investment. People stray. Circumstances change. Loyalties shift.

But think about it; if you were always guaranteed complete loyalty and compensation, the lower risk could conceivably translate into lower income, and our industry would significantly morph. Having said this, it's up to you whether you choose to accept a prospect as a client in the first place. *You* must trust *them* too. Normally, to a point, you do because the potential substantial remuneration is worth the risk; that's why you earn the big bucks. If you're not being appropriately compensated for that risk, you may want to address the issues by changing your method of operation.

I propose that most consumers would prefer to place their faith and trust in just one realty agent. After all, they traditionally trust one doctor, lawyer or religious leader. Why? Aside from being programmed, it's easier than assuming personal responsibility for their medical, legal or spiritual health. By trusting one honest agent, the home relocation process can be much simpler and more agreeable for everyone involved.

> *"A man who trusts nobody is apt to be the kind of man nobody trusts."*
> *Harold MacMillan*

BRA Comfort

If a new buyer customer wasn't recommended to you by their trusted friend, prior to their agreeing to become your client, you might have to jump through a few hoops to gain their trust. Until that occurs, they may choose to work with multiple agents. At some point during the preliminary relationship-building phase, it's a good idea to actually ask for loyalty by seeking a Buyer Representation Agreement (BRA). You might feel some trepidation about asking, but that speaks to a lack of personal confidence – or poor timing. After a certain comfort level has been established, just ask. With the right timing and a smart, honest presentation, you might be surprised with a yes.

In exchange for a promise of exclusivity, make sure they understand that you're also making a serious commitment *to them*. Don't be bashful about explaining the two-way commitment. Their forsaking all other agents is accompanied by your acceptance of full fiduciary responsibility – including the associated risks – to protect their interests. Not only will *you* feel more secure, but *they* will be comforted with the knowledge that you'll work harder and more conscientiously for them. It may sound ruthless or crass, but let's be frank; you're risking not only your legal neck, but also your time and money on the sometimes slim chance of being paid at the end of the day. Agents need to earn a living too. By working harder for your client than you might for a mere prospect or customer, you're more assured of a payday down the road. It feels great to know you have a serious and loyal client. Feel good about it because with a BRA, not only will your mutual bond be enhanced, you'll also not feel as inclined to pressure them into a purchase before they stray to another agent. Would you prefer your prospect to be just involved or to be committed?

"The difference between involvement and commitment is like ham and eggs; the chicken is involved; the pig is committed." Martina Navratilova

When you ask for a commitment and they baulk or outright decline your invitation, the ethical thing for them to do is to disclose this choice to all agents involved. Then all agents can make an informed decision whether to risk their time and effort. Perhaps, you might prefer to avoid noncommittal buyers altogether. But speaking plainly, by distrusting a realty agent, wouldn't it be natural for that agent to return that distrust? If all the agents choose to continue, you may want to forewarn your customer to be prepared for possible pressure tactics by competing agents in their hasty attempts to close them at any opportunity. Also, forewarn them about their possible commission liability if they mistakenly enter into multiple representation agreements.

It's nice to be their friend in the business, not only to answer occasional questions, but to enjoy the honour of their recommendations to friends. Most people move a few times in their lifetime. Once you've earned their trust and respect, they'll likely return to you for service every time because it's easier than interviewing agents all over again. It's a good feeling to know you've earned a trusting, long term relationship with a respectful client.

Courage and Competence

"Courage is resistance to fear, mastery of fear – not absence of fear."
Mark Twain

Why do so many agents fail? The easy answer is they fear rejection. It seems rather simplistic, but who enjoys being rejected time and time again? Because they don't want to be rejected, they often fail to commit to making the necessary effort to succeed. They don't try hard enough. They don't persist. Those whose defeats outnumber their victories usually don't enjoy the business.

And if they don't enjoy their work, why continue? But it's agents who face their fear, jump in with both feet, take risks and commit to doing whatever is ethically necessary to win that are ultimately rewarded.

Sometimes, new agents are almost immediately successful because they may not realize their low competency level, or they choose to ignore it. They're *unconsciously incompetent*, in other words, they don't know what they don't know. So, they just get out there and make mistakes, learn from them and continue to enjoy many great years in the business. Over time, as they grow through the various competency levels, they develop the skills and acquire the knowledge necessary to maintain at least a moderately lucrative business, if not hit the big time. And they seem to enjoy the business.

> *"Inaction breeds doubt and fear. Action breeds confidence and courage.*
> *If you want to conquer fear, do not sit home and think about it.*
> *Go out and get busy."* Dale Carnegie

Then there are those who are also busy immediately, but after serving those in their warm network, who were part of their motivation to enter the business, they hit a wall. Their productivity suddenly drops. Why? Because as they proceed to meet new people, be they already successful agents or savvy prospects, they begin to realize their perceived deficiencies, blame themselves or the world and crucially, fail to learn from their mistakes. They are fearful *conscious incompetents* and refuse to do anything about it. When a newbie meets a tough prospect, a fear of failure can surface into their conscious mind like a circling shark fin at dinner time. To avoid the stigma of failure and accompanying pain, embarrassment and sense of inadequacy, they tell their friends they quit because they weren't enjoying the business. They convince themselves, or at least their ego, that they weren't forced to quit; they voluntarily resigned. Thus, in an indirect way, it becomes a positive personal decision for them.

> *"Joy lies in the fight, in the attempt, in the suffering involved,*
> *not in the victory itself."* Mahatma Gandhi

A teenager is usually unaware that they're not competent to drive a car. It looks easy when they see someone else doing it, so they think it must be easy. They're an **unconscious incompetent**. The first time they get behind the wheel, they quickly realize they're incompetent, but they persevere and quickly transition to the level of a **conscious incompetent**. They're highly motivated, refuse to be discouraged and understand they have much to learn – and go about learning. After much practice, their skills improve to the point where they graduate into being a **conscious competent**. At this level, they must still consciously think before every operational decision, but they're learning from their mistakes and keep their goal in sight. Eventually, as their skills become honed, they move up to the final level of **unconscious competent** when, with the obvious exceptions, virtually all their driving functions are automatic. They don't have to think about how to perform every little mechanical function. Driving a car pretty much becomes habit.

> *"Bad times have a scientific value. These are occasions*
> *a good learner would not miss." Ralph Waldo Emerson*

After you've worked in the business for awhile and your skills become polished and no less important – you are aware – you'll move through the various competency levels and develop strategies for success. As competency increases, you'll be better equipped to earn loyalty. Having said this, honesty from the beginning is a great place to begin. Your reactions to common scenarios in the field will become increasingly automatic. You won't have to consciously think about what to say. You'll react according to habit stored in your subconscious in a manner that has brought you success in previous similar situations. And the more you operate on automatic, the more competent you'll appear – and become. It snow balls. The trick, though, is to maintain your sincerity. By reacting in a boring, disinterested fashion, you'll quickly discourage your prospect. Keep it fresh. Keep it candid. Continue to show you care. Even though eventually, you could perform the task with your eyes closed, nobody wants to be treated with a rubber stamp.

In today's real estate world, many consumers have forgotten all about the concepts of loyalty, trust and faith in their fellow man. They seem to have duped themselves into believing that it's all about the money. How much can they get at the lowest cost? Instead of searching for an agent in whom they can place their faith, they look for one who offers the best deal, be it a discounted commission or kick-back. And worse, some unscrupulous consumers fail to declare their intention up front that they intend to demand a deal when an offer is put in front of them. You can choose whether to accept such people as clients, but it was always my practice to reject that kind of business at the earliest possible moment. I refused to work from a place of fear and scarcity. If I felt I wouldn't enjoy working with them, I declined the business. Why? I had the faith that another prospect would be waiting for me just around the corner.

It's tough to maintain equilibrium in our industry because of its inherent nature of wins and losses. Just like cash flow management wherein you use revenue to pay debts, focus on chopping the emotional peaks to fill the valleys. Do your best to maintain a moderate, level frame of mind. Feeling down about losing or refusing a client? Don't, because tomorrow is another day with another prospect. The same thing applies to victories. It's fine to celebrate, but don't go crazy. Save some of that ecstasy for the inevitable sense of loss next week. Maintain your calm and appreciate your journey. Look at your practice from a broader perspective. Enjoy and learn from every experience. As the spiritual teacher, Eckhart Tolle says, "This, too, shall pass." It works both ways. People will come and go from your life, both those who upset you and with whom you comfortably establish honest, trusting and loyal relationships. With the latter, in many cases, you'll be The One. Have faith.

"Take the first step in faith. You don't have to see the whole staircase, just take the first step." Dr. Martin Luther King Jr.

SECTION II

NUTS and BOLTS

"Life is pretty simple. You do some stuff. Most fails. Some works.
You do more of what works. If it works big, others quickly copy it.
Then you do something else. The trick is the doing something else."
Leonardo da Vinci

Chapter Nine

Seeking Prospects

"Personal relationships are the fertile soil from which all advancement, all success, all achievement in real life grows." Ben Stein

Why a career in the real estate business? Was it the siren song of big bucks sung by someone in the industry? Perhaps it was the allure of personal independence, of being essentially self-employed or the flexible hours? Maybe the ticket was spontaneous vacations or long weekends. Or were you inspired to help people bring their home ownership dreams into reality because you love people? Good motivations all, from opportunistic to idealistic. Without a doubt, though, this business is definitely about people. As a matter of fact, unlike many who mistakenly think of it as a realty selling business, it's really a business rooted in human relationships. Often, it's more about *who* you know than *what* you know. Hence, the more people skills you possess, the more likely you'll enjoy a long and rewarding career.

I've always felt that the secret to success in this often misunderstood business is to build as many sincere relationships as possible. To do this, you have to actually leave your chair. Get busy meeting people. Prospecting for leads doesn't have to be laborious. It can be interesting and entertaining, fun and maybe even educational. Use your imagination. Put your heart into it. Without an eidetic memory, there's no way you can cope with the myriad details of a growing group. Enter the contact info of every likable person you meet into your contact management program for periodic contact.

Generating leads by spending big bucks can indisputably be effective, but here's the problem – it's expensive and becoming ever more so. Revenue is certainly important, but unless you thrive on fame, it's your net income that really counts. If you want to build a business without spending a lot of money, learn to improvise. Your ultimate goal is to build a referral business. The foundation on which a smart realty practice is built is not just competency in your trade, but repeat clients and referrals. People need people. So, get out there in the field where your charm and wit can win valuable connections – and business. When opportunity knocks, improvise.

> *"These are days when no one should rely unduly on his competence.*
> *Strength lies in improvisation. All the decisive blows are struck left-handed."*
> Walter Benjamin

Warm Calling

> *"The telephone is a good way to talk to people*
> *without having to offer them a drink."* Fran Lebowitz

It's the activity we love to hate. Unfortunately, this gold standard of lead generation is inappropriately referred to as "cold calling"; inappropriate because in reality, such calls should be warm. If they were some degree of warm, do you feel you might be more inclined to make them regularly? Probably, right? Nobody enjoys cold, unless it's a frosty beer on a hot day. Why do we hold this arguably necessary activity in such low regard? As I said earlier, nobody enjoys rejection. No one wants to expose themselves to a homeowner's disdain. But this timeless activity doesn't have to be awful. Consider this; maybe you receive the reaction you *expect*. If you anticipate the homeowner will be cordial, maybe they will be because you're already in that head space. If you're not worried about rejection, your chat, though brief, may be welcomed. Your voice is not the only thing that travels through the phone line; emotional energy is transmitted too.

Why do you make the calls? If you've been unable to fulfil a buyer's needs, maybe you're seeking an interested homeowner whose property is not yet listed. You know their preferred neighbourhood and house style, so it's an easy drive through the area to compile a contact list of prospective properties. You might first send a personally addressed letter of introduction and explanation, stating that unless you hear from them, you'll call or knock on their door to say hello. (This approach was very effective for me.) Since the homeowner anticipates your call or visit, you might find yourself engaging in a friendly conversation. If they're not interested at the moment, add them to your business network for future follow-up or maybe a future listing.

Not everyone will appreciate your initiative. For some, the timing may not be right. Some will be curt, others cordial. Many will fall into the latter group, but still not likely remain on the line for long, and that's perfectly fine. You may have mere minutes to deliver your message before they end the call. Prepare a script and practice a natural delivery – not like a recording.

Everybody hates automaton telemarketing because it's obviously disingenuous. Make it real. Be sincere. Role-play with a partner until you've developed a good comfort level. Your partner's attitude could randomly rotate between pleasant, civil and obnoxious. With practice, you'll learn to instantaneously adapt, to think on your feet. If you talk to people regularly, the odds will favour you and your devotion will eventually generate business.

If you had planned to make warm calls in the morning, but when rolling out of bed, the mere thought of it makes you nauseous, give yourself a break. Reduce the number of calls or delay to the afternoon or another day. If you're not in the mood, you may mess up anyway. By doing fewer, it may not seem so arduous. Focus on achieving the smaller goal and you'll likely complete them successfully. Who knows – maybe after you've reached the lower target and have found most of the homeowners congenial, you may feel like doing a few more. As time permits, press onward.

Farming and Charming

> *"Nature gave men two ends – one to sit on and one to think with.*
> *Ever since then, man's success or failure has been dependent*
> *on the one he used most."* George R. Kirkpatrick

Farming is great for developing leads. But it takes patience, perseverance and the will to get out into the field. Now, I'm not suggesting you start growing hemp. In case you're unfamiliar with this term in the realty sense, it refers to the tried and true practice of methodically working within a pre-defined area or people group. With regular systematic contact, personal high visibility and occasional distribution of quality promotional material, you'll grow to be the readily recognized specialist. For a neighbourhood, club or association where there's commonality, as your profile becomes increasingly commonplace, residents or members will begin to accept you as the local professional and hire you when they need realty service.

Periodically distributing postcards, flyers, calendars or inexpensive promotional pieces to a targeted specialization area or group is a great way to help build relationships. Early in my career, I delivered personalized spring flower seed packets throughout my farm area. And since it was such an unusual gesture, I became known as the flower seed agent. Well, you decide; during that first year, I generated a dozen listings from an area of about 250 homes. I had it "sowed" up tight and won every listing that came out of it that year. Not a bad return on my investment of a few dollars and a few hours of walking, knocking and talking in the sun.

It's important to choose an area with regular turnover, or where mature families are approaching the empty nest phase. And since enthusiasm breeds enthusiasm, it should also be one you find personally appealing. For example, it could be your own neighbourhood. You must like living there. Right? Who better to convince a prospect that it's a great place to live? Or it could be an upscale neighbourhood where you *aspire* to live. Further, by choosing your own backyard, you enjoy instant commonality with your neighbours, hence something communal to chat about. Topics could include local gossip or upcoming events at the community school or recreation centre. You might even organize a neighbourhood baseball game. From this common ground, friendly casual conversations may grow into long term relationships – and business.

Your area of specialization may not be geographical. It could be a network of people who belong to your particular cultural, ethnic or religious group. If you're a Smith, for example, you could contact all the local Smith families. If you hail from Holland, particularly if you're fluent in the language, check out the phone book for Dutch names. If you're a member of a club of some sort, networking with members can prove highly productive. People prefer to associate with others of their ilk. It's a comfort zone thing. Farm in your own community, wherever or whatever that happens to be. Commonality is magnetic because it immediately provides something to talk about besides the weather.

To avoid spreading yourself too thin and diluting your efforts, and to keep effort and expense reasonable, choose a sensibly sized group. Think quality versus quantity and note conversation details for future reference. You'll impress your new contacts with your great memory (and terrific notes). Someone once complimented me on my amazing memory; then they said unless I keep great notes. I admitted both. After awhile, when they get to know you in a non-threatening manner and you graduate to first names, you'll depend less and less on your notes. One day, you'll meet personally and realize you're no longer strangers. Your congenial attitude will have helped instil a mutual sense of camaraderie, if not modest affection. And you'll become their friend in the business.

> *"Sales are contingent upon the attitude of the salesman –*
> *not the attitude of the prospect." W. Clement Stone*

Scripts Tips

You may feel that scripts are insincere and unnatural, as I once felt. When first introduced to them by a seasoned professional, I immediately rejected the whole idea as unauthentic. When calling in my farm area, I wanted to be genuine. However, as time passed, I experienced an epiphany. I realized I'd unconsciously jettisoned phrases that had failed to elicit the desired response and had been repeating the more effective ones. Imagine that; I'd organically evolved my own "canned" presentation.

Well rehearsed scripts can help you deal with most objections or excuses. And the creative objections can be fun – so, loosen up. When you get a standard objection, choose an appropriate response from multiple choices and use natural language, the way you normally speak. Don't use someone else's phraseology. When reading aloud, most people fall into a monotone, especially if they're reading somebody else's words. Have you ever answered the phone and heard a droning telemarketer? To avoid sounding like you're reading a prepared script, use point form notes rather than prose. Bullet points will force you to ad lib, to be varied and natural. To be respectful of their time, keep your approach brief. Speak in short simple sentences because long ones may lose their attention – and possible interest. Actively listen – and respond. Have a conversation. With practice, you'll commit the scripts to heart, conversational skills will improve and effectiveness will sky-rocket!

When you make first contact, by phone or at the door, *don't* begin by asking if they want to sell their home. This aggressive approach may be immediately interpreted as *you* wanting something from *them*. They'll probably say no and hang up or shut the door. And since it rarely impresses anyone, skip the hyperbole. Ask if they've received your calendar. Distributing free gifts is usually a good ice-breaker. Tell them you're specializing in their area or actually living on the next street.

Without seeming to pry into their privacy, begin to ask about them. Commonality, such as shared locale, personal interest, ethnic surname or club membership, is important to the bonding process. To learn about shared traits or interests, entice them into a real conversation. Non-invasive questions, such as how long they've lived there or what they do for a living, are good starting points. Where were they from originally? Do they enjoy the neighbourhood? Why did they buy there? How do they find the local school? Ask for their view on recent local controversies or municipal infrastructure improvements and show sincere interest in their answers. Everyone likes to be heard. They may appreciate the opportunity to boast – or complain – about their neighbourhood and help you learn about it. This knowledge or opinion may prove valuable during your next chat with their neighbour.

A conversation is a gentle give and take. And *they're* giving to *you* – you're not demanding anything of them other than providing the opportunity to express their feelings. Occasionally, you may be fortunate enough to stumble across a homeowner who's aware of social events on their block, about who's planning or doing this and that with whom or what. As the local *Gladys Kravitz* (nosy neighbour), they may be willing to share local gossip and become your neighbourhood "deep throat".

After you've introduced yourself and chatted for a bit, almost as an aside or a "by the way", ask if they know anyone in need of your service. You're not directly asking anything of *them* other than for help. Most often, they'll probably say no, but sometimes they may have heard a rumour about a neighbour. However, if *they're* considering a move (previous complaining may have been a clue), they may say *they* are actually thinking about it. Obviously, if this is the case, your conversation will head in a new direction.

Set yourself apart from the competition and stereotypical biases by concentrating on creating a good relationship with a potential new contact. Delayed gratification has its own rewards. This timeless activity is referred to as "farming" for good reason; one doesn't sow and reap results immediately. A farmer must plant, nurture, weed and feed before a crop is ready for harvest. Because realty farming doesn't always produce immediate results, I suggest that a diminishing number of agents these days make the consistent and persistent effort to build neighbourly relationships with an eye to future business. If you invest your time in what I feel is a highly worthwhile endeavour – and you do it well – you'll harvest the long term benefits and maybe some short-term victories too.

You obviously can't dictate the behaviour of other people, but there's one thing you can control; your own reaction to external negative energy. Occasionally, a seemingly miserable person will abruptly end your call or after uttering a few foul expletives, literally slam the door in your face. Don't be discouraged. They may be having a bad day or suffering a difficult time in their life. Or they're angry with themselves and taking it out on the world. Forgive them. Don't take it personally; it's not about you. Rather than a personal rejection, consider them a challenge. Try a less intrusive approach such as sending something of value, like a newsletter, a flower or a complementary newspaper and try again. You may reap a reward for your polite persistence – or not. If you win their hearts, you could be their agent forever. However, after a few failed attempts, because life is short and there are lots of people, delete them from your database. As they say, onward and upward.

> *"The secret of every man who has ever been successful lies in the fact that he formed the bait of doing those things that failures don't like to do."*
> A. Jackson King

Mass Mailers

Provided they're professionally prepared and informative, newsletters are an increasingly popular method of maintaining regular contact with your network. Colourful postcards are another because they're less expensive and are, by their inherent nature, usually briefly viewed if not read. Calendars are also popular for annual mailers because they're usually displayed all year in a prominent place. If you choose to mass mail letters, keep them brief and business-like, maybe even point-form.

Some agents regularly blanket the town with junk mail. I happen to disagree with this method, not only because it emphasizes expensive quantity over quality, but because the vast majority of this stuff ends up in the recycling box or garbage where it contributes to our creeping ecological debacle. Also, I've found that it's usually the follow-up call that gets the business. And how can you possibly call thousands of homeowners? While your name is still fresh in their memory, make the call soon after distribution. At the end of the day, whatever you choose to mail, whether paper or electronic, the essential message is that you're there for them when they or someone they know need real estate service.

Door-Knockers

A wonderful way to meet people, especially in a farm area, is ringing doorbells. If it's not your farm area, recruit a colleague to accompany you and meet periodically for inspiration. You could share any business generated from the joint effort. If nobody's home, have a flyer, newsletter or door-hanger ready to leave behind so you've not totally wasted your time and effort.

If you actually have a bona fide buyer prospect for a particular type of property, don't be bashful. Scout their preferred neighbourhood and knock on the door, preferably on a Saturday when owners are more likely home. You might luck out and list and sell it yourself. Plus your new seller may buy another home. If they're not interested in moving, however, you may add another contact to your network.

I once door-knocked a small court and met the owners of two homes. After regular contact for a couple of years, one called to say it was time to move. After listing their home, I got a sign call from a fellow on the next street who wanted to move from their semi-detached into a larger single on that court. Well, they bought my new listing and I listed their semi which sold soon after. A little later, my buyer's brother called me and bought the neighbour's house. My point is that whether you're knocking doors or ringing phones, think future business. Build relationships because they can pay dividends later.

"Men are anxious to improve their circumstances, but are unwilling
to improve themselves; they therefore remain bound."
James Allen

Seminal Seminars

Due to the cost of the pamphlets and hotel room, first time buyer seminars can be expensive, but also highly lucrative. If your office has a sizable boardroom, get your feet wet and reduce costs by holding smaller sessions there. Keep them manageable in the beginning with no more than a dozen guests. Effective preparation, presentation skills, industry knowledge and experience are obvious prerequisites. When you have a sea of eager and inexperienced faces before your podium, you'd better be well prepared.

If you're newer to the industry, solicit the help of a credible veteran agent. Depending on anticipated guest numbers, consider inviting several agents to join you. This will permit the efficient handling, not only the higher volume of curious participants, but also leverage the expense. If you opt to underwrite the expenses, you may generate a good return on your investment. If you're able to produce several prospects, each of the participating agents would owe you a percentage of any resulting business. I've seen a referral as high as 50 per cent. Now, that's leverage.

Tired Expireds

There are three certainties in life; death, taxes and expired listings. Before making the call, ensure they're not on the DNCL, haven't re-listed with the same or another brokerage or already sold. A homeowner may make disparaging remarks about their previous agent. Obviously, you mustn't join in the unabashed bashing session. Listen respectfully and make your own independent professional approach. What can you do for them? How are you unique? Build rapport. Rather than pitch them on the phone, close for a personal presentation appointment. It might take more than one call because they're frustrated and prefer to cool their jets for awhile. Agents in general may not be in their good books. But the motivation for moving probably still exists. Don't burn your bridges.

When any property fails to sell, it usually boils down to the price. It doesn't matter what's purported to be wrong with it or local market conditions; *everything* is usually a function of price. Your competitor, whose listing has expired, had probably recommended a price reduction at least once, but the sellers were stubbornly steadfast. And when you convincingly advise the same lower price, they may concede. Sometimes, it takes more than one opinion. And you win a more realistic listing.

Write it Right

"Many a small thing has been made large by the right kind of advertising."
Mark Twain

Print advertising is expensive. With the exception of magazines and weekly papers that enjoy a little longer shelf-life, each ad is usually ancient history the day after it appears. Because of the brief window of opportunity to grab a prospect's attention, to maximise the return on your investment, writing effective copy is essential.

What publication is most suitable? For example, you wouldn't choose a high-end magazine to advertise property in the local trailer park, nor promote a recreational property in a newspaper that caters to city dwellers. Then again, maybe that might be a sound strategy since everyone occasionally enjoys escaping the concrete jungle for the land of the iconic loon. Nevertheless, whatever print media you choose, write your ad copy with fastidious forethought by following the decades-old formula of attention, interest, desire and action, traditionally referred to by its acronym "AIDA".

➢ **Attention** – In the vast array of ads, you must attract reader attention. No easy task. A bold heading and enticing property photo may do the trick. Avoid clichés like "just listed", "handy-man special" or the thoroughly exhausted "gleaming hardwood floors". Prime or unique features or benefits such as renovated gourmet kitchen, high-demand neighbourhood, special architectural design, large heated workshop, tranquil waterfront, spectacular mountain vista or close proximity to subway can be highly effective. Or it could be a real bargain, but make sure it is before saying so.

➢ **Interest** – After you've seized their attention, you want to hold it. To entice them to continue reading, use alluring comments about other elements of the property such as the number of bedrooms and baths, garage size, great room, acreage, western exposure or high-demand location. If the property doesn't have the features they're seeking or you neglected to mention them, they'll quickly assume that the property doesn't meet their requirements and move on to the next ad.

➢ **Desire** – Here's where maintaining interest is even more challenging; you must elicit desire. Needs are the cake, but desire is the chocolate frosting that will motivate them to call. It's vital to appeal to their emotion, arouse curiosity and stimulate excitement by including benefits of a few of the property's prime features.

If winter winds are blowing, it could be the wood-burning fireplace. In warmer climes, it might be the luxurious tree-shaded cobblestone patio with subtle illumination for summer evening gatherings. Parents may be drawn by the safe fenced garden, the short walk to school or the greenbelt with trails and stream abutting the property. The well-insulated detached garage-workshop with radiant in-floor heating may appeal to the hobbyist. Recreational property? Try something like the easily accessible sandy beach and shallow water for frolicking in the surf, plus a dock for the ski boat – perfect for the whole family. A fantastic terrace view over acres of treed parkland, riddled with running trails, may attract a fitness-oriented city dweller. Or a quick one block walk to public transit. Anyway – you get the idea. It's the sizzle that sells – not the steak. Make 'em drool.

➢ **Action** – Tell them what to do and when, to contact you *now* for more info or to reserve a private viewing.

> *"Creative without strategy is called 'art'.*
> *Creative with strategy is called 'advertising'".* Jef I. Richards

Don't err by providing so much information that you satisfy their curiosity without having to call. Keep it brief. As is often mistakenly believed by sellers, ads are not designed to sell the property. Rather, they're intended only to make the phone ring and expand your stable of prospects. I recommend, though, that you *always* include the asking price. Agents who think they're being clever by forcing a prospect to call for the price are barking up the wrong tree. I suspect most prospects won't call unless they believe the home is affordable. Include the list price and save everyone valuable time.

Also, if your ad is a small spot in the classified section, don't waste the space with a personal head shot or slick slogan. It's not the highest and best use of paper and ink. Spot ad callers don't care what you look like. However, for larger display ads, including a professional headshot is a good idea. It gives the caller a real person to call, plus it's good self-promotion.

Aside from advertising to the public, a listing agent's most critical marketing function is to expose the property to colleagues. Our Multiple Listing Service® system provides near instantaneous exposure to the absolute best source of potential buyers, those already actively searching the market. Bearing in mind the high potency of this historic system, carefully complete the data entry forms, including the comments section, with serious forethought. Think AIDA. The Remarks for Clients section is like a newspaper ad, but arguably more effective. That information, exactly as you create it, is uploaded onto not only the industry MLS® system, but also the public websites of

REALTOR.CA®, REALTOR.COM®, probably your own corporate website and possibly countless other optional data-exchange realty marketing sites.

I've noted on innumerable occasions that agents apparently invest little thought to this section. This not only weakens their business, but does their sellers a disservice. They may not understand the importance of this responsibility, lack copy-writing or language skills or don't care. Aside from being widely viewed by prospects surfing the Internet, these brief but potentially powerful capsule remarks provide your colleagues with a listing synopsis, but more importantly, a subtle sales pitch. Remember – enthusiasm breeds enthusiasm. If the agent reading your copy is excited, they'll more easily convey that enthusiasm to their buyer.

To improve public and peer response, when completing the listing data form, don't just tell – sell! Public sites garner a huge amount of traffic and the costs are included in your board and association dues. Write it right and they will call.

"Expensive advertising courts us with hints and images.
The ordinary kind merely says buy." Mason Cooley

Roller Coaster

When agents get busy with new clients, deliberately or otherwise, they often suspend their prospecting activities. The problem with this policy is that once they've finished working with those active clients, there are none waiting in the wings, so they have to kick-start prospecting efforts again. Forgive the cliché, but these agents find their incomes going up and down every month like a fairground roller coaster. A coaster ride requires a lot of power to slowly reach the top (prospecting) and then speeds down (client busy) only to repeat the process at the bottom. A month of slow prospecting activity is followed by a month of busyness, followed by another slow prospecting month. That equates to a half year of being busy with clients and a half year of slumping, resulting in a somewhat lacklustre annual production, maybe half your potential income. Even when busy with clients, prospecting should be part of your daily routine, part of your business plan. What's better – six hectic months with clients and six tough ones without – or twelve steady months?

"In sales, a referral is the key to the door of resistance." Bo Bennett

In my view, the absolute best strategy for building a solid and sustainable practice is to build a network of people who refer to you as their friend in the business. It's called networking. Building a referral base can be a whole lot easier, considerably less expensive and probably more enjoyable. It certainly takes time to kindle trust relationships and foster a solid reputation of integrity and dependability. But the long term rewards, with less worry and frustration about the source of your next commission, are well worth the effort.

In an industry where a majority abandon the business within their first few years, those who survive this crucial period have likely mastered the process, at least to the point of being moderately successful. Your business volume may build slowly, but it will build on a strong base. Even if you don't have a lot of money to spend on marketing, there's nothing to prevent you from building personal relationships. This methodology contributed to a highly successful four decade career for me. And it can for you too.

"Empty pockets never held anyone back.
Only empty heads and empty hearts can do that." Norman Vincent Peale

Chapter Ten

Fizzbo

"Luck is only important in so far as getting the chance to sell yourself at the right moment. After that, you've got to have talent and know how to use it."
Frank Sinatra

Luck and Happenstance

At first blush, one might think that buying and selling privately, commonly referred to as "for sale by owner" or by its acronym "FSBO" (fizzbo), is advantageous to both parties. But it rarely is. Why? By their inherent nature, private sales are rife with challenges and usually wholly dependent on luck and happenstance. If a seller prospect is wondering about advantages of going private, or your buyer is contemplating the private path under the dubious belief they can save money, they may have a surprise in store. Think about this; if trading privately is so easy, how could a dynamic real estate service industry with millions of worldwide members exist? The numerous disadvantages far outweigh the single possible, but not probable advantage.

At least to those in the business, and unquestionably to all who've made the attempt, it's common knowledge that the vast majority of FSBO's end in defeat. As a matter of fact, studies have concluded that a large portion of the relatively few homes successfully marketed privately in an average market are actually sold to acquaintances. Therefore, general statistics may be skewed. Homeowners obviously like the idea of getting a high price with a low cost, but the old adage about getting what you pay for usually applies.

Nowadays, though, thanks to the introduction of mere postings by private sale companies on the MLS® system *we* built, combined with a recent strong sellers market, private sales have realized, to some degree, relatively favourable results. However, most sales are still orchestrated by organized real estate. I'll opine here that as the market evolves into more balanced or buyer-favoured conditions and competing sellers demand more action, FSBO's may once again fall further into fringe territory.

So, why do most fail? Think about the term "private sale"; it's private. Nobody is shouting from the roof tops. With the possible exception of a small lawn sign and maybe an expensive classified ad in the local newspaper, nobody is spreading the word. Sure, private sale companies offer minimal service for a minimal fee, including website insertion, but their visitor traffic doesn't hold a candle to that of our Multiple Listing Service® system. Nevertheless, websites are just advertising. And as I said in the preceding chapter, advertising doesn't typically make the sale. Once the phone rings, sales skills and industry knowledge – which are obviously as scarce as hen's teeth in the private sector – enter the picture.

"If you think it's expensive to hire a professional to do the job,
wait until you hire an amateur." Red Adair

Alternative Considerations

A homeowner could dupe themselves into believing that no one is better equipped to show and sell their own house than the person who knows it best – themselves. They make up a lawn sign (amateur) with their personal phone number (loss of privacy), submit an ad (amateur) in the local paper (expensive) and wait for the countless calls (naive) from eager prospects (rare) ready to pay whatever the homeowner wants (I'll have what they're smoking). Well, good luck with that. It's like representing yourself in court. And you know what they say about that; you have a fool for a lawyer.

A possible alternative is a reputable "sell your own home" company that charges a non-refundable flat fee (whether or not the home sells) to advertise on their website and post basic descriptive details and photos on our MLS® system. They usually supply a lawn sign and maybe a brochure guide, possibly even telephone or on-line support. Optional services might be available, such as market value analysis and open house guidance, but levy additional fees. That's fine, provided homeowners are informed regarding the entire sale process, including the risks and responsibilities, understand when it's wise to seek professional advice, ask the appropriate questions at the right time, and critically, possess the skill to close the prospect.

Discount brokerages are another option. These companies usually charge a flat fee in advance or a low percentage commission to upload the property onto the MLS® system. The homeowner may think they›re smart until they realize that many serious buyers prefer their own representation, which means a seller may still have to pay a buyer brokerage commission on top of the listing brokerage's fee. And they may have to deal directly with the buyer›s agent at the negotiation table without the guidance or protection of their own representative.

Here's another challenge for a private seller. The discount listing agent may promise that if they bring their own buyer and double-end a sale, the entire commission will be only one low rate. Fantastic! But think about it; with ethics aside, why would that listing agent sell a buyer into their own listing for an extremely small commission when they could sell another brokerage's listing for a higher commission, plus still earn the advertised low fee when another agent sells that discount agent's listing? Come on – get real. But hey, the private seller is saving a little bit of money; just not as much as they believed.

Now, having said all this, the well-intentioned services provided by these alternative brokerages and private sale companies are indeed appreciated by a certain segment of the market and I commend them for their initiative. They do succeed in filling a gap. But prior to embarking on the private path, an industrious homeowner is well-advised to make an informed decision. Here are few other issues to consider:

Market Value: A seller requires a dispassionate evaluation from someone familiar with the area. Without hiring an accredited appraiser or obtaining a letter of opinion of value from a knowledgeable realty agent based on a detailed Comparative Market Analysis (CMA), a private seller would have to do their own Registry, Land Titles or Tax Assessment Office research to arrive at what they *impartially* believe to be an estimate of Fair Market Value (FMV). In many cases, a homeowner has tricked an innocent agent into providing an opinion for free. But unfortunately for the would-be seller, agents often talk list price rather than probable sale price because nobody has a crystal ball. Or they could have opined high in error or in a misguided attempt to win the listing. And since people hear what they want to hear, the homeowner might assume that's what their home is actually worth.

The seller may be basing their purely subjective value on the asking prices of what *may* be comparable homes that haven't yet sold. Key point – they've *not* sold, probably due to a stratospheric list price. They could also be relying on erroneous or exaggerated information delivered by a neighbour over the fence, or on property tax assessed value. But since there's no personal inspection of each property prior to uploading data, those amounts fail consider general physical condition and "show-ability" of the building and property, including furnishing, deficiencies and recent improvements.

Private sellers lack any credible proof of market value and often hold unrealistic subjective expectations. They may ask ridiculous prices, just to test the market. And market-savvy buyers generally refuse to pay those subjectively high prices.

Setting the Stage: Since it's virtually impossible for a homeowner to be objective about their own home, who'll advise them on how to properly prepare it for market? They'll need to hire a staging company – at some expense – or unwittingly suffer the consequences of a lacklustre home. How about photographs and a virtual tour? Unless they're a pretty good photographer and videographer or the private sale company offers such service, they'll have to hire one; more up-front expense.

Viewing Availability: Let's say the private seller finds someone interested in a viewing. Sometimes, it's difficult to coordinate an appointment. Thus, a seller must be available virtually all hours to facilitate a prospect's schedule, including having to leave work if there's no one home to tidy up and secure the dog. Or the family might have to postpone dinner. The caller might not even appear as agreed! Imagine the homeowner having made special arrangements to be home and nobody shows up. Frustrating? Absolutely, but hey – they chose to forego professional service.

The Show: If the parties agree on a time, the homeowner must lead them through the house and as expected, will do most of the talking while pointing out features, identifying rooms, maybe introducing family members watching TV, finishing supper, doing laundry or exiting the washroom. Because the buyer is courteous, the seller thinks everything's going fine. But they're not trained to effectively show the property or read the signs. Does a typical homeowner possess the necessary communication skills? Not usually. Can they answer questions about the structural, mechanical, electrical and plumbing soundness of the building? Or on the contrary, are they anxiously saying too much? Nevertheless, the prospect naturally distrusts any info offered or at least suspects exaggeration. Normally, personalities enter the picture too – from both sides – which can lead to unspoken or expressed conflict and ultimately to failure.

At the completion of the viewing, can the homeowner close the prospect? If the buyer senses seller anxiety, and unilaterally declares that they'll offer, the price will be low. Since both parties lack the skill and software to draft the documentation, they'll have to hire someone to prepare it. Since this isn't normally accomplished the same day, the buyer has a chance to cool off. In real estate, for more reasons than one, time is of the essence.

A buyer may feel uncomfortable invading an owner's privacy. It's easier to hire an agent as front person. Or a buyer may immediately hate the place. But they can't politely flee fast enough without offending the homeowner. So, they serve up pleasing platitudes and waste everyone's time.

Hard Questions: The owner obviously has no idea of the buyer's wants and needs or affordable price range. Do they qualify to buy the home? How's their credit rating? How much cash do they have? Are they serious or just nosy? Must the buyer sell their present house before buying? Do they honestly like what they viewed or were they just being polite? Do they have any objections to discuss? If such questions arise, how does the homeowner handle them? Does an amateur seller have the nerve or the capability of asking hard questions? When the prospect initially called, or before they departed after the showing, did the seller get their contact information? If not, how will the homeowner follow-up for feedback which could permit them to better address potential objections from future prospects?

Protection: A buyer's agent with specialized software and equipment usually prepares the APS. But in a private sale, it's the legal representative for either party who must draft the contract. And lawyers don't usually work for free. With no assurance of a successful negotiation, unless the alternative real estate company offers such service, someone is going to incur up front costs. Also, a lawyer is not typically a professional negotiator, marketer or evaluator. They usually see the final contract after it's all been completed by realty agents. Plus the lawyer doesn't usually inspect the property, so is incapable of advising about disclosure of possible latent or patent defects or about inclusions and exclusions. Without a lawyer or competent agent, private sellers risk erring with potentially serious ramifications. And so do buyers.

Safety and Security: What about safety? How secure would a homeowner feel being alone inside with a stranger? For all they know, the visitor could be a dreamer, thief, nosey parker or an axe-murderer! If the entire family arrives at the door and disperses pell-mell, how can the homeowner contain the sudden crowd scene? With complete strangers scattered throughout the house, stealing or damage is a distinct possibility, especially with uncorralled little ones carousing around. Also, how safe would a *buyer* feel being alone inside a stranger's house, particularly if the seller is indeed strange?

Formula for Disaster: Without a cushioning middleperson, a private seller, who obviously wants the highest possible price, must negotiate directly with at least one buyer whose position is diametrically opposite. As in union/management negotiations, where skilled professionals intercede, each party demands the most favourable terms. In a private sale, the absence of an agent to mediate fair terms is no different from labour conflicts; a major handicap.

A homeowner's *only* rationale to forgo the services, knowledge, guidance and security of a professional realty agent is to save commission. But here's the problem; that's usually the sole motivation for a buyer to sacrifice the same benefits – which usually cost the buyer nothing. Thus, if not for a lower price, why would a buyer chose the private route? Each party wants the monetary advantage of no commission. Before negotiating even begins, the parties are divided by an entire sales commission! At best, *reasonable* parties will split the difference. Also, without representation, how does a buyer determine offer price? Trust the homeowner? Offer too low and they insult the homeowner; offer too high and the buyer over-pays.

If a FSBO gets this far, the negotiation stage is often when things fall apart. While sitting across the table from each other and the inevitable small talk winds up – concurrent with stress levels – imagine the two opposing parties and the ensuing conversation: "Well, here's our offer," says the nervous buyer. And the seller, without even getting past the price says, "Well, thanks, but that's not enough," as they leave the table. "But you've not read the rest of our offer!" We don't need to," replies the seller in a stern tone, and with arms crossed, says, "Will you pay more?" "Maybe another $2000, but that's it," replies the disappointed buyer. "Thanks for your offer." End of awkward scene; exit buyer. No sale. Egos, sensitivities and technical ignorance of both parties come into play, with the expected results. By acting as a buffer in this emotion-packed scene, a mediator could have made a huge difference.

"Negotiation means getting the best of your opponent." Marvin Gaye

Conditions: Let's say, miraculously, the parties agree to enter into an APS, conditional upon the buyer arranging a mortgage. Before signing the contract, did the seller ask about pre-approval? Does the buyer qualify for the loan and will they do everything reasonable to fulfill the condition? While the loan application is being considered, the homeowner may be wasting valuable marketing time since their home is effectively off the market. Ditto for any category of condition. What if the buyer already owns a home and has to sell it? Who advises the seller if the back-up property is well-listed? Is it even listed, or is the buyer also planning to market privately? The seller may have tied up their home for months with a sale destined to fail.

Capitulation: After wearily suffering from the associated stress and critical remarks casually cast by strangers about their home during showings and open houses, a private seller may finally capitulate to an aggressive or unscrupulous buyer. When the dust finally settles and they tally up the not insignificant fees and expenses for advertising, staging, photography, appraisal, legal, private marketing company and maybe even a buyer agent commission, they could actually end up netting nearly the same money (or less) as they might have with the help of a full-service realty agent. Due to pressure or market ignorance, they may even have unwittingly undersold. Are they further ahead? Maybe, but it's doubtful. With the money aspect aside, I feel that the stress endemic to the private process isn't usually worth the meagre possible savings.

Private sellers make great prospects. They obviously want to sell, but at least initially, prefer to brave the hazards alone. Fortunately for our industry, when they realize it's no easy task, most ultimately surrender and hire a professional. As soon as you see their newspaper ad or private lawn sign, invite them to contact you for free advice. However, since they may still be in the honeymoon phase, don't try to discourage them. They may resent your negativity. If they agree to give you their guest list or present your business card to disinterested visitors, offer to do their paperwork. Volunteer to drop over to suggest staging enhancements or minor home improvements. You might even prepare a CMA and recommend an asking price.

To help cement your growing relationship, call them now and again for an update. Or offer to hold an open house and negotiate any resulting commission. By offering to help, when they finally concede that they need help (they usually do), they may call you. Work on building a trusting relationship. Even if the FSBO succeeds, they may still acquire your services for their purchase. Opportunities often dress in worker's clothes.

"Surely there is a time to submit to guidance and
a time to take one's own way at all hazards." Thomas Huxley

Chapter Eleven

Espousing Open Housing

"Many men go fishing all of their lives without knowing
that it is not fish they are after." Henry David Thoreau

Have you ever met a prospective buyer who said they're just looking and prefer to remain uncommitted to any particular agent? They'd rather just visit open houses or respond to ads or lawn signs that catch their attention. They clearly lack the benefit of knowing a trustworthy agent or may be innocently unaware of the value of your usually free buyer service. For a serious new buyer, searching solo is not a bad way to begin, but like fishing, they may catch something or may not. To continue the metaphor, if they enjoy fishing for a home (or a fish) as an amusing pastime, then that's fine. But dragging themselves around town every weekend with methodical intent, plodding through house after house, maybe with kids in tow, certainly isn't my idea of a joyful way to spend a weekend. It can consume a lot of time and be exceptionally frustrating, plus an unrepresented buyer may be exposed to pressure sales tactics. After all, many agents hold opens hoping to sell that particular house.

While unrepresented buyers are awaiting lawn sign installations and open house announcements, they may miss potential golden opportunities. A listing agent may have placed an open house ad for a hot new listing, but due to a quick sale, didn't have time to hold it. They may not even have installed a lawn sign! Buyers could completely miss the boat. If – and that's a big if – they find and respond to the ad and arrive at the house, they could find a big red sold sign on the lawn. It's a clear case of the early bird catching the worm.

On the other hand, exploring opens affords a buyer the opportunity to determine preferences. They can develop a feel for a special neighbourhood, learn what their money might buy and where to focus their search. They're able to investigate various styles, sizes, floor plans, features and price ranges, as well as local schools, parks, recreational facilities and other public services. Seeing lots of homes up close can also help a couple clarify their individual and collective wants and needs, leading to agreed objectives. Visiting open houses can also provide an informal interview process wherein they have the chance to meet, question and learn from more than one agent.

When they finally comfortably connect with an agent – hopefully you – a serious search can begin in earnest. With hands-on guidance, your new buyer can satisfy their quest more efficiently and usually with a lot less stress. In a hot market, they can now be amongst the first to view sharp new listings in their target area and price range. Your MLS® system's search and email program can automatically notify them – on their smart phone – as soon as new listings and price reductions are uploaded, possibly even on an hourly basis. They could be doing a drive-by moments later.

If you're able to establish the beginnings of a friendly relationship with a guest, before you send them on their way to visit more opens, suggest they inform the attending agents that they're no longer "orphans". The agents will likely still show them the property and answer questions, but may be reluctant to invest their time with another brokerage's client. Or better yet, instead of wandering through inappropriate opens, they simply contact you for details. If it meets their pre-screened needs and affordability, you can arrange a private viewing. Since you're working for them now, tell them they can take the weekend off and let you do all the legwork.

To Have and To Hold

Let's now explore open houses from another prospective – holding them. If you're an abstainer, you may be missing good fortune. If your goal is to increase the size of your business network, you must meet people. Aside from oodles of leisure reading time, nothing is gained by being a secret agent. Given the right training and attitude, you can enjoy a healthy "visitor to client" conversion rate and build a great business.

Do you have a certain style, format or methodology for your opens or do you treat them haphazardly? Do you sit impatiently in someone's living room on sunny weekend afternoons and pray for the quick passage of time while quietly slipping into slumber? Do you hold them only to help justify the rather large potential commission, or as a legitimate lead generation tool? Some enjoy great success with this traditional practice, while others consider them a complete waste of their precious time. Early in my career, I was a member of the latter group; I disliked their passivity. They reminded me of my days sitting in a new home sales office. If a new seller asked me about opens, I'd usually reply that they were a waste of time and an invasion of their privacy. Some were relieved and others disappointed, but that was my view.

However over the years, as I witnessed the gradual proliferation of this promotional practice, my attitude began to change. When I considered that, unlike open visitors, disembodied responders from passive newspaper and Internet ads could easily hang up the phone or ignore or block emails, I figured I'd give them a try. And I'm glad. Open houses provide tangible opportunity to personally meet and greet real people with whom you have immediate commonality – real estate. Plus you're on your own turf in an environment you control and critically – where people come to you. They presumably want a home and you're a provider, a facilitator of wishes. You have access to the product and the ability to bring their dreams into reality.

Opportunity Knocks

Some visitors may be nosy neighbours or dreaming drifters out for a Sunday drive, seeking decorating ideas or fanaticizing about home ownership. That's fine; at least you meet people. And people know people. Regard it as a chance to kindle connections and expand your business sphere. Collect names and numbers – even from non-prospects – because someday, they may become prospects.

Or your visitors may be serious searchers. Some may already be established with agents, but most may be orphans. Yes – in this modern digital age, where most buyers begin their search on the Internet, people still get in their cars to circulate the circuit. Internet virtual tours and slide shows are great, but there's nothing quite like feet on the ground. And if they don't care for your open house, you're gifted with a tiny window of opportunity to connect with them.

Frankly, in my experience, it's rare for an agent to sell their own listing from an open house, but many guests will ultimately buy *something*. People are regularly attracted to property beyond their monetary means and tour homes completely out of their affordability range. I'd often meet *more* people who *weren't* qualified to buy my medium to high-end listings! If someone looking unsophisticated, maybe roughly attired, walks through the door of your luxury listing, don't arrogantly (and possibly mistakenly) judge them unworthy. Make an effort to connect and convert them into prospects for another more affordable property. They may respond favourably to your respectful attitude. If the luxury home *is* within their financial means, odds are they won't find it suitable anyway. Then again, they might. If they fail to buy it and you're able to establish the foundation of a good working relationship, you may sell them something else that more suits their wants, needs and financial capabilities.

As you'd prepare for ad callers by having listing details of comparable properties close at hand, you should be aware of other current listings similar to the property on open. This way, if your visitor doesn't like or can't afford your open house, you can immediately tell them about other listings.

To permit guests to relax and view a slide show of assorted comparable listed properties, bring your laptop or tablet and connect it to the flat-screen TV. Or have your MLS® search engine open to other listings in the area. While they're in the house, show them your wares and what you can do for them. It's time to sing and dance, so to speak. You might catch their interest with a competitors listing they'd been wondering about, or even a home of which they were unaware. Plus if they're already homeowners, if they were impressed with your respectful, professional demeanour and expert presentation and marketing skills, you might earn the listing. The longer you're able to keep them interested, the greater the likelihood you'll establish the beginnings of a strong connection.

You may hold opens simply to appease a seller or to look busy. On the other hand, a homeowner may have to be convinced of the merits of opening the doors of their home. Well, allowing strangers into one's inner sanctum is indeed an invasion, but that's the whole idea. You want as many people as possible viewing your listing. So, they'd better get over it. By restricting your marketing to more passive promotion, they're essentially tying one of your arms behind your back. Ask for their trust.

Opens are also a great way to placate a frustrated seller who may have over-priced their property and as a result, aren't getting much action. With warm but disinterested bodies meandering around, oblivious of the high asking price – and still no offers appear – your stubborn seller may finally get the message. You get a price reduction and a more realistic listing in exchange for a couple of hours of your time sitting on your fanny. And an otherwise free opportunity to develop a few leads. I'd say that's a fair exchange.

Some homes are suitable for an open house and some are not. If the listing is a showplace – particularly the exterior – then it's more likely to attract visitors. Provided of course that it's priced right, once a qualified buyer sees it up close, the chances of an offer are good. However, if the listing is plain, tired or rough with poor curb appeal, an open may not be the right marketing method. In such case, the only possible benefit of holding one is the slim chance of generating leads. But a butt ugly property is unlikely to attract attention. It's a classic example of judging a book by its cover. Buyers will believe that an unattractive exterior likely means the same for the interior.

It's common practice for newer agents, who have yet to become busy listers, to "borrow" suitably attractive listings from other agents. If this applies to you, instead of using the personalized open house signs and feature sheets or brochures of the listing agent, buy your own. Promote yourself; it's *your* business practice.

Hear Ye, Hear Ye!

Advertising an open house in the local newspaper or by distributing professionally printed invitations around the neighbourhood are good ideas, but once advertised, you must commit to holding it even if the weather is gruesome. Well, if a tornado strikes, I think you'd be forgiven for cancelling at the last minute. Even if the home has sold conditionally or you have a hot prospect wanting to view other homes that same afternoon, you or a replacement must attend. Otherwise, you lose credibility (as does our industry) in the neighbourhood. Newspaper ads can indeed spawn visitors, but I've found strategic placement of numerous professional-looking signs at main intersections usually attracts sufficient traffic to justify the time and effort. And by not having committed to a newspaper ad, if you think you might be busy with buyers, you can cancel or postpone your open at the last minute. Plus you've saved a few ad bucks. Obviously, though, you might have to deal with a disappointed seller.

Before the day arrives, both you and the property must be properly prepared. Set the stage. Recruit your sellers to do their part, making sure the home is groomed and polished, inside and out. Ask them to mow the lawn, manicure the gardens, trim the bushes and sweep the walk. Stow bicycles, toys or refuse from around the property in the garage or shed. Insist the place be spotless, including windows and doors. Advise them to put away valuables or anything fragile that's precariously perched and might be knocked over by a rambunctious child. It's unlikely this will happen, but why tempt fate. This is all standard stuff that sellers should do anyway prior to even listing their home. If you lack staging skills, recommend professional help. The closer the property resembles a model home, the greater chance of achieving the mutual goal of a sale. Remember – you're a team. Work together.

Limited Entry

*"I keep my ideals because in spite of everything,
I still believe that people are good at heart."* Anne Frank

Have a sign ready to display in the front door announcing that you're showing and asking arrivals to await your greeting – and lock the door. Now, this isn't because you believe everybody is dishonest. Since it's supposed to be an *open* house, though, this policy may seem extreme. And you may lose some lookers. However, you should focus your undivided attention on any interested prospects already inside. If the new arrivals are truly interested, they'll wait for you. You could briefly break away from your presentation to greet and escort them to the living room to wait for an accompanied tour. A slide show of the subject and other homes could be playing on the TV. Or you could add a few words on your "busy showing" notice, welcoming them to wander through the garden or enjoy a walk around the block to investigate the immediate neighbourhood. Or simply relax in some comfy chairs on the porch to get a feel for the place while perusing strategically placed feature sheets. Weather permitting, as a welcoming gesture, have a closed thermos of coffee or lemonade with cups and glasses for them. Leave a covered dish of cookies to sweeten them up. If the visitor is unable to wait, have a sign-in list at hand for them to request an emailed brochure or feature sheet, or a call to arrange an exclusive viewing appointment. And follow-up with them!

The reasons for restricting the number of visitors at any one time are two-fold – security and opportunity. Security dictates that you avoid having countless strangers wandering unaccompanied through your client's home. I believe all people are basically honest, but one shouldn't gamble with another's property. Secondly, curiosity is a powerful motivator. You want the chance to bond with your guests and that won't happen if you station yourself in the kitchen while everyone rambles alone around the house. They'll probably notice the main features, but miss small innovative elements and leave without the advantage of your explanation of the *benefits* of those features. Just because it's an open house doesn't mean you don't properly show it. Use your presentation skills. Your priority is to grow your business and possibly sell your client's property – in that order.

How does one connect with a prospect? Aside from being professional, skilful, charming, courteous, curious and genuinely considerate, it helps to be patient, persevering, proficient and prepared. When someone arrives, greet them warmly at the front door. Most people are not completely comfortable walking into someone else's home. They may ring the bell and await your answer or may enter on their own. Either way, if you're not currently showing another party, ensure you're in the foyer immediately to welcome them. Yes – haul your ass out of that restful easy chair and enthusiastically do your job.

Introduce yourselves by first name. Offer your hand and most importantly, make a point to remember their names – including those of the kids. A person's name is music to their ears. It's personal. The fact that you made the effort to remember may impress your guests. And using the kid's names will impress the parents even more. You want them to like you. They want to know you care. Illogical as it may seem, many buyers and sellers make their hiring decisions based on the likeability factor. Often, it doesn't matter if you're a top agent or the ink on your registration certificate is still wet. If they don't like you, they won't hire you.

"Charm is a way of getting the answer yes without asking a clear question."
Albert Camus

Registration

Before you proceed with the tour, ask them to register in your guest book. Don't ask them to *sign* the register, since that could have a negative subliminal effect. It might infer they're somehow making a commitment. Use the words *register* or *complete* the guest registry or something similar. Casually observe as they put pen to paper. If they fail to add a phone number, postal or email address or answer any question, politely ask them to be thorough. If they refuse to comply, you could courteously explain that for security reasons, you must identify all visitors. Either they complete the form or you refuse access to the home. I've personally never had any difficulty in this regard. Most people don't mind cooperating. Some might supply false information, but hey, at least you tried. Perhaps you'd prefer to not work with such deceitful people anyway.

Ask if they're currently under contract with a brokerage. If they are, then your showing can be brief. They may be interested in the property and contact their own representative to arrange a more thorough viewing. If it's your own listing, you'll still benefit. If it's not your own listing, then the listing agent owes you a favour. However, if they're realty orphans, they're fair game.

As you start the tour, begin to ask casual questions. Don't make it sound like an application form or an interview. Intersperse your questions with information about the home's features and benefits. Offer them some tidbit about the house or neighbourhood and at the appropriate place during the viewing, follow it with a question. Make it a conversation with questions such as:

➢ Are they interested in this particular neighbourhood?
➢ How long have they been searching?
➢ Have they viewed many homes?
➢ Are they perusing websites and newspapers? How's that working?
➢ What features are important to them?
➢ How many bedrooms and bathrooms would they prefer?
➢ Do they presently own a home? Is it sold or listed for sale?
➢ Do they have kids? How many? School age?
➢ What type of school do they need – public, separate or private?
➢ How many cars in the family? Do they need a garage?
➢ Do they enjoy gardening or entertaining?
➢ Do they prefer separate rooms or open-concept?
➢ Do they need a mortgage and if so, are they pre-approved?
➢ What's their preferred possession date?

I've found that most people don't mind sharing their wants and needs, and this is an ideal time to gather such information. By sharing, they've begun the bonding process. If they're sincere buyers and your approach is agreeable, sensitively asked questions at appropriate moments can transmit a message of care, that you're not just trying to sell them something. As a matter of fact, if you genuinely care about them, that's even better.

During the showing, you have the responsibility to maintain some semblance of order. So, watch, listen and keep everyone together. If someone wanders off, politely ask them to stay with the group. By doing so, you may instil the feeling that the owners love their home – a definite benefit. If you sense any discomfort in this regard, ask them to put themselves in the owner's shoes. How would *they* feel about having strangers wandering unattended through their own home? Explain that if you agree to accept them as clients, they'll receive the same secure, quality service. This implies they must *apply* to work with you, that you practice selectivity when choosing clients.

You've shown the main floor, upstairs and finally the basement, pointing out the main features, improvements, details and of course, the many benefits. By the way, this is the best floor order; it's far easier to climb one flight of stairs at a time and then descend two flights to the basement as the last phase, rather than have to trudge from the basement to the second floor in one strenuous effort. A panting prospect is not a good prospect. This is particularly important with large multi-level homes, or large or senior people.

Don't skip any detail because you never know what small element will make a strong impression. But if you sense a lack of interest, don't bore them. Tune in to them. Focus. If they seem to be lingering, that's a good sign. On the contrary, it they appear anxious to keep moving, it's likely they're not interested. Aside from the periodic questions, don't feel compelled to talk too much. Converse – yes, but listen more. Observe. Ask questions. To assist the bonding process, use their names often, including those of the kids. If you sense interest, at the appropriate time, you can even ask trial closing questions. (See the chapter on closing techniques.)

Bond or Bomb

You're nearing the end of the showing, been gently asking probing questions and have deduced a lack of interest. Before even asking how they feel about it, you might voluntarily opine that this property is probably not for them. The couple may have exchanged a momentary look during the showing that shouted their longing to escape at the first opportunity and may be pleasantly surprised and relieved that you sensed their feelings. Released from the unpleasant task of telling you it's not for them, they might hang around a little longer to chat. Once again, it's about bonding, about connecting on an emotional level.

As you approach the front door, if you're unclear about their feelings, ask them how they *feel* about the home – not what they *think* about it. The two questions will illicit distinctly different answers. Ask for their thoughts and they'll probably reply that it has most of the basic ingredients they're searching for, but they're unsure. Inquire of their feelings, however, and they'll often honestly say whether or not they like it or that it's lovely or they hate it. Thoughts will be about the *property*, whereas feelings will be about *them*. Make it about them – not the house. Buying decisions are based primarily on feelings – not thoughts. Feelings rule. If you feel you understand their wants and needs, as you all return to the foyer, in a natural and spontaneous way, verbally summarize the answers they gave to your various questions sprinkled throughout the viewing.

"So, John and Jane, you want a large master suite with private bathroom and three other bedrooms for Jimmy, Judy and Jodie. You prefer a main floor family room with a gas fireplace, and a more spacious family-sized kitchen. You appreciate the benefits of main floor laundry and prefer the spaciousness of a double garage for all the family bikes. You definitely don't want a swimming pool, but a finished basement would be a definite plus for a kid's play area. Because of your daughter's allergies, you prefer hardwood floors instead of broadloom. Walking distance to a public school is a priority. And it's a bit more than you prefer to spend. Have I got that about right?" I guarantee they'll be impressed. They may not show it, but they'll be pleased that you made the conscious effort to not only remember their names, but all they had shared during the showing. They'll appreciate that you paid attention. You may even have helped them clarify their own needs. This is your chance to shine.

Close and Propose

Ask them if they'd permit you to save them a ton of time, effort, frustration and fuel exploring a never-ending series of open houses held at unaffordable or unsuitable homes and constantly perusing newspaper ads and websites. Offer to email them every new listing, including details and available photos and virtual tours of homes that might meet their specific needs, price range and preferred neighbourhood. They'll not have to lift a finger (except for their mouse) or load the kids into the car on futile jaunts every weekend. If their wants and needs are unusual or unique, or they're luxury or rural home buyers, offer to personally preview the listings for computer-unsearchable features to filter them further. For example, your visitors may be avid non-smokers who cannot tolerate odorous smoke residue. This isn't normally indicated in the listing data (yet). You can save them precious irreplaceable time. Your quality service is all about them.

If they already own a home, do they have an estimate of its market value? To provide further opportunity to enhance your bond, offer them a complimentary CMA. By agreeing to accept your service, they'll have a more accurate estimate of how much they can realistically afford to spend. Unbeknownst to them, they may qualify for an even better place! The clincher is that your buyer agency service will not likely cost them a dime. If you've impressed them with your charming attention, how could they refuse?

Dress comfortably to suit the environment. Be yourself. If you're able to establish a congenial connection, they'll recommend you within their sphere of influence – and be less likely to demand full service with discounted fees. And charging full fees is how one builds a profitable real estate practice.

> *"Everybody has a world and that world is completely hidden until we begin to inquire. As soon as we do, that entire world opens to us and yields itself. And you see how full and complex it is." David Guterson*

Chapter Twelve

Fees, Commissions and Discounting

"Self-worth comes from one thing – thinking that you are worthy."
Wayne Dyer

The Third Shoe

A former client called to say they wanted to list their home for sale. Since I'd served them nearly 30 years ago and had faithfully stayed in touch, I happily accepted their invitation. During the initial phone chat, while I gathered details about their situation, motivation and property, they inferred they'd be listing immediately. Consequently, I prepared a detailed CMA and to save them time, prepared most of the listing documentation in advance. When I arrived at their front door with lockbox and camera in hand, I noticed the property's rather unkempt condition. And that first impression was immediately confirmed upon entering the foyer. With the exception of a new roof, they acknowledged that little effort had been made to improve the place. Even the mechanicals were being coaxed well past their designed obsoletion dates.

After I'd finished my presentation and offered a candid considered opinion, they dropped the first shoe. To my dismay, they'd already sought the opinions of several other agents. Well, I'm accustomed to forthrightness from the outset and unaccustomed to direct competition, particularly in the case of former clients. Either out of ignorance or anxiousness, my esteemed colleagues had apparently unanimously opined a much higher market value. Then the second shoe made its debut; how short of a listing term would I accept? And yes, there was a third shoe; what would be my fee? They understood and agreed regarding the merits of offering a competitive commission rate to the buyer brokerage, but disagreed with my own fee. When they said all the other agents had promised a lower rate, I tried to justify my fee, but all they saw were dollar signs.

Our meeting ended abruptly when they said they had to think about it. While packing up to leave, I summarized their expectations by asking if they felt it reasonable to expect a highly experienced broker who is confident in his self-worth and truly cares about his clients, to accept an over-priced, minimum term listing of a sub-standard property owned by someone who doesn't seem to value loyalty or expertise, and with a heavily discounted commission rate? Significantly, they laughed it off and refused to answer.

Later that day, I was not surprised to receive their call to thank me for my time, but they had chosen to list with another brokerage. I was sure that without a significant price reduction, their property would not be sold any time soon. Hence, I felt I'd lost nothing but a few hours of my time and a troublesome seller. I candidly said that perhaps, to be fair, they should have disclosed during our first phone conversation that I was to be competing on price and commission rate because, honestly, I'd have respectfully declined the invitation. I cheerfully wished them luck. By the way, after more than three long months in prime market conditions, with dreadful marketing, amateur photos and several price reductions, it finally sold by a cooperating brokerage for an even lower price than what I had predicted.

For some time, it's been a common but unwise practice for property owners to hire a listing brokerage based on the highest asking price. But it's becoming more prevalent in recent years for that choice to be based on commission rate. But be forewarned; a client who is obsessed with the fee usually has little respect for you, your services or our profession. They need you, but out of fear, refuse to be fair. How desperate are you? Do you rationalize competing on fee by convincing yourself that a piece of the pie is better than none? It's your choice whether or not to accept an agency. Whenever I succumbed to a seller's demand for a fee reduction (extremely rare), they ironically and almost consistently proved very unreasonable, sometimes downright obnoxious. They could not be pleased. Or after I'd invested a lot of time, effort and expense, they'd spontaneously change their minds about selling. Suffice it to say that if – a big if – someone like this later refers anyone, the referred party will likely expect the same full service at a discounted rate. Birds of a feather flock together.

Many agents charge a popular local competitive rate. (I'm not supposed to imply this, but let's be real.) However, in a strong seller's market when demand exceeds supply, a seller could expect to negotiate a rate, especially for high-demand property. When supply and demand are more in equilibrium, or when supply exceeds demand, to attract more attention, a seller should offer a *higher* commission rate – not a *lower* one. Plus they should provide *you* with sufficient incentive to invest your time and effort on their behalf. They can't realistically expect you to work for less *and* to spend tons of money advertising it. It simply wouldn't be fair, nor under those circumstances, would it make business sense to accept the listing. Thus, if a seller demands a discount, they should expect discount service.

Meddling Media

Over the past few years, our fees have been a hot topic, and the controversy has been irrevocably altering our traditional business model. Media articles have intimated that, considering our services, we're grossly over-paid. But either by design or gross ineptitude, to grab reader's attention, columnists often neglect to get all the facts. And what draws that attention and its often affiliated ire more than reader's pocket-books? The adverse effect of such stories on public attitude is palpable.

Have you ever noticed sympathetic stories about our industry? Agents are often depicted as bungling, greedy, narcissistic egomaniacs taking advantage of innocent people. Have you seen any impartial articles stating, for example, that buyer services are normally free, or that many agents generate a mere handful of sales annually – or none, even though constantly on duty? On average, agents earn about the same as a typical office worker who gets a relatively secure regular paycheque with no business expenses and critically – works with significantly lower risk and weekends and holidays off! If we're all so exorbitantly paid, why do legions fail after a few struggling years? You'll not likely see such articles because truthfully depicting our members serving satisfied clients without drama would not be entertaining. Okay, okay – I'll stop ranting now, but I'm a little sensitive to unfair and usually unanswered criticism of our industry.

> *"The news media are, for the most part, the bringers of bad news and it's not entirely the media's fault; bad news gets higher ratings and sells more papers than good news."* Peter McWilliams

Surmounting Discounting

A prospective seller asks you to lower your fee. How do you handle this increasingly common tactic? Do you charge the same rate as the cooperating brokerage? If your seller agrees to buy through you, do you charge a lower rate on the sale? Do you lower your rate for a "double-ender"? Do you negotiate your fee at offer time? Do you chop services to reflect a lower rate or offer various services from a limited menu? Or do you even have a clear policy? Maybe you haphazardly surrender whenever the subject rears its ugly head? Or do you refuse to budge?

If negotiating your fee is normal practice and/or you're registered with a discount brokerage, that's obviously quite understandable because your business practice is presumably structured accordingly. You anticipate providing incentives and hopefully enjoy sufficient volume and profitability to justify them. But full service agents, often with higher expenses and lower volume, must generate relatively higher commissions to reflect their business model. And until a dramatic shift in our industry, for a business to stay solvent, it must remain this way.

Did you reduce any of your fees last year? How many times? A reduction of $2,000 for each of 10 transactions totals $20,000. If you're an average producer, after expenses, that may represent a large portion of your net annual income. Did your generosity generate any referrals? If you'd refused to reduce, would you have lost that client? Did they demand full service anyway? Whenever I was asked, I'd normally respond by asking why they need a lower fee – and calmly await their reply. If unable or unwilling to respond, I'd ask if they were under financial duress and desperately needed my charity. If they denied being needy (usually the case), I respectfully refused and moved on. But if they persisted, I'd ask why they contacted me. If they said because they trust me, I'd ask what that trust was worth. Often, this would nip the problem in the bud.

Rather than automatically capitulate to a prospective seller's demand, which is obviously the easiest thing to do, defend yourself by justifying your fee. Start by differentiating between *your* actual fee and that of the buyer agent. You may have to explain that you don't receive the whole commission, that your company takes its share and pays the buyer agent. Offering an attractive buyer brokerage commission is just as important as establishing a realistic asking price. The list price is designed to attract buyers, and the posted commission rate their agents. When selecting properties to show, it's so easy to skip a listing offering a low cooperating brokerage fee.

Once your would-be seller sees the logic, you no longer have to justify the full rate – only half – and hopefully, you'll have diminished their objection by half. If, however, they still balk at your share, ask why they'd even consider paying *you*, who'll have contractually undertaken to be legally and ethically bound to protect *their* interests (and spend *your* money and *your* time promoting *their* property) a fee less than that being offered to the buyer's agent whose intent is the exact opposite?

Ask how the seller would feel if forced to face aggressive buyer agents without your strong representation; what's that assurance worth to them? Why would they want to hire a weak agent who'd easily yield to their demand for a lower fee, and then expect that same agent to behave any differently under argumentative assault from a buyer's representative? If you so readily surrender during the listing presentation, what will happen to the sale price when the rubber really hits the road and you have an aggressive, skilled buyer agent sitting opposite at the negotiation table? Cave for one – cave for all.

It's *your* fiduciary responsibility to do everything possible to obtain for them the most favourable terms. Selling realty is not, as they may believe, just a matter of signing up a standard form, sticking an ad in the newspaper or on a website and jamming a sign in the lawn. If that were it, you couldn't begin to justify the traditional fee structure. The lion's share of the fee is earned during the advice stages; establishing an estimate of fair market value, the original and if required, amended asking prices, effective property preparation and offer negotiation – sometimes more than one – are the most critical services. The other marketing activities, while important, are secondary.

By accepting the listing contract, you and your brokerage agree to assume significant financial obligations as well as a substantial commitment of other resources. Hopefully, they'll appreciate that marketing expenses already lower your net compensation, at least if the property sells. And if for any reason it doesn't, remind them that you'll be in a loss position. The risk is all yours and unfortunately, they're in the "profit" driver's seat. You have control of the marketing gas pedal, but they control the brakes. Their level of reasonable cooperation and your risk of loss are inversely proportional.

Risky Business

"If you don't risk anything, you risk even more." Erica Jong

When sellers see the big commission number on their lawyer's statement of adjustments, they sometimes resent parting with such a sizable sum for a service period that might seem to have been (and maybe was) quite brief. They may not have appreciated the service provided or more importantly – the risk you undertook. They may not appreciate the fact that for each listing that sells, there are many more that don't. And agents incur marketing expenses on *every* listing.

There must be sufficient compensation for assuming *all* the risk. That alone justifies higher fees. You assume contractual fiduciary responsibilities and marketing obligations with all associated expenses without any guarantee of a return on your investment of time, money and expertise. There must be a reasonable profit incentive, and not just compensation for your time and reimbursement of expenses. Otherwise, why be in the business? Key word – business. It's not a job where you trade time for money, nor are you a charity or not-for-profit organization. You make the commitment with the hope that the market will favour you with a sale so you can not only be satisfactorily compensated, but make a profit. If it fails to sell, *you* lose – not the property owner. You're out of pocket, both in money and what's even more valuable – your time. Upon expiry, they can re-list with you or another brokerage without any penalty. For any investment, be it money or time, risk and rate of return should be directly related.

For understandable reasons, a commission based on a percentage of the ultimate sale price is an important agent incentive. It's also an attractive inducement for a homeowner because it provides them with an opportunity to attempt a sale without any risk or expense and with minimal effort. That's a huge seller advantage! Here's something else to think about. When accepting a listing, by charging a lower rate, you're not actually reducing your fee because there's no fee yet; it's merely a percentage of nothing. What you're really doing is devaluing your service, your worth. You're ultimately lowering your effective hourly rate – maybe to zero, or less – and reducing the chance of generating a profit.

You're entitled to make a reasonable living, just as the homeowners are. Usually, they're paid a salary or hourly wage, whereas you're paid by commission. If you fail to generate a sale that closes, you don't get paid. Period. Ask your seller how they'd feel if their employer instructed them to do their job, but without their normal compensation unless the company sold some product or was profitable. In such case, because of the risk of not being paid, your prospective seller would no doubt demand a higher compensation from their boss or even a share of profits. Here's a more realistic example; to provide adequate compensation for the higher default risk, a second mortgage interest rate is usually higher than that of a first mortgage. As I said, for the risk you agree to undertake, your fee is higher. It's not complicated. You don't work for free. Well, actually you often do. Greater risk goes hand in hand with higher fees. And the risk is normally spread out over all your listings.

Commission Impossible

The legal profession, particularly in the United States, regularly utilizes a compensation system based on contingency fees. If an American litigator fails to obtain a court award for damages, they usually don't get paid and are typically out of pocket for the expenses incurred. A Canadian lawyer also might not readily collect their fee if they fail to obtain an award for their client, who as a result, lacked the resources to pay their legal bill. In law suits south of the 49th parallel, these fees can be as high as 50 percent of an award. In this light, a real estate fee of 5 or 6 per cent seems quite modest. Obviously, our risk is considerably lower than that of a lawyer and their litigant, so to expect such high fees would be ludicrous, but the principle is similar.

Realty commission generation is also based on contingencies. In other words, if a sale occurs, you get paid. No sale – commission impossible. You work, spend, hope and pray the listing sells. If it doesn't, for whatever reason, including homeowner change of plans, you've laboured and spent with no return. You toiled for free. Nevertheless, for our traditional fee structure, we've always accepted such risks as an integral part of the business because we normally generate sufficient "pooled" commission income from multiple listings to rationalize the individual risks. When you replace that long-established fee structure with lower rates or small flat fees without a major boost in volume, are those risks still justified? At some point, our traditional business model will no longer make sense. And that's when the public will begin to notice a changing industry – possibly not a better one. Actually, I feel our industry is already evolving in that general direction.

Industrial Evolution

In these changing times, there seems to be growing resistance to our industry's traditional fee structure and a trend toward lower fees. To meet this demand head on and help increase professionalism, maybe it's time we seriously explored revolutionary new business models with alternative service options and fee calculation methods. To maintain industry viability, we may need a complete overhaul – from the top down.

Let's say a prospective seller objects to your normal rate, payable on completion of sale, with no fee if there's no sale. (Listing contracts used to state that a full commission was payable for simply procuring an offer per the terms of the listing, even if the seller rejected it.) Naturally, you're reluctant to discount because you have mouths to feed. You also know how challenging it may be to sell their property, not to mention the expenses. All sorts of options may be available to handle this scenario in a mutually satisfactory manner:

> ➤ Charge a percentage relative to estimated market value; the higher the value, the lower the rate. However, that could be a problem since it's often more time-consuming and expensive to market luxury property.
> ➤ Charge a lower percentage or flat fee with reduced services. After explaining your service menu and everything you do, they choose from basic, intermediate or deluxe.
> ➤ Charge an hourly fee plus reimbursable expenses, whether or not the property sells, for which you invoice weekly based on methodically docketed activities. Demand a non-refundable deposit as a retainer, payable when the listing contract is signed, and deduct any invoiced fees paid from any percentage commission ultimately payable. The deposit could serve as a guaranteed minimum fee if for whatever reason – including an arbitrary change of heart by the seller – the listing fails to sell.

Under this scenario, for a faster sale with lower costs, homeowners would tend to list realistically. On the other hand, we'd welcome a higher asking price because the longer a sale is delayed, the higher our revenue. We'd pray for long term listings and no sales. Arguably, with such low incentive, the existing system would collapse. Just think about open houses though. They'd not be so boring knowing you'd enjoy billable time for every dreary hour on their couch.

➢ Charge a variable commission rate calculated on a sliding scale. They acquire your services to buy another property and list their old home, and you earn a full fee on that purchase. In exchange, you agree to reduce the total commission on their sale by, say, one percent if the property sells within two weeks. If unsold after this period elapses, the rate is reduced by only a half percent, and with no reduction if unsold after another two weeks. To be fair, after yet another two weeks, the rate could *increase* by a half point and finally by a full percentage point if unsold after another predetermined period.

The length of seller incentive periods could be determined by your area's average Days on Market (DOM). List at the highest rate and provide the seller with a signed addendum spelling out the formula. Since the seller would save money if the property sold quickly, they'd be motivated to price correctly from the start. You'd earn a quick, but reduced commission. And regardless of how long it takes to sell, your fee would be reasonable, provided it eventually sells.

If your seller agrees to list and sell their property before buying another, and you feel it necessary to offer an incentive to work through you on the purchase, list at your normal full rate. Provide them with written confirmation that you'll reduce the commission as agreed after they've unconditionally bought another property using your services. This sliding scale program could obviously apply with or without an accompanying purchase. But with this option, it would seem prudent to ask for a BRA contemporaneous with the listing contract.

➢ Charge according to an association fee schedule. Apparently, medical and dental associations and insurance companies provide fee schedules for their members, so why couldn't our trade associations do the same thing? When real estate boards fixed its member's MLS® commission rates, we all played on the same level field. Then politically-motivated governments intervened to "protect consumers" from "unscrupulous" realty agents. And on that day, our traditional industry model began to die.

We could employ any of these formats or any combination, but such evolutionary changes would probably need to begin at the top levels of the industry.

If your would-be sellers steadfastly demand a lower fee, bring up the non-monetary value of services offered. Consumers are usually aware of the many obvious benefits offered by members of our industry, but are unaware of the unseen. We pay fees to provincial, state, national and local bodies that regularly lobby on behalf of our industry, from which the public derives direct benefit. Think about our collective efforts with respect to maintaining Canadian tax-free capital gains on home equity, eliminating municipal Land Transfer Tax and numerous other issues over the years. We've built, financed and evolved much of the infrastructure for the dissemination of information on the renowned Multiple Listing Service®. And national and provincial/state real estate associations and legislated administrations are funded by realty agents – not taxpayer dollars.

You're not a retail salesman awaiting the arrival of customers through the front door. You're a self-employed entrepreneur who's operating a small business. You've accumulated a great deal of experience which permits you to offer valuable, objective, professional guidance. You're an expert in your field who *must* make a profit. Unfortunately, unless you have a solid relationship with your prospect, there will probably be another agent, ready, willing and more anxious to take the listing at a reduced commission rate. But with what level of service?

It helps to understand your prospective seller's motivation. Why are they insistent on a discount? Because down deep, they fear being broke and dying poor. Therefore, they take any opportunity to squeeze people for as much as they can. If you can get them to admit this and to see things from your perspective, you might be a step closer to their appreciating your value, and respecting your fee.

> *"I do believe that in order to be a successful negotiator, that as a diplomat, you have to be able to put yourself into the other person's shoes. Unless you can understand what is motivating them, you are never going to be able to figure out how to solve a particular problem."*
> *Madeleine Albright*

Dearth of Worth

A fellow patron recognized and approached the famous artist, Pablo Picasso, while he was quietly enjoying a coffee in his favourite café. She was effusive in her praise of his work. Mr. Picasso thanked her and politely waived her off. Ignoring his wish for privacy, she persisted and asked for his autograph. Again, he demurred. When she refused to go away, he courteously said he preferred not to be disturbed, but she was relentless. The woman asked him if he'd do a quick sketch on her napkin and offered to pay him whatever he felt it was worth. Realizing she would not be vanquished, he finally yielded, snatched the napkin from her proffered hand, did a small sketch, signed and returned it to her. The woman was vociferous in her gratitude and asked him how much she should pay him for his effort. "Ten thousand dollars," he replied. Nearly fainting, she said, "Your price is much too high," she said. "It took barely a minute." Picasso said, "Yes, madam, this is true, but it took me nearly 30 years to learn how to draw like that."

Let's say you were in need of a serious life-threatening surgical procedure and had the choice of going under the scalpel wielded by an automobile mechanic, a newly graduated medical student or a highly credentialed veteran surgeon. Here's the catch; the mechanic offered to do it for $1000 and the graduate agreed to charge a third of the veteran's fee. Any thought required here? I think not. Price would be no object. It's somewhat an exaggeration, but it makes my point. Your potential fee may seem high to a buyer of your services, but you bring the benefit of accumulated knowledge, experience, skill, trustworthiness and enthusiasm into serving them. That's worth a lot. You should charge whatever fee you feel you're worth. If you're a newbie, maybe a discounted fee may be more justifiable. On the other hand, if you're a highly experienced senior agent, a full fee is certainly well warranted.

To win the listing in a competition, if you're hungry, you may feel inclined to cut your normal fee or in lieu of a discount, offer cash back or pay for certain services such as the lawyer's or stager's fee. I suppose if you're immersed in a hot seller's market and know beyond a shadow of doubt that the property will immediately attract multiple bids, hence your expenses and time will be minimal, you could rationalize a lower fee. But in a balanced or buyer's market, value added would arguably be perceived more favourably than cutting your fee. But what exactly did you win in any case? A chance to spend your time, money and expertise to market a property with the *hope* you can sell it. It's roulette. Spin the wheel and you might win – or not. What is your worth? It's a business decision and it's your choice.

"When your self-worth goes up, your net worth goes up with it."
Mark Victor Hansen

Buyer Agency

When do you ask your buyers to sign a Buyer Representation Agreement (BRA)? When you meet for the first time? After you've shown a few homes or immediately prior to signing an offer? Do you ask for a short-term commitment such as 24 hours and include only the specific properties you intend to show them? Or a longer term general contract? Do you even ask for a commitment – in writing or otherwise? Maybe you rely on an implied, trusting verbal arrangement. Or maybe before you step out the door, you flatly refuse to invest any time unless they commit. The practice of buyer agency has certainly been controversial since its inception, and largely inconsistent.

Normally, I ask for a commitment once my buyers and I are mutually comfortable. Unless they're old clients or friends, I need assurance they're serious and sensible. I need to know if I can work with *them* before I formalize our agency. You've no doubt heard the expression "buyers from hell". Well, they exist. Usually, I get a signature on a BRA contemporaneous with the offer. It just makes sense to me. However, to protect yourself and comply with legislated requirements, you're supposed to obtain their written commitment as early as is practically possible in the process.

When drafting a BRA and inserting your commission rate, you must once again decide your worth. To preclude my buyers from having to pay additional fees, I set my rate to coincide with what is typically offered to cooperating brokerages. However, if they choose to offer on a listing that advertises a lower rate, I obviously advise them of the additional fee they'll have to pay if their bid is successful. Fortunately, this is a rare occurrence. But without a BRA, this option would be unavailable to you. Unless the seller agrees to pay your normal rate, you'd be forced to accept the lower fee.

Dual Duel

"It ain't what you don't know that gets you into trouble.
It's what you know for sure that just ain't so." Mark Twain

Many agents avoid the potentially lucrative scenario of dual agency. Why? Well, I've been told they're afraid of erring and placing themselves in legal or financial jeopardy. Or they say there's no point in taking the risk because they'd be forced to cut their fee anyway. Accordingly, they steer clear of navigating these potentially hazardous waters.

But consider the proverbial man against the sea. If you're familiar with fundamental seamanship, are well-trained and equipped to handle the operation of the ship, then the odds are greater that you'll arrive unscathed at your destination. Dual agency is no different. If you understand the process and follow procedure, you'll most likely satisfy both clients' needs. It's just a matter of mediating a duel, thinking and carefully choosing your words, maintaining appropriate confidentiality and caring equally for each party. However, when a brokerage represents two competing buyers for the same property, the possibility of a conflict can more easily arise. Challenges can be further exacerbated if the subject property is listed with the same brokerage that represents the buyer. But as I said, dual agency seems more problematical than it really is. Just ensure you understand the procedure and your responsibilities.

Seller expectations of a reduced commission for a double-ender is another issue altogether. It's commonly perceived that the charging of a double commission is unreasonable. Technically, it may seem like a double fee, but it's actually two separate commissions on a single property. Remember when I discussed dividing a full commission into two parts – half for the listing agent and half for the buyer brokerage? Well, let's bring that concept into this discussion.

Opposition exists to the whole concept of dual agency. Amongst other concerns, it's been suggested that when representing the interests of multiple parties in a transaction, our services are degraded. Therefore, they argue that our fee should be lower because we provide less service. Well, I happen to disagree. Nevertheless, realty agents unfortunately often discount their contractually agreed fee when double-ending, not necessarily because they want to, but because they feel obligated since a full commission is a lot of money. Or they do so to win the listing or are coerced into doing so during a competition. Or during an offer presentation, an unscrupulous seller or buyer demands it. But think again about risk.

Naturally, with any agency, there's always risk, but it multiplies with multiple agency. More opposing clients and more potential conflict equates with higher risk. In a single agency, you normally assume the risk of what might ultimately prove to be a futile attempt to win the listing or generate income. And of course, there's always the risk of liability due to technical error. Also, on rare occasions, you may not be paid. Well, with dual agency, you can double that risk and then some.

If the multiple-agency transaction is skilfully and conscientiously organized, *more* agent expertise is required – not less. To effectively execute the riskier role of dual agent and discharge your professional fiduciary responsibilities correctly, you must do *more* work, provide *more* disclosure, carefully and cautiously communicate and mediate between and expertly advise *more* client parties and create and manage *more* documents than if a cooperating brokerage were involved. Plainly expressed, doubling the number of parties equates with doubling the complexity. Consequently, under such circumstance, a full fee is quite justifiable.

Commission Conundrum

An ethical challenge exists with respect to the discounting of fees for a "double-ender". Let's say the total commission payable by the seller is

$20,000. You present an offer to your sellers who say they'll accept it if you reduce your commission to $15,000. They complain that your commission is still a lot of money, especially if it's only been a couple of weeks on the market. If you comply, the seller is happy, the buyer is happy, but you – not so much. You just lost $5000. If you had not introduced your buyer to that listing, which you're ethically compelled to do, and instead, sold your buyer another agent's listing of the same value and in the meantime, another agent sold your listing, you'd have generated the full $20,000 commission; half from your sold listing and half from the sale of another brokerage's listing.

Clearly, this is a practical disincentive to do your best for your seller client. To collect your full fee, either you not show your own listing or your buyer must make up the $5000 in lost commission under the BRA. Complicated. It gets even more so when the buyer demands a "kick-back" of commission for agreeing to work with you as the listing agent. Or the buyer expects to buy the property at a lower price because they think, rightly or not, that you're earning a double commission and will reduce your fee to "make the deal happen". But the seller wants the entire benefit of a lower commission for themselves.

Everybody wants a piece of your fee. Since when did the agent become a third party contractor to the APS? For all practical purposes, that's exactly what happens when you throw in your fee. Under common law, this isn't permitted. I mean, think about it. You're participating as a *party* to the contract by contributing your fee to the price negotiation, but without the accompanying equity interest. It's not much different from you paying part of the purchase price to the seller or *giving* money to the buyer for their down payment – but without the benefit of a lien or titled equity interest. In exchange for your financial donation, maybe you should demand a collateral mortgage be registered on title in the amount of your fee reduction and see what happens. I can hear the howling as the parties fervently object to such an "unreasonable" proposal. Kicking in is a slippery slope indeed. To enjoy a solid business, I suggest you avoid it whenever possible. If the sale is meant to be, then it will be – and without your sacrificial contribution.

Mediate or Advocate

People have expressed the concern that an agent cannot honestly represent the interests of two or more rival parties simultaneously. There may be some truth to this, and the risk of conflict of interest is certainly a possibility, but it all boils down to how the situation is handled. In any case, you're not a secret agent acting for one side or the other. The objective of both parties to the proposed contract is the same – an agreement.

If a dual agent can successfully negotiate mutually agreeable terms with full and appropriate disclosure, why should they not be rewarded for their efforts by receiving both commissions – one for representing each of the two sides? After all, for all intents and purposes, there are two deals involved, a sale and a purchase. When you're doing double duty, what's wrong with a double commission? You're worth every penny. Both parties want the deal. Both want to reach an agreement, maybe one more than the other. And the one who wants it the most will do the most bending.

But if you feel you must reduce, at least wait until you're dealing with real money, when you're working with an offer – not when you first accept a listing. When you take the listing, it's intangible, merely a percentage of nothing. If you await a sale, you'll have a better idea of the extent of your time, effort and expense required to achieve the sale. Then, when the finish line is within sight, you can make an informed decision regarding your value.

As you're probably aware, a double-ending agent can discuss every aspect of the APS with both parties except for price and motivation. Confidentiality is critical in this regard, but to a limited degree, you must still remain dutiful to each of your clients. However, in such a multiple agency scenario, your role effectively changes from one of advocate for one party to mediator between two. All parties know and expect you'll essentially be mediating because you obtain their informed, written consent. If either party refuses consent, then one of the parties (usually the buyer) would have to seek the services of another brokerage. There's no "Chinese Wall" in a real estate brokerage.

Sometimes, it's collectively advantageous for the seller and buyer to acquire the agency services of the same expert agent. A mediator handling the negotiation process can sometimes more effectively arrange a meeting of the minds than two aggressive, adversarial agents trying to out-negotiate the other. While trying to get the best terms for their respective clients, combative agents can sometimes blow the sale simply because their own egos get involved. Everybody wants to be a hero. Mediation has worked effectively and successfully in many other industries, such as family law, for a very long time. And it can and does work well, albeit informally, in our business. Maybe it's time we officially embraced the concept in our industry.

In the realty world of ever-rising expenses and falling revenue, where will our industry end up? If we survive at all in any recognizable form, I suggest we'll likely evolve into one that may offer a menu from which a seller or buyer can acquire specific services for prescribed fees, possibly paid in advance, maybe set by our associations. Standard procedures could change to reflect a new protocol reality. Maybe homeowners would complete and submit the requisite forms to the brokerage and perform all other services typically provided by a full-service brokerage, with fees varying accordingly.

There would probably be fewer real estate sales people and brokerages in this brave new world. In any given market, there's just so much revenue to be generated. To limit the number of sales people in any particular region, maybe a cap on applicant registrations could be imposed. With fewer participants, the remaining professionals might generally earn a comfortable living. There'd be no more superstars. Maybe a university degree requirement will facilitate a significant transformation. In any case, there's no doubt in my mind that our industry is evolving. I mean, think about how we did business not that long ago, before the introduction of computers, the Internet, smart phones, flexible commission rates, franchises, independent contractors and government meddling. It was a different era and so will the future be. And consumers will collectively get what they pay for.

If the public continues to demand lower and lower fees, then it must accept more of the burden of responsibility for risk and marketing expense. In the meantime, you decide what your services are worth and charge accordingly. It's your money.

"You must accept that you might fail; then, if you do your best
and still don't win, at least you can be satisfied that you've tried.
If you don't accept failure as a possibility, you don't set high goals,
you don't branch out, you don't try – you don't take the risk."
Rosalynn Carter

Chapter Thirteen

Callers, Clients and Prospects
Oh My!

"Half the money I spend on advertising is wasted;
the trouble is, I don't know which half." John Wanamaker

Ad and Switch

If asked by a new seller if I intend to advertise their listing, I always say yes. At my discretion, though, unless I feel the property worthy, I don't usually promise print promotion. Why? As I said, the primary purpose of expensive advertising is general call generation. And if I feel a print ad won't produce sufficient calls to justify the expense, I advertise another listing that will, and switch the caller to their listing. Some properties just don't have what it takes. If you feel the house is unsuitable, don't waste your money.

Even during newspaper's heyday, I refused to rely on them. Aside from the Internet, I usually got a better response from direct mailers to and personal contact with my own client network and farm area. And I improved the odds by habitually asking for referrals. Whenever I placed a newspaper ad, it was for one of three reasons; to promote myself, to appease a seller or as a last-ditch and usually futile attempt to generate prospects. Tell your sellers you'll certainly promote their listing on multiple Internet websites and via a lawn sign, open house, office window display and verbally through your personal business network. If you offer a clear explanation – and your seller trusts you – you'll have no problem. After all, who's the professional?

Fishing and Wishing

Don't assume your new seller understands the workings of our industry. You might have to explain that most sales result from our incredible MLS® system – by far the best advertising venue – where nearly all buyers begin their search. When a sold sign appears, chances are the home was sold by a cooperating brokerage. Explain that agents don't search the newspapers for property to show. They peruse our proprietary MLS® database and consider any suitable listing with any brokerage.

Some agents advertise their listings in newspapers by way of small classified ads, while others resort to regular personally-branded display ads. The humongous advertisers, though, are just fishing for listings and legitimately focus mainly on that end of the business. Sometimes, they refuse to even work with buyers, instead delegating callers to junior agents or team members. Homeowners, who mistakenly believe that it's advertising that sells homes, are often attracted to big advertisers believing they'll receive superior marketing service. They might indeed, but not necessarily, since it depends on how they define superior. As a matter of policy, some big volume producers anticipate expired listings, chalking them up as acceptable losses, and may not have the time for regular personal contact with their numerous clients.

The fact remains that, to my knowledge, there's no official correlation between promotional dollars spent and a successful sale. Since buyers aren't normally duped, if the property isn't properly prepared and/or priced correctly, *no* amount of advertising will move it. If you're legitimately trying to generate buyer prospects, however, intelligent selective advertising in a property-appropriate venue can produce good results.

What's your commission generation ratio between buyer sales and listings sold? My practice was usually 70/30 favouring buyers. I normally preferred to work with buyers, but early on, I realized that listings are a great buyer generator. List to last, they said, or don't be listless. Consequently, I usually spent about a third of my time prospecting for listings and two thirds on buyers. Not only did lawn signs, open houses and Internet inquiries create buyers, but my sellers became loyal buyers too. And rarely did any of my listings expire unsold. I *personally* sold real estate and wasn't just a listing agent who sat around waiting for an offer. Prospect for listings, and buyers will knock at your door – and without spending a dime in the newspaper.

Trading Information

> *"When you meet people, show real appreciation, then genuine curiosity."*
> *Martha Beck*

Home seekers call for one reason – curiosity. It's an extremely powerful motivator, but intrinsically short-lived. Once satisfied, they no longer need you. You have a tiny window of opportunity to connect in a meaningful way before the call ends. Thus, you'd better be prepared. Have something scripted and well practiced in advance. For many reasons, callers are often not interested in the advertised property. Therefore, as I've said, be familiar with local inventory and have the details of alternate listings at your finger-tips.

When your phone rings, identify yourself by name and immediately ask for theirs. First names are acceptable and subliminally perceived as friendlier and less of a commitment. Sprinkle the conversation with their name because a name has magical powers. Have you ever been called over the drone of a crowd? We're instinctively drawn to familiarity. The bonding process begins with the exchange of basic info, directly and indirectly. Theory goes that if you give them something, they may be inclined to return the favour. It's a trade.

Thank them for calling and ask how you can help. If they ask the whereabouts of the property, tell them the town or neighbourhood, not the specific address, and immediately ask if that's where they prefer to live. If they answer yes, you've got a good prospect because they've begun to give *you* information. They've also confirmed their intention to buy and aren't "just looking". Answering a question with a question instead of an answer is patently evasive and potentially offensive. If that happens, you're toast. Briefly respond to their question and follow-up with *your* question. Here's a sample conversation:

- ➤ *What's the asking price?* (Share it.) Is that in your range? (Wait.)
- ➤ *How many bedrooms?* Three. How many do you need? (Await reply.) Do you have children or other family members living with you?
- ➤ *Yes, we have two kids.* Are they in public school or separate?
- ➤ *Public.* Great. The public school is located a short walk away.
- ➤ *Is the basement finished?* Yes, it is. There's a cozy rec room with stone fireplace that warms the room nicely. Plus there's an additional room that could serve as a hobby or extra bedroom. Would extra rooms be useful? (Await answer.) How long have you been home searching?
- ➤ *We've really just begun.* Do you own a home now or are you renting?
- ➤ *Yes, we own a home now.* In town here?
- ➤ *Yes.* (If they're renting, to give you an idea of urgency and timing, ask when their lease matures.) Have you had it evaluated recently?
- ➤ *No.* Knowing how much you can afford to spend is a good place to begin. So, it would be wise to know how much equity you have. Would a free no-obligation market evaluation interest you?
- ➤ *Well, I guess so.* (Early in the conversation, ask if they have an agent. If so, ask if they've entered into a BRA and if applicable, if their home is listed. If they're under contract, the call can end quickly, but professionally. Be courteous, answer questions and ask if you can email listing details to their agent. If they're not committed to another agency, then continue with your dialogue.)

> ➢ *No, we've just been calling on ads and lawn signs.* You must be growing a little frustrated when they're already sold, in the wrong area or price range. (Pause briefly for any forthcoming reply.)
> ➢ *No, it's not bad. We're not in a hurry.* That's great, but if an exciting home that met with your wants and needs were newly listed, you'd like to hear about it right away. Right? (Wait for a response.) Well, I provide a free service to a select group of clients wherein I email listings of interest that meet the search criteria in the preferred locale, including details, photos and virtual tours, immediately they're available. My buyers get in early and usually long before those listings hit the papers or open house circuit. Do you see the benefit of this early notification?
> ➢ *I don't know. We like the idea of just calling on a house if we like how it sounds.* As I said, this is a free service. It'll save you a ton of time, effort and frustration. If you see something you like in your email-box, you can just email, text or call me with questions or for a viewing. A map is included so you can drive by to check out the exterior and neighbourhood. If you like what you see, contact me to arrange a private viewing. We can go from there. You don't need to await a newspaper ad or open house. How would you feel about that?
> ➢ *That sounds nice. I guess I've nothing to lose.* (How could it be otherwise since there's no real commitment and their search just got easier?) Great! It'll be a lot easier for you. What's your last name? Email address? Phone number? I'll set it up today and call you to confirm that you received the first email. You'll not regret placing your trust in me. I promise. (Sign off using their name once again.)

After you've sent the first email, don't forget to call to confirm that they gave accurate contact information, that they received the listings and to ask for feedback. The follow-up is an ideal time to learn more about them and strengthen your bond. A second exchange means you're no longer strangers, so it'll be more relaxed.

During the initial call, if you're able to confirm a personal consultation appointment, detailed questions can await that meeting. If not, take your best shot on the phone. Engage them in conversation and give something of value, such as key benefits of the home or of working with you. Ask for their technical maximum price as well as their comfort maximum, which could be considerably lower. (See chapter 23 for more detail.)

Convincing them to have enough faith in you to officially hire you usually occurs in baby steps. And if you fail to take that first step, you've wasted your resources. Talk *with* them and demonstrate genuine interest by actively listening. You're learning about them, and by responding to your questions, they're learning about and investing in you too. Every minute you share on the phone adds to the natural conclusion that they'll work with you. What else could happen? They've calmly conveyed their requirements, one at a time, to help you help them. Giving you their contact info and acknowledging informal representation is almost anticlimactic. Remember – you're not trying to convince them to buy; you're initially selling *yourself,* building rapport. Earn their respect. Gain their confidence and the rest is simpler.

Polish comes with experience. Since practice makes perfect, using a script, rehearse different scenarios with your spouse, a friend or colleague. Ask your role-playing partner to change their level of cooperation from easy to challenging to obnoxious. Eventually, you'll be an expert at handling anybody.

The longer you can comfortably keep them on the phone, the more likely you'll establish the beginnings of a good relationship and convert them from caller to prospect to client. But you must take that first baby step to building faith.

"Faith is taking the first step even when you don't see the whole staircase."
Martin Luther King, Jr.

For an Internet inquiry, it's a little different in that at least at the outset, you have to rely solely on a variation of a phone script. Digital messages are notoriously misinterpreted because of the intrinsically cold anonymity. It's almost impossible to emote in print, to inject warmth, charm and natural magnetism – your charisma – particularly for someone with deficient writing skills. However, the intent is the same; trade information. Because there's no voice inflection or casual remarks, no smiles thrown into the mix, choose your words and phrases carefully. You may have one fleeting opportunity to connect. But look on the bright side; you got a request for more information. And unlike a possibly anonymous phone caller, by default, you got their contact information – their email address – and sometimes their name.

If they gave you some contact info like a phone number or last name and where roughly they live, prior to contacting them, learn a little about them. For example, perform a reverse phone number search and determine if their home is for sale or sold. Check the sales history of their property. Knowledge is power. If they ask for a reply by phone or email, call them. The odds of establishing a personal connection with your digital *voice* are far greater than with anonymous digital *ink*.

In a written reply, skip the boasting verbosity. Be courteous and succinct. Introduce yourself and thank them for their inquiry. Carefully answer *all* their questions and, as with a phone inquiry, follow each of their questions with your own. Don't be too aggressive or personal. Keep your questions general and few. Since many people don't read much beyond restaurant menus, a long reply may not even be read past the first answer to their most pressing question. Offer your help with any other properties, no matter with whom those homes are listed. You could provide a little information about yourself, adding that you're there for them, and include a link to other comparable listings. Offer to call or meet with them for a personal, free, no-obligation consultation. Here's a sample reply:

> Dear Jane:
>
> *Thank you for your email inquiry. Here is the information you were seeking.* (List their questions, followed by direct answers in a straightforward point-form or narrative format. If you've created an e-brochure with photos, include it as a link or attachment in a popular file format. Or offer to mail it to them, for which you'd need their postal address.) *Due to a hectic schedule and ample showing activity, I have no open house planned. However, at your convenience, I would be pleased to arrange a private viewing for you. This home has numerous quality features, so many that a quick inspection during an open house would not do it justice nor provide you with all the information necessary to make an informed decision.*
>
> *It's situated on a pie-shaped lot on a quiet court located in the heritage district of Small Town. Is this the focus area of your home search? It's a short walk to the theatre, schools, public transit, a wonderful park system and several fine restaurants and shops. Do you have children? They'll love the amenities close by. When would you require possession? The owners vacate date is flexible. If you wish, I have an extensive colour brochure that I could mail to you (or it's attached). Would you be interested in receiving it?*
>
> *I realize you might only be at the information gathering stage and not yet ready to share information about yourself or your needs. Be assured that I will respect your online privacy. Aside from one follow-up contact to confirm successful receipt of this message, I will only reply to your further requests.*
>
> *If and when you are ready to explore your real estate needs, I will be pleased to help. Thanks for your interest. I hope to hear from you again soon.*

Offer your complimentary search service as described earlier. To personalize your message, attach a head-shot to your signature. A link to your website where they can view a virtual tour or more photos is also a good idea. If they don't within a day or so, contact them, preferably by phone, to ask if they received your message and if you answered their questions. If they reply, you're in the game. If not, at least you got off the bench to bat. Now, let's talk about what is sometimes a major issue with buyers – whether to buy brand new or a previously loved home.

> *"Anything can be achieved in small, deliberate steps. But*
> *there are times you need the courage to take a great leap;*
> *you can't cross a chasm in two small jumps."* David Lloyd George

Chapter Fourteen

New or Used?

"I was seldom able to see an opportunity until it had ceased to be one."
Mark Twain

Soup Can

Have you ever lost to a newly built home what you felt was a solid resale buyer? Even though you presented them with what you felt was an ideal opportunity and lots of logical reasons to buy a unique home in an established neighbourhood, they failed to see it as such. No matter what you said, they were determined because they loved the idea of brand spanking new. They were hooked.

Production builders play a siren song to the uninitiated with trendy words like stone, wood, peace, sky, green, meadow, desert, coral or mountain. A fabulous array of professionally staged, upgraded model homes beckons strategically from within corralled capture compounds, accessible by way of richly carpeted sales pavilions with artist's renderings, resplendent with non-existing grass, mature trees and designer flower gardens. Buying brand new is made easy; it's like choosing a can of soup from the grocery store shelf. However, once one gets past the somewhat different floor plans and frontal elevations of rapidly constructed building-blocks on empty, characterless lots, unless a sizable premium is paid for a premium lot, many of the cans are pretty much the same. Is my bias showing already?

A prudent buyer should, however, carefully consider the numerous potential drawbacks to new – major and minor – before leaping into the fray. Then, if they choose to pursue that option, at least it'll be a fully informed decision. Before heading over to the builder's sales office, all starry-eyed with pen and chequebook in hand, you can provide them with valuable tips.

Not all new home purchases are burdened by the following issues, but be prepared. In some areas, a purchase is subject to the unpopular Harmonized Sales Tax (HST), usually buried in the purchase price. Builder contract terms, including the price, are rarely negotiable, the possession date, especially a high-rise condo, is usually many months, if not years away, and options can be surprisingly exorbitant. Builders often levy a hefty premium for upgrades to rationalize breaking their production schedule. Now, these should be sufficient justification to avoid buying new, but they're often not.

If the main house fixtures haven't already been ordered or installed, a new home buyer can usually choose kitchen and bathroom cabinetry and counter-tops, paint and plumbing fixture colours, flooring, exterior cladding, roof shingles and maybe even the exterior elevation (architectural style). Everything will be shiny and new when they move in. Plus, they get a limited warranty, the fee for which is usually included in the price. But that's pretty much where the fantasy ends.

"The big print giveth and the fine print taketh away." Fulton J. Sheen

The Fine Print: In most cases, the buyer must enter into a purchase on the builder's own custom contract. Prudence dictates that your soon-to-be former client have their lawyer review it *before* they sign on the dotted line because, unlike a generic resale APS, builder contracts are typically blatantly biased in favour of the builder. Since the house is a manufactured product in a relatively closed market, this is certainly justifiable. Also unlike a resale contract, the deposit required by a builder is usually very large and sometimes divided into multiple payments over a prescribed period of time. Your buyer should be prepared to make the instalments when due, failing which, they may be declared in default of the contract and responsible for possibly substantial penalties, including forfeiture of all monies already paid. And check for additional "hidden" buyer expenses in the fine print.

Delayed Gratification: Due to disasters waiting to happen, builders usually reserve the right to postpone a completion on as many as three occasions. From the builder's perspective, this is totally understandable since they're at the mercy of labour, suppliers, municipal government and weather conditions, not to mention the fickle buying public and the general economy. If sales are slow, construction may be delayed – sometimes indefinitely and occasionally permanently. Under such circumstances, buyers are often permitted to cancel a contract, usually without penalty, after a certain number of delays. The buyer must be given a predetermined amount of notice, but their special day gets delayed or eliminated. This can be particularly problematical if they've already served notice to their landlord, or worse, they've sold their old house and must vacate on the contractually agreed closing date. They'll be forced to seek temporary accommodation or totally change their home plans. It happens.

The would-be buyer suffers through the infamous double move. Not nice, not convenient and not cheap.

Value Volatility: The chances are relatively low that market values will fluctuate dramatically during the 60 to 90 day closings typical of resales. However, the risk of values plummeting during the traditionally longer closings associated with new homes is much higher. A buyer can only hope the market continues to at least maintain current values, if not rise. On closing day, they could be forced to hand over their hard-earned money in exchange for a key to a new house whose market value is lower than what they paid a year ago. It's a bitter pill to swallow. Ramifications? You bet, and potentially serious ones. A buyer who refuses to close could forfeit their deposit, plus be held liable if the builder sues them (very likely) for specific performance (to close) and/or for damages in an amount determined after the builder is forced to resell the house at a lower price, including any additional expenses. Depending on how the market fares, this could be big bucks. Is the gamble worth the benefit of being able to pick colours?

Just in Time: Let's say their new home purchase went well and there were no postponements, or they've lived with the grief. They've undergone the scheduled inspections with the builder's superintendent and any deficiencies, touch-ups and repairs have been made or promised. Moving day arrives. Large production builders follow the "just in time" practice wherein construction details are frantically finished immediately prior to the scheduled completion date. The builder doesn't want the expense of carrying the property any longer than absolutely necessary. The buyer has delivered the balance of their down payment to their lawyer, paid the typically higher closing costs and after a long wait, the sale is finally completed.

Everybody – including the team of movers – arrives at the shiny new front door, ready to crack open the traditional celebratory bottle of champagne or a case of beer with an extra-large pizza. But, surprise – they're welcomed by a crew of construction workers scampering about in a frenzy to finish and get the place "broom-swept" ready for occupancy. With frustration settling into their hearts, your former buyers are praying they made the right decision. The glossy shine of the "brand new" part has already begun to tarnish.

> *"Don't pray for rain if you are going to complain about the mud."* Proverb

Mud and Dust: If there's been little rain, when they move in, the "lawn" is a dusty, garbage-strewn cracked mud desert. And if it's rainy, sloppy mud everywhere is no better. The new homeowners are reluctant to let their kids and pets into the backyard because it's still a construction site, replete with nails, discarded building materials and assorted sharp objects. And of course, there's no fencing; that's the happy homeowner's dime. Usually, they can forget about having any large trees unless they agreed to buy a landscaping package or paid a greenbelt premium. It'll be like living in a big brown field. The driveway is a rutted gravel mess because it can't be paved until the ground settles (if asphalt was even included). The unassumed municipal road is mired in mud, littered with masonry skids and choked with roaring, fume-belching construction vehicles. And since it probably won't have the finish asphalt for months, keeping their car clean is mission impossible.

Opening the windows? I don't think so, unless they want a perpetual film of dust enveloping everything in the house. Inside, the kitchen cabinets are dusty and the basement concrete floors and walls smell damp because, well, they're still curing. You know that damp basement odour. Oh, and it's advisable to delay finishing their dream recreation room for at least a year (not that they can afford to anyway) because if the foundation walls crack or leak – which is known to happen in the first year – they must obviously be repaired. Collateral damage to any basement improvements is normally not warranted. The house usually experiences structural settling, with wall cracks above door frames and drywall rippling in corners. However, such damage is typically warranted and repaired by a reputable builder, but it's still a mess. So, there's no point in personally decorating their love nest because the builder won't repair it beyond standard original paint or primer.

Fumes and Follow-Up: Many new construction materials such as paint, cabinets, hardwood and laminate flooring, particle board sheathing and plywood sub-floors, broadloom and vinyl windows – most materials in a new house – off-gas toxic fumes. That new home smell definitely won't contribute to health and wellness, particularly during the heating season when windows of the tightly sealed house are closed. Before occupancy, to reduce the toxicity in the air, it should be thoroughly ventilated for several weeks.

For days and sometimes weeks afterward, workers return to finish small projects. If the house next door was sold later, the builder and his heavy equipment may still be busily excavating and building there for weeks, months or years if sales have been slow. Therefore, they better get used to construction noise, dust and mud. And here's a bonus; they may be serenaded occasionally by one of the construction guys next door! Let's hope he sings like Pavarotti.

New House Roulette: It's been said that good neighbours make for a happy home. Buying a home in an established neighbourhood certainly carries a similar risk, but at least prior to buying, they can meet the neighbours and check out their property. In a brand new subdivision, the risk is obviously far greater. If the neighbours have already moved in, hopefully they'll be likable because, well, they'll be living right next door. Maybe they won't be loud and obnoxious and take as much pride in their home as your people intend to do in theirs. If not, their deteriorating property (or unimproved) condition may adversely affect the market value of your buyer's new home, not to mention their quality of life.

"A good neighbor doubles the value of a house." German Proverb

A Different Animal

To make my point, I obviously used a wide brush to paint a grim nightmare new house scenario. Nevertheless, aside from grown trees and green grass, I honestly feel that existing homes are the better choice for one simple reason – a buyer can actually see what they're buying. It's less of a gamble. Unlike having to rely on floor-plans and artist renderings, a prospect can walk around the block and get a solid feel for the area – before buying. They can meet the neighbours, confirm the absence of motor-homes and tow-trucks next door, inspect the existing schools, shopping centres, parks, bus stops and hug the maple on the front lawn.

Since previously loved homes have often been improved, each is special in its own way. Landscaping, fencing, finished basements and a host of other improvements – most of which aren't normally part of a new house purchase – are often included. Buyers don't have the luxury of choosing their own cabinetry and plumbing fixtures, but then again, they do because they have the choice of offering on a particular home or not. If they don't like the kitchen cabinets, they can buy and renovate or pass. If the bathtub is avocado, re-finish or replace it. The cost of a small renovation is far less than that of the numerous improvements necessary with a brand new basic home.

Since the seller is obligated to maintain the property in the same condition as when viewed, there should be no surprises on moving day. Everything they bought, including the lawn, will be there. No mud or dust! What they saw is what they get!

A resale contract is usually a lot simpler and normally balanced between the parties. Also, since all contract terms, including a fixed completion date, are agreed at the outset, a homeowner can't unilaterally alter any of the terms – including postponing the closing – without the buyer's express consent. And unless it's substantially renovated or on large acreage, there's no HST applicable. Pretty much all the potential risk and hassles associated with a new house purchase are eliminated.

Now, having said all this, keep in mind that brand new and resale are totally different animals. The former is a newly manufactured product on which a builder must make a profit. He's got his challenges and all things considered, typically upholds his end of the deal. If your buyer prefers everything to be brand new and they can live with the potential disadvantages, they should go ahead and make the deal. There is, however, another option.

Nearly New

Try a last ditch effort to divert their path from the builder's pavilion by suggesting a *nearly* new home. Sometimes, family plans change and someone who'd bought from a builder was forced to list it not long after closing, or even before. Or the original buyer was a speculator who bought to flip. Your buyer client has the opportunity to enjoy many of the advantages of a brand new home (except finishing choices) without many of the disadvantages, including the long wait and accompanying risks linked to extended closings. If they like the idea, send them a few sample listings. You might be pleasantly surprised. What's to lose?

If they're determined to buy from a builder, visit a few new home sales offices in the locale of interest to ask if the builder or its brokerage is cooperating with realty agents. You might recover some costs by way of a referral fee for registering your buyers. They're not typically very generous, but something is better than nothing. Plus you can still provide your former client with helpful tips. Remember – one day, they'll want to list and sell that house.

"One generation plants the trees and another gets the shade."
Chinese Proverb

Chapter Fifteen

Challenging Clients:
Love 'em or Leave 'em?

"Don't be afraid to fail. Don't waste energy trying to cover up failure.
Learn from your failures and go on to the next challenge. It's okay to fail.
If you're not failing, you're not growing." H. Stanley Judd

Triggers & Rigors

Do you ever experience situations in which an obdurate client refuses to heed your advice? Maybe they unreasonably reject what you feel is a fair offer or insist on something that seems completely devoid of logic. You know in your gut that their course of action is wrong for them, but with all your experience, you're unable to help them understand. And if you press too much, you might elicit a reaction you prefer to avoid; bigger divisive walls or worse, a boot fits figuratively against your butt as you're impolitely encouraged to exit their home.

Humans are naturally emotional beings. And with major decisions involving large sums of money, they can certainly be volatile. You'll undoubtedly meet people who are belligerent, arrogant, cantankerous, argumentative, sarcastic or narcissistic and some that are *really* not nice. You seek qualified teachers from whom to learn business skills. So, why not endow yourself with the skills to handle such destructive emotions and maintain inner peace and harmony?

Their negative feelings are a result of *their* issues – not *yours*. Therefore, don't make them your own. Resist being embroiled in their personality issues because you'll not change them. Learn to identify the behaviour in others that triggers a negative reactive emotion in you. And when this happens, step back, witness and acknowledge it, silently count to ten and let it pass.

Conflict Resolution

To assist during moments of conflict or even its potential, you may want to consider developing skills in the field of conflict resolution. Marshall B.

Rosenberg, Ph.D. wrote several books, one of which is entitled *Nonviolent Communication; A Language of Life. Create Your Life, Your Relationships and Your World in Harmony with Your Values*. Here's an excerpt:

"Most of us have been educated from birth to compete, judge, demand and diagnose – to think and communicate in terms of what is 'right' and 'wrong' with people. At best, the habitual ways we think and speak hinder communication and create misunderstanding and frustration in others and in ourselves. And still worse, they cause anger and pain and may lead to violence. Without wanting to, even people with the best of intentions generate needless conflict. We express our feelings in terms of what another person has 'done to us'. We struggle to understand what we want or need in the moment and how to effectively ask for what we want without using unhealthy demands, threats or coercion ... 'What others do may be a stimulus of our feelings, but not the cause.' At best, thinking and communicating this way can create misunderstanding and frustration, or simply keep us from getting what we want. It can also keep us from the fulfilling relationships we deserve. And still worse, it can lead to anger, depression and even emotional or physical violence."

If you're interested in learning to "transform the thinking, moralistic judgments and language that keep you from the enriching relationships you dream of", more easily resolve conflicts, to *ask for* instead of *demand* what you want, more easily understand the true needs of others, strengthen personal and professional relationships and begin living to your fullest potential, I encourage you to study NVC. How would possessing these skills help your real estate practice? You'd be better equipped to avoid reacting (or suppressing) and instead, deal more calmly with any stimulus or conflict that might arise in your professional and personal life. Your level of life success is directly related to and highly dependent upon your attitude, which in turn depends upon your happiness, peace of mind and self confidence. Learning new interpersonal relationship techniques can improve your life in general – and your business in particular.

Occasions may arise when a client reacts angrily to your attempts to dissuade them from a particular path. Why do they behave so? Anger is a derivative of fear. Why are they afraid? What's the source of their inner conflict? Do they not trust your advice? Do they object to the quality of your service? Is it a credibility issue? Are they disappointed? Do they have a hidden agenda which they guiltily perceive you may be inadvertently close to discovering? Have you missed a signal from them? Are they feeling overwhelmed? Maybe they simply need reassurance that you know what you're talking about and that they can trust you. Maybe they feel you're just not hearing them or failing to sincerely understand their wants and needs. Since many people lack the ability to articulate their feelings, they might be deliberately suppressing their anger. Or they may be afraid to express themselves out of a fear of being judged. Life could be a whole lot easier if we were all mind-readers, but we're not. However, if you're equipped to read the signs, at least you might lesson the chance of being deceived, if not improve your level of service.

Sometimes, a clarification of the common goal and the logical steps toward attaining it will be all that it takes to resolve the situation. Talk about it – and listen. Pay attention. You have the same objective; the sale of their home and/or the purchase of another. If you're unable to resolve the problem, often they don't move and you don't collect a commission.

The old adage that the customer is always right went out the window with the stereotypical slick, cigar-smoking salesman who couldn't care less about the customer's needs. For a fast buck, they'd press anybody into anything. Whatever was right for the salesman was *made* right for anybody with a pulse. Unfortunately, many of this breed still exist – maybe without the cigar. The fact is, though, that the client is *not* always technically right. To professionally serve them, when appropriate, it's imperative to tactfully tell them so.

Your client is always right, I suppose, in that they have the right to express their feelings, be it fear, anger, love, gratitude or whatever. But don't try to convince them of their error before understanding the truth behind their behaviour. You certainly want to avoid a heated argument. You may be dealing with a powerful ego too, both theirs and yours. Ego gets us into trouble almost every time. How do you convince a client to see your point of view without offending them?

> *"The components of anxiety, stress, fear and anger do not exist independently of you in the world. They simply do not exist in the physical world even though we talk about them as if they do." Wayne Dyer*

Certainty & the Closed Mind

If your client thinks they're right and you think they're wrong, then from their perspective, you're wrong to think they're wrong because they feel they're right and you're wrong even if you're actually right. Let me restate that. Though absolute truth is another matter (truth relativism), when it comes to belief, right and wrong are relative. Belief is a powerful force and if someone believes they're right, then in their mind, they are indeed right, even if their belief is a violation of Universal Law. Their belief may be diametrically opposed to yours, but from their perspective, they're right. It may be mission impossible, but you must convince them to open their minds. If they continue to insist their mind is open and remain certain of their position, tell them that certainty exists only with a closed mind.

The best way to begin this process is with active listening. Encourage them to express their thoughts and feelings – uninterrupted. Then gently remind them that you have a common goal, whether it's to buy or sell, and ask for their acknowledgment. You're on the same team. You win only if they win. Express yourself calmly, clearly and most importantly, sincerely. Impress them with your thoughtfulness, consideration and wisdom. Try to get the underlying reason for their choice, which may be fear-based. Address each of their concerns in whatever form they appear, and seek their acknowledgement. Respond enthusiastically, but gently, with intelligent logic – not emotion. Patiently try to help (not coerce) them to understand the reasoning behind your expert advice and the possible adverse consequences of their own fear-based decision. Lay it out for them. You need a genuine trust connection. Otherwise, your relationship will continue to be stressful – if it continues at all.

Trust is extremely valuable, but unless they were referred by someone *they* trust, you may have to work hard to be deemed worthy of theirs. Earning it will likely be necessary anyway, but at least with a recommendation from their friend or family member, you have a leg up. You may have to backup your opinion with facts. For example, use a properly prepared CMA with market statistics to substantiate price advice. Impress them with your knowledge and maybe toss in a few testimonials from previous satisfied clients.

The best way to gain trust is to be completely honest, and make it patently obvious that you're placing their interests ahead of your own. Explain that to help them effectively, you must tell them what they *need* to know and not just what they *want* to hear – and do that. If their home is a mess, tell them so. If your new buyer's eyes are bigger than their belly, enlighten them. At an appropriate moment, share a little about yourself, your business and life experience. Get to know them – and allow them to know you. Gradually lower your defence shields and build a solid, honest – authentic – relationship. All of this is crucial, but trust is often earned by giving it first. Trust them and they may trust you in return. Once you have it, trust can last a lifetime. And guess who they'll contact every time they need real estate service? The big shot agent in town or someone they know and trust?

> *"The best way to find out if you can trust somebody is to trust them."*
> Ernest Hemingway

Retain or Refrain

There may be instances when you're not the right person to serve a particular client. Call it a personality conflict. You may not like them or they may not seem to like you. (How's that possible?) Before entering into a business relationship, formal or otherwise, determine whether you're all compatible enough to work pleasantly in concert for potentially many months, if not years. Will you enjoy regular contact? If you don't like them now, just imagine how you'll feel in the future. It's your call, but life is short. I advise against allowing obnoxious people into your life. Have a heart to heart up front, before the paperwork and prior to investing any serious resources on their behalf. They might surprise you. Your forthrightness may bring out their better selves. Defensive walls could crumble and a bond could begin to bud.

After you've exhausted every tool in your intellectual arsenal, and your client continues to adamantly insist on a particular position, or you shudder every time you're exposed to their negative energy, make a decision. Do you keep the client or terminate the relationship? Tough choice – or not. Under the circumstances, if you're emotionally unwilling or technically unlikely to fulfill your responsibilities – and enjoy the experience – consider expressing those feelings and seeking a release from the agency contract. If you feel it's just a personality conflict, you could ask if they'd prefer to be represented by a colleague within your own brokerage or a competitor. If they eventually enter into an APS with that peer, you'll at least recover some costs from a referral fee.

During my career, I've taken this route with a few difficult people and been delighted with the result. After once offering to release a particularly challenging client, they seemed to find my advice more credible and me more trustworthy. When they realized I wasn't just after their money, they magically transformed into pleasant, cooperative clients and respectfully asked me to continue as their representative.

On the other hand, if your client accepts your proposal for a new agent, process the paperwork and if necessary, introduce them. Or if they stubbornly refuse to release you, document the advice they rejected. And depending on the gravity of the situation, have them sign a detailed acknowledgement. It might come in handy later if, for example, their property remains unsold. Or as I said, it might impress upon them the seriousness of the situation and motivate them to accept your counsel. If you're unable to resolve the problem, they may have a hidden agenda. In such case, you may not want to trust *them* and limit your investment of time and effort.

During the initial consultation, do your best to determine the odds of successfully satisfying their wants and needs. Are their demands realistic? Are they of serious intent? Will they sell or buy for fair market value or only if they get their price? Is that price expectation realistic? Will they make their home readily available and presentable for viewings? If buyers, are they committed to owning a home and available to view on reasonable notice? These are all serious matters to be considered prior to accepting an agency.

Get to know them as best you can. Discuss your intentions and offer candid, honest advice. But above all, maintain your personal integrity and professional standards. If you sense trouble, let them find another agent. Set them free. If they return, they're yours. If they don't, they never were. If you wish to successfully remain in business, keep the bottom line in sight. Make this protocol part of your business plan. Our industry suffers from a huge turnover. Don't be a statistic. If you accept someone as a client, whether stranger, friend or family, you decide if you'll be able to work with them – happily and profitably. If you accept someone you don't like, will you still love yourself in the morning?

"The first step in exceeding your customer's expectations
is to know those expectations." Roy H. Williams

Chapter Sixteen

Kith and Kin

"Insanity runs in my family. It practically gallops."
Cary Grant

Connections and Affections

Why do you invest so much time and expense staying connected with people in your business network? Because you want the ideal real estate practice wherein people remember to contact you for real estate service. Why would they call you and not the neighbourhood "specialist" or another agent who happened to serendipitously cross their path? Two reasons – familiarity and trust. By diligently staying in regular contact, you hope to establish and maintain a familiar, durable and trusting relationship. Simply expressed, your goal is to be their friend in the business.

Here's the thing, though, about family and close friends. You obviously share at least semi-regular contact, so familiarity and trust are hopefully ingrained. You'd presuppose they'd seek your services, if for no other reason than your close relationship. Naturally, they'd anticipate extra special care while having a great time working together, and trust that the potentially stressful process of home relocation would be secure and more relaxed. Since they must pay somebody anyway, you'd expect they'd agree to your usual fee. After all, keeping the wealth in the family rather than paying a stranger makes perfect sense. Unfortunately, though, this isn't always how things turn out.

In many cases, they suffer from the belief that you should perform your skilled services – surprise – for a reduced fee or even free of charge. Why? Because you're family. They conveniently ignore the fact that unlike them, you don't enjoy the benefit of a regular weekly paycheque. They fail to appreciate that the sometimes considerable investment of time, money and expertise puts food on your family's table, a roof overhead and fuel in your car. They fail to grasp that for you, time is money. While you're labouring for them and critically, *not* for other *paying* clients, they're at work earning *their* daily bread. To a somewhat lesser extent, it's not unlike their volunteering to help build your new sundeck, unless of course, they happen to be a carpenter by trade. In such case, to avoid a double standard, pay them for their skilled assistance or at least barter services.

To impress a new stranger prospect, you don your best clothes and professional (hopefully genuine) behaviour, and strive to get to know them, to gain their trust and bond as quickly as possible. Since relatives already know you, you'd think the process would be easier, but it ain't necessarily so. There's usually no need to convince them to trust you *personally*, but *professionally* may be an entirely different matter. When it comes to serving loved ones, particularly for the first time, you may still have to jump through a few credibility hoops to earn their professional trust. It won't necessarily be easier just because of your personal long term blood relationship, which could actually become a hindrance when crossing over from auntie to agent. Though serving family may be more relaxed, keep in mind they're still clients for whom you've undertaken a solemn responsibility, including associated agency risks.

Representing relatives can be more stressful because, I suppose, of the dynamics of long term relationships. It could be argued that you should be charging a higher than normal commission rate since they'll probably expect a superior level of service *because* you're related. Since they're comfortable with you, don't you think they'd contact you with questions, concerns or complaints more often than a non-related client – and at any hour of the day or night? Remember – they've got your home phone number! Wouldn't that eventually drive you crazy? Professionally, if they become a pain in your posterior, you can't tell them to take a hike. Well, I suppose you could, but by carefully following appropriate professional protocol.

Holding or Folding

"If you cannot get rid of the family skeleton, you may as well make it dance."
George Bernard Shaw

If your sibling believes you're failing them, you can watch any chances of a commission fly out the window. And since emotions are difficult to avoid in family situations, maintaining professional decorum can prove problematic. Firing can be as easy as hiring. Compounding the problem is the resulting family gossip, ridicule, conflict and enduring hard feelings within a potentially polarized family. Rumours can travel like a grass fire and family won't be vanishing after the business relationship is over. Professionally or personally, you *really* don't want to disappoint a relative. Also, in addition to lost or damaged relationships, you could lose opportunities for future family business.

New closeted skeletons are given the breath of life, to be rattled periodically and never forgotten.

Throughout my career, whenever I was asked for service by a relative or close friend, unless unusual circumstances prevailed, I'd normally accept the agency and charge my usual fee. They typically agreed without argument because they appreciated the value of our trust relationship. Occasionally, however, after calling me for professional advice, a couple of them proceeded to hire a hungrier agent who readily acquiesced to their demand for a chopped fee. Did I find this disturbing? Oh yes. Did I ever forget this betrayal? Nope. Have I forgiven them? The jury is still out, but I'm working on it.

If you're asked for a discount, without raising an eyebrow, calmly refuse and without missing a beat, move to the next step. At that point, they might drop the issue and the problem is resolved. However, if they persist, ask them why they asked you to represent them. If they reply that they thought you'd work for free, then it might be time to fetch your hat and head for the door. But if they say they trust you, ask if they know another agent they trust as much. In most cases, they'll say no. What's that trust worth? What's the value of being represented by someone with whom they share a familiar loving relationship, someone they completely trust to protect them unequivocally and who'll conscientiously do absolutely everything in their power to fulfill their wishes? In my book, that's worth a lot.

If they refuse to drop the issue, tell them to begin interviewing agents. They'll likely respond by saying they don't want to go to the trouble or wouldn't trust them as much. Point made. Hold your ground. Or to preserve the relationship, you can fold, take a hit in your income and do your best in the following years to suppress your resentment or better yet, forgive them. Their motivation isn't that they don't love and respect you. They may suffer from the virulent and increasingly common Money Madness and be driven by a fear of scarcity. And that fear may be stronger than their innate ability to love. It may be hard for you to handle, but you must accept that they're hard-wired to think that way. If you allow yourself to violate your customary fee policy, then you'll be aligning your own loving higher vibrational frequency with their lower fear frequency. (More later on this topic.)

By strictly following this protocol, most prospective clients, whether family, friend or trusting stranger with whom you have a solid mutually respectful relationship, will be satisfied. If not, then consider what you may have lost as you walk out the door. Remember – relationships are more important than money.

"Treasure your relationships, not your possessions." Anthony J. D'Angelo

Meets and Boundaries

It's arguably in poor taste to blatantly prospect at family gatherings. However, during such events, if a relative seeks your advice, and you're open to helping them, prior to accepting the agency, clarify your policy of no discounts. If they grumble, save everyone a lot of time and frustration by politely refusing their business right then and there. The personal relationship must come first. By treating your business relationships with family professionally, you'll improve the odds of keeping the personal element intact.

Early in a relationship with stranger clients, you normally delineate mutually unambiguous boundaries as determined by personal feelings and social and business mores. Since boundaries with family can naturally be blurred, it's best to establish similar clear limitations, professional boundaries and expectations *before* entering into a principle/agent contract with loved ones. Don't wait until a perceived transgression occurs and someone is upset, either expressed or suppressed. Obviously, all industry rules, codes of ethics, standards of practice and provincial or state statutes still apply, but a healthy working relationship is more than that. A personal connection is great, but to avoid damaging a familial relationship, it's *really* important for both sides – prior to putting pen to paper – to recognize what would constitute inappropriate behaviour, unreasonable expectations and unwelcome trespass.

In your business life, disappointments will be forgiven or forgotten fairly quickly. Aggrieved clients will vote with their feet and never do business with you again. They're gone from your life. However, family will always be family. You can't divorce a sibling. When boundaries or expectations are not clearly understood or reciprocally respected, the result could ultimately be disastrous. For example, prior to accepting a family member as a client, your professional availability should be established. Advise them that unless it's an emergency – by *your* definition – they may contact you with business questions or concerns only during regular business hours. Or you could insist that when you have a report ready, you'll contact them.

Treat all your clients, be they family, friend or stranger, in the same professional manner and expect to be treated the same in return. Yes, it may be a little softer around the edges with family, but it's a good idea to stay within your preconceived and usually unwritten boundaries. It's not always possible, though, because regardless of the relationship, some people will cooperate and others won't. But at the end of the day, you want your family to be happy.

Sew Quid Pro Quo

I believe that people are fundamentally honest and trustworthy, hence I trust people until they give me a reason to do otherwise. And fortunately, I'm usually trusted in return. Life is definitely easier when you're so blessed. More often than not, you get what you give and reap what you sew. I've earned the faith of my clients – kith, kin and otherwise – by providing honest, dependable service and by trusting them. Of course, I've been betrayed occasionally; it's hurtful, but it happens. However, I've never betrayed the trust of a client, for without integrity, you have nothing.

In most situations, your relatives and close acquaintances will hire you. And they'll do so for one chief reason – they trust you to take extra special care of them. They know in their heart that you'll not allow them to be cheated, that they can sign documents without worry. Key decisions during the home transition process are made much less stressful with the thoughtful loving guidance of trusting counsel. Again, what is that trust worth? A lot. And it's worth your full fee.

"A happy family is but an earlier heaven." George Bernard Shaw

Chapter Seventeen

Buy or Sell First?

"The 50/50/90 rule: Anytime you have a 50/50 chance of getting something right, there's a 90 percent probability you'll get it wrong." Andy Rooney

Unless you work exclusively with first time buyers, you're destined to deal with clients in the quandary of whether to buy before they sell their old home or sell prior to buying another. It's an essential decision wrought with potentially taxing emotions. During their deliberation, no matter which option they choose, they must understand that a calculated risk is unavoidable. Their choice will depend on circumstances, including their financial capabilities, their home and the current marketplace, and of course – their nerve. To protect yourself against potential liability, I advise you *not* to encourage them either way. Ultimately, it must be *their* informed decision. And it's your job to provide that information so they can make the wisest choice with the lowest risk. A worried client is an unhappy client.

"Worry does not empty tomorrow of its sorrow. It empties today of its strength."
Corrie Ten Boom

Buy First

Because it's considered the safest, most conservative route to trading homes, buying first is probably the most popular. After searching for days, months or longer, a buyer finds the right property and submits and hopefully successfully negotiates an offer subject to the sale of their old home. The next step is to list and sell the old place, following which they remove the sale condition from the APS. In a perfect world, it's neat, clean and in theory, relatively stress-free.

However, it's not without potential challenges. After investing all the time and effort (and your money) searching, your buyers may be met with an exasperating situation; the seller of their dream home flatly rejects their conditional offer. Oh no! Unreasonable or otherwise, some sellers refuse to even consider sale conditions, regardless of the proffered price. Why? Because they don't really consider them a bona fide sale. From their perspective – a view often shared by the listing agent – it's like an option to purchase. They think of it as a "pretend" purchase that will become a "real" purchase if the buyer succeeds in selling their old place. And sometimes, that's a big if. The seller refuses to tie up their property with a "non-sale". The result? Crushed hopes – theirs *and* yours.

If a seller takes this stance or your client is competing with another buyer who has no house to sell or who sold first, your buyer must decide whether to buy unconditionally and gamble they can list and sell their old home in time to close on the new one. Or do they surrender and begin the search all over again and pray they find another satisfactory home belonging to someone who'll entertain their conditional offer? They may elect to start over from scratch, but history sometimes repeats.

Escape: Let's say you find a property owned by someone who agrees to accept your buyer's sale condition. It's standard practice to include an escape clause in the contract which allows the seller to continue marketing their home and to consider other offers during the conditional period while your buyer is attempting to sell their old home. Since this period is typically longer than for other conditions, it would be unreasonable to expect a seller to accept such a condition without the right, under certain circumstances, to cancel the contract. In Ontario, it's usually 30 to 60 days, but varies depending on local market conditions. If it weren't for the escape clause, the seller's home would be effectively off the market.

Bump: If a second buyer wants to offer on the property conditionally sold to your buyer, they must "bump" your client's APS. The second buyer's offer would include a clause stating that the acceptance of their offer by the seller is conditional for the number of days or hours, depending on the escape clause, upon the seller being released from your buyer's contract. The seller then delivers a Notice to Conditional Buyer to either waive (remove) your buyer's condition on sale (depending on terminology, possibly all conditions, whether or not they've been fulfilled), thereby forcing them into an unconditional purchase as per all previously agreed terms, or to execute a mutual release and have their deposit returned.

Whether or not your buyer has sold their own home, if they elect to waive instead of release, they assume the risk of successfully selling their own home prior to having to complete the APS on the new place. Stressful? I think so. On the other hand, if they release, your client's dream home becomes that of the second buyer and your task begins again. Time and effort wasted.

Educated Guess: Since evaluating property is an educated guess, no one can accurately predict the ultimate sale price of your buyer's present property. If their conditional offer is accepted, obviously they've agreed to pay a particular price on the new place that depends upon them getting a minimum price for their old digs. And if they don't get it, they may have insufficient funds to complete their purchase. Or if their property is over-priced, it might not sell during the conditional period. Once again, time and effort wasted. The seller will also have suffered because of a doomed condition.

Sellers don't readily accept sale conditions. When they do, they're coaxed into it, perhaps by a premium price, or they aren't in a hurry or their property has been on the market forever. Sometimes, their agent feels the buyer's property will likely sell easily. Having to pay more, your buyer may insist on a higher price for their old home, which may render the entire transaction unfeasible. Having said this, in markets where home sales are slower, homeowners are often more amenable to such conditions.

Here's something you mightn't have learned in the classroom. If a seller agrees, there's a possible upside for your buyer. Depending on market conditions, once the conditional sale is reported to the board, interest in the conditionally sold property can wane. Buyers are discouraged from viewing it, preferring not to wait even the average 48 hours to learn if their offer was successful. Why? They prefer to avoid the hassle of viewing, negotiating and becoming emotionally attached, only to lose it when the first buyer firms up.

> *"The only thing that interferes with my learning is my education."*
> Albert Einstein

Guaranteed: A seller has accepted your buyer's conditional offer, but soon after, you receive a Notice to Conditional Buyer on their behalf to firm or release within 48 hours. Your buyer (as the seller in this example) has just accepted an offer on their old home with a one week condition that won't become firm (if it does at all) until *after* your 48 hour notice period has elapsed. Now what? It's risky decision time. Does your buyer gamble that their sale might firm in time and waive the condition(s) in their purchase, or refuse to gamble and release it? Tough choice.

If they decide to waive and the sale of their old home falls through, they've bought the new place without a sale of their current property and will be contractually compelled to close on their purchase, even if they fail to sell their old house. The other route is to refuse to accept the risk and release their purchase, thereby losing the new home. But if the conditional sale on their old house firms up afterward, they've sold it and lost the new one. Hmm – another challenge. All you can do at that point is ask the selling agent to convince their client to firm up before the notice period elapses. Or offer their buyer an incentive to firm up immediately; lower purchase price, extra chattels or some other concession. Or you could personally guarantee their sale. So, either the home search begins anew or there's pressure to sell their home before the closing date of the now unconditional purchase. And pressure could mean being forced to accept a lower than planned sale price on their old place.

String Unravels: If you have a series of homes all connected together via conditional sale agreements and the first in the string firms, all is well and good; each subsequent sale firms like a row of falling dominoes. But in reverse, if the seller at the opposite end of the series receives an acceptable offer and serves notice to the buyer of their home, it's possible that the entire string could begin to unravel. Or suddenly, some of the parties could be under unexpected pressure to expedite a sale. If your commission earnings are substantial enough, to save the string from fraying, you could guarantee the sale of the first property, maybe partnering with a participating agent who shares a sizeable interest in the successful conclusion of the connected contracts. With such a series, you may feel you're laughing all the way to the bank. But be forewarned – the situation can change in the blink of an eye.

> *"If you're in a bad situation, don't worry it'll change.*
> *If you're in a good situation, don't worry it'll change." John A. Simone, Sr.*

Sell First

The opposite approach entails the listing and selling of your client's present home before the serious search begins. Though viewing homes during its marketing is an option, offers on a new place are postponed until after it's sold, at least conditionally. Your clients avoid the nail-biting challenges, financial risks and possible heartache described earlier, as well as the pressure to entertain an otherwise unacceptable offer. Nevertheless, this home transition technique is also fraught with potential risk.

After they've sold and not yet bought another, you can calculate their exact equity for transfer; no guessing. And if fortunate, you already spotted an interesting property and can immediately offer without a sale condition. They may enjoy a stronger bargaining position and negotiate more attractive terms, particularly a lower price. By choosing to sell first, though, if you're unable to find a satisfactory home before they have to close their sale, your client's worst case scenario may be renting until the right place comes along. The double move is the major drawback, but it may be a lesser of two evils.

But there's another upside; while renting worry-free with cash in the credit union, after a leisurely stress-free search, when you find their new home, they're perfectly poised to pounce, with the added bonus of being able to accommodate any seller's reasonable possession date request. No matter which option they choose, coordinating closing dates is a common challenge. Selling first may commit them to a fixed date on the sale to which the seller of their new home may be unable to comply because of their own commitments. If your client buys first, they must commit to a closing date on their purchase that the subsequent buyer of their old home may not be able to accommodate. Imagine losing a great deal over a closing date! During negotiations, closing dates can be as critical as the price.

What's the best option for your client? Well, it depends on local market conditions as well as their emotional and financial resources. If the market is balanced or there are few buyers with lots of listings, the traditional route of buying conditionally may be the better choice. However, if you anticipate difficulty with their property, to save everyone a lot of frustration, sell first. On the other hand, if there are tons of buyers and few listings, maybe there's no cause for concern. They can buy first, but because of the highly competitive conditions, may have to do so without a sale condition. Disregarding the market, they may prefer to buy first for purely emotional reasons or because what they want is in short supply or you're in a locale where sale conditions are more common.

If they can handle the financial obligation of owning two properties simultaneously, you can *suggest* they buy without a sale condition. Before proceeding, though, counsel them to be fully prepared for the consequences by having finances in place to handle any scenario. Hope for the best, but prepare for the worse. And if they elect to buy unconditionally, ask them to sign an acknowledgement that you thoroughly explained all ramifications of their decision and that you advised *against* that riskier route. It's called protecting your posterior. Nevertheless, unless they're well-heeled, whatever route they choose, there's no way for your client to completely avoid stress.

The Great Swap

When two homeowners agree to exchange properties, for obvious reasons, there's no requirement for conditions on sale. Once you understand the process involved with these extremely rare trades, they're not difficult to organize. Be exceedingly careful, though, about multiple agency and its required confidentiality and disclosure.

To protect the interests of both client parties, ensure the two contracts are carefully prepared and executed on a timely basis. If you're unfamiliar with the procedure and clauses, seek professional advice. One lawyer can act for both parties, provided nothing is remotely anticipated that might create a conflict of interest. If one arises, the lawyer will probably drop both clients. The haggling can be tricky, but a skilled mediator can save everyone a lot of stress and frustration.

After you've shown each party through the other's home and have confirmed mutual interest, prepare a detailed CMA for each property to assist everyone involved with the evaluation process. Since full disclosure is the best policy, share the results of both CMA's with each homeowner. Once verbal negotiations have concluded and an understanding reached with respect to prices, common completion date and other assorted terms, draft the two contracts with the usual clauses, including all normally appropriate conditions. Usually, the condition expiry dates and the completion date would coincide with its counterpart in the other APS. It's not important for the two properties to be of equal value since each buyer will use their own resources, including mortgage funds, to complete the purchase.

To avoid a serious legal conflict, both contracts should include an identical clause stating that each is subject to the successful completion of the other. For example, let's say Dick and Jane agree to a trade. For whatever reason, if Dick refuses or is unable to close on Jane's property, even though Jane is ready, willing and able to close her sale, then Jane is no longer obligated to close on Dick's house. But technically, she must still be prepared to close her purchase or risk being declared in default. But due to Dick's default and the consequential absence of Jane's sale proceeds, she should have back-up emergency financing to complete her purchase.

It sounds risky and complicated, but in common practice, the double transaction just falls apart, with mutual releases all around. No sane person wants litigation. Nothing ventured, nothing gained.

"Take a chance! All life is a chance. The man who goes farthest is generally the one who is willing to do and dare." Dale Carnegie

Chapter Eighteen

Investor: To Be or Not To Be?

"Successful investing is anticipating the anticipations of others."
John Maynard Keynes

Introspect Before Inspect

After hearing their friend boast about a huge profit on a real estate investment, your client excitedly announces they want to do the same. Obviously, you relish the idea of earning a commission or two, but as a professional, you must be the calm, objective voice of reason. Before they leap, remind them that those who boldly boast of their good fortune tend to shout it from the roof tops. But there's always a flip side; embarrassed losers don't normally loudly lament their losses from lofty levels. Lottery wins are heavily publicized, but never is there a peep from the legions of habitual victims of decades-long gambling who have incrementally suffered the storied "death by a thousand cuts".

When investing in real estate, even though one hopes for the best, your client should prepare for the worst. Prior to diving blindly into the investment pool, they should think thrice and test the water by doing a little introspection, along with some research and planning. And to grease the cogs of cognition, start a conversation by asking a few probing questions:

> ➤ What's their motivation and ultimate aim?
> ➤ Do they want retirement capital or an income stream?
> ➤ Is their preference a long or short term investment?
> ➤ If short, will renovate prior to re-selling and if so, to what extent?
> ➤ If long, could they tolerate being a landlord and all that entails?
> ➤ Have they consulted with an accountant or financial advisor?
> ➤ What are their available financial resources?
> ➤ Do they have construction skills or must they hire contractors?
> ➤ Can they cope with the stress of property management?
> ➤ Does their spouse support their intention?

The Plan, Stan

A lack of forethought, compounded by delays and unexpected expenses, is a recipe for a postponed or even abandoned project. Therefore, creating an investment plan and budget, including calculating the capital required to complete the entire project on a timely basis, is the next logical step. How much money and time will be needed to complete the renovations? In this case, time is definitely money. From the closing of the purchase to the date of tenant occupancy or the property's resale, the cost of fees, materials and labour as well as payments for the mortgage, property taxes, utilities, insurance and if condominium, monthly condo fees, must be factored into the equation. Calculations should also include legal fees, disbursements and land transfer tax on the purchase, and excluding the tax, the same on the sale. And one mustn't forget real estate fees for its eventual disposition. Then there's the tax man; unless it's to be a principle residence, when sold, they may be liable for capital gains or income tax on any net profit. If you're not a fiscally savvy investment agent, your client should consult with their expert tax advisor.

Hopefully, your client has the skills and free time to undertake the remodelling themselves since contractors don't work cheap and good ones aren't always readily available. Many a buyer has bought a handyman special, maybe a power-of-sale, foreclosure or a house nobody loved, believing they could profit after a quick professional renovation. But after the hefty contractor fees and assorted surprises, they realized a net loss, or a small gain sufficient to recuperate some of their time. Prior to signing on the dotted line, especially if they're a novice renovator, to improve the odds, invite a trusted building contractor or home inspector to attend the second viewing. Not only might they may spot an expensive problem that you missed, your client will be better equipped to determine project viability.

Flip-Hip or Flip-Flop

A significant advantage to the quick flip is the *quick* part, with the flipper in and out cleanly – and hopefully profitably. With no tenants involved, your client won't have to deal with all the implications of being a landlord. Also, since rented homes often fail to completely survive a tenancy unscathed, by flipping it, your investor escapes the potential heartache of discovering their newly renovated property damaged by an irresponsible tenant. Anyway, when major renovations are involved, they'll not easily rent it for the short term. So, naturally, there'd be no rental revenue to off-set the expenses.

After the construction is complete and while awaiting a sale, your client might find a short-term monthly tenant. However, since most buyers want vacant possession, not only will your investor need the tenant's cooperation for viewing appointments, they'll also need them to vacate promptly. To ensure compliance, a carefully worded clause should be included in the lease agreement. If your seller is unable to provide vacant possession to the buyer on completion of a sale, they'll be in default of the contract. Thus, a sale could be lost. Tenant trouble or a delayed sale due to unexpected renovations or an unforeseen longer closing could bring unbudgeted carrying costs, adversely affecting the profit margin.

In my experience, the higher returns on reno expenses are usually the result of more modest beautifying projects such as fresh paint, replacement kitchen cabinets, minimal bathroom makeovers, flooring upgrades, gas fireplaces and minor landscaping such as sod and shrubs – the showy stuff. Unless your client is a contractor intending to do a major renovation, the odds of a profit are lower if they embark on bigger undertakings. Choose upgrades that will have mass market appeal. Having said this, if your qualified investor/contractor is interested in a small older house in a locale that would support a major renovation, or even a replacement with a larger home, then go for it. In any case, much depends on getting a bargain property during a strong seller's market – in the right location. You've probably heard the common cliché about the three most important things about real estate; location, location and wait for it – location.

Does your client intend to live in the house during the renovation? Obviously, it's not exactly a great experience being immersed in construction every day. It's called "divorce dust" for good reason. There are better ways of generating excitement in a relationship.

"Investing should be more like watching paint dry or watching grass grow.
If you want excitement, take $800 and go to Las Vegas." Paul Samuelson

Regression, Progression and Substitution

Choose a fixer-upper in a great area over one in a less popular neighbourhood. You can live in or rent either, but from an investment perspective, they're far better off in the great area. Why? Market value is affected – positively or negatively – by the market values of neighbouring properties. The Principle of Regression is the decrease in value when the surrounding houses are smaller or inferior in some way. The Principle of Progression is clearly the opposite; the increase when the surrounding houses are larger or superior. The argument goes that a shack in a prestigious area is a better investment than a castle encircled by hovels. If your client wants to buy a handyman special on a prime lot in a prime neighbourhood, over-improving it would be difficult. As a matter of fact, a total demolition to build a luxury home to align with the stature of adjacent houses might be financially feasible. In the less desirable neighbourhood, however, one must renovate more frugally. Upon finishing the project, they can't just magically move it to a better location. Buying a potentially luxurious home in a rough neighbourhood would be unwise unless they plan to live in their own fiefdom.

The Principle of Substitution refers to the actual value of a property feature or amenity. It states that the value is not determined by the cost of an improvement, but the value derived from it. For example, two adjacent homes are identical except that one homeowner spent twice as much to drill a well because the house was built on solid granite, whereas the neighbour's was on clay. Even though the costs differed substantially, the market values for the two properties would be virtually identical because the value is based on the water produced – not the cost of obtaining it. This is definitely something to consider when calculating a budget for a renovation relative to an anticipated market value.

The Long Winding Road

"Life is inherently risky. There is only one big risk you should avoid
at all costs, and that is the risk of doing nothing." Denis Waitley

If they intend to keep the investment property as a long-term rental or personal residence, in all probability, even if costs prove higher than expected, they'll likely be okay because typically, market values go in one direction – up. The property becomes a great "land bank" with a positive cash flow (income less expenses) for a monthly retirement income. Also, the cost of more extensive renovations may be recovered by higher rents and a higher sale price down the long road.

Money lenders often have a policy regarding minimum down payment for rental properties. But unless your would-be investor is looking for a loss and accompanying tax deduction, recommend enough down payment to permit sufficient positive cash flow to pay all regular monthly and annual expenses, thereby making the investment revenue neutral, hence no immediate income tax liability. And the bonus? If they keep the property long enough, along with a sizable capital gain upon its sale, their tenant(s) will have paid off the mortgage debt!

Being a landlord isn't all roses though. For example, your client is responsible for ongoing maintenance, repairs and improvements due to mechanical and structural breakdown and normal or potentially abusive wear and tear by tenants. To handle both planned and unplanned expenses, advise them to build a reserve fund into their budget. Generally, a small investor, who buys a single condominium unit where all exterior and building maintenance is handled by the corporation's property management, would just have to manage the leasing, rent collection, occasional inspections and perform periodic interior repairs and maintenance. Freehold property would demand somewhat more time and expense, but for most small investors, this could easily be handled.

But the numerous, often daily, responsibilities associated with multiple unit residential buildings (MURBS) demands delegation to professionals. Property management companies can take care of regular repairs and maintenance, collecting rents, dealing with complaints, defaults, evictions and advertising. They also thoroughly screen replacement tenants by obtaining critical employment and income confirmation, credit reports, criminal record checks and references from previous landlords. But be forewarned; such companies often charge up to 10 percent or more of the rental income.

Whatever your would-be investor may be contemplating, make sure the area is popular for rentals. Prime residential, recreational, university or hospital neighbourhoods are good prospects. A property with schools within walking distance would be favoured by families, whereas singles and students appreciate close proximity to colleges, public transit and entertainment. A condominium townhouse or apartment, typically linked with singles and couples, could translate into less physical labour, but make sure rentals are permitted under the condo corporation's rules.

To protect your client's property and themselves, a well-drafted lease is crucial. Properly prepared documentation will improve the odds of successfully evicting a defaulting tenant or holding them accountable for property damage. Whether neophyte or experienced, a landlord should be familiar with local legislated requirements, including those associated with multi-family buildings and basement apartments. Be forewarned that many of these technically multi-family homes are in violation of local zoning, fire and building codes. If the property violates local by-laws, they may be unpleasantly surprised after closing by a municipal order to evict the tenant and remove the cooking facilities. If it's considered legal non-conforming use, then it was constructed prior to the enactment of the by-law restricting such housing. In such a case, they may be okay. But be informed before taking the plunge.

ROI

*"I'm more concerned about the return **of** my money than with the return **on** my money." Will Rogers*

During the planning process, your enthusiastic investor should understand the concept of "Return on Investment". ROI on an investment property or renovation project is dependant on the type and calibre of the project as well as the condition of the local economy and real estate market. When the property is sold and closed, after all costs and expenses have been deducted from the sale proceeds, how much money will be left in their jeans? Certain projects, such as a sundeck addition, kitchen or bathroom renovation or landscaping, often have a greater ROI than, say, the installation of a swimming pool, new roof shingles or an upgraded electrical panel. Shingles and breakers just don't seem to excite most buyers. A shiny new kitchen, on the other hand, is a different story.

ROI is a performance measure used to evaluate the efficiency of an investment. Basically, to calculate an ROI, the benefit or return on an investment is divided by the cost of the investment with the result being expressed as a ratio or a percentage. Simple gain or loss is calculated by subtracting the purchase price from the sale price. However, calculating the cost of an investment is a more complicated matter. Real estate can generate capital gains not only from market value appreciation, but also from rental income, which must be added to the gain as it's realized. From this total, deduct the initial cost of the investment, including any and all expenses incurred to acquire, renovate and maintain the property during the ownership period. Property taxes, mortgage interest, insurance premiums, utilities, repairs, improvements, general maintenance and the cost to rent or sell the property, as well as management, legal and accounting fees, would be included in expenses.

If an investment does not have a projected positive ROI, maybe they should pass on it and seek another that promises a better return. For example, if the annual return is expected to be only 4 percent, because of the effort required – along with the ever-present risk, they should probably put their money into a conservative investment vehicle such as a GIC. The return is guaranteed and there's no risk, expense or maintenance. It's more about the numbers and less about the property.

Unless your client prefers to be renting when they're old and grey, investing in real estate, at least in a family home or long-term rental property, is a great idea since it can be quite profitable. But without meticulous preparedness and organization – and avoiding buyer competitions – investing in flips might be disappointing. They may regret their decision – or they may kiss the ground under your feet. Either way, it's an interesting ride!

> *"How many millionaires do you know who have become wealthy by investing in savings accounts? I rest my case." Robert G. Allen*

Chapter Nineteen

Bidding Wars: Win or Walk?

"You have to learn the rules of the game.
And then you have to play better than anyone else." Albert Einstein

Feeding Frenzy Afoot

In an ideal world, your buyer is the only bidder on their dream home. However, unless all the planets are impeccably aligned and you're in the midst of a balanced or buyer's market, you and your buyer may find yourselves in the unenviable position of having to compete with another anxious buyer (or several) who shares your client's ideal of what constitutes a dream home. When should you encourage your buyer to walk away from a war? Does the procedure involve a logical strategy for buyer or seller, or does it all boil down to gut feeling? How can a seller maximize the benefit of a multiple bid?

When accepting a listing, there are two basic options. The traditional conservative approach involves establishing a reasonable asking price marginally higher than perceived fair market value. Individual offers ensue and are presented on a first-come-first-served basis. The other more aggressive approach normally requires not only a market wherein buyer demand excessively exceeds supply, but also the trifecta of a suitable property, a mutually trusting agent/seller relationship and nerves of steel.

To incite a competition and hopefully generate great terms for your seller, list at or below fair market value. The remarks section of the MLS® system listing should include a specific date and time, usually a few days after the listing is uploaded, when all offers will be presented to the seller during the same assembly. This hard-hitting option permits all interested buyers and their agents with the chance to be notified of and, like a furniture auction preview, leisurely view the listing prior to presentation day. It also affords the interested parties the time to improve the attractiveness of their upcoming offers by fulfilling any conditions in advance. Offers can then be submitted without the typical frenetic feeding flurry on the day the listing appears. It *can* be a more civil procedure for obvious reasons, and certainly great for a homeowner, but the competition is often a nightmare for anxious buyers and their agents. Be careful with this marketing method, though, because it can backfire. If you don't have an appropriate property during the right market conditions, the result can be a sale price below market value – and an unhappy seller.

Before your buyer even begins to view property in a competition-prone market, they should confirm – in writing – their ability to finance a purchase by seeking an *unconditional* pre-approved mortgage. A good practice anytime, but it's particularly so when competing. The lender will need confirmation of employment income (financial statements or tax returns if self-employed) and down payment as well as a credit report. Insist on an approval letter that doesn't just state they're approved subject to confirmation of all the aforesaid. If you can assure the seller and their agent that the financing condition is a mere formality and that your client has been unconditionally pre-approved – and you can prove it – you may be in a stronger bargaining position.

Depending on circumstances, to enhance the attractiveness of your client's offer even further, you might exclude the financing condition. However, if your buyer elects to include it, during the negotiation, clarify to the seller that only *their* property must be approved by the lender by way of a realistic appraisal. If the lender thinks the buyer was overly generous and they have a minimum down payment, the buyer had better have more cash in the piggy bank. The loan may be approved, but at a lower principle amount because the purchase price excessively exceeded the lender's appraised value. Arguably, though, the best reason to seek a pre-approval before entering a bidding war is to confirm your buyer's absolute maximum affordable price. Then, they *can't* go nuts in the heat of the moment. Reasonable heads may then prevail.

To avoid further conditions, your buyer could arrange for technical inspections to be performed prior to the offer presentation date. It means upfront fees for a potentially losing bid, but as they say, better safe than sorry. Unless your buyer's offered price is exceptionally higher than a competitor's, or all competing bids include the same condition, and the seller is confident that their home will easily pass an inspector's scrutiny, the seller is unlikely to even consider accepting such a condition.

It's really easy for a group of competing buyers sitting on the edge of their seats to agree to pay an unreasonably high price which, under calmer circumstances, would be considered ridiculous. Winning the bid may be emotionally satisfying, but from a money perspective, it's crazy. Leave impulse shopping for the grocery store check-out. If their emotions get the better of them, they may ultimately buy a lovely home, but at an exorbitant price. To get the best possible deal, they must steer clear of emotionally attaching to a particular outcome – or property. It can certainly be exciting at the time, but also painful if they lose a bid – or later when they realize they grossly over-paid. Tell them to be cool. If they're successful, that's great; celebrate. If not, then at least they tried. Move on. There's always another house. It's just sticks and bricks.

> *"The only competition worthy of a wise man is with himself."*
> Washington Allston

Ministration, Deliberation and Orchestration

In a bidding war, buyers are deliberately kept unaware of the terms of competing offers. To ensure it remains a blind bid, all offers are typically presented in one session, but separately, and in the same order as they were registered with the listing brokerage. Each buyer agent is given a brief private opportunity to argue the merits of their client's offer. To help develop a feel for each buyer's intention and position, a smart listing agent will take advantage of these moments by asking questions of each agent (who often disclose too much) regarding their client's offer. The length of each presentation will obviously depend on the quantity and complexity of the offers. Afterward, each agent is asked to leave a copy with the listing agent for later comparison during a private consultation with the seller. This continues, usually with all agents (and sometimes the buyers) waiting elsewhere in the home or outside, until all bids have been presented.

With a copy of each offer spread before them, the seller and their agent compare the pros and cons of all bids. Sometimes, the seller may reject the least acceptable and work with only the best few, or they may accept the best one. If the irrevocable dates permit, they might counter one while holding all others in abeyance. If that counter-offer is accepted, the show is over. However, if it's rejected, the seller may repeat the procedure with the next best offer until an APS is executed.

When countering, it's *critical* to be ever mindful of irrevocable dates and times. If a seller counter-offer is *verbally* rejected by a buyer, but the seller irrevocable time and date haven't strictly expired, that buyer could change their mind prior to the technical expiry of the seller's offer and accept the counter-offer. Assuming a verbal report of its rejection to be binding, if the seller proceeds to deliver another fully executed counter-offer to a second buyer while the first counter remains officially valid, and the second buyer accepts it, the seller has risked contractually committing to two separate buyers. Be very careful – this is really easy to do. And you may pay the price for your negligence, maybe a big one.

Nevertheless, sellers often elect to return all offers untouched to the respective buyer agents, thereby allowing each buyer a chance to improve their bid. In this event, the listing agent should forewarn their seller of the possibility of some or all of the offers being withdrawn. When the remaining offers are re-registered, the entire process begins anew in the order of their return. After a brief private consultation with the listing agent, the seller usually chooses one.

When given the chance to enhance the terms of their offer, if a buyer is unable or prefers not to increase the price, they should re-submit anyway. One never knows; some or all of the other buyers may feel the same way and refuse to alter their offer terms or even withdraw from the competition. It would be a shame to lose a bid because your buyer gave up, especially since it costs nothing to persevere. Instead of quitting, consider other ways to improve their offer. Removing conditions, adjusting the closing date to comply with a seller's preference, excluding chattels, eliminating seller requirements or increasing the deposit might do the trick. Usually, though, it comes down to conditions and price. When a buyer unwisely shuns all competitions, they miss out on the possibility of acquiring an obviously desirable home. It's like not buying a lottery ticket; you can't win without playing the game. Rather than be frightened or intimidated, they should proactively commit to a maximum realistically affordable price – in advance – that's not ridiculously over what you collectively agree is fair market value, and faithfully stick to it. Don't budge.

During a competition, if offer prices soar into the stratosphere and well over your buyer's previously determined maximum, encourage them to resist the temptation to join the frenzy. Bidding wars can be emotionally challenging and exceedingly expensive. If they lack sufficient financial clout or the stamina to continue, and/or prefer to avoid paying top dollar, tell them to walk away. There'll be another property somewhere sometime that they'll love just as much and maybe more.

Big Bad Bully

"Competition brings out the best in products and the worst in people."
David Sarnoff

During my career, I orchestrated many multiple offer scenarios for my sellers. In earlier days, board rules permitted us to delay the showing commencement date as well as offers. I'd organize showings to begin – and offers to be presented – on the same day, usually a Saturday. On that first day, the property was usually a buzzing beehive of activity, with appointments scheduled every half hour, sometimes overlapping. Aside from the first and last showings of the day, the lockbox usually remained untouched. I also occasionally threw a public open house into the mix. Typically, during the presentation that same evening, the street was clogged with cars, anxious agents and lingering buyers, all caught up in the competitive frenzy. Even back then, though, some agent would seek to sneak in early with an offer conditional on satisfactory buyer inspection. Thankfully, my vendors normally adhered to the plan and rebuffed them. And did those overtly aggressive agents show up at offer time? Always; I don't recall ever losing one.

Ignoring your carefully formulated plans, with the deliberate intent to avoid a competition, an aggressive buyer agent may contact you to register on your new listing what has become known as a "bully offer". They demand an appointment prior to the officially announced presentation date. Since you're convinced of the merits of your marketing strategy, you encourage your seller to make this insistent agent wait.

A seller certainly has the right to refuse to see this "short-circuit" offer, but curiosity sometimes gets the best of them. It's mystifying why they'd sacrifice an opportunity for multiple showings and offers by surrendering to a bully's attempt to evade a fair competition. Obviously, you must comply with your principle's instruction. However, before committing to an earlier date and all that entails, ask the buyer agent about the offer. If the major terms are unacceptable, advise your seller to stick to the original plan. But if it's full asking price or more, with no conditions, they may not gamble losing it.

In accordance with industry rules – and prior to viewing the bully offer – the MLS® listing must immediately be amended with the new presentation date and time. Plus all agents who have already shown the property, have confirmed but outstanding appointments or have expressed interest must be promptly informed of the new arrangements. If they haven't already done so, all buyer candidates must quickly scramble to view the property and register their offers. Unfortunately, some may be unable to act swiftly enough. So, your seller might lose them. By caving to a bully's demand, they'll never know if that lost buyer might have been The One.

Given such short notice, the buyers who weren't able to act in time are grievously disappointed and sometimes very angry with our industry and its members. It could be argued that your seller was formally tendering for competitive bids, but at the last moment, chose to dishonour their commitment to await all comers. What can a disappointed buyer do about it? Well, it's been opined that an aggrieved buyer could sue the seller and their agent for damages. I'm unaware of any precedent-setting court case to date, but it could happen anytime. All it will take is a sufficiently disturbed buyer with deep pockets. Listing agents beware.

Does greed get the best of people? Yes, I suppose it sometimes does. Some argue that buyers who dodge the rules of fair play for their own advantage are indeed avaricious and iniquitous. Is a bully buyer innocent? Do they have the right to be aggressive? Obviously, the technical answer is yes, for they certainly have the right to buy at the lowest possible price. The same argument could be made for an aggressive seller who wants the highest price possible. But if a bully buyer deliberately ignores a seller's clearly stated procedural request regarding the marketing of their *own* property and attempts to circumvent the system, are they behaving morally? They're demonstrating a complete lack of respect for not only the seller's wishes, but potentially, our rules of service. In my view, this is not representative of innocence. Bully buyers are no different from movie patrons who butt into line ahead of other people patiently waiting their turn.

It's also been said that sellers could refuse to comply with a bully's demand, that those who agree to this marketing strategy are also selfish and greedy and knowingly contribute to the inflation of market values, not to mention a highly stressful and potentially devastating experience for many buyers. Some have suggested sellers can be bullies too. However, are homeowners not entitled to attempt to maximize the sale price of their own property by any available legal means? And by agreeing to a viewing period and delayed offer presentation day, are they not being fair by providing *all* interested buyers an opportunity to make a bid? Further, is it not a major responsibility for a listing representative to do everything legally and ethically possible to get the best terms for their seller client? The strategy is designed to stimulate fair competition which should result in a fair sale price based upon supply and demand in a free democratic society.

Is the bully offer system undermining consumer confidence? Absolutely, especially with buyers willing to respectfully comply with the posted protocol, but are caught with their pants down by a bully jumping the queue. Nevertheless, until the rules change yet again, fair buyers must be prepared to respond to bully offer scenarios by viewing the property at the earliest opportunity. And as their representative, you should have your buyer's offer documents prepared in advance and ready for presentation on short notice. To contribute to consumer confidence in our industry, listing agents who practice this legitimate hot-market strategy, which is more prevalent for city or suburban than rural, should carefully prepare their new seller for the distinct possibility of a bully offer. Ask your seller to adhere to the plan or risk trouble for both you and them. The reputation of our industry is at stake.

"When a resolute young fellow steps up to the great bully, the world, and takes him boldly by the beard, he is often surprised to find it comes off in his hand, and that it was only tied on to scare away the timid adventurers."
Ralph Waldo Emerson

Chapter Twenty

Concrete or Cornfields?

"Happiness is having a large, loving, caring, close-knit family
... in another city." George Burns

Bright Lights, Bright Stars

"I have an affection for a great city. I feel safe in the neighbourhood of man
and enjoy the sweet security of the streets." Henry Wadsworth Longfellow

Do you have a client who's dreaming about living in a rural paradise and forsaking the many benefits of city or suburban life? Are they country novices? Are you? Before plunging head first into the outfield, or for that matter, offering to represent someone on a quest for country, there's much to consider. To dispense reliable advice, you should thoroughly understand the differences between city and country living. The information contained in this chapter is far from exhaustive, but it offers some of the basics your would-be country gentry should contemplate before buying a rural home or an undeveloped piece of paradise.

Countless people count themselves fortunate to reside in a big bustling city or sprawling suburb. They're drawn by the hum, hustle and handiness of absolutely everything. Your prospective serenity-seekers would be abandoning the substantial selection of shopping outlets, extensive public transit system and the fabulous array of entertainment and restaurants serving a delectable selection of foods from a multitude of ethnicities. Country living may mean no more handy public recreation facilities, including grids of inter-connecting parks, bike paths and roller-blade trails; no more throbbing mix of diverse cultures. Concrete canyon dwellers appreciate the close proximity to friends and jobs, often travelling about on foot. Some rarely take those feet out of town. Some don't even own a car! Why bother when everything is close at hand? They couldn't imagine a rural lifestyle with its relative silence and solitude. Enamoured with city living, some choose the reverse commute to the suburbs or beyond for employment and trek against the heavier opposite traffic flow.

Because city realty prices and property taxes (including municipal land transfer tax in some areas) have increased to skyscraper heights, others are abandoning the city womb for more affordable housing in the suburbs or small towns and villages in the hinterland. However, unless they're okay with a humble abode on postage stamp, rural living can also be expensive. As you'd expect, price will depend on the locale, proximity to metropolitan centres, municipal services and the size and topography of the land. Premium and large acreage, majestic vistas, lake and river frontage, forests and rocky outcrops don't come cheap.

"In the country, the darkness of night is friendly and familiar, but in a city, with its blaze of lights, it is unnatural, hostile and menacing. It is like a monstrous vulture that hovers, biding its time." W. Somerset Maugham

Many people love the whole idea of living under an immense country sky devoid of polluting city lights. It's usually much quieter, cleaner and obviously has less traffic because, well, there are fewer people. They prefer to raise their family away from the stifling heat of the concrete and asphalt, the long shadows of monolithic towers, the smog and water pollution, the never-ending screaming sirens and chronic noise of ever intensifying high-density living. They get no satisfaction from the rocking lyrics of the *Rolling Stones* reverberating from the house virtually an arm's length away. Some are disturbed by the obnoxious odours of industry and commerce, adrenalin-infused quick tempers and quicker horns, snarled traffic and daily visual reminders of the pathetic plight of the poor and homeless souls shielding their shopping carts of meagre worldly possessions while keeping barely warm and alive, huddled, lonely on city subway grates or in dark, dank alleys. Is my bias showing?

Your clients could be just trading the intolerable sounds and sweltering smells of the city for those of farm animals and agricultural equipment. They could be swapping city congestion and convenient services for wide open spaces and running up the car odometer. Unless they're in a small town, leisurely strolls to the local Italian restaurant or the neighbourhood pub or popping into the corner store for daily essentials will be history. There are no poop-and-scoop rules on a country road or in the back forty, but taking Spot for a walk around the block will hold a whole new meaning. And utilities aren't always reliable in the middle of nowhere; hence the popularity of emergency electricity generators and sump pump battery back-up systems.

Do they have children or plan a family? Since most kid's activities will be in town, rural living demands regular parental shuttle service. Big yellow school buses will normally cart their kids to and from school. That's okay, unless they're involved in extra-curricular school activities. If it snows and blows and the roads aren't promptly cleared of the big white drifts (yes – snow is very white in the country, and sometimes voluminous), they could be snowed in for days. There's always the chance that buses won't be running. No doubt the kids will be very disappointed about missing school, but "snow days" may be more frequent in rural areas. With school-age children, your clients must be prepared to take a day off work too. On second thought, maybe this isn't so bad. Of course, school closures occur in the city too when streets become choked and rutted with snow-blanketed cars parked helter-skelter.

Do the Due

Before loading up the truck and heading for the hills, with your expert guidance, your client would be wise to do some due diligence. What should they know *before* beginning the process? Buying a suburban home is usually pretty straight forward. However, a city core or rural purchase can be a little more complicated. City realty can involve rights-of-way, easements, encroachments, mutual driveways, parking pads, street parking permits, common lanes, surveys and land leases. Proximity to public transit, railway tracks, electricity transmission corridors, flight paths as well as distance to schools, recreation facilities, churches, employment and shopping may also be factors. Local development plans and zoning may be applicable. Is the greenbelt ravine at the rear a happy place or is it reputed to be rife with crime? Also, since they're so near, how's the physical condition of adjacent properties? Does the neighbour's back yard look like a garbage dump or a party pad? Though city and rural realty share several potentially negative issues, rural property presents some that are unique.

Lots and Land

"Having land and not ruining it is the most beautiful art that anybody could ever want to own." Andy Warhol

Many people wonder about designing their own home. I've personally seen some exquisite creations, architecturally and aesthetically designed to naturally meld into the local picturesque landscape or neighbourhood. I've also watched as a lovely site was desecrated by the construction of an unholy disaster that clearly materialized from the strange machinations of a sufferer of nightmares.

If your clients are interested in buying vacant land or a suburban building lot for a custom home, aside from the exceptions of the planning, coordinating and budgeting process, the considerations are pretty much the same as shopping for an existing house. One obviously must first find a suitable piece of it. How much acreage or frontage? How large a home do they want to build? What price range, general location and topography? If they want a ravine, river or lake-frontage, the price will be higher. Mixed bush? Ditto. Rocky outcroppings or a million dollar view? Prestigious area? They'll need to dig a little deeper into their pocket. An already utility-serviced lot? Up it goes. If a flat corner of a farmer's field or a typical building lot in an unpretentious neighbourhood is fine, the price may be more reasonable. Prior to submitting an offer on that little patch of rural heaven, here are a few more things to investigate before they leap into the deep:

> Any garbage dumps, industrial manufacturing, high-tension electricity corridors, nuclear waste facilities or industrial wind turbine farms?
> Any planned municipal road widening?
> Any air traffic flight paths overhead?
> Any pig or poultry farms with machinery noise and bad odour?
> Any aggregate quarries? Behind the tree-covered berms, operators steadfastly rape the landscape. Rock is dynamited and regularly carted away in rumbling diesel trucks shrouded in clouds of billowing dust.
> Is any portion of the subject or adjoining land zoned environmentally sensitive and under greenbelt or conservation authority?
> Any wetlands close by? Any flood potential? Bull rushes in the ditches are a sure sign of potential trouble. Imagine the beautiful birdsong of red wing blackbirds mixing with the incessant buzz of voracious mosquitoes.
> Is tree removal permitted? This could affect where they'll be permitted to site their custom home, outbuildings and septic system.
> Any environmental concerns like car-wreckers, buried fuel tanks or pipelines?
> Is the zoning suitable?
> Any fencing restrictions?
> How deep must they drill for water? Deeper means more expense.
> Is the local water potable without expensive treatment systems?
> Where are the shopping centres, schools, public transit depots?
> Is the lot accessible via public thoroughfare or private road or across the neighbour's land? The latter necessitates a right-of-way.

➤ Who maintains the private road and at what prorated share of costs?

➤ Do neighbours have any rights to cross the subject parcel of land?

➤ Any road access restrictions?

➤ What are the exact boundaries of the parcel?

➤ Any current encroachments?

➤ Is there an existing survey? Acquiring one can be expensive. The municipality may insist on one prior to approving any building permits.

➤ Any development plans for abutting property? Will that peaceful country retreat be surrounded by subdivision homes some day?

➤ Is that beautiful lush mixed bush abutting the rear of the property on public or private land? If the latter, it might disappear some day.

"Buy land. They're not making it anymore." Mark Twain

Needs and Feeds

Your client may be innocently unaware of the differences between city and rural water supplies. Unlike the city, where municipal pressurized water arrives at the property via an underground city pipe, rural water is typically sourced from a private (or communal) dug, bored or drilled well located on (or near) the property and pressurized by a small private on-site tank. When buying a vacant city lot, one must only address the cost of connection to the water supply at the street. But for rural, they should check with a local well driller to get an estimate of the drilling cost to install a well. If he must drill deep or through solid granite to reach the water table, expect a higher fee.

Total coliform, a group of bacteria present in animal waste and sewage, can be found in soil and on vegetation. In minute quantities, they're not usually considered disease-causing organisms, but it's a good idea to eliminate them from the water supply. Bacteria in the water are usually the result of surface water run-off entering the well or by contamination from a nearby source such as a septic system or animal barn. Look for good drainage away from a sealed, water-tight well cap, which should be at least a foot above grade. Water may be treated and/or filtered using a chlorinator, ultra-violet, distiller, ozonator, activated charcoal or reverse osmosis system. Whether serviced by municipal or private well, having a sophisticated filtration system to remove the chlorine, fluoride and other toxic contaminants and bacteria would also be health-smart. At the time of sale and annually thereafter, the local Public Health Authority can perform a bacteriological analysis or water potability test to check for coliform and E.coli. Depending on municipal policy, this test may or may not be subject to a small fee. After removing the small aerator screen from the kitchen faucet and letting the water run for a few minutes, carefully fill a special sterilized bottle supplied by the laboratory.

In areas with municipal sewers, grey or black water flows into the public sanitary system and homeowners don't have to give it another thought, except when the sewers back up. Hey – it happens. With the exception of estate subdivisions or towns where building lots are often fully serviced, rural homeowners are personally responsible for the treatment and disposal of sewage on their own property. Effluent flows by gravity down the drain into a private septic tank buried close to the house and well away from the well. The sludge settles in the tank and the remaining water flows into a tile bed to dissipate into the ground. Look for a large flat and sometimes raised open area. Due to the warmer earth atop the bed, the grass may be greener and dandelions earlier. Depending on usage volume, your client will need a septic service to pump the tank every two to five years. It could go longer between pump-outs, but the sludge tends to compact in the tank, rendering a cleaning service more expensive, especially if the bed is choked. When planning a septic system, your client should seek assurance they'll not have any difficulty installing one.

A brand new city or suburban home is normally connected to the utility-provided natural gas line, electrical, telephone and if available, cable distribution systems. It's not usually complicated. However, for most rural properties, natural gas isn't usually available. Typical fuel options are oil, wood, electricity, propane gas or a combination. There's also been a growing interest in ground or water source heat pumps or geothermal systems. The latter is more expensive, but your clients will be less dependent on the main supply grid. Unless the property is an estate area or close to town, there's usually no cable television service available, leaving satellite as the only option. If they're a big Internet user, check to make sure high-speed is available because sometimes it's not. Cell phone coverage may not even be available.

Permits and Planning

Prior to submitting an offer, make sure the lot meets the requirements for what they want to build. Is it large enough to accommodate their new home plans? What's the maximum building footprint permitted? What's the lot-line setback requirement? Are there any easements or mature trees that'll affect the building site? Is the grade suitable for the house style? Will the architectural style aesthetically suit the neighbourhood or region? If they want friendly neighbours, perhaps they should avoid building a behemoth in a cottage area or an ultra-modern in a heritage district. The local municipality may restrict such elements, so best to check early.

Before breaking ground, they'll need municipal building and entrance permits; no access driveway – no construction. Not only must they comply with the requirements of the local Building Code Act, they'll also benefit by having their plans reviewed and approved – and the construction of their house periodically inspected – by the municipality. This ensures the minimum construction standards established by the provincial or state building code are met or exceeded to protect the health, safety and welfare of your client's family. Yes, there are fees associated and many people resent paying them. But the strict protocol is designed to protect them from unscrupulous or unqualified builders. If your client buys land in an area regulated by a conservation authority and their project is all new construction or work that's not wholly contained within an existing building, they may need approval from them. They can still apply for a municipal building permit prior to obtaining this approval, but a permit typically can't be issued until such approval is granted.

If not already paid by the previous owner, development charges – lot levies – must also be paid when the permit is issued. They're typically collected on behalf of the municipal, provincial or state governments and boards of education. Levies can be substantial, but are a one-time expense. Any previous payments for earlier buildings constructed on the site will often be taken into account by way of a re-development allowance. Several other items from an extensive list, available at the local municipal office, must also be submitted with the application.

Building a rural or recreational home could present another practical challenge; finding a builder who's willing to travel. Also, the building designer who'll prepare the plans may be required to be registered and/or have specific qualifications, without which, your client's permit application may be declined.

Your client's favourite city builder might not appear when expected at the newly acquired rural or recreational lot, or want more money to compensate for the travelling distance, island property or heavily wooded lot. Shipping materials to the island paradise or isolated construction site is more expensive because of the added labour and expense of long-distance shipping, barging and extra handling. A custom builder will likely take care of the permits and include this in a written cost estimate. If a neighbourhood builder exists, check them out. They may know someone personally in the local building department who might more easily facilitate the plans.

"Land is the only thing in the world that amounts to anything, for 'tis the only thing in this world that lasts, 'tis the only thing worth working for, worth fighting for, worth dying for." Margaret Mitchell

The Offer

You've found a suitable property and with your expert guidance, your client has researched everything they need to know to make a fully informed decision. Perhaps they even went so far as to ask the neighbours about the area. Now you're ready to get down to the fine stokes.

Particularly for country, there may not be an existing survey document. You can ask for one in the offer, but if one doesn't exist, it's not likely that anybody is going to assume the hefty expense of producing one. Thank goodness for title insurance. For larger acreage, ask the seller or listing agent to walk or drive the property boundaries with you to clarify more or less what's being offered. In any event, the offer should contain the parcel dimensions and if applicable, a clear description of the acreage. During the walkabout, the homeowner might be willing to share the property's history or a few interesting anecdotes that might help your client develop a better feel for it.

Due to the potential complexities of buying rural, especially acreage or vacant land, before submitting the offer, your client may want to seek counsel from their lawyer. Aside from the more common financing, home inspection, insurance or the sale of the buyer's home, several rural-specific conditions may be appropriate.

Building Permit: Obviously, when offering on vacant land, your buyer will want the assurance that they'll be able to obtain all permits required to construct their new home. Therefore, it's imperative to include appropriate conditions to allow them sufficient time to apply for and obtain them. If they don't intend to build right away, you might at least include a condition that allows them to satisfy themselves that the property meets all the current requirements necessary for the issuance of all appropriate permits and approvals.

Well, Well: A bad well could not only make the home uninhabitable, but preclude the approval of a mortgage loan. Thus, it's vital to include a condition to allow your buyer to perform a water potability test and determine if the well provides a sufficient quantity of water for their family's needs. For convenience, arrange the home inspection appointment to coincide with that of the well technician, and encourage your client to attend with you. For a nominal fee, a qualified well driller can check the well and equipment for flow rate. The less common dug well will also require a recovery rate test to determine the speed the well re-fills with water after use. If it's a dug or bored well, he'll inspect the cap to ensure it's properly sealed. If not, the well may be subject to frequent contamination from decomposing insects and worms creeping and slithering into the well to meet their fate. Also, the location of the well relative to potential contamination from the septic system, outbuildings or paddocks where manure is handled is important. What's the grading like around the well; can surface water drain into it? The technician will also inspect the pump motor and pressure tank for good physical condition and proper operation.

The Septic Skeptic: If the house is newer, chances are the septic system is fine. But if you're concerned, especially if it's an old home, add a condition allowing the buyer to determine satisfactory condition and have the system inspected by a specialized technician. The local municipal office might have the original application, plan and use permit. At least get the seller to agree to either provide your buyer with such documents or include a seller representation and warranty. The well, equipment and septic system are expensive to repair or replace.

Wood and WETT: To confirm correct installation and safeness of any wood-burning stove or fireplaces, include a condition regarding a satisfactory inspection and report by a Wood Energy Technology Transfer technician. Before approving a policy, an insurance company may insist on a copy. If your buyer can't get insurance, their lender will refuse to advance funds. For convenience and time-saving, arrange this appointment to coincide with the other testing and inspection appointments.

The Environment: It's important to know there are no environmental problems or hazardous conditions or substances existing on the land. For most properties, there's little cause for concern. A careful visual inspection combined with a seller warrant can easily allay any fears. But if you suspect a buried fuel tank or garbage dump or there's an auto repair shop out back or the abutting property is a junkyard, better safe than sorry. Better yet, investigate prior to submitting an offer.

Animals, Access and Assorted Affairs: Do your buyers plan to keep farm animals? When maintaining livestock, there are often special requirements such as manure storage protocols, minimum acreage and setback distances for outbuildings from the subject and neighbour's houses.

Taxes: A ruling from Canada Revenue Agency (CRA) may be required to determine if Harmonized Sales Tax (HST) will be applicable on the purchase price. When buying large acreage, the house and a small plot of land immediately surrounding the house will normally be exempt, but the larger portion of the acreage may not.

Sensational Recreational

Awhile back, I took a break from city life to practice in the land of the iconic loon, the paradise that is Muskoka, Ontario. Hollywood and professional hockey stars retreat there for fun, sun and hobnobbing with chief execs and others of their well-heeled ilk. It was a brief, but interesting and certainly educational experience into the world of casual ostentatiousness. Breaking into a new marketplace is never easy, but that market proved particularly arduous. I quickly learned that *who* you know out-trumps *what* you know. It's all about established connections.

Aside from discovering more about myself, I learned a few things about luxury real estate and the people who own and trade in it. The biggest lesson? That lifestyle wasn't for me. During our one very long wearisome winter after the sidewalks were rolled up, we witness the local population drop dramatically. After Labour Day and Thanksgiving, little moves but the occasional local wild inhabitant. If one doesn't snowmobile, ice fish, hunt or covet the neighbour's spouse, there's not much happening. After such a winter, sandwiched between two long, arduous and extremely frantic summers of seven-day work-weeks amongst the fracas of mosquitoes, black flies and summer tourists, we returned to the real world. Don't get me wrong; it is indeed a paradise. But to enjoy a successful recreational realty career, to have been born to that lifestyle with solid connections is a huge advantage.

During this foray, I learned about shore road allowances, wetlands and the significance of western waterfront exposure. I discovered that the steepness of a waterfront lot and whether the access road is private or public and winter-accessible are serious factors for discriminating buyers. Introverts appreciate the solitude of island life, whereas extroverts love the social hubbub of the mainland. Shore and lake bottom characteristics, shallow or deep, sand, rock or gravel, are important matters. Is the dockage sheltered sufficiently to protect boats from wave action? How's the privacy from neighbouring cottages? Any annoying traffic noise from the main road? And never tell your buyer, particularly if negotiations are being handled by a California lawyer, that they can have completely vacant possession in the winter; boathouses often can't be emptied when the lake is frozen.

There's a lot to know. It's definitely a speciality. And no less important than having the realty skills is the knack to screen prospects. Countless dreamers, who typically arrive on weekends, sometimes with a gaggle of kids in tow, are eager for a boat-ride to view luxury waterfront homes. If you're a city slicker who like's the idea of a road trip to cottage country to put a quick deal together, save your resources and refer to a local who specializes in this complex category of real estate. Otherwise, you could be in for a world of hurt.

*"It is better to have your head in the clouds and know where you are
than to breathe the clearer atmosphere below them and think
that you are in paradise." Henry David Thoreau*

Before Listing

Mend and Tend: One thing shared by rural and city property is putting your seller's best foot forward by staging both inside and out. One significant difference, though, is that anybody interested in buying rural or recreational property is definitely going to be an outdoors person. The condition of the lot, land or waterfront will be of great import. Bigger lots can mean bigger messes. Are there outbuildings? Does the fencing need repair? Are there large dead trees or limbs on the property that need removal? Ask your sellers to perform minor repairs prior to listing. With a larger piece of land, sometimes there's a tendency to accumulate stuff that sits around in various states of repose and decomposition. Even if they must hire someone, encourage a clean-up of the junk. It may be sentimental treasure to your seller, but a buyer will see only old rusting vehicles, building materials and assorted paraphernalia that they'll be forced to remove. Help your seller visualize the property from a buyer's perspective. Any obvious work a buyer feels they'll have to do will have a negative impact on their decision whether to offer and how much to pay.

Water and Waste: Since the drinking water likely comes from a well, it would be wise to have the equipment, including the sump pump, pre-inspected by a technician. To lessen the chances of any challenges arising after an offer is accepted, before marketing begins, do a well potability test. This is something the homeowner probably does on a regular basis anyway, but you may want to have it tested immediately before listing so you can offer assurances. Because the property is not on a sewer, if they've not done so recently, recommend a septic tank pump-out. The specialist can inspect the tank at the same time. Then a buyer won't be guessing whether it's necessary after they take possession. It's all about value-added.

Survey: Since it would be an exceedingly expensive proposition, a seller needn't hire a surveyor to create one unless negotiated with a buyer. But if they have a survey document, note its availability on the listing. It could even be accessible to fellow members as a download from the MLS® system. With guidance from the seller, particularly with acreage, mark the land boundaries at least at the corners using fluorescent ribbon that's clearly visible from a distance. It's annoying, at the least, for a buyer agent to be unable to point out the lot line to their buyer.

Animals: Even though there may not currently be any farm animals, if the property is sufficiently large and has suitable zoning, a buyer may want to have a few chickens or llamas. Ask a local municipal official about restrictions regarding minimum acreage requirements, what type of animals and the maximum number that are permitted on the property and about outbuildings. For promotion, you'll have to know anyway.

Quiet Enjoyment: Be aware of any possibly adverse proceedings or municipal applications that might affect the area. Is there any planned road construction that could affect quiet enjoyment of the property? Are there any significant changes coming up for local farming operations that might affect a buyer's decision?

Timing: As in the city and suburbia, at least in Canada, the busiest time of year for marketing country real estate is spring and summer. But with rural, it's even more important since the land is a priority. Any buyer is hesitant to buy what they can't see. So, if the ground is snow-covered, they're generally disinclined to even look, let alone buy. People normally want to enjoy their new country home after school is out, during the summer and autumn. If it's possible, list it when the spring flowers begin to peak their noses out.

"An investment in knowledge always pays the best interest." Benjamin Franklin

Rural real estate is a specialty. If you intend to be involved, I suggest you begin by taking as many courses as possible. Ask a rural expert if you can apprentice with them or be mentored. Meet with a well driller or septic service company. Stay informed about pending applications in your area for quarries, industrial uses and proposed road expansions. Contact the boards of education to ask about schools, policies, bus routes and boundaries. And know your market. If you try to sell rural or recreational property without this specialized knowledge, you may be assuming significant risk.

Rural life or city living? What attracts you personally? Whatever market category you choose, to be satisfying, it should be your personal paradise. If it's the nurturing womb of the city with its countless condo corridors and smaller efficient spaces cloistered in noisy cohesion, where one can reach out and touch a neighbour, then you should probably stick to city or suburban real estate. A great living can be earned in the speciality market of condominium apartments and tree-lined city streets. Refer your country prospects to a qualified agent.

However, if the wide open peaceful spaces and big sky of the countryside are your siren song, where you don't have to pay for parking, where you're lulled to sleep at night by the gentle chirping of the crickets, maybe rural real estate is for you. If you love what you do wherever you do it, you'll never work a day of your life. Either way, it's a great business.

"Burn down your cities and leave our farms, and your cities will spring up again as if by magic; but destroy our farms and the grass will grow in the streets of every city in the country." William Jennings Bryan

Chapter Twenty-One

Ups and Downs

"A market is never saturated with a good product,
but it is very quickly saturated with a bad one." Henry Ford

Does the idea of working in the condominium market raise your crane? It's certainly a speciality, particularly in larger metropolitan areas where already jagged skylines, crenellated with hi-rise buildings, are prickled with countless construction cranes seemingly springing up over-night. With the relatively rapid transition toward population intensification of both major cities and smaller recreational and retirement communities serving the greying boomer demographic, it's a rapidly expanding segment of our industry. Do you think you know everything there is to know about condominiums? Maybe – maybe not. Here's a basic primer to get you started or to top up your knowledge tank.

Condominium ownership is usually residential, but can also be found in the commercial and industrial sectors. A specific part of a piece of real estate, usually an apartment building or townhouse complex, is individually owned, while the common element (halls, elevators, heating system, tennis courts, playgrounds, driveways, etc.) is executed under legal rights associated with the individual ownership and controlled by the association of owners by way of a board of directors which jointly represents ownership of the entire building or complex. Expressed more simply, a residential condominium is a multi-unit dwelling where each unit is independently owned, with the common areas jointly owned by all the unit owners of the building or complex.

Individual home ownership within a condominium encompasses the air space within the walls, floor and ceiling of the unit and includes all fixtures such as cabinets, flooring, plumbing, lighting, heating and cooling units. Details are specified by a legal document called a "declaration". Owners are usually allowed to make interior modifications as long as the changes have no effect on the common element. Renovations to the exterior, such as balconies or patios, may require management permission. Anything outside the boundaries of the unit is held in an undivided ownership interest by the corporation established at the time of its government registration. Since the condo corporation itself cannot own property, it holds this property in trust on behalf of the group of homeowners.

The primary difference between a condo and a rental apartment is how the occupant holds legal ownership. A residential condominium may be defined simply as an apartment that the resident owns as opposed to rents. If the property reverts back to the owner of the land after the lease period has expired, it's referred to as leasehold. And just like freehold, a condo unit is still subject to easements, rights-of-way or restrictive covenants that may be registered on title. By the way, the term "condo" is commonly incorrectly used to refer to the space itself in place of the word "apartment", "unit" or "suite".

Condos can take various forms, but most common are the traditional apartment in a high or low-rise building and the conventional row or stacked townhouse. Though rare, there are detached or semi-detached condos. "Whole lot" or "lot line" condominiums, known as site condos, permit owners to have more control and possible ownership over the exterior appearance and are often the preferred form for gated communities and planned neighbourhoods. Underground parking spots are either owned by the unit owner or restricted to their exclusive use. Townhouse backyards, driveways or terraces are also normally designated as exclusive use, meaning no one else can legally use them, and are typically maintained by the property management under contract to the condo corporation.

The Money, Honey

Besides their mortgage loan payment and unit municipal property taxes, condo owners must contribute monthly into a fund from which numerous regular and extraneous common element expenses are paid. These may include major and minor improvements, repairs and systematic maintenance to the building structure, recreation facilities, elevator, underground and surface parking lots and roadway, and for landscaping, snow removal, security service and accounting. Utilities, municipal taxes and insurance for the common element, as well as property management fees, are also paid from this fund. Under the Condominium Act, a portion of each month's condo fee is credited to the reserve fund to maintain it at a certain minimum, to be used mainly for future significant expenditures.

When listing a condominium, realty agents commonly err by stating that the municipal taxes payable by the condo corporation on the common element are excluded from the monthly condo fee paid by the unit owner when normally, the taxes are included. The agent erroneously believes that the little check-box on the listing form refers to the municipal taxes for the individual unit. This widespread error usually goes undetected or ignored by everyone involved in the transaction, including apparently, the lawyers.

When you're showing condos, keep in mind that a mature and possibly deteriorating building might require extensive repair or renovation expenditures in the near future. For sufficient funds to be available for such work, management might have to impose significant increases in the monthly fee or levy a special assessment against each owner for their prorated share of the expense involved. This can be a significant amount of money. Before your buyer signs the offer, be sure they're aware of what they're buying. Also, tell them that the monthly fee is usually adjusted on closing, which could add a little to their closing costs.

Unlike many recently built towers, apartments in older buildings are not usually individually metered for major utilities, hence, the monthly fees are generally higher for those mature beauties. Your client may prefer the simplicity of one larger payment to the condominium management instead of separate invoices from each utility supplier. However, here's the caveat; the size of the annually adjusted all-inclusive fee is subject to the whims of group usage as a whole. If several residents prefer hot suites, for example, or use a lot of electricity, even though your client may prefer cooler temperatures and uses energy-saving bulbs, the monthly condo fee may reflect a higher cost for your buyer than what they might have experienced with individually controlled utilities. Obviously the building as a whole will benefit from your client's conservation efforts, but separate billing allows them the opportunity to have some degree of control over their total expense. Condo townhouses normally have lower monthly fees, not only because they're usually less expensive to maintain than hi-rises, but because each unit owner is usually invoiced separately for most of their utilities.

Your client will be responsible for insuring their own unit with a policy specifically designed for condominiums. Whereas a rental apartment policy covers only chattels, personal effects and liability, a condo policy covers everything within the unit, including interior finishing materials, furnishings, fixtures and flooring. A policy on a *freehold* townhouse, on the other hand, usually includes all of the above as well as the building.

Besides using a slightly different contract form to buy a condo, a buyer will have a slightly different loan qualification calculation to deal with because the condo fee is usually factored into the mortgage approval process. When calculating the gross and total debt service ratio on which, in part, a lender decides on a loan application, a lender will typically include at least half of the condo fee along with the usual one twelfth of the annual property taxes.

Status Certificate

Is the condominium financially solvent? Are there any unpaid condo fees or special levies registered against the unit? You certainly don't wish your buyer to unwittingly assume any pending litigation, outstanding judgments or executions against the corporation. Does your client have a pet? They may not be permitted. Prior to committing to an unconditional contract, knowing the rules and regulations is important. Don't make any assumptions. Make sure they know what they're buying by insisting on the production of a Status Certificate (SC) for the unit.

Formerly called an Estoppel Certificate, a SC is a detailed report on the current financial and legal health of the corporation. Prepared by property management under the Condominium Act upon the written (or on-line) request of the seller, buyer or one of their agents, management has up to 10 business days to comply. In Ontario, for example, it must be accompanied by a bank draft or certified cheque (or credit card) for $100 inclusive of HST. Accompanying documents normally include:

- Declaration details the structure, rules and regulations
- By-laws explain corporate functioning
- Corporate financial statements with actual and estimated costs indicate fiscal stability, expenditure trends with receipts from prior years
- Current budget identifies corporate income and reserve fund balance
- Contracts list (available upon request) to which the corporation is a party, such as management, security and maintenance
- Insurance certificate for the common element
- Statement declaring number of known leased units in the complex indicates condo stability. Ratio of renter to owner occupied units may affect buyer's decision whether or not to proceed with the purchase
- Information on monthly fee arrears or planned increases for the unit and major building work scheduled and if reserve fund is sufficient
- Details of outstanding legal judgments, executions and legal proceedings against the corporation. If insurance is insufficient for any major claims, the board of directors can increase the common expense fee or levy a special assessment against the individual unit owners

When buying a resale condo, include a condition in the APS to permit your buyer to seek a legal opinion of the corporation's health *before* they commit to the purchase. I've witnessed a few agents assume this approval responsibility; big mistake. Why assume the potential liability when you can pass it along to a lawyer who is likely more qualified to opine? Blunder and it's your neck on the proverbial chopping block.

As buyer agent, you normally control the phrasing of the clause regarding which party must provide the SC at their own expense. It's no longer necessary for it to be ordered in the name of the buyer for it to be legally reliable for them. Usually, you'll make the formal written request on your buyer's behalf and ask them for payment. Or you can be a hero and pay for it yourself. Who pays the fee is certainly negotiable. But to be fair, since the buyer's lawyer might have to order an updated SC if the closing is longer than 60 days, it seems only fair that the seller pay for the first one.

When you list a condo for sale, it's good practice to order a SC right away. A buyer will request one anyway and the seller can save valuable time after accepting their offer. Instead of waiting up to two weeks for a firm sale, everyone can carry on with their plans. Plus, by ordering a SC in advance, you'll have an opportunity to clarify with the property manager any possible issues, and be prepared to satisfy objections from a prospective buyer.

Moving In

There are all sorts of ways to impress a buyer client in both macro and micro ways. Handling the entire process in a professional and thoughtful manner is certainly the best way. And they expect that you will. But it's the managing of the small details that will help reduce stress levels and subsequently earn you their gratitude – and referrals.

After all the conditions have been fulfilled or waived, if you haven't already done so, ask property management about moving policies and restrictions. Your clients may have to submit a refundable damage deposit, be prohibited from moving in on certain days or reserve the elevator well in advance. What a shock if they arrived at the main entrance with the mover's clock ticking, only to be refused entry to their new home because they couldn't use the elevator or it was the wrong day!

Everyone prefers to live a prosperous and happy lifestyle. And such prosperity usually includes the ownership of some type of real property, be it condominium or freehold. And condominium permits less affluent buyers the opportunity to own a piece of that property. However, sometimes, bad stuff happens to good people. We've discussed a lot about acquiring realty; now let's move on to an unpleasant alternate flip-side – losing it. It happens, and you should be prepared to deal with it, technically and emotionally.

"You cannot spell prosperity without i-s and p-r-o-p-e-r-t-y."
Bradley J. Harrison

Chapter Twenty-Two

Losing It

"The best way to guarantee a loss is to quit." Morgan Freeman

Possessed

With the gargantuan amount of property repossessed around the world by money-lenders, I'm sure you've encountered the terms "power-of-sale" and "foreclosure". You may even be personally familiar with someone who has suffered this tragic misfortune. When a financially distressed homeowner defaults on their contractual responsibility under the terms of their mortgage, the lender usually seizes the property. No one wishes to be victimized by this emotionally catastrophic tribulation. Nevertheless, in our society, such losses are all too common. As an agent acting for buyers and both private and institutional sellers, it's important to thoroughly understand the processes.

In Ontario, Newfoundland, New Brunswick and Prince Edward Island as well as several American states, power-of-sale (POS) is a mortgagee's (lender) primary debt recovery method. Judicial sale, a more costly and time-consuming method, as it requires legal action against the mortgagor (borrower), has been adopted as the primary method in British Columbia, Quebec and the Prairie Provinces. In Nova Scotia and most American states, foreclosure leads in lender popularity, but it's still considered judicial since the court is still involved. Because of the lender rights incorporated in the mortgage, POS proceedings in Ontario are fairly fast. Two different types – contractual and statutory – are referenced in the Ontario Mortgages Act. The former applies if the mortgage document includes a POS provision, and the latter rarely used procedure applies if not included, and the mortgagor has defaulted for at least three months.

Same Difference

Foreclosure and POS differ significantly. Ultimately, though, both recovery methods have the same result for a defaulting homeowner – they lose their home.

A POS is a forced sale of a property by a lender, with the homeowner maintaining title, due to a default of one or more of the mortgagor's obligations. These would include paying principal, interest, municipal taxes, providing adequate property insurance and maintaining it in good repair – pretty much anything a proud and financially competent homeowner would normally do. The lender in possession has the right to sell the property, but contrary to foreclosure, has to attempt to get fair market value. Once sold, the lender must account to the mortgagor and all subsequent encumbrancers such as second mortgagees. The Mortgage Act requires that the sale proceeds first be applied to sale costs such as legal, property management and real estate fees and then to debt interest and costs owing under the mortgage. These are followed in priority by the outstanding principle, monies due to subsequent encumbrancers and if the property had been rented during the marketing period, to return any security deposits paid by a tenant. (Renters beware: if little equity, your security deposit may be at risk.) Since municipal governments have first claim for property tax arrears, their hands are first into the trough. Finally, the lender must return any net sale proceeds to the titled owner who defaulted and lost their home in the first place.

For the more common contractual POS, the mortgagor has 35 days (45 for statutory) to redeem the mortgage. If the mortgagor fails to comply, the lender can seize the property and evict them. Once the redemption period expires and the mortgagor has failed to rectify the default, the lender can legally sell the property by auction, private contract or by tender. Typically, though, it's listed with a real estate brokerage on the MLS® system.

A foreclosure is the process wherein a mortgagee loaned money to a property buyer in exchange for a registered lien against it, and repossessed and gained title to the property after the mortgagor failed to fulfil their responsibilities. To recover their outstanding debt, the lender has absolute discretion regarding the terms of the sale. Unlike a POS, the lender actually owns the property and normally retains any residual equity from the sale proceeds. When a homeowner defaults by more than 15 days, the foreclosing lender has the right to deliver a written Notice of Sale under Mortgage, which contains details of the mortgage, including a payment demand with a deadline, to anyone with an interest in the property. This group might include subsequent encumbrancers such as second mortgagees, statutory lien holders and those who have informed the lender in writing of their interest. The notice must contain a warning that if the mortgagor fails to redeem by the deadline date, thereby bringing the debt current, the lender intends to evict the mortgagor and sell the property. However, the process can't proceed any further until this redemption period has passed.

In both cases, the promissory note in support of the debt usually contains a recourse clause which provides the lender with a remedy for default. When the lender gains possession of the property and sells it, if the sale proceeds generate insufficient funds to pay what's owed, the lender can file a claim for a deficiency judgment and commence collection proceedings against the mortgagor.

Definitely Maybe

Are there any savings for your client to buy a property being marketed by a lending institution? My standard reply is definitely maybe. Your buyer may have heard that it's a chance to buy cheap. Well, it's a common misconception. Such properties could have a lower market value because of their poor physical condition. The previous owner or tenant could have neglected or maliciously destroyed it. Or while vacant for a lengthy period without utilities, vandals or harsh climatic conditions may have done a number on it. They're often advertised as fixer-uppers or handyman special. It's important for your client to thoroughly understand what they're getting into – literally and figuratively.

Since there are no worries about hurt feelings with an institution, a buyer usually has no qualms about offering a really low price, commonly referred to as a "low ball". That's fine and it's certainly their privilege. However, depending on how long it's been on the market, the lender may counter or even reject the offer. If they counter, along with a higher price, to protect themselves, they typically add and amend numerous clauses, both in the custom clause section and the standard pre-printed form. This doesn't necessarily mean they'll refuse to further negotiate, but they must maintain a paper trail to show they attempted to get a higher price. It's standard procedure. Advise your buyer to sign back the lender's counter-offer and try again. In my experience, POS sellers will negotiate price and possession date only, and not accept any conditions beyond financing and possibly home inspection. If your client has a house to sell, unless they're prepared to buy without a condition pertaining to its sale, they should probably forget about buying a repossessed property.

And don't expect things to happen quickly. Corporations work at their own plodding pace and traditionally only during regular business hours; certainly not on weekends. Negotiations might take several days or longer. You're dealing with a seller who has absolutely zero emotional attachment to the property; it's strictly business.

Redemption Risk

Where available, POS is normally preferred by lenders over foreclosure. Under the latter, once possession is obtained, the lender owns the property, so there's no redemption possible. But with POS, the lender enjoys the possible benefit of either a sale *or* redemption. The mortgagor's paying off the loan or bringing it current, of course, would preclude the necessity of having to pursue such remedy at all. And because of this possibility, lenders traditionally include clauses that allow it to terminate any uncompleted APS.

The problem arises for a buyer when the mortgagor redeems while the buyer, who has successfully negotiated an APS, is preparing to close and move into their new home. Because they prefer to avoid committing to a purchase that could be cancelled by the lender at the last minute, buyers resist the inclusion of such termination clauses. Courts have decided, however, that a homeowner who has lost their home under POS does not have the right to redeem *after* the execution of a bona fide *unconditional* sale. If this were not so, the exercise of the POS remedy would lose significant credibility as an enforcement mechanism. If a buyer could not rely on the ability of a POS seller to complete the sale under such circumstance, the demand for POS properties would fall – along with sale prices obtained to compensate a buyer for assuming such a significant risk.

Since there are usually no rights of redemption for a foreclosed mortgagor, there are no worries for the new buyer in this regard. However, there are potential disadvantages for the lender. In a declining market, if the property remains unsold for a protracted period, falling prices and extensive maintenance costs could result in a substantial loss. In such a case, it might be prudent for the financial institution to agree to a loan holiday, forgive the homeowner part of the loan and/or permit them to remain in possession. This would be both an intelligent and compassionate step towards a more just society. On the other hand, in a booming real estate market, if the bank holds the property long enough, it could generate a hefty profit for the "banksters".

No Promises

Because the repossessing lender has little or no knowledge of the property, they usually don't warrant anything. For example, even if there are appliances in the house, they typically refuse to reference them in the APS. Nor will they warrant the furnace or air conditioner to be in good working order. Sometimes, they even refuse to include the lot dimensions on the APS, instead inserting that the dimensions are as per registered deed.

Unlike buying a non-repossessed property where both parties share in the risk and make mutual promises, buying a POS or foreclosure property is pretty much at the buyer's risk. If you successfully negotiate what you feel is a price below market value, it's probably not only because of its poor physical condition, but because your client is assuming *all* the risk. By the time the proud new homeowner has made all the repairs and renovations to bring the property up to reasonable standard, in many cases, they might just as well have saved their time, effort and expense and bought a similar property in better condition from a non-institutional homeowner.

"It's just as unpleasant to get more than you bargain for as to get less."
George Bernard Shaw

Chapter Twenty-Three

Getting To It

"Always be smarter than the people who hire you."
Lena Horne

Nurturing a Neophyte

For a neophyte, buying real estate is usually uncharted territory. Worse, realty virgins sometimes suffer from misinformation from unreliable sources. As their trusted agent, it's your job to educate, to gently coach and coax them into appropriate home ownership with as little stress as possible. That means no unpleasant pressure. As I continue to emphasize, by winning their trust, your task is easier. Plus, you'll be rewarded – emotionally and financially. And if your service is exemplary, you'll earn referrals. Throughout my career, I've evolved and practiced the system detailed in this chapter with both novice and experienced buyers. Glean from it what resonates with you, whatever comfortably complements your present style, or try something new.

Seize the opportunity to learn more about your buyers. Find out what makes them tick by way of an extensive initial consultation. During this personal meeting with *both* spouses, ask numerous pertinent questions regarding *both* of their respective wants and needs. I emphasize *both* because they each may have quite different ideas – sometimes contradictory – as to what constitutes the ideal home. It's in your *and* their best interests to understand each of their individual as well as collective wants and needs. If you fail to satisfy both parties with the right home, one may block the other from offering on anything. If this occurs, you lose and so do they. Compromise means that neither party gets everything they want. But to remain within their budget, it may be unavoidable. And they'll depend on you to mediate and miraculously produce a mutually agreed outcome.

During the first consultation, I once asked a wife for her wants and needs. I recall her replying effusively with a long, detailed feature list, from kitchen cabinetry to floor covering and everything in between. She had obviously been envisioning her new home for some time. The husband, when asked, replied simply that he wanted a big master bedroom with a bathroom and attached double garage ... (pause) ... and whatever she wants. Smart!

EEE

The list of questions is limited only by your imagination and their affordability factor. What basics do they absolutely need? What would they *like* to have? As you make suggestions, they'll have a tendency to say yes to everything. So, it's a good idea to initially allow them to volunteer this info without your prompting. Often, the unprompted features are what excite them the most. Make notes throughout the meeting and categorize the list by "needs" and "wants". The needs become your primary search parameters and the wants are a close second, particularly those expressed at the outset. Satisfaction of the *needs* list will get them through the front door for a viewing, but it's the exciting stuff from the *wants* list that will ignite their Emotional Excitement Engine and get them to the offer table.

To ascertain a feasible target price range, it's important to include basic financial questions so you don't waste their time – or yours. How much cash do they have available for down payment? Is it from borrowed funds? What's their approximate gross combined income and outstanding debt with minimum monthly payments? Estimate their gross debt and total debt service ratios to ensure their dream home is within their financial grasp. You might be surprised to discover that they can comfortably afford a larger home. Their lender will repeat this procedure when they seek a mortgage pre-approval certificate, but at least you can do a pre-screen.

If they already own a home, to determine their net transferable equity, a property evaluation supported by a CMA is obviously a prerequisite, and as early in the process as possible. You should clarify any difference between how much they *believe* they can spend and what they can *actually* afford. Since homeowners often over-estimate the value of their homes, the figures could be quite different.

Your thorough and thoughtful inquiry will attest to your serious intentions to make their home transition a happy reality. Plus the sharing of their personal financial information, along with their feelings, cracks open the door to their inner trust circle and begins to nurture the growth of a mutual bond.

"He who does not trust enough, will not be trusted."
Lao Tzu

Dubious Maximus

For comfort and peace of mind, buyers sometimes prefer to spend well under their lender-approved maximum purchase price. Of course, do your best to accommodate their wishes – at least initially. But I've found they're often disappointed with the less expensive homes and end up increasing their limit somewhat. Perhaps you're uncomfortable advocating buying to their highest technical affordability level because they may feel you're just trying to increase your commission. But your prime motivation isn't self-serving. As a matter of fact, it's the exact opposite.

You don't want them to excessively compromise their wish list because the more space and features they sacrifice to remain within their emotionally preferred budget, the sooner they'll need or want to upgrade to a larger, more expensive home. Of course, this will entail a move sooner than later with all the stress and associated expenses – real estate commission, legal fees, land transfer taxes and movers – all over again. At least increase their maximum to include an estimate of these future expenses. It's arguably wiser to invest in a larger home now and stay put longer, provided of course they don't buy a home too big for their britches. They mightn't sleep well worrying about a bigger debt. Obviously, health is our first wealth.

"Worry is interest paid on trouble before it comes due."
William Ralph Inge

Background Busy

While they're lining up ducks, you're busy behind-the-scenes with research, market analysis and leg work, searching and sifting through listing inventory to create a list of homes that fit their parameters. Don't waste your client's time by having them view homes you could easily have eliminated in advance. Published listing data doesn't usually include *all* pertinent property details, so you may have to personally preview the short-listed homes. For example, allergies might preclude buildings occupied by smokers or pets. And you might consider having a sneak peek at larger, more complex homes, out-buildings or property. Depending on wants, needs and health concerns, investigate for such things as school boundaries, bus stops, high-tension electricity transmission corridors, micro-wave towers, quarries, industrial wind turbines, noise and exhaust from planes and trains and automobiles, rear ravine crime rate, soil quality, location of the well and septic and the apartment view. Just a few things.

Let the Show Begin

"Once you make a decision, the universe conspires to make it happen."
Ralph Waldo Emerson

The mortgage pre-approval is now in writing, you have an attractive selection of carefully scrutinized listings and they're available on Saturday. Prior to appointment day, email them the list of contenders with your personal comments and include several interior and exterior photos and any virtual tours. For more extensive properties, you might send an e-brochure obtained from the listing agent, or additional photographs or video that you took during previews. You might suggest they personally scope out the immediate neighbourhoods prior to viewing day. If the locale or exterior elevation doesn't excite them, there's no point bothering with the interiors. Shorten the list again.

To minimize driving time between homes, organize the final tour list in geographical sequential order. If distance is not an issue, sort the listings by each property's appropriateness, saving the best for last – like dessert. That way, they'll have had an opportunity to see several homes to which they can compare what you instinctively feel will be The One. If you're unfamiliar with the area, so you can focus on them instead of a street map in your lap, scout it ahead of time or program all the addresses into your GPS (Global Positioning System). You definitely don't want to get lost with clients in your car or following behind.

"Strive not to be a success, but rather to be of value." Albert Einstein

If the distance isn't prohibitive, meet the buyers at your office or other convenient location, maybe at their home if they live close by. If their party is large, they may follow in their family van. Don't lose them! If travelling in separate vehicles, the first home in the series can serve as a meeting point and go from there. You'll become quite adept at keeping them in your review mirror and correctly timing traffic signals and lane changes. It's best, though, to ride together in the same vehicle, not only for safety sake, but to have the chance to chat about the properties and life in general. It's an opportunity to commune, bond and obtain property feedback.

To avoid confusion, limit the number of listings to half a dozen or so. Too many and all the features and various emotions begin to blur together like ink and water. To simplify matters and to eliminate homes from contention, ask them to choose a favourite as you progress through the list and then compare each subsequent home to that favourite. The favoured home could change. At the end of the tour, a decision will be easier; either the final favourite is worthy of offering or not. Audio recording or written notes can also be a valuable memory aid. Some industrious buyers even snap photos, but some sellers might find this invasive.

Having seen innumerable properties over the years, you bring to each viewing an expert level of realty knowledge and experience as well as an extra set of senses. As their valuable realty resource, it's your job to not only point out attractive features and benefits, but also deficiencies, patent defects and possible symptoms of latent defects.

Aunt Ethyl and Uncle Harry

"No enemy is worse than bad advice." Sophocles

One of the most indispensable contributions to client care is *objective* advice. This should be far more precious to them than, say, the opinion of an unqualified friend or relative who has tagged along. Where you're impartial, a relative can bring a personal bias. And in my experience, their advice is usually negative.

It's easier to discourage with critically destructive remarks than encourage with constructive commentary. The so-called advisor, hoping to be a hero, may exuberantly try to protect their loved one by pointing out what "in their humble opinion" are the flaws. They normally don't easily slip into your client's shoes to see the property from your buyer's perspective. Aunt Ethyl may brazenly declare the price too high. It may be true, but it's often *how* the message is delivered. As does a destructively critical parent, it's easier to find fault. Unless Uncle Harry is an expert contractor, recommend that your buyers leave him out of the picture.

As if in a dream, buyers sometimes merrily float through the house and seeing only the pretty furnishings and decor, and not the physical details of the house and property. They see the forest and not the trees. Encourage them to go slow. Logically, the condition of the flooring, windows, cabinetry, furnace, roof and other accoutrements should be a high priority, but they're often overlooked. Buying a home in this manner is like choosing a new car by colour and comfort only.

They may be so smitten that they don't even hear your continuing commentary about features and benefits. Make sure you're heard. Get them to widen their scope for an informed decision, be it to eliminate a property from contention or make it a serious contender. Hopefully, the seller will be absent to allow you to deliberate freely and not secretly in whispers, or at all. Nobody wants to risk offending the homeowner. A constructive dialogue is critical to the decision-making process.

Depending on weather conditions and your buyer's priorities, normally, you'd show the interior first. If they don't care for the floor-plan, the exterior won't matter. If the interior is worth considering, guide them around outside to view the landscaping, swimming pool, garage and outbuildings. For viewing condo high-rise, be prepared to escort them confidently, with foreknowledge, through the common areas. If there's acreage, waterfront or forest and you're all suitably shod, walk the land to get a feel for it.

If you've qualified your clients well, properly pre-screened the listings and their requirements are not extremely specific, they may actually find their new home on the first excursion. On many occasions, I've actually shown only one property, obtained, presented and had an offer accepted, all on the same day. As a matter of fact, without the aid of an assistant, I once did two separate property transactions in the same way on the same Saturday. And yes – I fell exhausted into bed in the wee hours of the following day. But what a day that was!

Search parameters may change as you introduce them to new listings. Sometimes, they'll increase their maximum price because, as I said earlier, they often optimistically start low, but are disappointed with the calibre of homes or neighbourhoods. But if you continue to provide them with sensitive, thoughtful service, they'll not change horses and will continue with you. Don't pressure them; it's not about the quick sale. Closing opportunities will present themselves. Be professionally persistent and patient.

"Adopt the pace of nature: her secret is patience." Ralph Waldo Emerson

Intuition Volition

"In any moment of decision, the best thing you can do
is the right thing, the next best thing is the wrong thing,
and the worst thing you can do is nothing." Theodore Roosevelt

You probably already know what they *think* about the homes in question because you properly qualified them in advance and thoroughly vetted the listings. You know each home has the basic ingredients to satisfy most if not all of their practical wants and needs. Thus, rather than a logical decision, their final choice will be an emotional one. People can over-complicate things by thinking way too much by bringing all sorts of factors into the equation, including discussing it with family and friends. I've always believed that the longer one takes to make a decision – thinking about it – the more difficult it is to make. So, don't ask what they *think,* but how they *feel.*

While still in the favoured home, sit down together and relax. Are they comfortable? What are they feeling? Excitement? Disappointment? Indifference? Can they imagine living there and raising their family? Can they visualize their furniture in place? How does it look? What would they do to personalize it? Spend some time in the garden with senses at full throttle. Stroll the neighbourhood together or send them off alone for walk. Visit the parks, schools or recreation centres. Check traffic and maybe even meet the neighbours. When faced with a major decision, they should follow their instincts. What does their gut tell them?

If they appear to be waffling because of the list price, and it's still technically within their financial grasp, remind them that if they remain in their current money comfort zone, they'll not likely buy a home – period. Or if they do, they'll not be satisfied with it. Do they want a better home? Well, ownership costs. Growth always comes at a price. Stretching financially and being a little nervous go hand in hand. Obviously, they should exercise reasonable restraint, but encourage them to seriously consider extending themselves.

Cold Feet

> *"The risk of a wrong decision is preferable to the terror of indecision."*
> *Maimonides*

They seem very interested, but fearfully slam on the brakes. Buyers sometimes procrastinate, become disheartened and can easily change their minds over-night. If they lose their enthusiasm or confidence, they occasionally even go so far as to indefinitely postpone a purchase. They then step back, sigh with relief and fall back into their former comfy life. But at some point, maybe days or months later, it dawns on them that their motivation to move remains. They find themselves staring at the same rented apartment walls or over-crowded conditions or listening to the same obnoxious neighbour screaming at his kids. Nothing has changed. Then, with deep regret at permitting their fears to impede their path to home ownership, they contact you, if you stayed in touch, to begin the search anew.

In the trade, we call this "cold feet". While they were procrastinating, the home they loved was sold to another buyer. Prices or mortgage rates may have risen and they've not been able to save enough money to compensate. To lift their spirits, they may even have bought a truck with their down payment.

Consequently, they either end up settling for a smaller home or have a higher mortgage payment. But the entire process begins all over again.

"Procrastination is the thief of time." Edward Young

A charming middle-aged couple once walked into my office and expressed interest in buying a home. During a brief qualifying consultation, I learned they'd been renting for many years and had $100,000 ensconced in the bank. They'd never bought a home! This was incredible because, at that time, they could have bought a nice detached house in the suburbs for under $75,000. Even though they expressed a sincere wish to buy and escape the perpetual rental game, they'd obviously permitted their fears to determine their life path. Their love of the idea of home ownership was outweighed by their fear of failing. When asked why they hadn't bought years ago, they replied that they'd never found just the right place. Needless to say, they disappeared off my radar screen and probably passed away as tenants.

This is an extreme example of a decision postponed. The best advice you can offer your buyer is to face their fears and make the decision. Fears are not real; they're always fabricated. Make an offer – without delay – or move on. Procrastination usually doesn't pay.

"The most difficult thing is the decision to act, the rest is merely tenacity.
The fears are paper tigers. You can do anything you decide to do.
You can act to change and control your life; and the procedure,
the process is its own reward." Amelia Earhart

On to Offer

Prior to submitting an offer, you'll probably be asked to opine on how much to offer. It's your job to professionally advise them, but since the price decision is in large part emotional, determining where to begin is ultimately *their* responsibility – not yours. Ask how much they want it. What's it worth to them?

Opinion is purely subjective. And because subjectivity plays such a prominent role in determining fair market value (FMV), your opinion and the final sale price may be chalk and cheese. Due to their own preferences, biases and circumstances, your estimate may differ considerably from the value your buyer might apply to it. For example, someone who adores a home will value it much higher than someone who thinks it's merely satisfactory or hates it. Few would value a seller's home as much as the naturally biased homeowner because it's their castle, improved and decorated to their own exacting standards.

If you choose to provide price advice, keep in mind that estimating market value is like trying to nail jelly to the wall; it's virtually impossible. By its inherent nature, FMV will remain elusive until *after* negotiations – and the home inspection – are completed and conditions removed. At that time, FMV equals the market or sale price. You could give a quick "from the hip" guess or prepare a carefully considered analysis. It wouldn't take long to review recent local sales and apply your market savvy to arrive at a well-informed opinion of value. Instead of stating a specific figure, though, offer a range. You'll reduce the risk of being blamed if, following negotiations, they feel they over-paid or lost it in a harried competitive bid.

Whichever party is the least anxious will usually get the best deal. FMV can obviously be affected if one of the parties is under duress. The seller may have already bought another home, maybe unconditionally, or is immersed in an acrimonious divorce. A buyer may be competing with another bidder or under pressure to vacate their present home. A party under such stress is certainly not in a position to dispassionately negotiate favourable terms.

If they insist on your opinion, presuming the list price is realistic, you could suggest they offer 5 percent under the list price or whatever percentage is customary in your area. If you feel the property is over-priced, they could ignore the inflated list price and apply the same discount to what you believe is a realistic FMV. If the asking price is fair, suggest they offer fairly. An excessively low offer could alienate the seller who might counter-offer at a higher price than what they might have considered if your buyer's opening bid had been fair. Or the seller could simply refuse to sell their home to your client.

Contract Cruxes

To address the myriad situations that arise, it behooves you to be fully informed on the intricacies of drafting reliably accurate contracts and supporting documents. When creating custom clauses, ambiguity can easily result in misunderstandings, lost business or worse, litigation.

I once received an offer from a buyer represented by a cooperating agent and was stunned by the number of blatant technical and grammatical errors it contained. He had botched the chattels and fixtures, inserted a clause regarding a non-existent basement apartment and erred by reversing the two brokerages. I couldn't imagine asking a client to sign such an amateurish document. On a condominium offer, by not including a Status Certificate condition, another agent had irresponsibly committed his unwitting client to potentially buying into a corporation about which he knew nothing of its financial or legal status. If you find yourself deficient, seek help from your manager or more experienced colleague. We're all human and no one is completely infallible, but this is a major crux of our fiduciary responsibility.

Prior to signing, invite your buyer to read the entire agreement. If they demur, which is usually the case, emphasize what really matters – the information typed into the body and blanks of the contract. Various clauses are usually written in plain language and easily understood. But be prepared to paraphrase every clause, including the standards in the pre-printed form. I'll not dwell on the intricacies of contract drafting, but simply proffer a few points to ponder that I feel are sometimes not taken into account by realty agents.

"Clarity affords focus." Thomas Leonard

Deposit: Size matters – at least when it comes to the deposit. Be mindful that size is often directly proportional to the extent of faith the seller places in your buyer's offer. Do you want it taken seriously? $1000 won't have the same effect as $20,000. At today's ridiculously low interest rates, it doesn't really cost your buyer anything to offer a larger deposit, and it may motivate the seller to treat it more favourably, especially in a competition. I once won a multiple bid for a buyer with just a large deposit; it was the proverbial straw that tipped the scale in my favour. So, weigh it carefully.

Chattels and Fixtures: This may seem a simple subject, but it's rife with opportunity for misinterpretation. In most circumstances, the difference between the two is obvious. But sometimes, it's not. *Before* you list a property for sale or *prior* to drafting an offer, to avoid confusion, seek clarification.

Unless items that are mechanically attached (screwed, nailed, glued or hard-wired) to the house, outbuilding or grounds are expressly excluded on the listing and on the APS, when the owners vacate, they must leave these fittings behind. Also, anything that could be remotely perceived as being physically part of the property, even if it's not mechanically attached, such as a bathroom wall mirror hung on a hook, could also be expected to be included.

Thermostats, furnaces, central air conditioners, electrical panels, drapery tracks, window blinds or shutters, installed carpet, built-in cabinetry, attached swimming pool equipment, sheds, decks, fences, garage door openers, door bells, security and water filtration systems and pressure tanks, sump-pumps, garburetors, built-in workbenches, awnings, satellite dishes, exterior fireplaces, attached entertainment systems, built-in appliances, toilets and sinks, hard-wired light fixtures, central vacuum systems, affixed mirrors, docks and fireplace inserts would clearly be classified as fixtures. If a flat-screen TV is wall-mounted with a bracket and wired into the system, it's also a fixture.

On the other hand, an above-ground hot tub that rests on the deck could be considered a chattel except that the associated electrical and plumbing are mechanically attached to the property. Without written clarification, the parties could easily be in conflict prior to or after closing.

Free-standing large and small appliances, uninstalled carpets and area rugs, draperies and curtains, portable lamps, central vacuum utensils, furniture, mirrors and art hung on hooks, fireplace equipment, window air conditioner units, pool tools, patio furniture and free-standing barbecues would normally be considered chattels. Unless expressly included, they'd automatically be excluded. Specialized equipment or attachments could be collectively described as "all related equipment or attachments".

Warranty: In most offers, a seller representation and warranty should be included in an APS with respect to any chattels and fixtures. Since these items contribute to the over-all market value of the property, a buyer ought to have the assurance that what they're paying for will be in good working order and free of liens or encumbrances on completion. However, ensure that your buyers are not deluding themselves into thinking they'll have some kind of extended warranty.

A warranty and representation by a seller is simply a promise that the fixtures and chattels will be properly operational when the sale closes. Advise your buyer to check them immediately upon gaining possession. A judge will allow a *reasonable* amount of time after closing and in most cases, that's a day or so. If something is malfunctioning, they should inform you or their lawyer right away. The seller may be held liable for any repair or replacement.

Rental Contracts: Rented or leased equipment located on the property and not technically owned by the seller, such as a hot water tank, furnace, satellite receiver, air conditioner, security alarm or water treatment system, should be incorporated into the listing contract and APS. A seller obviously doesn't have the legal right to sell such equipment. However, they can usually assign the rental contract to a subsequent owner. If they're transferable, a clause must be included in the APS whereby the buyer agrees to assume the terms of the rental contract. If not, they'll believe they've bought the equipment and may successfully argue before a judge that they were included in the price. The seller could be held liable to the rental company for a penalty or the balance of a buy-out of such equipment. Or the buyer could be drawn into a legal conflict between the rental company and the seller. Either way, a messy, potentially expensive situation for everyone may ensue – including both agents.

Final Inspection: For many years, it's been standard procedure for buyers of brand new homes to accompany the builder's representative on a final inspection of the new house immediately prior to closing. Usually, the buyer is asked to sign an acknowledgement affirming their understanding and agree to accept the property as completed, with the possible exception of any deficiencies noted during the inspection.

A prudent buyer of a resale property will do a similar inspection before instructing their lawyer to complete the sale. Obviously, it's not the same formal inspection as performed by a builder, but the buyer should still want assurance that all the chattels and fixtures contractually included are still present and that the property is in basically the same physical condition as when they entered into the APS, save for modest wear and tear. To comply with contract terms, a vacating seller should leave the property and all chattels and fixtures in good physical condition. Besides being a contractual necessity, it's also the ethical thing to do.

> *"I know that you believe you understand what you think I said,*
> *but I'm not sure you realize that what you heard is not what I meant."*
> *Robert McCloskey*

Predilection for Protection

Buyers once relied on their own or their uncle's construction knowledge or sued the seller for the cost of unexpected major repairs. Most of those days of "caveat emptor" or "buyer beware" probably held few regrets. But over the years, the home inspection report has become a part of our industry's lexicon, with a standard clause finding its way into pre-printed forms. Why? Well, I suppose we've become a more litigious society and agents want to protect their clients – and themselves – from litigation. Our business costs are increasing every year, so who wants unnecessary risk?

Because they're clearly visible to the trained and often untrained eye, patent defects aren't usually critical. However, the latent variety is another matter. If a seller is unaware of, or innocently or maliciously attempts to conceal a major latent defect, they could ultimately be held liable. And if an agent becomes aware of such defect, s/he is obligated to relay this information to their client, or also risk liability. A seller's refusal to accept an inspection condition should be construed by cautious buyer as a "red flag", that there may indeed be a problem. If a seller accepts such a condition, they may still lose the sale anyway. Thus, they have nothing to lose by declaring and cooperating.

If the home is nearly new, maybe with a new home warranty still in effect, has been extensively renovated or is a condominium apartment or townhouse, a full inspection may not be as critical. But the fee is a small price to pay for the peace of mind in knowing there are no unseen problems. Before committing to a firm purchase, to protect your buyer from expensive surprises, to specifically inform them about the physical condition of the property and building and to give them the opportunity to learn how to properly maintain a home, encourage them to request one.

It must be made clear to your buyer that the inclusion of such a condition is not intended to give them the chance to escape a contract over minor concerns – or if they've just changed their minds. Let's be fair. When reviewing the report, they must reasonably consider that as a structure ages, the more maintenance and repair it requires. Thus, they mustn't expect a 30-year old house to be as pristine as one built yesterday. A report's purpose is to avoid major surprises and educate them regarding what they're buying.

If a significant defect is exposed, depending on the clause terminology, the seller may have the option of repairing the defect at their own expense or your buyer may serve notice of their intent to cancel the contract. Or the buyer can ask the seller to either remedy the deficiency or reduce the purchase price by an amount that reflects an estimated cost of repairing or replacing the defective component. A further inspection by a specialized contractor, such as a foundation damp-proof expert, roofer or mould specialist, may be necessary to provide a cost estimate. The seller may agree to perform and/or pay for the repair or insist that the buyer pay all or part of the expense by way of a higher purchase price. Once the parties agree, an amendment is executed to simultaneously remove the condition, specifically detail work to be performed at the seller's expense prior to completion and/or adjust the purchase price.

Normally, an inspection and report of any swimming pool and related equipment is beyond the purview of a home inspector. If there's a pool, consider a condition permitting your buyer to obtain a satisfactory report by a specialized technician. They'll pressure test the underground pipes for leaks, examine the pump, filter, heater and liner to ensure proper operation and generally ensure good order. They'll also check for local zoning, safety code and building bylaw compliance regarding heater exhaust, electrical safety, fencing height and boundary set-back requirements.

If the pool is relatively new, well-maintained and fully operational, and your buyer is pool savvy, they could accept the seller's representation and warranty that the pool and related equipment are and will be in good working order on closing. However, at offer negotiation time, if the pool is closed for the season, they'll want a guarantee that it will be in good working order upon spring opening. To give your buyer reasonable time in the spring to satisfy themselves of its proper operation and condition, the warranty period should survive the completion date until the pool is opened, with a late date to protect the seller. If there's a problem, your buyer will have a remedy – and you'll have a satisfied client.

Now let's move on to the really exciting part of our service, where we get to truly shine – the offer presentation.

> *"Truth is confirmed by inspection and delay;*
> *falsehood by haste and uncertainty."* Tacitus

Chapter Twenty-Four

Proffer an Offer:
Techniques and Methodology

"It is the nature of every person to error, but only the fool perseveres in error."
Marcus Tullius Cicero

Most homeowners are innocently unaware of the daily minutiae of our trade. They're ignorant of our industry's high attrition rate, meagre average income and the everyday anxieties faced bravely by our assiduous assembly. Understandably, they have no idea of our extensive expenses, nor do they feel our anguish over a lost client with whom we'd heavily – and speculatively – invested our resources. Some agents orchestrate magnificent thematic advertising campaigns, while others pursue expired listings and private sales, patiently farm neighbourhoods, sponsor athletic teams and adopt roads. Some trawl extensive social, business and family networks, while others patiently sit on their duffs and wait for the phone to magically ring. Whatever you do to earn your daily bread, unless those activities culminate in successful closings, there's no payday. And to better the chances of being paid, you need a competent offer presentation style.

Over the years, I've witnessed countless techniques, many of which were unprofessional, boring, disorganized, frustrating, inefficient, dumb and alas, sometimes hostile. A distinct lack of formal training is clearly evident in what is arguably our most important direct income-generating activity. Every time you find yourself in front of a client, be they your own or a competitor's, for durable success, you must make every presentation moment count. And no moments lead more directly to earning commission than during an offer negotiation.

Negotiation Innovation

*"Negotiation, in the classic diplomatic sense, assumes parties
more anxious to agree than to disagree."* Dean Acheson

Negotiation is an art form. In our industry, as in any other, such skills vary considerably from superb to abysmal. As clearly demonstrated by the industry's mediocre average income, many agents are not much more than couriers and order takers. I've met shoe salesman with presentation skills superior to those of many realty agents. It's no small wonder that a minority monopolize the majority of the business. If you're prepared to invest the time and effort to learn and polish new skills, to develop intelligent, repeatable and reliable negotiation techniques, you'll be better equipped to make every business moment count for more. Higher efficiency translates into fewer business hours necessary to generate the same or better income. Of course, this also means more time and energy for personal and family pursuits – the real reasons we're here; happiness and personal fulfillment.

The Dance

*"When you dance, your purpose is not to get to a certain place
on the floor. It's to enjoy each step along the way."* Wayne Dyer

Learning how to negotiate is like learning to dance. It's a sensitive balance, a gentle coordinated give and take between two shuffling partners. If the leader isn't comfortably familiar with the steps, the dance becomes awkward and unpleasant, sometimes painful. It's not a time for confusion and treading on toes. Many naturally excel at dancing, but to gain confidence, novices must learn the proper steps through study and practice. Any dance instructor will say that you can *think* about the dance steps, but to be a better dancer, you must *feel* them. Be sensitive to the subtle movements and emotional nuances of your partner. With good guidance and proper technique, it can be a highly pleasurable pastime.

When presenting an offer, it's a similar scenario. Be sensitive to the moods and needs of everyone around the table, including the other agent. See things not only from your own perspective, but also from theirs. Now and again, take the time to step into their shoes for a few moments. Being narcissistic, blatantly aggressive and unreasonably demanding usually fails to make the sale. Haggling happens and emotions flare, but you'll fare better with a scalpel than with a machete; even better if the scalpel is wrapped in velvet. Maintain your calm, your centre and be grounded. Focus. Do not permit any negative energy from the other parties to affect your serenity. If you do, you'll only be feeding theirs. Witness the events, but do not lose yourself in them. Be alert, aware and think before you speak. Make a respectful connection with the parties and your dance is more likely to conclude smoothly and successfully.

> *"I grew up with six brothers. That's how I learned to dance*
> *– waiting for the bathroom." Bob Hope*

Absentee Agents

Nowadays, it's becoming common practice for listing agents to refuse the buyer's rep the opportunity to personally participate in the presentation, and to insist that offers be faxed or emailed. That's a mistake – big one. These listers may have duped themselves into believing they're protecting their sellers from the mysterious pressure tactics of big bad buyer agents. Or they're heavily relying on technology and totally discounting the human factor. Or they're attempting to save themselves time and effort by circumventing a proven process that's been around since before they were born. Or they see the buyer rep as a mere courier and would relegate them to solitary confinement anyway while they privately consult with their seller. Whatever their faulty reasoning, they're doing their seller a serious disservice.

Beyond a shadow of a doubt, unless geography or weather makes it prohibitive, having both reps present increases the overall odds of a successful negotiation. The listing agent enjoys the good fortune of being able to ask questions about the buyer and their offer and to have the seller hear the answers – unfiltered – directly from the buyer's agent. And it allows the buyer's agent a fair opportunity to professionally plead their client's case. Prior to signing back the offer, to test the waters, the seller's rep can ask the buyer agent to call their client. In other words, it's a great opportunity to negotiate terms and to avoid having to make unilateral decisions in a vacuum.

If you intend to help your seller make the smartest decision, information is imperative. How the buyer agent responds – verbally and nonverbally – can speak volumes. You could ask questions by phone. But asking strategic questions face to face presents the valuable opportunity to witness and interpret body language, voice intonations and nuance which, in turn, allows you to more competently advise your seller. You get the chance to dance, to develop a *feeling* about the buyer, and to discuss various strategic counter-offer options.

Imagine for a moment what would happen in a union/management grievance meeting without a representative from each side sitting at the table;

not much chance of success. Without the buyer agent in attendance, your seller misses the chance to express themselves to someone who could perhaps directly influence the buyer. With only the listing agent present, there's no repartee, no professional jousting between the two sides. With polar opposite positions, your seller could push – often unreasonably – with no resistance. In my opinion, that's not negotiation – it's demanding.

Buyer agents should insist they be permitted to fully partake in the negotiation process. I encourage listing agents to get with the program. It's smart business. Now, let's move on to the steps involved in what has proven to be an effective personal presentation style.

Wrong & Right Way

> *"Admitting error clears the score and proves you wiser than before."*
> Arthur Guiterman

As I said, I've witnessed all sorts of presentation styles, most of them appallingly amateurish. Some listing agents have vainly attempted to justify their existence by simply reading the entire offer (and not well) to the seller as though their client were functionally illiterate. Others have respectfully encouraged the seller to read for themselves, and then proceeded to read it to them – out loud – just in case they missed something during their private reading. Boring, boring and did I say boring? It's time-consuming and maybe a little insulting to their clients' intelligence.

Upon receiving the offer, others have launched immediately into a brief abridgment of the terms, thereby not allowing the seller the opportunity to read and properly digest a document with which they're probably unfamiliar. After the seller has read the offer, some agents have brazenly declared the price unacceptable – without any client consultation – and without giving any due consideration to other critical terms. This introduces an aggressive, antagonistic spirit to the proceedings. I've observed a listing agent hand over a copy of the offer to the seller, wisely allow them to read it thoroughly, sometimes quietly, and then immediately upon their finishing, ask for their comments, opinion or decision without any questions, discussion or explanation. And of course, a list of terrible styles would be incomplete without the one wherein a listing agent just faxes or emails the offer to their seller for review; ridiculous and unprofessional. All of those agents – many of whom are probably long gone – neglected to take a professional holistic approach to what is arguably the most important aspect of our service.

A listing agent should arrive at their seller's home prior to the arrival of the buyer's agent for a brief coaching session. Walk them through basic procedure and ask that they follow your lead during negotiations. Answer any questions that might arise, and to help them be objective, review an updated CMA. Remind them that the other agent will almost certainly be representing the interests of the buyer. For this reason, they should not disclose anything of a confidential nature nor visibly react to the offer terms in the presence of the buyer's agent. Tell them to keep their cards close. Explain that once the offer has been reviewed and you've asked clarifying questions of the buyer's rep, you'll be asking the agent to leave the room so you can consult privately with your seller regarding the merits and shortcomings of the offer. So they'll be better equipped to choose the best course of action, you'll then explain all available options and make recommendations.

Since it's a business meeting with a fair amount of paperwork and hopefully document signing, ask that everyone gather around a cleared kitchen or dining table, and to do whatever is possible to avoid potential interruptions from kids, snuffling dogs, squawking birds and blaring TV. During the proceedings, unless it's an emergency, ask that all phone calls go directly to voicemail. If they live in a raucous menagerie, suggest a meeting in your office boardroom. You want a fully informed decision after both spouses have had the benefit of an uninterrupted presentation and discussion.

The Reading

After the buyer's rep arrives, to minimize a potentially adversarial environment, strategically seat everyone around the table by mixing it up a little. Avoid the table being a divisive boundary between two opposing sides. Maybe have a seller on each side and the two reps on each of the other ends. The agent will then hopefully hand you an offer copy for each participant. Astoundingly, they sometimes bring only a single copy. I recall a long ago presentation when an old-timer, after some social chatter, leisurely withdrew the only copy from his back pocket. With a wink and a smile, he gently unfolded a wrinkled, hand-written offer onto the table and casually slid it over. We made the sale, but it was memorable in its casual informality.

To set a respectful and optimistic tone, on behalf of your sellers, express your gratitude to the buyer agent for bringing the offer. Begin by explaining that the offer is prepared on a standard form, which is usually created and printed by the local association, on which most resales are created. Invite your attentive sellers to read the offer entirely. Since the standard form is generally unbiased, unless they have a specific question, suggest skipping the pre-printed standard clauses and review only the pertinent terms typed into the offer body and blanks.

Silence Alliance

Until the sellers are finished their reading, both agents should wait patiently – and *quietly*. Resist the urge to discuss the offer or engage in idle prattle. Such behaviour will only distract the seller and prolong the presentation by stealing their focus. And don't fidget in your seat like an impatient school kid waiting for the bell to ring. If your seller asks a question, ask them to save it until after your summation since all their questions will likely be answered at that time. Make it clear that prior to getting into details, you want them to get a general overview of the terms. Controlling the presentation is the name of the game. Even though it's their property, it's *your* party.

After confirming that *both* sellers have finished silently reading the offer, starting from the bottom of the last page and working your way up and to each previous page, briefly summarize each clause. In other words, start with the least important clauses which are typically those added nearer the end of the contract. (Offers should be drafted with clauses ordered in priority of importance – most to least.) Don't waste time re-reading the entire document because everyone has already read it, maybe more than once. If your seller begins to opine or complain about something, particularly of a confidential or strategic nature, or voices an objection, politely remind them to hold that concern for your private session. Proceed as you had coached them in your pre-meeting by asking for verbal acknowledgment of understanding – not necessarily agreement – of each clause and advance in reverse through the offer until you arrive at the price.

Question Period

Now, you can ask the buyer's agent to leave the room so you can have some privacy with your client. However, permitting them to remain a little longer provides the opportunity to question them. Before counselling your seller, it's prudent to know, for example, if the buyer is pre-approved for the mortgage, if the closing date is set in stone, if the deposit can be increased or even if the buyer is prepared to negotiate. Ask if this is their client's final offer; their verbal and/or non-verbal response can reveal much. They may prevaricate or say it's a starting point, either of which means the buyer is open to a counter. If the offer is conditional upon the sale of the buyer's home, it's critical to know the terms of that listing or if it's even listed? If so, how long has it been actively available? Is it priced correctly? If not, their offer may not be worth the paper upon which it's written. So, determine viability of any conditions.

Having the buyer agent present also gives you the chance to get some personal background on the buyer. Get a feel for them through "small talk" with their representative. How long have they been searching for a home? Do they have children? How suitable is the home? How excited are they? It's critical, though, to avoid this being perceived as an interrogation. To avoid alarming them, casually sprinkle the questions throughout the meeting. With such information, you're better equipped to sense the degree of buyer motivation. Many agents talk too much. And they may not consciously realize that you're not engaging in purely social drivel. If properly asked, subtle probing questions can provide answers that could prove pertinent to the negotiations and help you better advise your seller. Finally, so you can consult confidentially with your clients, ask the buyer's agent to leave the room and retain at least one copy of the offer.

If you're representing a buyer, I caution you to be selective about the information you share; don't gab too much. Keep your cards close. You don't want the listing agent to know, for example, that your clients are really excited. Delicately convey a subtle message that they're interested in buying the property. But unless your buyer finds the terms acceptable, they're prepared to continue their search. They may even have another home already in mind. It's all about position. Whoever appears the most anxious will lose the high ground and end up capitulating to the demands of the apparently less so.

Hot Iron

After the buyer agent has left the room, begin your private consultation by briefly summarizing the offer. It's important for the seller to understand and address the less significant terms before tackling what is usually the most contentious issue, the price. As you progress quickly through the clauses, once again beginning with the least important, ask your sellers if each is clear and acceptable. If an objection arises, make a note of it and say you'll return to it later. Objections aren't always genuine, but simply veiled attempts to slow things down. They may need time to think before making a decision and their ostensible objections may vanish into thin air. Then ask for their feelings.

Rarely do clients immediately accept all the terms without question. However, at times, it's merely their ego in play. They may just want to appear more confident and knowledgeable than they truly are. Or it may just be posturing. Never assume the seller fully understands or is comfortable with the procedure. Encourage them to ask questions; there are no dumb questions

– only dumb answers. Bear in mind that selling a home is a rarity for them. KISS – keep it simple sweetheart. (I know what you're thinking about this acronym.)

At some point, one of the homeowners may offer tea or coffee or even an alcoholic beverage. This may be an attempt to be a gracious host, but it's more likely an indirect effort to delay the inevitable decision. Let them do so, but for obvious reasons, politely decline the alcohol. Nevertheless, if they even hint they'd prefer to think about it over-night, encourage them to decide during the current meeting. Not only will the buyers probably be waiting anxiously, given sufficient time and in the light of a new day, buyers can lose enthusiasm – or even withdraw their offer. For best advantage as well as out of respect for the buyers, your seller should strike while the iron is hot.

More often than not, the seller will reject the price. If you haven't already gained acceptance of all other terms, try to narrow things down a little by asking if they approve of everything else about the offer. By so doing, you're sending the message, consciously or subconsciously, that the offer is valuable enough to treat seriously. If they restate an earlier concern, of course, you must address it. Or if they're disquieted about other lesser issues, obviously, you must deal with them too. Tackle those before getting down to the bigger concerns. But if they declare that everything else is satisfactory, they'll be hard pressed to raise those or any new objections again. Now you can focus on the main event – the price. However, if any unresolved issue is significant, such as the closing date or a condition, it may be appropriate to encompass that issue into the discussion about price.

It's important for your client to realize that just because the price is unsatisfactory, the offer should not be summarily rejected as homeowners are oft wont to do. The buyer has clearly demonstrated their sincere intent to purchase their property (don't refer to it as their *home* since that term can subliminally stimulate emotions that may only complicate matters), provided everyone can come to terms. And your sellers should return that respect by seriously entertaining their offer. After all, the buyers have affixed their signatures on the dotted line. All you have to do is negotiate the terms. In other words, it's a starting point.

Unless unusual circumstances prevail where one of the parties is under duress, or the local market strongly favours one party, the most effective method of negotiating a successful sale is to keep it balanced. Without compromise, there's normally no sale and neither party achieves their goal. To help your sellers maintain a calm demeanour, make sure they understand that it's a process, like baking bread. All the ingredients must be added in the correct proportions and appropriate steps followed to produce the final loaf. The offer is just the beginning of the negotiation process, with certain steps to be followed for the mutually intended result. Avoid any possibility of an adversarial attitude developing around the table because such a negative stance could ultimately ruin the bread.

CAR

For simplification, explain the three options: Counter-offer, Acceptance or Rejection. It would be great if all offers were accepted without contest, but alas, that's not how it usually goes in the "real" world. The order of the letters in the acronym "CAR" is typically the order in reality. Since opening bids are usually negotiable, unless the offer is ridiculous and totally unacceptable, sellers should not immediately reject them. Sometimes buyers are just greedy and stupid (or their agent was an order-taker or trying to be a hero) and typically agree to pay more. Thus, countering is normally the best response to a reasonable, but unacceptable offer.

To obtain the highest price for your sellers, try a two price strategy. During your private consultation, determine your seller's bottom line. This amount becomes their fall-back *secondary* price, below which they're prepared to lose the buyer. Then agree on a higher *primary* amount to present to the buyer agent when they return to the table. If the closing date on the offer is acceptable to your seller, have a secondary tolerable date to interlace into the counter-offer proposal. Remember that you're negotiating; it's a give and take and perception is four-fifths of reality.

When the buyer agent rejoins the presentation, tell them straight away, not that their client's offer is rejected, but that your client will *not accept* the offer. A flat refusal, which is how your news will likely be perceived, may shock them into acquiescence. Rather than accept a rejection, the buyer's agent will normally ask (beg) for a counter-offer. Make them ask for it because it will bring the power into your court; they become the supplicant. Maybe after another brief (staged) private chat with your seller (or even exchanging a predetermined code sign like a subtle mutual nod or a particular word) with a suitable preamble such as "upon further consideration", announce that your seller wants to be fair. They'll grant the agent's request for a sign-back at the higher primary amount (obviously without mentioning the secondary lower amount) and with your seller's preferred primary closing date. Expressly tell the buyer agent that your seller will agree to *all* other terms. Then, get the buyer agent's reaction – both verbal and non-verbal. Watch their body language.

"So when you are listening to somebody, completely, attentively, then you are listening not only to the words, but also to the feeling of what is being conveyed, to the whole of it, not part of it." Jiddu Krishnamurti

Fleet of Foot

At some point, you might ask the buyer agent about their client's priorities. Since the most important terms are typically price, closing date and conditions, ask which single term is most important to their client. If the buyer's priority is price and their agent seriously balks at your proposed primary counter price, ask the agent for a price proposal since they may have a glimmer of what their buyer will pay for the property. If they suggest an amount equal to or greater than your seller's already secretly established secondary figure, with a nod from your client, inform the buyer rep that the seller will agree to the agent's suggested counter price if the buyer will agree to the seller's primary closing date. Once the terms are verbally agreed, make the written changes and proceed to affix initials and signatures.

If the agent refuses or is unable to offer a suggestion, then your seller could give a little on their primary price proposal, but maybe not as low as their secondary price. Or in exchange for your seller countering at their secondary price, maybe the buyer would consent to dropping a condition or two and agree to your seller's primary closing date.

If the buyer must have a particular possession date, advise your seller to agree (if possible) to the buyer's demand for that specific date. In exchange, ask that the buyer be fair and agree to the seller's primary price, provided of course that all else is fair and reasonable. I often obtain the higher primary price for a seller just by "agreeing" to the buyer agent's request for their client's preferred closing date. This will involve your thinking quickly. Remember – it's a dance between the two variable positions – the ideal primary and the acceptable secondary. And that dance is sometimes a quick-step.

Commission Accomplished

If the buyer agent readily agrees to the initial verbal counter-offer proposal of the primary price and closing date, make the changes on the offer and proceed to the initialling and signing in a methodical manner, with the buyer agent double-checking the changes and initials. The buyer agent may not oppose your seller's primary terms, however, for a couple of reasons. They either believe their client will accept them, lack sufficient skill and experience to effectively handle the situation (they're just order-takers) or they don't care about getting the best terms for their client. If you suspect a lack of skill, to hopefully prevent a further counter-counter offer from the buyer and to save everyone a lot of time and effort, prior to making the changes on the offer, suggest the buyer agent call their client to seek verbal approval of the proposed terms. On the other hand, if your gut instinct tells you the terms may be acceptable to the buyer, be quiet and proceed with the formal sign-back.

If the buyer agent is an experienced negotiator, they may attempt to convince your client to counter at a lower price or with a closing date more acceptable to their buyer. If they sufficiently press the issue, keeping in mind the concept of give and take, with a nod from your seller, you can agree to counter at your seller's secondary price, closing date or both. Chances are you'll have just made a sale. The buyer's agent will often enthusiastically agree to present a counter-offer to their buyer with the lower secondary price and/or closing date because they believe they've successfully negotiated better terms for their client. They return to their buyer in the belief that they successfully convinced the seller to cave – and that they'll be perceived as a hero. They can boast that they saved them some money or got their preferred closing date in exchange for negotiating the price down from your seller's primary amount. The agent's enthusiastic energy usually generates acceptance.

"Aspire rather to be a hero than merely appear one." Baltasar Gracian

Fairness in Balance

If the buyer refuses to accept the secondary price, maybe your seller's expectations are unrealistic – or the buyer's are. Your seller may need guidance to objectively re-evaluate their property. If the market fails to give them their dream price, they mustn't blame you. If the market disagrees with their lofty and patently subjective estimate of value, they must accept that the market doesn't lie. They may have to adjust their expectations and reduce the asking price – or prepare themselves for no sale.

When all else fails, maybe that buyer wasn't meant to be the next owner of your seller's house. Unless it's a strong seller's market, making unreasonable demands usually proves disastrous. The same holds true for the opposite case in a buyer's market. During normal balanced conditions, however, it's give and take by both sides, like a gentle waltz. The key word is not to demand, but to negotiate. A successfully negotiated APS is usually a balanced one, a fair exchange scenario. In practice, unless duress or competitiveness due to market conditions is involved, a seller rarely gets exactly what they want, nor does a buyer usually obtain their perfect terms. Having said this, seller markets make very happy sellers and buyer markets the opposite.

"Fairness is not an attitude. It's a professional skill
that must be developed and exercised." Brit Hume

Ping Pong

If a buyer offers fairly, the odds are better that the seller will also be reasonable. If your seller refuses what you believe is a fair offer, question their commitment to selling or their understanding of their property's worth. Sometimes sellers or buyers prefer to play the multiple back and forth game, which I believe is a monumental waste of everyone's time and effort. In dual agency, of course, you have no choice since you're not permitted to intervene with price advice. Therefore, the ping pong process is inevitable. However, when acting for a buyer under single agency, and you personally participated in the presentation, you'll often have a fair idea of the viability of a counter-counter-offer to the seller. Share your opinion with your buyer. If you feel the seller's terms are unreasonable, encourage your client to sign it back or walk. On the other hand, if you feel the terms are realistic, but your buyer disagrees, that's another matter.

If your buyer must absolutely *steal* a property, you should have clarified their intention before accepting them as a client so you could have focused your efforts on finding an appropriate bargain-priced listing. If the seller is being fair, though, your buyer should be the same. If they insist that the seller's terms (especially a secondary position) are unrealistic or it's unaffordable and you feel another counter would be futile, perhaps they should re-evaluate, adjust their expectations and move on to something within their budget. Take it away from them. (See the next chapter.)

The listing agent may surprise you by calling the next day to request your buyer re-submit their offer because the sellers changed their minds. Maybe they were bluffing. It happens. Remember the two-position protocol? For a buyer to get the best possible price, they must be prepared to walk away. They mustn't attach themselves so much to any particular home that they'll agree to pay any price, especially if it's an unreasonable one.

By regularly following this negotiation protocol, your skills will become increasingly more natural and polished and your instincts more honed. Because you simplified what was likely perceived to be a complicated and uncomfortable adversarial process, you'll be a hero. And heroes get referrals. A solid and fair-minded offer presentation will mean a successful culmination of your laborious, persevering and creative efforts. The system works. Try it.

"According to the law of nature, it is only fair that no one should become richer through damages and injuries suffered by another."
Marcus Tullius Cicero

The Extra Mile

After the excitement of a successful negotiation, your "job" isn't really over. Well, I suppose, aside from processing any follow-up documents, technically it is completed. Maybe the average agent would leave it at that, but you want to be a cut above. Right? Go the extra mile for them. Unless they're numb in the chest cavity or you can clearly see the world revolving around their heads, they'll be grateful for any extra help. It's an opportune time to intensify your mutual connection. Why? They'll be even more impressed with any assistance *after* the sale is consummated because your commission has already officially been earned. Anything additional help will be perceived as kind and caring. You'll be cementing your mutual bond and with regular grooming, one that can last a lifetime.

Remind them to make arrangements for a moving service. Make sure they don't leave it to the last minute, especially if they plan to move at the end of a month, summer months in particular. Good movers are often booked long in advance. It's often less expensive to hire a moving service for a Monday through Thursday and not at month's beginning or end.

It's also a great time for homeowners to empty their garage, basement or storage locker of accumulated junk that's been around since Methuselah. Lend them garage sale signs. Why pay movers to move junk? It's time to purge, get rid of the anchors. Give your buyers a list of utilities, services, schools, local institutions and government departments to be contacted for registrations and change of address. If they're relocating to a rural property, ask the current owner for the contact info for their septic tank and well service, the guy who ploughs the laneway and if there's a pool, their service company. Garbage pick-up and recycling, the hours and location of the local dump and school bus routes and hours would be handy.

"It's never crowded along the extra mile." Wayne Dyer

When's moving day? According to a standard APS, the closing will be completed *by* 6:00 p.m. on the date fixed for completion. I've often found this misunderstood by clients as well as agents. It does *not* mean the seller has until that time to vacate the property, nor does it mean the new owner can take possession anytime that day. At the moment the actual closing occurs and title transfers, which can occur anytime *prior* to 6:00 p.m., the seller must be out and the buyer can move in.

A happy new homeowner is not so happy when their movers are forced to wait outside the house with ticking clock while the seller removes their belongings from what is now the buyer's property. The buyer may have justifiable cause for a claim against the seller, who agreed to deliver vacant possession *upon closing,* to recover these unexpected costs. To avoid this potentially expensive situation and avoid midnight moves, tell your buyer not to plan a move on the completion date. And advise sellers to ensure they've completely vacated by the expected closing time, often mid-day, or perhaps even the previous day.

Nothing says thanks more than a referral. Ask your buyers to let all their friends and family know they've bought a home! Help them (and win points) by giving them an appropriate supply of standard or better yet, custom-printed cards or an e-card with a classy exterior photo of their new home for distribution to everyone they know. Inside – beside your professional head-shot with contact information – can be *your* simple expression of gratitude for their trust and faith, along with *their* testimonial.

They may be unaware that referrals are a prime source of business. Thus, you may have to educate them. Think about this; if you generate only 10 sales annually and each of those satisfied and happy clients send you just one referral, you've doubled your volume. That's how to build a great business – without spending big bucks on advertising and promotion. And recommended clients are much easier to close because trust has already had a leg up. Be grateful for their faith and trust in you. Truly feel it and let them know. Congratulations! You're now just like a member of the family.

> *"The bond that links your true family is not one of blood,*
> *but of respect and joy in each other's life." Richard Bach*

Chapter Twenty-Five

A Manner of Closing

"I like to think of sales as the ability to gracefully persuade,
not manipulate a person or persons into a win-win situation." Bo Bennett

A Desire to Act

For as long as I can remember, the subject of closing has been controversial. Some say that consumers shouldn't be closed, that it's unethical and unnecessary. They believe in just serving – without coaxing or coercion – until a client is ready to make their own unassisted decision. Closing is sometimes viewed as a misguided attempt to unduly influence or improperly force consumers into doing something they'd rather not do. Well, nothing could be further from the truth. I've no doubt that unscrupulous agents regularly ensnare their prey and inveigle their way into getting signatures. The truth is, though, that when a buyer finally finds the right home or a seller is poised to sign a listing, when they arrive at the classic "desire to act" moment, they often need a little help with their decision. Even world political and corporate leaders, when faced with uncertainty, seek trusted counsel.

People sometimes don't realize their need for help, or their ego won't permit them to admit it. They may see a proposed move as logical, but are intimidated by the prospect of committing to it. They hesitate to make decisions, usually from a place of fear. They even sometimes make choices entirely opposite to their pre-stated wishes and intentions, including completely changing their minds about moving. (This common scenario spawned the offensive and erroneous idiom that "buyers are liars".) For some, making the emotional leap to act is a huge hurdle they may not be equipped to accomplish alone. In this chapter, you'll discover a few simple ethical techniques designed to gently assist a client – at the right moment – to make that critical decision to move forward.

"On the plains of hesitation bleach the bones of countless millions who,
at the dawn of decision, sat down to wait, and waiting, died." Sam Ewing

Since the inception of your business relationship, you've calmly, carefully and compassionately answered your client's myriad questions and gradually gained their trust and respect. Why have you gone to such effort? Because the more they trust and respect you, the easier it becomes to elicit a decision from them. When they finally reach a choice point, particularly since the early ones will be minor, a decision will happen naturally. Because you've served them honourably, their decision will seem serendipitous, as if it was meant to be.

It's far easier working with a knowledgeable client than one who's in a constant state of confusion, which is to say, a state of fear. This may seem counter-intuitive, but a knowing and confident client is far easier to close. Why? A fearful uninformed client must *totally* trust you because you'll be asking them to make a potentially frightening flight into the proverbial darkness. Unless your client is family, achieving that level of trust can take an exceedingly long time. An informed client, on the other hand, trusts you at least enough to have confidence in the reliability of the education you've provided them. So, with a subtle nudge from you – at the right moment – a decision is had. If performed with timely tact, they'll be unaware of the close. An added bonus is that a well-informed client clearly understands what they're getting into, therefore lowering *your* potential liability.

Once decision time arrives, they may suddenly ask you to draft the offer or prepare the listing, whatever the case, and that's great if that happens. But in my experience, a client exercising such initiative is as rare as a happy chicken in a poultry processing plant. Usually, I've had to ask for the offer or listing by saying something like, "Shall I draft an offer for you?" or "Are you ready to list?" or a simple "Shall we get started?" This is straight forward closing without any hype or pressure. Timing is critical, though, because they must be logically and emotionally prepared to proceed at that moment. A premature request might be perceived as a pressure tactic and be summarily rebuffed. They may even retreat completely from the precipice.

It's fairly easy to fulfill their logical needs. That's just a matter of showing them the practical reasons why it's the right choice. For example, there are no logical reasons to remain in their present house. Or the property you've shown them technically meets all their physical and affordability needs. But that's only part of the decision process. Because humans are predisposed to be change-averse, the other not insignificant challenge is the emotional decision to abandon their current comfort zone. To more easily accomplish *your* mission, they must believe they're accomplishing *theirs*, and feel reasonably comfortable with their choice. This is rarely achieved completely since any major life change is accompanied by fear and its common symptom, stress. To get as close as possible, though, you must empathically do what you can to establish a heart-felt, trusting connection.

*"The Comfort Zone is like an addictive drug. The pain of addiction
will paralyse you within its boundaries." Rodney Lovell*

Trial with a Smile

Unless you're familiar with the lake, before leaping in for a swim, do you dip your toe in to test the temperature? Well, I recommend testing your client's feelings before plunging ahead in an attempt to elicit a life-altering decision by using a trial or "small question" close. Get your toe in first.

You've found an affordable home that your timid buyers seem to really like. Instead of brashly blurting out a question about trying an offer, at the appropriate moment, ask if they would like the appliances to be included – not in *an* offer, but in *the* offer. Or if they ask if they're included, instead of replying that they *are* or *could* be, ask if they *would like* them to be included in *the* offer. Or ask a random question such as "Will you replace the broadloom with hardwood?" or "Which room will each of your kids claim?" Did you notice how I replaced the "would" with "will"? Subtle, right? That's a gentle segue from a hypothetical to actual. Or you could ask a question that can't be answered simply with a yes or no, such as, "Will your daughter attend the public school down the street or the separate school on the next block?"

A positive response, or a school name, tells you they're ready to make a decision, or very close to it. You're on the right track. Then, try another, maybe more obvious trial question such as "So, what possession do you prefer?" If they say as soon as possible, with a specific date or that it depends on what closing they can get on a sale of their present home, start preparing the offer. If they continue to demur, they're still not ready. Retreat a little. A collective silence says they're really thinking, or one spouse is quietly encouraging the other. However, with a positive response, you can say, "Okay, let's go back to the office to discuss terms." If they agree or just follow you out the door, you're pretty much there.

If a seller prospect is stalling, you could ask, "Do you want to leave the appliances with the house?" or "When do you prefer to vacate?" or "Do you feel the house is ready for market?" With a positive reply, get busy completing the listing forms. Whatever you do – don't pressure them. It's unnecessary and counter-productive. You may lose every bit of trust you've won so far. It can take ages to gain it and only moments to lose it. Use your God-given intuition; your gut will tell you when it's time. Don't miss these opportunities. Time and time again, many agents blindly jabber right past them.

*"The intuitive mind is a sacred gift, and the rational mind
is a faithful servant. We have created a society that honours
the servant and has forgotten the gift." Albert Einstein*

Groom to Assume

Another fairly self-explanatory closing method is the "assumptive close". Many people find it difficult to contain their excitement, especially if they trust you. You're quite confident you've found their postcard perfect home and the excitement in the air is palpable. Now, head back to the office without mentioning an offer and on arrival, start filling in the blanks of the draft you proactively prepared earlier that day. If they don't grab the kids and run, your mission is accomplished.

After an extensive consultation with a seller prospect, you're convinced they're ready to ditch their old digs. Don't ask if they want to proceed. Instead, casually remove the previously prepared listing forms from your briefcase and simultaneously ask for their final property tax bill, proof of ownership and survey documents and smoothly begin filling in the missing information. Once they get up to retrieve the requested documents, your close was successful.

It may seem presumptive but, well, that's the whole idea. If they're not ready to decide, they'll not comply. Just continue with your presentation until another closing opportunity presents itself. Don't be anxious. Remain unruffled and sensitive to their emotions. If they're not ready and you're too aggressive, it may backfire on you. Pay close attention. You're actually helping with their decision – one way or the other – without specifically asking for the offer or the listing. This close can also be used in conjunction with a trial close by asking the small question first.

> *"Nothing gives one person so much advantage over another as to remain always cool and unruffled under all circumstances." Thomas Jefferson*

Take Away

Here's another technique that has proven highly effective, particularly with buyers. If you feel in your heart they're ready, that the home is perfect for them, but they're hesitating from fear, try taking it away from them by saying, "Maybe this isn't the right home for you. Perhaps we should continue searching for something more suitable." If they're unsure, you'll have lost nothing and they obviously won't feel pressured into acting against their will. Move on until the next closing occasion arrives. However, if the home-buying decision-maker (usually the wife) loves it, as your secret ally, they'll overtly or covertly do their best to convince the more obdurate half to go along.

During an offer negotiation, your buyer dithers when asked to seriously consider what you've identified as the seller's final counter-offer, which you believe to be fair and reasonable. After a brief pause, tell them that since they seem reluctant to accept it, maybe they should reject it, that perhaps it isn't the right home. Or if it's your seller, suggest that maybe these buyers aren't right for their property. Usually, the decisive spouse will kick the prevaricating partner under the table and agree to accept the offer.

"In my house, I'm the boss. My wife is just the decision maker." Woody Allen

Puppy Dog

With the knowledge accumulated about your clients, combined with a solid, honest relationship, you sincerely feel the move would be really good for them, but the sound of their knees knocking under the table is clearly audible. What do you do? You've answered all their questions about listing or offering on a special home, as the case may be, and they seem keen to proceed. However, they're having difficulty with the final decision.

You've attempted a trial close, but the clear signals weren't yet there. You've asked a direct closing question such as, "Are you ready to list?" or "Shall I draft the offer?" and they're still hesitant. Maybe the question is too big too soon. Sometimes, the anxiety of moving quashes the original inspiration. Now what? Well, you already know their why; now remind them by trying the popular technique known adorably as the "puppy dog" close.

If it's for a listing, in a series of brief questions, seek verbal confirmation of their motivation. Now that the kids have moved out, maybe their home is too large. Or it's too small for their growing family. Maybe they want to escape their nosy noisy neighbour or the heavy maintenance of the gardens. Or they've grown to dislike city life. If they're downsizing, ask if they still like the idea of having a chunk of cash in the bank and owning a home mortgage-free. Would they enjoy spending more time on the golf course or travelling instead of maintaining a large property? Or would they appreciate each of their kids having their own room, with the associated absence of sibling rivalry? Whatever their motivation, wait for their corroboration between questions. Ask the questions to which you already know the answers will be yes. Obviously, you'll know what to ask since you've already established their prime reasons for moving.

After they've answered all these affirming smaller questions with yes, end the series with the big question; "Okay, shall we begin the paperwork?" Or don't even ask; use the assumptive close and start filling in the listing contract. If they don't stop you, then you've helped them make the final decision without them having to expressly say so. Once they realize they're over the hump, they'll be grateful. It's like a nervous automobile passenger who closes their eyes as they approach a big bend in the road. Before they know it, the driver has safely rounded the curve. Much less stressful.

The process is pretty much the same for a buyer, except the questions obviously differ. You've attempted to close using one of the previous methods, but they prevaricate. It happens, not necessarily because it's the wrong home, but because they're afraid of change. It's critical, though, for the property to be right, so don't try it on the wrong home. Start gently with a series of questions such as "It's affordable for you, right? Do you understand that if your lender believes you can't afford this home, they'll not approve a loan? You like the neighbourhood, right? You do like the architectural style? Do you agree that it's the ideal size? You like the hardwood floors? You appreciate the close proximity to schools, am I right? The garage is large enough for your purposes?" Ask as many of these small questions as you feel is necessary, one right after another – and await their hopefully brief reply between questions. Once again, because you qualified them so well at the outset, ask questions which you're already aware will be answered with a yes.

After they've answered affirmatively to this rapid-fire series, it would be extremely difficult for them to suddenly change direction from a repeatedly positive position to a negative one. They're unlikely to answer no when you finally pop the question whether to draft the offer. It's against basic human nature. At some level, be it conscious or subconscious, they'll realize it is indeed the right home because all their answers were yes. They may even begin to smile with that dawning realization. Then close with a small question such as "How much do you have for a deposit?" or "When do you want to move in?" or just use the assumptive close and start completing the form. Don't send out negative energy by showing any frustration. Be patient, calm and methodical. Maintain a light, positive attitude throughout the attempt. If it fails, they weren't ready or it's the wrong property. Then take it away from them.

"Excellence is not a skill. It is an attitude." Ralph Marston

Focus-Pocus

When presenting an offer or counter and your client refuses to accept it, they may be feeling overwhelmed. Try to narrow things down by asking them to specify the particular issue of concern. Then ask if that's their only concern. If there's another, ask if these are their only two concerns, and so on. Get them to focus their objections. At some point, they'll say they have no other objections. Then confirm that *all* the remaining terms are acceptable. Normally by that point, they'll say yes. If those few issues can be resolved satisfactorily, ask if they'd accept the offer.

Now deal with their concerns one at a time, beginning with the least important. Discuss it thoroughly to determine if it's really an objection and not just a stall tactic. Dig into it to see if it can be eliminated; issues can vanish into thin air. Repeat for the other objections. If unable to clear them, perhaps a counter-offer is necessary, in which case you've now established its terms. Conversely, if you gain their agreement to these previously objectionable terms, as I said earlier, they can't logically raise them again, nor any other objections since they already admitted everything else was fine. If they had previously declared that they'd proceed if a resolution was found, their rational minds understand they have a deal. If they continue to procrastinate, they're just fearful, and that's a different kettle of fish. It may be time to move on to another property or for you to accept that your seller isn't truly committed to moving. Try taking it away from them.

When communicating with a potential seller, use the objective term of house or property instead of home. For buyers, it's the opposite. Home has an emotional connotation, a warm, fuzzy feeling. For a seller who needs to emotionally detach themselves from their home, the use of a more dispassionate term will consciously or subconsciously help them separate from those sticks and bricks.

Practice makes perfect. Regular exercise of these effective communication techniques – for that is essentially what they are – will bring you a step closer to being a great closer. Practice with a colleague. You'll both develop that muscle and reap the seemingly magical benefit of ethical and honourable influence over others. Be a gentle persuader.

"Take advantage of every opportunity to practice your communication skills so that when important occasions arise, you will have the gift, the style, the sharpness, the clarity and the emotions to affect other people." Jim Rohn

Chapter Twenty-Six

Presentation Persuasion: Winning the Listing

"Motivation is the art of getting people to do what you want them to do because they want to do it." Dwight D. Eisenhower

Realty agents are usually happy, if not thrilled, for the chance to present to a prospective seller and gratefully do so free of charge. They hope to convince them to list – realistically – and hope the property sells and hopefully closes successfully, after which they hope to finally receive a sizable fee for their efforts. That's a lot of hoping. As expert entrepreneurs, they operate on the premise that the potential reward is worth the risk. I suggest, though, that you not rely so heavily on hope.

Before accepting an invitation to consult, it's smart to discern why the homeowner wants an evaluation. They may be serious about selling; if this be true, go for it. They could, however, just be curious about their home's market value and have no immediate plans to list. They may need a CMA or Letter of Opinion of Value for a credit application, matrimonial conflict or court case. Ask if they're seeking opinions from other agents. Sometimes they choose to list with the agent who promises the highest price or the lowest fee. So you can be properly prepared, it's only fair they disclose their intentions. Or perhaps you might refuse to play their game; it's always your choice. In any case, you should make an informed business decision.

If they honestly disclose they have no plans to sell anytime soon, before you commit to the task, you could request a flat fee for service, to be deducted from any commission if the property is listed and sold with you, say, within 6 months. If they agree, to prevent possible future conflict, confirm in writing. You may not mind working for free, but don't allow them to take unfair advantage of you. Of course, you could still do the work and hope they remember your generosity, but don't count on it. Memories can be short, especially for those infected with Money Madness.

Educated Guessing

What's a property worth? It's a common question not easily or always accurately answered because it demands the conversion of *subjective opinion* into *objective fact*. Unless you possess physic foresight, it's impossible to foresee. The inherent nature of an open market, hence market value, is dependent upon the Law of Supply and Demand. This most basic law roughly states that an increase in supply can *deflate* market values, whereas an increase in demand can *inflate* them, and of course, the opposite holds true. And supply and demand boil down to subjectivity. Nevertheless, even though a CMA is far from definitive, it's one of the foundational pillars upon which our industry was built and can undoubtedly provide clues to establishing a *rough* estimate of value.

Offering a verbal opinion without research is just an unsubstantiated guess. It might ultimately prove accurate, but why amateurishly gamble with a homeowner's foremost asset? If a prospect insists on your best informal estimate, at least preface it with a disclaimer that it's just that – an educated guess. Since you may be unaware of a recent sale that could significantly affect their property's value, favourably or otherwise, it shouldn't be relied upon for a major decision. Also, without thorough research, why would they necessarily believe you? A meticulous investment of resources is the path to credibility and trust.

What you create for a prospective new and sometimes existing seller (or buyer) is not unlike a report prepared by a certified appraiser. However, there are a couple of significant differences. A residential appraiser is paid a flat fee to produce – with or without a personal property inspection – a written standard form report containing a precise considered opinion of value based on historical data. For lenders and lawyers, whose needs normally demand specific and easily substantiated calculated amounts, form appraisals are considered standard procedure. But unlike appraised value, market value is more abstract, more subjective. The same basic methodology is involved, but the evaluation process goes to what I feel is, at least for agents and most consumers, a more practical level.

Since you're actively working the market, your instincts may be more honed than those of someone mining data from behind a desk. You're familiar with competing or sold listings because you actually viewed them. The ultimate sale price of your prospective seller's home may differ substantially from an appraised value (or even your original estimate) since a formal appraisal doesn't involve exposing the property to a competitive marketplace where virtually anything can happen. Just as stock market bidders can frantically push a share price beyond its arithmetically calculated book value, fervent realty buyers can drive prices into nose-bleed territory.

Buyer agents often prepare either a formal or informal CMA to help their clients settle on an offer price. Usually, it's a verbal opinion, but could be substantiated by actual data. It's a great tool, not only to help a buyer make an informed decision, but to help you earn credibility and trust.

> *"I'm not upset that you lied to me; I'm upset that from now on,*
> *I can't believe you." Friedrich Nietzsche*

As an active trader who's familiar with the local market and prevailing economic conditions, you have a fair idea of the approximate value of a prospective new listing before even starting the work or entering the foyer. However, it's important to polish your opinion by carefully analyzing the neighbourhood sales history. You begin by checking the active, sold and expired listings of properties most closely resembling the subject in building and lot size, architectural style, age, features, upgrades, physical condition and most importantly, location. Keep in mind that a comparable property, virtually identical to the subject but backing onto railway tracks or edging a busy corner or poorly maintained could have a lesser value.

Although CMA reports can vary in scope, from brief summaries to multi-page tomes, on paper or in pixels, a typical report will contain the following:

> ➢ **Actives:** Listings currently for sale in the same or similar area. Resist drawing direct conclusions solely from these because competing sellers can subjectively set their own list prices, which are often unrealistically high. A competitive listing can, nevertheless, help determine an asking price for *your* new listing. Take advantage of the other agent's experience with *their* listing. If it's been exposed for a protracted period with no sale, it's likely overpriced. Don't duplicate their mistake.
>
> ➢ **Conditionally Sold:** A property is reported conditionally sold when a seller accepts an offer in which the buyer needs time to fulfill a specific requirement before committing. Terms of the APS are kept confidential until conditions are fulfilled, but such sales can denote market trend. Since an offer was generated, assume the asking price was fair. Therefore, it may still serve as a comparable.
>
> ➢ **Sold Firm:** The best comparables are recently sold listings in the same area. Adjust your estimate to reflect improvements or deficiencies relative to the subject. Consider the Days On Market (DOM) before selling. If long, they may have initially been over-priced. When checking listing history, if they had to reduce, avoid the same mistake. Create an average sale price report and compare your new listing to the average. Superior subject? Expect more money. Inferior? Less.
>
> ➢ **Unsold:** Expired, cancelled and suspended listings are properties that failed to sell. Usually, it's for one reason – they're overpriced. However,

listings are withdrawn for various secondary reasons such as change of plans. But normally, the market disagreed with the seller's opinion of value and buyers saw insufficient value to justify the list price.

➤ **Conclusion:** After reviewing the data, made the necessary calculations with adjustments, finalized a statistical analysis and applied market savvy, you arrive at an estimated market value range.

Arrange a Range

After your diligent deliberations, to further enhance your opinion, prior to your consultation appointment, consider scoping out the exterior and streetscape. Is the front garden neatly manicured? Is the garage door updated or the original rust-scalloped door? How's the general neighbourhood? Are the adjacent properties well maintained or dishevelled? Depending on the severity of the symptoms, your preconceived opinion might migrate in a southerly direction.

After you've researched and refined your preliminary opinion of value, resist the urge to narrow it to a specific amount. Such pinpointing may open the door to future seller disappointment, bad feelings – and no sale – because homeowners often tend to cling to that original promised amount or base their moving plans on it. As bearer of bad tidings, if you later have to inform them their house is worth less than you thought, they may feel they're losing money, which actually never existed. Of course, it was just an opinion, not a guarantee, but they might not understand.

Instead, offer a *market value range*, the breadth of which is determined by the relative uniqueness of the home. Is it a typical production-builder house on a postage stamp lot, not unlike all the others in the row? Or is it a custom-built or heritage home on a leafy lot? Or maybe it's a distinctive country property. The price spread will also depend on how active your local market is at the moment. Slow market or custom or country home? Broad spread. Busy market or "cookie cutter" home? Narrow spread. By avoiding specificity, if a price reduction becomes necessary, it can still be within or close to that spread. And a reduction within a previously discussed range is often more easily obtained. In any event, forewarn them of the possibility (or inevitability) of one or more price adjustments.

The Consultation

With appropriate forms in your briefcase, a lawn sign and lockbox in your trunk and hope in your heart, you're confident and fully prepared. As you step through the front door, you're greeted in a beautiful foyer with a fantastic mosaic tile floor, rich wood paneling and etched bevelled glass doors to an elegant dining room. Suddenly, your opinion heads north. Okay, the owners of an outwardly unkempt property aren't outdoorsy and they fired the gardener. But while inspecting the basement, a whiff of dampness brings another negative tweak. Down it goes again. Oh, but you're then left breathless by the sight of a dazzling gourmet kitchen featuring Brazilian granite counter-tops and rich cherry cabinetry. Up goes your yet unspoken opinion.

My example is clearly exaggerated, but I'm sure you get the idea. Think like an impartial buyer, but consider the emotional element. Will the property enthuse or bore? In the final analysis, your ability to view objectively, and think on your feet, is where you justifiably earn a large portion of your fee. It's that important. If you like percentages, try 40 percent at this stage, another 40 percent during offer negotiation(s) and the remaining 20 percent with everything else.

Once you've completed the inspection, with or without the homeowner traipsing around after you, gather everyone at the dining table for your carefully prepared CMA presentation. Its format might be a sophisticated *PowerPoint* production on your tablet or the homeowner's television. Or it might be a collection of unpretentious hi-lighted print-outs of comparables, scribbled with notes upon which you reason your case. Or it could be a full-colour customer-friendly portfolio with appropriate charts, graphs, testimonials, business bio and services rendered, along with feature sheets of *your* previously sold listings (with private information redacted). If they choose to defer their decision, leaving an expertly prepared booklet behind serves as a silent sales aid that, in your absence, will reinforce your professionalism.

To thwart any possibility of their summarily bringing the meeting to an end, don't lead with your value judgment. Remember the power of curiosity. Keep them wondering. Even though you've already done the mental arithmetic, reserve your opinion until you've had more opportunity to bond. By reviewing the comparables with them, working up from the lowest sale prices, you'll not just be *telling* them; you'll be *showing* them how your opinion evolved. Going through them again will also serve as a refresher for you and at the same time, ease them into drawing a similar conclusion. Your opinion, when finally given voice, will become not just the view of a stranger, but a conclusion based on a solid, honest rationale and credible substantiation. If they're rational, your prospect will reach a similar conclusion. In summarizing, don't pull any punches. Tell them what they *need* to know which isn't necessarily what they *want* to hear. Honesty is always the best policy.

You may perchance find yourself competing with other agents who have unknowingly erred or deviously opined with an excessively high opinion. Agents in the latter group rationalize their behaviour by thinking that if it fails to sell, at least they'll benefit from sign calls and Internet hits. Avoid both practices; the former because it's obviously incompetent and the latter because it's unethical. Don't "buy" the listing with the intention of seeking a price reduction a few weeks later. Since the market is the final arbiter of value, even with a realistic opening list price, you may need that price change anyway. By innocently or maliciously misleading a homeowner, you'd not only be ill serving them, but also accepting a listing that's doomed to expire. A faded lawn sign on a stale listing does not enhance your neighbourhood reputation, nor earn you a commission paid by a happy homeowner.

At the best of times, evaluating real estate is an inaccurate science. Reinforce the fact that an opinion is simply an educated guess, and that in an open market, anything can happen, favourable or otherwise. When all is said and done, whatever price their property obtains will be fair market value. Assure them that you'll do everything practically possible to make it as high as the market will bear. You're on the same team.

Wishful Thinking

"It is psychological law that whatever we desire to accomplish, we must impress upon the subjective or subconscious mind." Orison Swett Marden

It's impossible for a homeowner to escape their personal bias about their private home. And because of this lack of objectivity, they're unable to rationally evaluate it. After all, their castle, furnished and decorated to their own exacting standards, holds memories and emotions. Perfect, but perhaps not for an average buyer. During my career, out of thousands of proud and not so proud homeowners, I recall only two who needed gentle persuading to list higher than they'd anticipated. Fortunately, they trusted me, because I succeeded in obtaining the higher price. Were they happy? You bet. Virtually every other former seller has held unrealistically inflated opinions about their property – some ridiculously high. By the way, when assessing your own home, you're no exception.

Your seller's subjective estimation is like a cake, baked with haphazard exposure to newspaper ads, neighbourhood rumours and iced with wishful thinking. They could have erroneously concluded that their *superior* home was worth a lot more than those *inferior* ones on the next street. They might be shocked by the suggestion that the high tension power corridor abutting their yard might adversely affect its value. They may have disregarded their old leaky concrete pool, corner lot with no rear yard or the messy backyard over the fence. They may be desensitized to their home's low level of hygiene or threadbare broadloom. Or they expect a 120% return on the cost of improvements as claimed feasible by certain TV "reality" shows. Or they base their opinion on a perceived need to affordably make a move. Or they originally over-paid for the property. It's your responsibility to objectively assess how an impartial buyer – who lacks any emotional attachment – will perceive it. A homeowner needs an honest and objective, hype-free opinion from someone they trust.

By definition, fair market value (FMV) is the highest price estimated in terms of money which a property will bring a willing seller if exposed for sale on the open market, allowing a reasonable time to locate a willing buyer who agrees to purchase with the knowledge of all the uses to which the property is adapted and for which it can be legally used and with neither party acting under necessity, compulsion or peculiar and special circumstances. Wow! That was technical. Allow me to simplify; to determine FMV, the homeowner must list it for sale.

Your new seller must fully understand that unless you're able to foretell the future, your estimate is just that – an estimate. It's an informed guesstimate based on researched facts combined with instincts, market knowledge and experience. At the end of the day, though, FMV is determined only upon a sale. At that moment, it usually becomes market price, which is an accomplished or historic fact as the amount paid or to be paid for a property in a particular transaction. In an efficient market system involving willing, informed parties acting rationally and prudently, given reasonable periods of time without undue influences, market price tends to closely align with FMV. However, in a hot seller's market, when buyers are acting aggressively and emotionally – that is to say subjectively – market price often excessively exceeds fair market value.

> *"To look at ourselves from afar, to make the subjective*
> *suddenly objective: this gives us a psychic shock." Julian Barnes*

The Gist of List

Once you've established an anticipated sale price range, move on to the critical – completely separate – conversation about asking price. Whereas the estimated market value range includes the "hoped for" sale price, the list price is the bait, the inducement for buyers to view the property.

There are two schools of thought here. The first is to list high and periodically reduce the price until a sale is achieved or your sellers voluntarily or involuntarily change their plans. This is the more common method because it's easier to placate a naive seller who wants to *try* first for a higher price. But without a price reduction, listings often end in expiry. Because you seemed to share their inflated value perception of their home, your seller will love you during the honeymoon. But as weeks crawl by with no nibbles, love rapidly fades to frustration, anger or indifference. And a loss of faith usually translates into a loss of listing. The second school of thought involves putting your best foot forward, so to speak, by listing realistically at the outset.

If you perform a statistical analysis of the list prices of sold comparable properties, the original asking prices prior to any reductions and the DOM, you'll probably discover that the properties that were realistically listed from day one, all sold relatively quickly – without the need for price adjustments. Typically, the listings that lingered longer started out too high and had to be reduced, sometimes more than once, before finally attracting a sale. There's only one conclusion; presuming that every sold listing gets FMV, the list price merely determines how long it takes to get it. In other words, the more over-priced the listing, the longer it will take to sell. In an average active market, with a realistic original list price, a property should sell fairly fast. Or after one or more price reductions, it should sell when the asking price finally reaches sensible territory.

Even though you or your seller may not consider it important, setting the right asking price is, after market evaluation, your second most critical function in the entire listing process. Whether they reject your opinion or you opine incorrectly, if a homeowner fails to list right, they may grow long in the tooth waiting for a solid bite. They may believe that asking price is almost irrelevant because a buyer can opt to offer whatever they choose. This is true, but it most certainly is *very* relevant. Generating an offer early in the game often renders a higher sale price because the seller – with a brand new listing – is in a superior negotiating position. The property has not been long on the market; it's not a stale listing. Also, in a hot market, the odds are higher that with an enticingly fair asking price, a buyer competition could ensue. And since buyers prefer to avoid a competition, if the list price is realistic, they'll get out early to view it before a feeding frenzy forms – and offer fairly, sometimes generously.

The asking price can make the difference in not only how long it takes to sell, if it even sells, but also indirectly, what final sale price is actually achieved. It's not complex; price too high and there's no interest from buyers. By setting the listing price lower, but still too high, your listing may get attention and showings, but buyers refuse to waste their time or risk insulting a homeowner. Remind your seller; as *they* have the advantage of your sage price advice, buyers have the same benefit from their own agents. In years past, naive buyers were more easily duped by unscrupulous agents. But thanks to the Internet, our evolving industry standards and the popularity of buyer agency, buyers are no longer so ignorant. Of course, set a list price too low and your client could conceivably under-sell their home, or depending on market conditions and the property, generate multiple bids.

Plainly put, list price determines the volume of buyer activity. And a high volume of viewings obviously increases the chances of a quick sale at a better price. To demonstrate, here's an exaggerated example: if a home is realistically valued at, say, $400,000 and you price it at $700,000, how much action would it generate? Obviously not much. And conversely, what kind of interest would result from a list of $100,000? Point made.

The problem with the policy of accepting over-priced listings is that the seller loses the advantage of typically the most active period in the selling process – the first couple of weeks, or longer, depending on your local market conditions. There's always an average DOM; know it and use it. Statistics can be powerfully convincing. Unless your market is depressed, there's usually an existing pool of buyers scouring the marketplace for new listings and price reductions. Thanks to the fantastic exposure provided by the Internet, they've already discovered, maybe viewed and rejected current inventory. When a new listing appears, but in their or their agent's opinion, it's not priced competitively, they ignore it and/or await a price reduction. However, if the asking price is fair, they contact their own or the listing agent to arrange an immediate viewing.

Have you ever had a buyer ask how long a home has been listed for sale? I'd say you'll answer yes, many times. If you told them it's a brand new listing and they liked it, they often made a reasonable offer immediately – or should have if they were smart. If they'd felt that the DOM was excessive, they may have automatically wondered or even asked why no one else wanted it. A stale property listing, even at a subsequently realistic lower price, often brings buyer indifference because they suspect it's over-priced, has serious defects or is owned by an unreasonable seller – or all three. If they're still interested, count on any bid being low. Innumerable listing contracts expire due to improbable list prices and associated unreasonably long market exposure. Listings that have been around for months on end with numerous price reductions – or none at all – if they sell, will attract a price below what might have been obtained if the seller had listed reasonably in the first place. Expired listings abound.

When your market strongly favours sellers, a homeowner can – within reason – price their property however they wish. The actual asking price is less critical when there are oodles of eager buyers chomping at the bit to bid. But when a buyer or balanced market prevails, when listings are plentiful, the list price is definitely a key factor in attracting attention. A reasonable asking sends the message to your peers that your seller is fair, serious and accepts your professional advice, which in turn, encourages showings. No agent truly enjoys negotiating with a stubborn or ill-informed homeowner or with a listing agent who, out of ignorance or apathy, failed to accurately advise their seller. Without viewings, you're guaranteed no sale. Do you want your listing to attract buyers? Thoroughly educate yourself, and when establishing list price, advise your sellers to be fair and reasonable. Often, all it takes is to be courageously better at your job.

"Don't wish it were easier, wish you were better." Jim Rohn

List or Sell?

To win a listing, hungry, unprepared or unskilled agents sometimes succumb to a homeowner's demand for what is an improbable sale price, and proceed to pray for a miracle. It's the easiest route, but rarely the wisest. Or not expecting it to sell without a price reduction, treat it as a lead generator. Pragmatically speaking, even though I believe the latter to be an ignoble practice, it can be a cheaper way to add to your stable of buyers than newspaper advertising.

Sellers fall into two categories; those who are genuinely committed to selling and will negotiate FMV for their property, and those who refuse to sell unless they get their price. Most expired listings obviously fall into the second group. Before accepting a listing, determine into which category your prospective seller falls. If the odds of selling are poor, seriously consider declining the listing. Or if the would-be, but unrealistic sellers are of earnest intent, you could relent and accept it, but with provisions. In exchange for consenting to list their property, they understand and agree that you'll extend a minimum of effort and expenditure during the marketing process. Or if the listing fails to sell within sequential time frames of, say 30 days, they agree in advance to a series of price reductions, one for each of those frames.

In most circumstances, however, the agent accepts the listing and implores the seller to be realistic. The problem is, though, that without a solid trust relationship, the seller refuses to accept any responsibility for the failure and blames the agent for not performing a miracle. They reject your expert advice and rebuff your assertion that their listing was effectively exposed as much as every other MLS® system listing. They refuse to accept that the market doesn't lie and that nobody was interested. They desperately cling to their fantasy that the right buyer with faraway eyes has yet to discover their listing. And when the listing expires, after they're given the same lower estimate by a competitor, they're finally convinced. They then list with your competitor, often at the same lower price you'd recommended. To add salt to the wound, following the installation of your competitor's lawn sign, the property sells quickly! Surprise! You lost the listing and all your time, effort and expense was for nought. The other brokerage gets the credit for the sale and in the minds of the neighbours who watched your sign fade in the sun, your agency failed.

Before accepting a listing or even a re-list of a competitor's listing, so that you can make an informed business decision, ask your prospective new seller if they're interested in selling or just listing. And when they look at you with a puzzled expression, explain the difference.

> *"Nothing is worth doing unless the consequences may be serious."*
> George Bernard Shaw

The Perfect Storm

In a strong seller's market, a popular strategy, as described earlier, is to deliberately encourage a buyer competition by under-pricing and delaying the presentation of offers for a week or so. Critical ingredients are a trusting seller, an expert and trustworthy agent and a special property. Call it the perfect storm. It's usually a hectic, revolving door week. But if the strategy works, you'll be presenting multiple offers to a very happy and possibly overwhelmed homeowner. But beware; without the correct conditions, it could back-fire. If only one buyer offers because the hotly anticipated perfect storm proves to be a washout, then you misjudged. The property could end up selling at a lower price. Or you may have to raise the list price, which can discourage future activity.

On the other hand, sometimes a seller prefers to steer clear of an invasive storm in favour of a calm sale. An exclusive listing may be more appropriate for a fragile elderly homeowner, for example, who may not be able to handle being besieged. Or if you already have a prospect, there's no need to share with competitors. Your seller, of course, must agree to the limited exposure. But you could be disserving your seller. Yes, the fee may be a little lower. But by not exposing the property to the much larger marketplace, they could miss a chance for a multiple bid or even one enthusiastic buyer with deep pockets. Maybe a higher sale price could have been realized to make that small commission savings seem paltry.

Realty Reality

At no other point during the listing term will you have a greater opportunity to have an impact in the marketplace than when your listing is first uploaded onto the MLS® system and you hammer that sign into the lawn for the first time. It's in the best interests of your seller – and ultimately your own – to be sensible when estimating FMV and setting an asking price, which as I said, are two distinctively separate functions. It's the perfect time to strategize, clarify expectations and set reasonable goals. It's also the smartest time to get a price reduction.

Be honest and candid during the evaluation process and help them slip their feet into the cool objective shoes of a prospective buyer. For optimum results, the opening list price should be fairly close to the anticipated sale price. If your seller expresses higher hopes, they'll be reluctant later to lower those expectations because they'll perceive the reduction as a loss of equity. Since you›ll not sell the property without buyers viewing it, choose the right bait. After a prolonged period of little activity, you certainly won't enjoy seeking a price reduction from a disgruntled homeowner. And if that request happens to serendipitously coincide with a bona fide offer from your own buyer who feels their offer terms are fair – and you entirely agree with them – you may have a major challenge convincing your seller that the offer is realistic. They may feel your allegiance has shifted to your new buyer client or that you selfishly want to earn a double commission. Tough sell. Pricing it correctly in the first place might have been easier.

Be worthy of their trust and fulfill your marketing responsibilities as promised. But if those efforts prove fruitless, your seller must understand that the market alone will be the decisive arbiter of FMV. If they refuse to accept responsibility for their decisions or disregard your price recommendations, they can blame the market and themselves – not you. After all, you're only the interpreter of a market that is never wrong. They'd be wise to accept realty reality by setting a fair asking price up front and move on with their life.

"Few delights can equal the presence of one whom we trust utterly."
George MacDonald

Chapter Twenty-Seven

Daddy-More-Bucks

*"Any man who can drive safely while kissing a pretty girl
is simply not giving the kiss the attention it deserves."*
Albert Einstein

Bees & Butterflies

For a plant to procreate, it must entice pollinators to come hither. This miraculous feat of nature is accomplished by producing attractive fragrant blossoms. If you want to sell your car, what better way to improve the odds than a good shining, maybe even tune-up, so it looks and runs its absolute best. What do you do to prepare for a first date? Ensure you're well coifed and groomed. Well, to best attract passing buyers, wouldn't it make sense to apply the same logic by ensuring your seller's property is as appealing as possible?

Many new sellers mistakenly let nothing, including the marketing of their home, interrupt their daily routine and do absolutely zilch to improve its show-ability. Hence, they typically need coaching on how to effectively prepare, prettify and maintain their home prior to and during the listing term. In addition to more significant undertakings, this guidance should include homework to be done immediately prior to each viewing, such as vacuuming, making beds and polishing plumbing fixtures. A seller's contribution – be it enthusiastic or lackadaisical – helps or hinders a sale and has a direct effect on not only how long their property remains unsold, but also the ultimate sale price.

Remember that a buyer's decision is based primarily on how they *feel* about it. Their level of excitement about making your seller's home their own is, within reason, directly proportional to how deeply they dig into their pockets. Successful marketing preparation and culmination relies upon a simple formula: a pinch of cash + a dash of imagination + a stirring of creativity + a pound of effort + a dose of objectivity = a successful sale.

Renovate & Elevate

When someone buys a principle residence, they don't primarily think of it as an investment, but as a home. Thus, any major improvements are usually for lifestyle enhancement. How those renovations might affect the eventual sale price may not even occur to them. Nevertheless, owning a home is indeed a great investment vehicle. But unlike a corporate stock, the investor can physically live in it. And unlike the return on a passive stock investment, upon which the casual investor has zero influence, an owner's home improvement choices – as Goldilocks would say may be too small, too large or just right – can critically impact the final return on that realty investment. The eventual sale price will obviously depend on market inflation, but also on the quality, extent and frequency of maintenance and upgrades.

There's no doubt that major endeavours can be expensive. The good news is, though, that renovating can be done at least in part, at someone else's expense. By shrewdly choosing projects reputed to generate higher returns, such as kitchen, bathroom or landscaping, a significant portion of the costs may be passed on to the next owner by way of a higher sale price. It's common knowledge that sharp, updated homes usually command premium prices. But over the years, if a homeowner habitually neglects their property, when the time comes to sell, to optimize a sale price, they may have to play expensive catch-up by swiftly spending some serious cash that could have been incrementally invested – and benefits enjoyed – during their occupancy. If they refuse to spend a dime on their home before listing, since many buyers prefer to avoid the time and expense of renovation, you'd better prepare your sellers for possible lower buyer interest and corresponding sale price in the lower end of your recommended value range.

A homeowner often has resources from which to draw for renovation expenditures, such as a home equity credit line. A buyer, on the other hand, may not be able to afford to do the work because all their available cash is necessarily devoted to their down payment. Thus, even if they see the potential in the house, they may have to pass on the property. If they choose to offer anyway, with the guidance of their agent and home inspector, a prudent buyer will discount the offered price to reflect the cost of doing those repairs and renovations personally or with the assistance – and expense – of a hired contractor. And to compensate for the nuisance factor, they may even deduct a little extra.

There are two categories of buyers who typically show interest in a deficient property. The first wants an affordable home to live in while doing the renovation work personally as resources become available. They'll probably have a minimum down payment and will justify offering on a "fixer-upper" if they can buy it cheap enough. The second is a shrewd investor/renovator who's looking for a bargain and refuses to pay anywhere near the asking price because they plan to "fix it and flip it". Their carefully calculated offer would probably be even lower than that of the novice renovator.

Should your seller prospect invest their resources before listing? It depends. If the property is physically substandard, they should do *some* work. If they've neglected it during their tenure, it's safe to assume it's at least tired, if not in desperate need of tender loving care. Things wear out. Fashion and styles change. New trends appear, become popular and then disappear, only to be engulfed by the next big consumer crave wave. If their home exhibits pride of ownership and has been periodically upgraded and regularly maintained, you may have few improvement recommendations. It may be market ready without significant effort or expenditure.

Your seller should be careful about over-improving for the neighbourhood. They don't want to spend so much that they're forced to demand a price that excessively exceeds the average market value range of neighbouring properties. I've seen incredibly beautiful homes languish for months at a price that would have been a fair asking price or even a bargain in a more upscale area. How much is too much? It's difficult to say with any accuracy. However, unless you're in a declining market, it's likely that whatever reasonable amount they agree to spend, they'll recover at least some of it. And they may be blessed with a quicker sale.

Care to Prepare

An easy way to attract a buyer's eye and enhance market value is to improve the property's curb appeal. Forgive the cliché, but one never gets a *second* chance to make a *first* impression. Due to the emotional element, it's important that a home not only look great on-line, but that it imparts a favourable first feeling on a buyer's initial approach. Upon entering the home, they'll wander around and – consciously or unconsciously – seek to justify that first impression. If they're disappointed at the curb, they'll instinctively look with a critical eye for more off-putting aspects to justify that first ghastly impression. Of course, the opposite holds true if their first inkling is encouraging.

Your sellers needn't necessarily spend a bundle, but a few basics might really add to the allure and help project pride of ownership. While minor front elevation improvements may not add much monetary value, they may add a little. And if the home is well priced, attractive curb appeal and great exterior photos can contribute to more activity in the form of sign and website calls – and a speedier sale.

As you know, most buyers these days insist on a home inspection. Any major or minor damage or deficiencies – patent or latent – will be noted on the report. So, if an ancient, yellowing list of repairs is clinging tenaciously to your seller's fridge, it's time to get crackin', especially if it's a lot of small stuff. If an inspector's report includes no *major* problems, but is littered with *minor* stuff, the buyer may still waive the condition, but only if the seller does the work at their own expense or reduces the purchase price. Anticipating this, your seller might as well take pre-emptive action and get it done at the outset.

Do your sellers have a cat, dog, turtle, fish, snake or other exotica? With the possible exception of clawed door casings, unsightly fur-balls, carpet urine stains or conspicuously soiled litter trays, a cat is usually not a problem, unless it's one that roars. Dogs, however, present other challenges. Few people enjoy being welcomed by a slobbering, sniffing, barking canine, friendly or otherwise, trying to jam his snout into their crotch or jumping all over them in sheer delight that someone (who cares who it is!) is finally home. Obviously, if Rover is defensive, your sellers will have to be home for every showing or make arrangements with Uncle Herb. Small dogs can be a problem too, if for no other reason than being irritatingly yippy.

Make sure the homeowners clean up after them – inside and out. A buyer accidentally stepping sock-footed on a warm, squishy offering will not endear them to the house. Fish are okay if aquariums don't reek, but anything outlandish such as monkeys, lizards or pythons might be a bit off putting. Banish them from the premises along with all traces of their residency. If Polly, the squawky bird with personality, shares the perch, she might annoy the prospects too; give her a cracker at somebody else's house. Recognizing unfriendly terrain, people with allergies will head for the door in a flash.

If your sellers are smokers, aside from their chronically deteriorating health, they may have another problem. Many people are avid non-smokers and will be immediately disinclined to even view, let alone offer on a smoker's house. As is the case with UFFI and handicap accessible, it's just a matter of time before a required "smokers" check-box is added to the MLS® listing form. Your sellers should refrain from further partaking of their malodorous habit inside or anywhere near the entrances. If a thorough washing and steam-cleaning of virtually every interior surface fails to eradicate the insidious residue, carpet replacement and a complete paint job may be a prerequisite.

Because of their chemical nature, air fresheners are offensive and intolerable to many people. Their purpose is to mask, not eliminate, and in my opinion, fail miserably at both. Even if a buyer can only smell the artificial scent, the toxic chemicals are still present in the air. Actually, the same often holds true for scented candles. Better to eliminate the source of the smell, be it pets, smoke or lingering after-odours from foods such as fish or spicy dishes.

One man's fragrantly delicious scent is another's flagrantly obnoxious odour. On the other hand, I've never met anyone who didn't love the aroma of baked bread or cinnamon rolls (cinnamon is an acclaimed aphrodisiac). Your sellers might even leave them fresh and warm on a plate with an invitation for guests to help themselves. Nice touch! Make those endorphins soar!

They say cleanliness is next to Godliness. Well, I'd add tidiness to the proverb. Not much else more commonly and unfavourably affects market value than dirt, bad odour and an unkempt house. Nobody wants somebody else's filthy, untidy mess, even if their own is in the same sorry state. Buyers want a clean slate. Before listing and while on the market, your sellers should thoroughly and regularly clean – inside and out. And let me make this perfectly clear; window glass must be perfectly clear. No nose smears from exuberant Eddie on the patio door.

The kitchen is a home's heart. And if the cook doesn't like that heart, it's no sale. Clean and shiny is a must. Forsaken dirty laundry, a cluttered kitchen and soiled bathrooms send a pretty clear message that the homeowner is not house-proud. The buyer may wonder what else needs attention. Prior to leaving for work in the morning (forget about weekend sleeping in; that reward comes after a sale), your sellers should invest some time and effort into last-minute tidy-up. Load the dishwasher, make beds, give bathroom sinks, faucets, shower and toilets a last minute polish, close and flush toilets, organize counter-tops, vacuum carpets, close closet doors and hide dirty laundry in a hamper.

Before the guests arrive, your sellers should open all window blinds, drapes and interior room doors and turn on all lights – everywhere – even on a sunny day! To avoid stuffiness, let the light and air flow. Unless the buyer is a cave dweller, not only does a bright and airy atmosphere make the home more welcoming, it also means the agent doesn't have to search for light switches, which allows them to focus on their buyers. If your seller agrees to vacate the house for an after-dark showing, it's *critical* to turn on *all* lights – inside *and* out. It's unwelcoming, not to mention irritating and rude, to arrive at a dark doorway and have to open a lock-box to find the key, the key hole and then stumble and fumble for light switches in an unfamiliar foyer. Ask your seller how they'd like to be greeted after dark at a stranger's door. If they leave during daylight hours and an appointment is booked for after dark, remind them to turn them on before heading out. Or they can install a light timer or motion/light-detector.

With so much free online information available, it's not always necessary to hire a professional home stager. However, if you or your clients have no fashion sense, it may be a good idea. Scrutinize your new listing as would an objective, discriminating buyer. Ask yourself a few simple questions. Is the house over-furnished? Crowded? Is traffic flow inhibited in any way?

Minor staging can be done last minute, but properly preparing a house for agreeable viewing takes time, planning and maybe purging. Their home may need to be de-personalized, de-cluttered and de-junked. Or to beautify it, they may need to add or remove furniture and/or decor pieces. If possible, store excess furniture off premise. To dress the principle rooms, a stager may have a contact from whom they can rent needed furniture and décor. An uncrowded room, though, may appear larger and more inviting. Think minimal when it comes to decoration and ornamentation.

Stow away family photo collections, trophies, model airplane collections and the like. Clear out the clutter and organize the closets and cupboards. The strategic addition of fresh-cut flowers is a nice touch. And by all means, to avoid offending anyone, unless your listing is a hunting or fishing lodge, hide the stuffed marlin, bear skin rug and Rudolph's head.

Snow country? Shovel, de-ice or sand the driveway, sidewalks and porch. You don't want buyer prospects slipping and sliding away from your listing – or into a courtroom. Ensure the furnace programmable thermostat is not in off-set mode at a lower temperature. Few people enjoy a cold house. Ignite the gas fireplace or build a fire in the fireplace (provided they have safe equipment). Summertime humidity? Activate the air conditioning, but not at an excessively low temperature. Frost bite won't endear the buyers to their home.

Without vacating and roping off the rooms or hermetically sealing in the kids and pets, having a house perfectly ready for showings is not easy. But while the house is on the market, it's important for it to always be as close as possible to a state of readiness, necessitating only a quick tidy tour for last-minute details. Short notice happens, especially during evenings and weekends. And don't miss a showing because that rejected appointment could be "The One". It may be a lot of work, but your seller should be prepared to keep their property consistently clean and presentable at all times. By its very nature, last minute organizing must be accomplished in the last minute – oh, all right, 30 minutes.

Cloak of Invisibility

If your seller prefers to remain in the house during viewings, beseech them to vacate before the prospect arrives, or greet them at the door and exit immediately. Invading someone's privacy can be quite uncomfortable. Buyers may not linger or open cupboards and closets, which is an integral part of a thorough viewing, especially if the sellers are going about their normal routine, or worse, following visitors around the house. Hovering may also make your seller appear anxious or untrusting; not a nice message or good bargaining position. You want buyers to feel welcome, relaxed and stay awhile. As I continue to say, it's not so much about what they *think*, but how they *feel*.

Vacating the house may result in a better offer since the buyer agent can address concerns, such as room size, technical deficiencies, furniture placement or sunlight direction that buyers might more freely disclose while still in the house. And it's far easier to resolve contentious issues on site rather than in the car on the return trip to the office. If there's moderate interest, the longer the showing lasts, the better the chance of developing an emotional attachment to it.

For whatever reason, if your seller is unable or unwilling to exile themselves from their domicile during showings, advise them to don a cloak of invisibility and stay out of the way. After they've completed all last minute preparations, including powering off noisy entertainment systems (except maybe soft music) and ensuring that no one is sleeping, eating or in the bathroom and the prospects have arrived, your sellers and their family must disappear. Direct them to remain in one room (or weather permitting, go outside) and then move to an already viewed room and remain there for the duration. With the exception of *briefly* and courteously answering specific questions, sellers should never ask questions or volunteer information. Warn them not to engage in lengthy conversations because not only might they accidentally offend the buyer, they may innocently divulge confidential information. Minimal chatter is usually better.

To improve market value, invite your new sellers to participate in the marketing by transforming (and maintaining) their house into a professionally designed, decorated and furnished model home. Their extra effort will pay off. The buyers will appreciate the obvious pride of ownership as well as your seller's efforts to make them feel welcome. Your listing will likely achieve a higher – and possibly sooner – sale price. And happy sellers refer their friends and family. Isn't that what it's all about?

> *"You may not like the idea of putting money into a home when you're moving out. But it's demanded by the market. You need to show it off. You don't have to rip out the kitchen and bathroom, but maybe replace the tiles or the countertops. Get professional advice."*
> Barbara Corcoran

Chapter Twenty-Eight

The Tough Listing

"The rung of a ladder was never meant to rest upon, but only to hold a man's
foot long enough to enable him to put the other somewhat higher."
Thomas Huxley

Blame Game

Oh, happy days. After all your effort, you've finally planted your sign in the lawn of that long-promised listing. Everything looks terrific and you and your splendidly cooperative sellers are anticipating an anxious throng of interested buyers. Everyone is a perfect picture of contained excitement, bursting with optimism, and the sun is shining brightly on your little green patch of Mother Earth. But after a few weeks of disappointingly little activity, to your dismay, your carefully orchestrated plan goes awry – the phone fails to ring. No one shows it and the few inquiries fizzle. Your open houses, including a blitz with agents of competing listings, have yielded no results. You've compared notes with your colleagues, but to no avail. What went wrong?

It's not an uncommon scenario. As you know, a rather large percentage of listings remain unsold for weeks, months and in many cases – never sell. Do you tumble into the ever-popular trap of searching for something or someone to blame? Oh, it's the slow market. There's too much competition or too few active buyers. It's a quiet time of year or the weather hasn't been conducive. Interest rates are too high or banks are too tight. There's been too much bad press or buyers refuse to recognize good value when they see it. The variety of seemingly viable excuses is astounding and limited only by your imagination. I've heard them all.

But here's the thing; blame is completely non-productive. Don't fault outside forces. Why? Because you can't do anything about them. All you control is how you respond and adapt. Assuming for now that your seller is amenable, as the CAO (Chief Activity Orchestrator) of your own business, you must accept personal responsibility for the lack of activity and seek strategic solutions to the conundrum. What are you missing? What can you do differently? What are the addressable causes for the failure? The indicators are there if you look for them. Answers may be found by reviewing and updating your original CMA and marketing strategy, if you even had one. Re-think the asking price, re-examine the property's physical condition, consult with your peers and confirm seller motivation and cooperation. Think of it as a process. Once you develop possible solutions, re-strategise and take the next step up the ladder toward a sale.

"You can't blame gravity for falling in love." Albert Einstein

Annoyed or Anointed

When you accepted the listing and asked about their motivation, did your seller say they were seriously committed to selling for fair market value, whatever that might prove to be? Or did you judge them to be conditional sellers and only sell if they got a certain minimum price? Has their position changed since then? Are they as committed to a move? It's no easy task to persuade a homeowner to get serious since motivation is an inside job. And since it's essential to understand their motives, you must persuasively pry your way into their thoughts and feelings.

If they're convinced their expectations are realistic, the only thing that might dissuade them is a lengthy span of quiet time on the market. Depending on the degree of their conviction, this could consume weeks, months or longer. The problem is, though, that no amount of time will persuade *some* sellers. Many flatly refuse to accept personal responsibility for their mistaken subjective conclusions and dump the blame squarely onto your shoulders. Were you aware you possess miraculous powers, capable of generating an offer on over-priced listings? Hopefully, they trust you – their temporarily anointed one – and remain enthused enough to dispassionately review the situation. You're on the same team. Their interests mesh perfectly with yours. If the property fails to sell, none of you achieve your related goals. They don't move and you don't get paid. Actually, they'll come out financially even, but you'll have invested your money, time, effort and expertise with no return on investment.

If you erred in your original FMV opinion and are unable to manifest a miracle, you have an obligation to apprise them of this fact. Or conversely, if they hold surreal expectations, have been uncooperative for viewing appointments, too rigid during negotiations or exert minimal effort to maintain their home in optimal marketing condition, even though your efforts may prove futile, you must make your best effort to shatter their value delusions and enlighten them of their inadequate contributions.

If the odds of selling it are slim to none, it may be time to reassess the value of retaining the listing. If you originally accepted it primarily as a lead-generation tool, you can certainly continue. However, if your intentions had been to help them sell – and they now seem to be acting wishfully rather than purposefully – you should candidly declare your reluctance to continue and request a release. Why invest your resources on an unsaleable property? They might agree, in which case you can cut your losses. Or your sudden request might stun them into realizing that they're dreaming. Trust could rekindle, and in light of that renewed faith relationship, they may reduce their expectations along with the asking price.

In the meantime – and prior to requesting a price adjustment – let's explore how you might create something from what may be shaping up to be potentially nothing more than a hole in your pocket and a dent in your professional reputation.

"Great minds have purposes, others have wishes." Washington Irving

Stimulate – Not Satisfy

When your listing was first uploaded, it should have attracted near immediate attention from buyers and their representatives. Well, that was the plan anyway. If it had been priced correctly, the photographs of professional calibre and the accompanying MLS® ad copy craftily prepared, you'd have accomplished that mission. That's a lot of "ifs", but each is an integral part of a successful outcome.

I'll not get into the merits of taking a basic photography course. Suffice it to say, though, that if you possess a modicum of photographic talent, by all means, take your own shots. However, if you lack digital camera proficiency, it's well worth the relatively low cost to hire a professional to re-shoot. I've seen innumerable listings with ludicrous photos of inadequately furnished room, cluttered kitchens with chaotic counter-tops and warped shots of disappointingly groomed exteriors with car-choked driveways. I've even seen photos of unfinished basements and unkempt bathrooms! Don't upload shoddy distorted wide-angle or fish-eye lens photos in a well-intentioned attempt to encapsulate an entire room. Having said all this, even the world's best photographers can't make a silk purse from a sow's ear. The subject must be worthy of the photographer's skill. If the place is a disaster and your seller refuses or is unable to do anything about it, skip the photography.

To lure prospects, use only clear, well-composed, exposed and amply lit photographs of features and highlights of attractively staged principle rooms. And make sure you don't catch yourself or the flash in a mirror. Sunny days are perfect for capturing a room beautifully illuminated with warm natural light. Include a colourful bouquet of flowers in the foreground and deliberately exclude a car or truck parked in the driveway; better yet, remove it. Don't snap a careless shot from the street. Instead, fill the frame with your subject. Include an eye-catching and well-framed perspective of the front elevation and if appropriate, a welcoming front entrance. Take your time. Create a work of art. Remember – you want to make your phone ring.

Photos are not intended to inform consumers of property features, but as tools of enticement. As I've said, inquisitiveness is a powerful motivator. Try to stimulate curiosity – not satisfy it. Too many detailed photos typically tend to satisfy it, if not deter it. Also, if the photographs are amateurish, prospects will often skip the listing. During the few seconds of attention you might garner, ignite their fire. The same holds true for virtual or video tours. Frankly, I'm not a big fan of these pretend tours since they lack the essential element of personal guidance. Video tours might save you from having to show to potentially disinterested buyers, but you may miss a prospect that mistakenly misjudges and rejects your listing based on a sequence of poorly prepared and presented pixels. Besides, by meeting them, you might add a new contact to your prospect stable. If they don't like your listing, you might hit it off and sell them another home.

I suppose virtual tours are exceptionally convenient for buyers since they needn't get off their backsides to personally view property. But I suspect many might make unfavourable decisions based solely on that video tour. You lose a showing and the buyers may lose too because the video may not do the home justice. How can one make a sensible preliminary decision involving huge sums of money based on a virtual tour? I suggest that a slide show is arguably a better idea. Nevertheless, it's impossible to get a reliable feel for a home without kicking the bricks, so to speak.

Re-visit the ad copy in the client remarks section of your listing. You may believe that our industry site should be loaded with basic data, without any forethought or pizzazz. But agents are susceptible to pitches too. Also, keep in mind that the public domain of the MLS® system – primarily an advertisement medium – receives the identical data. Is your ad copy strictly factual or could it be considered provocative? Have you used trendy hot words and phrases and avoided tired clichés such as "gleaming hardwood floors" and "handyman's dream"? Or because of space limitations, to encompass numerous features, chattels and improvements, did you invent short forms or use cryptic industry acronyms or codes that nobody but another agent *might* decipher? You're better off choosing only the major features and enhancing them to poetic standards. Then add all the other stuff, in prose or point form, to a feature sheet uploaded as a listing attachment for emailing to prospects. Advertise first

– inform second. Treat it as an opportunity, not to educate but to stimulate prospect curiosity on the busiest realty promo website in existence.

"It is a miracle that curiosity survives formal education." Albert Einstein

ADOM

Computer-generated reports of the "Average Days On Market" statistics for your local area are an indispensable tool. If the property has already been available for the ADOM, in the absence of extraordinary circumstances, I can say with conviction that your listing is incorrectly priced. Unless there's a huge over-supply (which actually depresses prices, in which case, it's still over-priced), there's normally a buyer for any property – at the right price. Sparsely populated rural, small town and recreational markets can take longer. However, for typical residential listings in most active suburban and city markets, if you've not been able to manifest an offer within the first two to four weeks, you've got some serious re-evaluating to do.

Is the home special in any way or just another "cookie-cutter" house like countless others in an average subdivision? Is it situated in a popular area or does it back onto a railway track? Does it front onto a busy four-lane road or a quiet crescent? If there are even remotely objectionable attributes, you may have underestimated their potentially adverse effects. If your listing refuses to attract an offer, to get it sold in or around the ADOM, those negatives must, if possible, be eliminated or factored into the estimate of market value and list price. Sometimes another perspective can be helpful. Have you made the effort to obtain feedback or opinions from colleagues? Why have buyers viewed it, but not offered? Did you ask? Maybe there's a common denominator that could be affordably addressed. The price may be acceptable for the general category, but something is deterring prospects. Identify and remove the obstacle – or adjust the price.

Have you been keeping tabs on the competition? Since you listed the property, how many competing listings have appeared? Have any sold? Are any of the comparable listings from your original CMA still active at the same list price, been reduced or expired unsold? How long have they been for sale with the current and previous brokerages? A review may provide you and your seller with strong dose of reality. It might be a bitter dose, but to make an informed decision, it's info you both need. Perhaps a CMA update and re-presentation might prove beneficial. Keep your sellers involved by communicating with them regularly regarding local market activity. Persevere. Don't abandon them. If you do, they may abandon *you* when the listing expires.

"If your determination is fixed, I do not counsel you to despair.
Few things are impossible to diligence and skill. Great works
are performed not by strength, but perseverance."
Samuel Johnson

Stale to Sale

Sometimes, the best way to change the outcome of a situation – to transform your listing from stale to a sale – is to *not* try to impose fundamental change on the listing, but to alter the way in which you approach it or how your listed property may be perceived by consumers and colleagues.

What elements of your seller's home originally attracted *them*? Was it the neighbourhood, architectural style, mature garden or proximity to schools, shopping or public transit? Was it the local golf course or adjacent park system? Maybe it was just the low price. Whatever features inspired them, which may be different than those you've been emphasizing in your marketing, may entice someone looking for similar features. Over the years of living in and improving their home, your clients obviously became emotionally attached to it. For them, it's not a house, but a home. Thus, they'd be the perfect buyers for it. It's your task to find their clones by targeting your advertising and carefully choosing your phraseology to reflect the features that they've appreciated and grown to love.

Companies often develop new consumer products, but they also continue to successfully market older ones. Some are *really* old; consider the marketing changes instituted during the 20th century by Coca Cola. To entice new buyers or reignite customer interest in an established brand, they set about to revitalize that product's packaging and re-stylize the brand. Think about the fast-food restaurant chain, *Kentucky Fried Chicken*. Because of the growing trend away from fried foods toward healthier eating, they successfully acronymed their name to *KFC* to disassociate from that established and perceptively unhealthy image. *Dairy Queen* did the same with their new brand *DQ*. It's all about public perception. Now, consider your listing as a product you've undertaken to market and adopt a fresh perspective. To revitalize a stale listing, before adjusting the price, try a different marketing approach with different features, different descriptions and different photos. Remember what they say about repeatedly performing the same actions (i.e. advertising) while expecting different results – you're nuts!

"We cannot solve our problems with the same thinking
we used when we created them." Albert Einstein

Gauge and Restage

Did your seller stage their home prior to commencement of viewings? If not, it's time. There's nothing like a makeover and fresh look to accentuate the positive. Is the space warm and inviting? Does it still have the "wow" factor? Or due to minimal activity, has your seller become apathetic in their housekeeping efforts? Is it time to re-clean the windows and re-organize the garage? As people are wont to do with everyday living, have they allowed rooms to become cluttered and untidy? Are any decor items dated or too numerous? Sometimes, all that's required is a fresh coat of paint, new trendy decor pieces, maybe some neutral stylish furniture and artwork or a general re-tidy. It's never too late to bring in a staging specialist.

How's the curb appeal? Is there something about the front exterior that could immediately deflate a buyer's balloon? Is it kept tidy? Is the lawn mowed regularly? Is the snow consistently cleared and the exterior maintained and in good repair? As mentioned earlier, a buyer's mind is often made up as they approach the house and enter the front door. It's that first impression thing. Anticipating your listing to be the one, a buyer's hopeful feeling is either optimistically reinforced as they approach the home or it immediately diminishes. You can obviously improve those odds by asking your sellers to put their backs into some front garden improvements or hire a specialist. Perhaps one shouldn't judge a book by its cover, but in most cases, buyers do just that.

Re-List Trickery

With the immense popularity of REALTOR.ca® and REALTOR.com® and countless brokerage websites, buyers nowadays are often relatively market savvy. Even if you or your seller are in a state of ignorance or denial, buyers will know that the asking price is somewhere in the stratosphere, if not the ionosphere. When a home has languished for too long on the market, buyer interest typically wanes because they commonly perceive that it's over-priced or there's something wrong with it. Pulling it off the market, even just for a brief respite, may be all that's needed to rekindle interest. And while it's suspended, your sellers will have the opportunity to rethink their previous participation and make a few improvements.

When the "cancel and re-list" strategy was in its infancy, it was fairly effective. But since it's become more commonplace, it's lost much of the shine because the now popular process is often unwisely short-circuited by cancelling and re-listing the same day. This blatant attempt to trick everybody, with no intervening period for property improvements or marketing changes, usually fails to impress peers or public. Unless a substantial price reduction is processed contemporaneous with the re-list or there have been upgrades to the property or your marketing efforts, this ruse fools nobody. It's the same stale re-listed property.

Re-listing can create a new beginning for a reconditioned home. Existing buyers, or those new to the market, may not recognize it as "that stale over-priced property" that's been on the market forever. And you can take advantage of the break to re-evaluate your product, upgrade the photos, re-write the MLS® ad and analyse alternative marketing methods. It could be the beginning of a fresh phase of marketing with renewed vigour.

The Big Buffer

Is the property listed anywhere near Fair Market Value? Was your hasty evaluation done incorrectly? Or did you build in too big a buffer between the asking price and your guestimate of value? If your listing has failed to attract an offer, the number one reason – by far – is a sky-high asking price. There could be holes in the roof, a flooded basement or a freeway traversing the back yard. The place could be so disastrously decorated that it would induce horrific nightmares for Martha Stewart. At the end of the day, the house's physical condition doesn't really matter. Unless extenuating circumstances exist, at the right price, there's a buyer for *every* property – period. It all boils down to price. That's normally the single biggest secret to selling real estate. Price it right.

You've exhausted all other avenues to get your listing sold. Since extraordinary times call for extraordinary measure, even though nobody wants to hear or serve as the harbinger of bad news, it's time you had a serious discussion about the price. A seller requesting a price reduction would be like a politician honouring their election promises; it ain't going to happen. Therefore, to fulfill your responsibility to deliver competent professional service, it's up to you to broach the subject. Armed with candid feedback from your peers and updated market research, you have a pretty good (revised) idea about its market value. At least, you realize the price must come down. During the presentation, get them to set personal values aside and slip their feet into the objective shoes of a buyer. Hopefully, they don't expect someone to pay an unrealistically high price to help pay for their next property.

A seller ignores trustworthy qualified advice at their own peril. Just imagine a patient lying on an operating room table, conscious but numbed, and telling the surgeon how to proceed with the operation. I don't think so. Who's the expert? The patient at least listens to the doctor's advice and if acceptable, trustingly heeds it. Even REALTOR® homeowners sometimes hire a colleague to objectively evaluate and market their personal residences. Since it's their property, a homeowner can technically demand whatever price they choose and instruct you how to do your job. But to make an informed decision, they should at least listen to your impartial expert advice. If they refuse, maybe you need to improve your communication skills or be more discriminating when accepting clients.

Without a doubt, the absolute best time for a price reduction is when you first list it. Many agents, though, fall back on the old practice of listing at whatever their new seller asks – just to capture the contract – with the conscious intention of seeking a price reduction later. Reducing later is better than never, but unfortunately, your listing is no longer new and fresh and may not receive the same buyer attention as it might have it had been priced properly from the beginning.

If your listing remains unsold and your clients are faithful, and you feel you've tried everything under the sun to attract an offer, leave it for awhile. If a solution remains elusive, relax and stop thinking about it. Go do something else. Take a walk in the rain. You may feel a sudden flash of inspiration – a gift from your subconscious, your higher self, from the Universe. You may have a "eureka" moment! Then return to the challenge with renewed vigour from a different and creative perspective.

Section III takes you in a completely different direction, into the more esoteric aspect of life as it relates to our business and personal lives. If your mind is open, your life could conceivably make a right turn. But first, I'll finish up this section with a short glossary of industry terminology.

> *"We should be taught not to wait for inspiration to start a thing.*
> *Action always generates inspiration. Inspiration seldom generates action."*
> *Frank Tibolt*

Chapter Twenty-Nine

The Lingo

Listening to a realty agent, lawyer or mortgage broker describe the various clauses contained in an Agreement of Purchase and Sale (APS) and associated documents, the uninitiated may feel they're listening to a foreign tongue. Common terms can certainly seem that way to those who don't trade property every day. Fortunately, the older confusing legalese lingo has more or less evolved into user-friendly language. Part of your professional responsibility is to ensure that your clients are fully cognizant of the abundant technical terms and phrases associated with their realty transition. The following far from exhaustive list represents a few of the terms I've found confusing to both novice consumers and inexperienced agents alike:

Consideration: For a contract to be legally valid, an exchange of something of legal value must occur between the parties. For an APS, that value is represented by a promise. In exchange for the buyer's promise to pay the agreed sum of money, the seller promises to transfer title to the real property in accordance with the contract terms. It's the exchange of promises that constitutes the consideration – not the deposit – which is merely another term of the contract. If a buyer refuses to pay the agreed deposit, they're in default of the agreement, thereby making the contract voidable – not automatically void – by the seller.

In contract law, consideration refers to any negotiated exchange. A court will generally not inquire into whether a particular form of consideration is sufficient. If a seller agreed to sell their home for $100 and after completion, realized their error, they usually cannot successfully argue in court that due to no consideration, the sale was invalid. Provided they freely agreed to the sale, the fact that the price was absurdly low is irrelevant. However, if the APS truly lacked consideration, it's invalid and cannot therefore be enforced. For example, if a seller enters into a written contract to give their house to someone for free, they can change their mind anytime. The buyer cannot sue the seller for breach of contract because no binding contract existed since it was unsupported by consideration from the buyer; no funds were *promised* in exchange for the title transfer. Any time before the gift transfer occurs, the seller could unilaterally cancel the deal, but once title transfers, they cannot. The need for consideration is why you'll occasionally see transfers, essentially gifts, for insignificant sums such as $2. If the transferor tries to renege on their promise, the token consideration ensures a legally binding agreement.

Deposit: Monies normally submitted with or upon acceptance of an offer are often confused with the funds paid by the buyer on closing. A deposit is not the down payment. A deposit is typically remitted to the listing brokerage, held in its trust account and upon closing, is credited to the buyer as part of the purchase price. Although a deposit, usually a fraction of the purchase price, isn't required for a valid contract, it bestows to a seller a level of comfort and confidence that the buyer will honour the terms and close.

Easements: A non-possessory interest registered on title to use somebody else's real property for a specific purpose. For example, utility company easements permit entry onto a property to service equipment. Unlike a lease, an easement doesn't grant the holder a right of possession. As a lesser interest than an easement, a license gives a holder a personal privilege to use the land belonging to another only for a limited purpose. For example, a license, which can be terminated more easily than an easement, is given when a landowner gives his neighbour verbal permission to park their car in his driveway. An easement also differs from a license in that the benefits of most easements flow to an adjacent parcel of *land* rather than a specific *person*. As such, the owner of the adjacent land who benefits from the easement will continue to enjoy the easement even if they're not the initial owner of that property. Other examples of easements are rights-of-way, support (pertaining to excavations), light and air and rights pertaining to artificial waterways.

Encroachment: An unauthorized intrusion onto someone else's land and property. The right to an encroachment by one landowner over an adjoining owner's property is sometimes granted by express written agreement. For example, particularly common in older urban areas with narrow side yards, a window sill, eave, deck, porch or chimney may extend over a side yard area. When the overhang disappears, the encroachment ceases to exist and no right to substitute an encroachment exists if one is lost except by further agreement. Under an encroachment agreement, the owner whose land has been encroached upon by the improvement essentially foregoes from exercising their legal right to require the improvement be removed from the land. Such agreements, normally registered against title of both affected properties, may be encountered where one owner has inadvertently constructed a building, fence or driveway over adjoining land. They may contain provisions that call for the removal of the offending improvement upon the occurrence of some future event (i.e. destruction by fire or wind) or by a specific time.

Environmental Issues: Also known as hazards, such issues can be significant factors in realty transactions. Ensure that your clients and customers receive accurate information by seeking expert advice from appropriate authorities. No easy method exists to categorize significant hazards. In some instances, hazardous conditions have not gained widespread public awareness or condemnation. Somewhat contentious issues are associated with property in close proximity to industrial wind turbines, high-tension power corridors, landfill sites, quarries, airports, some agricultural uses, meat processing plants and micro-wave transmission towers. Consequently, agents are challenged with everyday marketplace negotiations complicated by vagueness and ambiguity.

Highest and Best Use: The use which, at the time and over a given period, is most likely to produce the greatest net return in money or amenities to the land. Net return may be monetary, as with an income property, or with a single-family dwelling, as amenities such as pride of ownership, comfort and convenience. In cases where a site has existing improvements, the present use may fail to meet the defined criteria. Potential highest and best use may differ from existing use. Present use will typically continue, however, unless and until land value in its highest and best use meets or exceeds the total value of the property in its existing use. In opining on market value, an appraiser must consider not only the current use, but also the likely uses to which it is adapted and is capable of being used in the foreseeable future. Purely speculative future uses may not be considered.

Since owners normally use their property as advantageously as possible, and since economic pressures usually dictate the optimum or most profitable use, the highest and best use is usually, but not always, its present use. For various reasons, instances exist where owners fail to use their property at its optimum use, especially along major new highways, busy thoroughfares and rapidly expanding areas where changes in demand occur suddenly and over time.

Lawyer's Title Opinion: A service letter provided by a buyer's lawyer that states the lawyer's view of whether or not the buyer has good and marketable title to the property. It includes search and inquiry results along with outstanding issues that may affect future title.

Legal Description: In any transfer of real property, including related documents, a complete and accurate legal description is essential. This entails adding the municipal lot and plan numbers, possibly a block or reference plan number or in the case of a condominium, the corporation, level and unit number. For rural property, the concession and lot or part lot numbers, possibly east or west half or something similar, the municipal emergency number, approximate acreage, frontage, depth and any lot or parcel irregularities are pertinent. A brief description of the property, structures and main improvements may also clarify the description.

Liens and Encumbrances: A lien is a form of non-possessory security interest granted over a property to secure the payment of an outstanding debt or performance of an obligation. There are countless types, but most common are mortgages, secured credit lines, mechanics or those given as security for installed rental equipment. An encumbrance is a legal term for anything that affects or limits the title of a property, such as a mortgage, lease, easement, lien or restriction, as well as any that could make title voidable. For example, a court charging order on behalf of a creditor or a municipal work order could indefinitely delay a title transfer until it is satisfied.

Mortgage: A loan secured by real property uses a document which evidences the existence of the loan and encumbrance of that realty through the granting of a mortgage. In other words, a mortgage (or the equivalent in law, a charge) is the transfer of an interest in property to a lender as security for a monetary debt. Even though the word "mortgage" alone is now commonly used for this type of loan, it is in itself not a debt, but the lender's *security* for a debt. This transfer of interest from owner to lender is made on the condition that said interest will be returned to the owner when the terms of the mortgage have been satisfied.

Notice of Fulfillment: When a condition is fulfilled by a party to an APS, a NOF is executed and delivered to and signed by the other party to acknowledge the condition has been fulfilled. When a buyer wishes to remove a condition, such as that pertaining to an unperformed home inspection or sale of their unsold home, a Waiver is the appropriate form. In common practice, however, a Waiver is erroneously used in both cases. The two forms ultimately accomplish the same result, but in a different way. However, if a legal conflict later arises, such as a misunderstanding regarding mortgage approval, an agent might regret not having used the proper form. A seller agent should demand the assurance that the condition has technically been fulfilled.

Null and Void: In law, both of the words "null" and "void" mean "of no legal effect". A voided contract is an absolute nullity and is treated as if it had never existed.

Right-of-Way: A ROW lawfully permits one party to pass over land owned by another by a specific route in both directions, more or less frequently, according to the nature of the easement.

Representation and Warranty: Contained in virtually all contracts, a RAW is basically the underlying matters or facts as presented in the contract terms. Sellers *represent* themselves to be the owners with legal authority to sell the property and *warrant* the property to be as they represent it. A representation is an account or statement of facts, allegations or arguments, everything from its *past* to its *present* status, and is created to induce a party to enter into a contract. A warranty moves from the *present* to the *future*. When a seller warrants something, they're promising that the item is presently free of defects, will be for a specified period into the future and if found otherwise, will repair or replace it. The warranty obligates the seller to the terms of the contract and can be either expressed (written) or implied (verbal or assumed), but the latter has less force in court. Since it's an assurance from a seller to a buyer who relies on it as factual, a buyer should insist on warranties being written into the APS.

Requisition Date: Sometimes referred to as title search date or deadline, it's the last date upon which a buyer's lawyer can require the seller to clear up any title problems. This is important particularly if the buyer intends to mortgage the property since the lender will require clear title before advancing the purchase funds.

Sheriff's Execution Search: A vital function of the law office or closing service handling the completion of an APS, it's performed for the current owners and all named buyers of the property. It discloses any unsatisfied judgments (claims) that may have been filed which might create a lien or interest in the subject property. If any of the parties to the transaction are aware of any judgments against them, they should so inform their lawyer on a timely basis.

SPIS: This highly controversial Seller Property Information Statement is designed in part to protect sellers by establishing that accurate property information is disclosed to prospective buyers, and in part to assist buyers with their decisions regarding the subject property.

Spousal Consent: Under the *Family Law Act*, if a spouse is not named on title, to give full force and effect to a sale, the non-named spouse must consent to the sale by affixing their signature to the APS and all pertinent documents. It applies to both married and common-law relationships, provided the non-titled spouse has resided in the property for a certain period of time as described in The Act. No spousal approval means no sale. Anything otherwise could be deemed fraudulent and may be voidable by a court.

Survey: This term is generically used to refer to a Survey, Surveyor's Real Property Report (SRPR) or Reference Plan (RP). A survey is defined as the process of determining the measurements/boundaries of a plot of land by way of dimensional relationships, horizontal distances, elevations, directions and angles on the earth's surface. An SRPR shows the location of all improvements (buildings, decks, pools, fences) relative to property boundaries and usually includes an illustrated plan and written report of the surveyor's opinion regarding concerns. In a realty transaction, it may be relied upon by all transaction parties as an accurate property representation. An RP, which is necessary for a severance, is a graphical representation of a description of land. It shows the boundary, dimensions and any physical or documentary evidence that could affect title (location of fences, hedges, retaining walls, overhead wires) as well as evident or registered easements and ROW. Buildings and any improvements would generally not show unless they were used for boundary positioning or encroach on the subject property.

Survive and Not Merge on Closing: In an APS, a buyer wants assurance that any chattels or fixtures included will be as represented by the seller and in good working order on closing. However, once a transaction is completed, under the Doctrine of Merger, unless some provision otherwise is included in the contract, all obligations by both sides are extinguished, merged or considered fulfilled. To make a seller warranty practically effective, a buyer must insist that some reference for a warranty to *survive* closing be included in the APS. Such inclusion allows a buyer *reasonable* time following closing to ensure everything is in good working order.

Title Search: Normally performed prior to closing and before the Requisition Date, such searches are primarily designed to ensure that a seller has the legal right to sell, transfer or encumber a property. They provide information regarding any restrictions or allowances pertaining to the use of the land (real covenants, easements) and reveal any existing liens that must be discharged at closing (mortgages, municipal tax arrears, mechanic's liens).

Vacant Possession: A property is for sale or lease on the understanding that prior to completion, the occupant will vacate with all chattels not included in the sale. It doesn't apply to property sold to a buyer who agrees to assume an existing full or partial tenancy. If a buyer wishes vacant possession of a tenanted property, since prior to completion, the buyer isn't the landlord, the buyer must appoint the seller, the current landlord, in writing to act as their agent to provide appropriate notice to vacate.

SECTION III

REALTY REALITY MANIFESTING SUCCESS

"Heed these words, you who wish to probe the depths of nature:
If you do not find within yourself that which you seek,
neither will you find it outside. In you is hidden the treasure of treasures.
Know Thyself and you will know the Universe and the Gods."

Oracle of Delphi; Ancient Greece

Chapter Thirty

Who Are You? Who, Who?

"When everything seems to be going against you, remember that the airplane takes off against the wind, not with it." Henry Ford

A Short Long Story

The man is no stranger to loss. During a painful period of adversity more than a score of years ago, he lost custody of his two little girls whom he'd parented essentially alone since one was in diapers and the other not long out of them. After reaching a certain age, they had unexpectedly – and courageously – expressed their wish to live with their somewhat estranged birth mother, to get to know her, they claimed. Many years later, they told their father that part of their motivation had been to escape their step-mother, the man's second wife. To this day, the sorrowful sight of their little faces looking forlornly through the rear window as they were driven away remains indelibly etched in his memory. Not long later, the man also found the courage to liberate himself from the viscous web of that unhappy marriage. He was unaware at the time, however, that he was fleeing one web, only to be caught in another far more malevolent.

With essentially nothing but his car, the clothes on his back and a fleeting flicker of freedom in his heart, the man vacated his home of many years. Adding salt to the wound, his relatively comfortable lifestyle virtually vanished over-night when he was abruptly informed by his commercial bank manager that the security for his brokerage's operating credit line – his matrimonial home – had been withdrawn without warning. Since he had no control over any of the material assets deemed acceptable by the bank as replacement collateral, to the dismay of his loyal agents and support staff, he was forced to close the doors of his brokerage – even though there was no bankruptcy. To further dishearten him, under the personal guarantee in the corporate lease, he was compelled to pay a substantial penalty for breaking the lease. Coordinating the unwinding of his business, one into which he had poured his heart and soul, only compounded the most depressing period of his life.

With slower market conditions, maxed out personal credit line and a sluggish re-start of his sales career, he was forced to pay the rent on his sparsely furnished apartment by way of cash advances on his only credit card. He felt the bottom and it was not a good feeling.

Over the next 20 years, an epic matrimonial litigation and mitigation ensued wherein the man patiently struggled within the complex and combative web of the judicial system. He endured countless court hearings and a stressful string of adversarial meetings with expensive suits gathered around mahogany boardroom tables. After a complicated week-long divorce trial, the judge dithered for nearly two exasperating years to produce his reasons for a favourable judgement, which not surprisingly, the man soon found uncollectible. During the process, he also unjustly lost his treasured sport yacht, a recent acquisition which had been the achievement of a life-long dream. And to top things off, after a lengthy illness, his father passed away. The man lost most of what had held any significant personal value for him. He felt destitute and alone.

> *"Our greatest glory is not in ever failing, but in rising up every time we fail."*
> *Ralph Waldo Emerson*

Though he'd abandoned personal sales several years earlier and the economy had plunged into what has been referred to as The Great Recession, the man was able to overcome many hurtles during that devastating period of his life. To help survive the early lean times, he'd accepted an invitation from an acquaintance to sell boats at a local marine dealership. With the support of his new loving partner and loyal former clients, and with gradually improving market conditions, he was able to rebuild his practice with another brokerage. It wasn't long before he once again rejoined the industry's upper production rank. Why? Because he continued to believe in himself. His strength of conviction could not be stolen or diminished.

How did I manage this challenging feat? For the same reason I was successful when my career began over 40 years ago; I *knew* I could do it. I was becoming more conscious and more aware of my authentic self. With far fewer material distractions, it began to dawn on me what all these tragedies and personal losses were – a continuing message from the Universe. I could have allowed myself to fall victim to the evidently easily manipulated judicial system, not forgiven the perceived perpetrators, and quit. Instead, I chose to finally learn the lesson that life isn't about fear of scarcity or the acquisition of more and more things that don't last. As I painfully discovered, stuff can be easily and unjustly stripped from you at any moment. Life is about love, joy, happiness, compassion, forgiveness of others – and self – and about expressing daily gratitude for our abundance.

Paraphrasing G. Gordon Liddy, the famous Watergate burglar, from his best-selling autobiography, *Will*, anything that doesn't kill you will make you stronger. Well, I grew to understand why I underwent such misfortune. Without destroying me completely, the experience rattled me sufficiently to collectively contribute to a clearer understanding of what constitutes a happy person. The price – including virtually every major tangible asset I'd worked for and accumulated during the first half of my adult life – was certainly substantial, but well paid. It took several years, a great deal of suffering and considerable introspection, but I came to realize that we mustn't attach our happiness to physical possessions. Sustainable joy is not the result of insatiable acquisition, be it material or social. If you depend on those things, or even your spouse or children, for your happiness and suddenly lose them, happiness vanishes too.

"It is prosperity that gives us friends, and adversity that proves them." Proverb

To rely on anything outside of yourself for your happiness, be it things or people, is a recipe for disaster. Happiness must come from within where no one can steal it – unless you allow them. Happiness is not about bigger being better. I had lots of money, so I can unequivocally testify that financial wealth does not buy lasting joy or inner peace. Sustainable happiness also doesn't come from a romantic relationship. A truly wonderful partnership results from two independently happy people equally and positively contributing; the whole is greater than the sum of its parts. Just because someone thinks you're great doesn't mean you are – unless *you* think so too. What others think or say about you is actually irrelevant; it's about how *you* feel about yourself. And to discern those feelings, you must know who you are, at your core.

Soon after I had left that failed marriage, I received an unexpected phone call from one of my daughters who timidly asked, "Daddy, can we come home?" Hallelujah! The world is right again! In hindsight, their fleeing the unpleasant fall-out from much of the initial legal shenanigans and the chance to get to know their birth mother had indeed been a blessing in disguise. And as a consequence of all the hardship undergone, I now have a much clearer idea of who I am; a much stronger man than I ever imagined possible.

"Adversity is like a strong wind. It tears away from us all but the things that cannot be torn, so that we see ourselves as we really are."
Arthur Golden

Face in the Jar

"The walls we build around us to keep sadness out, also keeps out the joy."
Jim Rohn

Do you know who you really are? Have you ever thought about it? Introspection is a valuable tool but I suggest, not often utilized. Are you more focused on the fearful, competitive world of separateness – a "me against them" philosophy – or on the loving, compassionate realm of connectedness – a "me with them" belief? When you step outside your door in the morning, do you expose your genuine self to the world? Or to paraphrase the *Beatles* from their classic song, *Eleanor Rigby*, do you put on a face that you keep in a jar by the door? If you're like most people, you instinctively don your mask, your protective egoic shell commonly referred to as public persona or false self. The problem is that pretending to be that imaginary person – living a charade – can be highly stressful and with accumulative adverse health effects. Such foreign behaviour conflicts with your basic and usually private nature, which is normally shared only with those within your inner trust circle.

Everyone has their personal spheres of trust. Try this exercise. On a piece of paper, draw three concentric circles. Inside the innermost circle, write the names of those with whom you have a strong bond, such as your spouse, sibling, parent or best friend; only those in whose hands you'd *completely* entrust your life. If you're guarded or have undefined personal boundaries, maybe nobody or everybody qualifies. In the second, middle ring, insert the names of those whom you trust to a lesser degree – neighbours, clients, colleagues or casual acquaintances – who have done nothing as yet to earn your distrust. Nevertheless, from them, you cloak your warts and hide your dirty hair. Finally, everyone else in your social sphere is in the outer ring. You might trust these folks a little, but not very far. As your feelings change, it's normal to promote or demote from ring to ring.

Resist giving anyone in the outer two rings (or the inner circle, for that matter) the power to hurt you. If you choose to relinquish your power to others, they may maliciously or innocently usurp that power for their own perceived personal gain. Be they clients, children, associates or spouses, people will occasionally betray your trust. But don't allow them to adversely affect your attitude, your joy of living. Maintain your harmony. And most importantly, don't depend on them for your happiness. Be happy *with* them – not *because* of them. As I've said, their behaviour reflects on *their* personality, *their* fears, *their* issues and not *yours*. Don't allow their issues to become yours.

Think of the boundary between circles as a pliable, semi-permeable membrane (not a wall) through which suffering from toxic words or actions cannot penetrate, or as a polarized lens that filters out the harsh rays of sunlight. You can regularly interact with people through your self-applied protective mask, but no pain can pierce that barrier. Destructive elements are filtered out. Along with information, only positive thoughts and feelings, such as love, joy and compassion, are permitted to permeate. By all means, be yourself as you truly believe yourself to be. And maybe, one day, you'll feel comfortable enough to leave home without your mask.

> *"To be yourself in a world that is constantly trying to make you something else is the greatest accomplishment." Ralph Waldo Emerson*

Heart Afore Head

The great writer and poet, William Shakespeare, famously and correctly claimed that all the world is a stage. If you equate acting with artificial behaviour, then most of the time, you act. When you're with clients, do you *naturally* behave in a manner that exudes confidence? Or to gain their trust and cooperation, do you fake it? Is your behaviour authentic or do you play a part based on your programmed personality and how you think you *should* behave? Do you conduct yourself in a manner *expected* of you, as you were conditioned by your elders? If so, then you're an actor whose behaviour is derived from the fear of losing their love, respect and/or approval, not to mention a commission. But don't worry – it's a rather large club. It's ironic that to be loved, many innocently behave dishonestly by denying their true – and most lovable – selves.

In business, we do everything we can to create and maintain a professional, confident and competent image. That's obviously important. But to reduce the stress of such an undertaking, try composing that image around your authentic self and not a simulated, artificial clone. Don't *pretend* to be an honest and knowledgeable agent; *be* that person. Hiding behind a manufactured personality is no different than a short, balding man with a serious comb-over and lifts in his shoes. It ain't natural and most people will see through the artifice. Uncomfortable? Stressful? What do you think? How long could you sustain such a taxingly false facade before a chronic physical or emotional "dis-ease" invades your cells?

Remember my example earlier about holding your arm up in the air for an extended period? Well, artificial behaviour is no different. It's a lot of stress for your psychic muscles to maintain for very long before emotionally and/ or physically collapsing. It's been reported that persistent stress invites the creeping onslaught of chronic illness and is the root cause of many of today's major health concerns. Acting is merely defying nature, that is to say, your natural self. So, what to do about it? That's easy; stop it, at least for prolonged periods.

Your behavioural decisions result in part from intentional present thoughts; you choose to act a certain way. But they're also rooted in memories of lessons learned from previous experiences and according to theory, earlier incarnations. You behave mostly due to subconscious programming where learned fears skulk in the shadows. Sometimes, you behave a certain way – consciously and unconsciously – to produce a favourable outcome based on a similar previous experience.

For example, nobody has to remind you not to touch a hot stove because stored deeply in your memory is a childhood lesson from an actual burn or a stern warning from your mother. You don't think about it; you just instinctively avoid the hot element. Or there's the classic metaphor about never forgetting how to ride a bicycle. Your instincts automatically instruct your body to continuously micro-lean or incrementally turn the wheel enough to maintain your balance. Life is like a tight-rope and you're the wire walker, ever balancing and arbitrating with people on your path. It's a continuous, often unconscious repartee, a give and take, an energetic harmonizing.

When you have an epiphany, a heart-felt idea to do something, before making the conscious decision, it's certainly prudent to first think about it, at least for a moment or two while you consider its ramifications. But when it comes down to the crunch and you must choose a course of action, instead of following your logical head, follow your emotional heart – your gut – for that's where the abundant knowledge of micro-leaning is unconsciously accumulated. That's the conduit to Universal Knowledge. Trust your instincts. To be successful in your endeavours, resist living subject to the conditioned limiting beliefs usually long held in your memory vault. Make your behavioural decisions, not based on habit or ingrained limiting beliefs, but on heart-felt convictions. Before you can do this, however, you have to discern the difference. It's time for some long overdue self-examination.

> *"The unexamined life is not worth living."* Socrates
> *"The unlived life is not worth examining."* Alphonso Lingis

The Mirror Reflex

> *"Everything that irritates us about others can lead us to an understanding of ourselves."* Dr. Carl Gustav Jung

What distinct qualities do you most admire in others? Why are you attracted to them? What makes them likable? Such an observation may provide insight into that facet of yourself that you most value. Conversely, attributes in others you find repugnant, you also possess, but may have suppressed into your subconscious. You might dislike someone, but not understand why. At some level, they remind you of a dormant trait buried in your own character that never felt quite right.

For example, have you ever been accused of having a quick temper? A lack of the protective membrane mentioned earlier results in your instinctively responding in kind to somebody's expression of anger. Buried in your subconscious is a dark side, a powerfully suppressed dark energy current seething beneath the civil surface. Or you might be unconsciously angry at yourself for living a false life, one not in sync with your authentic self. If you relish those moments when someone expresses respect for you, *you* may lack self-respect. If you melt at romantic movies, then love – requited or unrequited, of self or another – may be deficient or ostensibly absent from your life. The effects of external stimuli are similar to those of an addict's drug fix. Deliberate or innocent suppression of feelings can spontaneously manifest stressful, undesirable behaviour. Once recognized, a healing and forgiveness can begin.

Do you long for a romantic partner and wonder why you're unable to attract the right mate? Is each new suitor a carbon-copy of their predecessor? Why do you feel so unloved? Why do you fear being alone? Why do you long for respect? Why are you shy? Why do you talk a lot or feel unable to freely express yourself? Why are you nervous about meeting new people? Why are you subservient or on the contrary, need to dominate? If you can answer such questions and identify undesirable hidden traits, you may be able to delve into the core causes, begin to make some changes and love and respect yourself more. Allow any positive traits to emerge into your conscious mind and make them a habit. If you're able to objectively witness and cease undesirable behaviour, and instead, build your life and business practice on those loving traits, people will flock to your door – with love and respect in their hearts.

> "*When people do not respect us, we are sharply offended; yet in his private heart, no man much respects himself.*" Mark Twain

If you sat down for a coffee and a friendly interrogative chat with yourself, how would you describe you? (Do this in private; fellow coffee shop patrons might not understand.) Take some quiet solitary time to reflect and record a specific, detailed and heart-felt statement of who you believe yourself to be. Dig deep. Pretend you're gazing into a magical mirror that reflects deepest inner-most feelings. Go beneath your artificial veneer that believes happiness is the unambiguous consequence of earning the big bucks.

Who are you really? I don't mean your formal education, letters following your name, former or present occupation, professional or familial title, trade or designation. And I definitely don't mean the name on a government-issued permission document like a birth or marriage certificate or driver's license, which are simply control mechanisms associated with the body you're currently occupying. I'm referring, not to your egoic self but to your genuine heart-centric spiritual self – the true being behind your ego.

Ego is an artificial societal-conditioned construct, a personality or public persona, a counterfeit identity that automatically serves as a self-imposed brick-wall defence mechanism built to protect your authentic self. And unless identified and objectified, the face you apply daily – literally or figuratively – is usually reinforced throughout a lifetime. (It's also interesting to note that your authentic self, which is so much smarter, doesn't really need protection.) Being fear-based, the ego believes its very existence depends on maintaining its power over your life. It accomplishes this by preserving a "safe" alienating distance from other people. Sadly, it blocks valuable vulnerable human connections and strenuously buttresses the life-long delusion of separateness. Hmm – not good for either business or love relationships.

A growing number of people refer to ego as a joint mass delusion. A powerful ego is particularly prevalent with men who, as boys, play *alongside* other boys instead of as girls do, *with* each other. (It's been suggested that since women are usually better communicators, they're more enlightened than men.) Unfortunately, due to multi-generational conditioning, we men come by our powerful egos and resulting sense of separateness quite organically.

Neil Kramer, philosopher and teacher in the fields of consciousness, metaphysics, shamanism and ancient mystical disciplines, in his insightful book *The Unfoldment, The Organic Path To Clarity, Power and Transformation*, offers a great metaphor in the chapter *School Bus of Selves* about the complex reasons why we sometimes lose it and behave contradictory to our conscious personal preferences. He talks about our psyche consisting of 3 components – the composite self (bus driver), various character selves (archetypes) and the survivalist ego – and how they interrelate during our bus ride through life. It "demonstrates how different elements of our psyche can unexpectedly leap to the fore in challenging situations"; a very interesting read.

If you ever wish to achieve enduring happiness and success in life, materially or spiritually, self-inquiry is enormously important. Question *everything*, especially your own convictions since they may unconsciously be founded on inherited untruths from, as Dr. Carl Jung called it, the Super

Consciousness. Those falsehoods – and your ego – are probably holding you back from achieving your wildest dreams.

What are your dreams, your longings? What brings you joy and delight? What makes your heart sing? What gets you through the night and springs you out of bed like a jack-in-the-box as dawn cracks? Where do you feel you might find your bliss? If money were no object, how would you aspire to live? Mentally go where you may not have gone before. Just imagine – without any fearful restraint. How do you want to contribute to our beautiful world? What legacy do you wish to leave behind after you return home, or do you even care about this concept? Maybe you prefer to live hard and fast, and leave behind a trail of shattered promises, broken hearts and rubber tire skid marks.

Are you okay to die without having taken any risks, without figuratively climbing your own Mount Everest? When you're alone, do you love the one you're with, or at some level, are you angry and self-loathing? Do you feel victimized or out of control? Do you relish solitude or thrive in a crowd? Do you feel worthy of success – in business or in love? Does being judged disturb your personal harmony? There are so many fundamental questions, but without questions, there would be no answers. And it's answers that germinate growth, which is why we're all here. Hopefully, they'll stimulate even more questions, but that's the whole idea of the exercise.

Through maturation, experience, education, research and most importantly, personal choice, your current beliefs may be different from those of your childhood, but still rooted in that kid's world. Obviously, your personal 3-dimensional reality – your current embodied life – is ultimately your responsibility, but you may have to wrestle with your ghosts. Awareness comes first, followed by critical thinking, followed again by more awareness and more independent thinking. To grow, you must become consciously aware of individual beliefs, including the limiting variety (which I'll get into later) entrenched in you without your approval and in many cases, even your awareness. In the meantime, let's do some more introspective analysis and get to know who that is staring back at you from your bathroom mirror.

"It's not what you look at that matters, it's what you see."
Henry David Thoreau

Intro or Extro

"One of the things that is assumed about actors is that they are
extroverted, which is almost never the case, in my experience." Bill Nighy

A purported misperception is that all sales people are extroverts. Even though many surely are, just as many are highly sensitive people, introverts. Various studies claim that anywhere from a third to half the population are introverted. In my travels, I've encountered legions of these self-proclaimed quiet ones. In a society that has propagated and glamourized the desirability of its opposite, extroversion, in business and social life, just the word "introvert" unjustly conjures a negative connotation. Introverts are commonly and usually falsely pictured as lonely loners, agoraphobic wall-flowers who fear socializing or even stepping out the door of their secure sanctum.

In her highly-researched New York Times bestselling book, *Quiet: The Power of Introverts in a World That Can't Stop Talking*, Susan Cain states: "We're told that to be great is to be bold, to be happy is to be sociable." Well, let it be known that if an introvert understands and appreciates the advantages they possess, they can be happily social without being bold. Rest assured that no matter your type, reserved or audacious, you can enjoy a rewarding real estate career. To my knowledge, no direct correlation exists between vociferousness and financial or social success. So, if you're a closet introvert, you can lower your shields, the extroverted façade, and stop pretending to be someone you're not. Just know when and how to seek an energy fix. In the interest of knowing who you are and living a lower-stress lifestyle in alignment with your genuine self, it helps to understand the group to which you naturally belong.

"Being solitary is being alone well: being alone luxuriously immersed in doings of your own choice, aware of the fullness of your own presence rather than of the absence of others. Because solitude is an achievement." Alice Koller

When home alone, do you feel restless and bored? Do you regularly long for social interaction, and after an energy dose, return home energetically satiated? Branded as outgoing, extroverts seek crowd energy and enjoy the excitement of hosting and participating in big house socials where they're often the life of the party. Or do you fret about future social events looming like lingering wraiths? Even though a highly skilled small-talker, you're exhausted by the ordeal and gratefully return to the quiet solitude of sanctuary, to re-charge like a plug-in electric vehicle with a limited travel range. (The proliferation of home offices might be due in part to a rise of introverted agents.)

To be happy, vibrant and energized, not everyone wants or needs to live in a boisterous beer commercial, constantly immersed in frivolous social drivel. However, to be accepted, introverts sometimes bravely pretend to be much more gregarious. And like an elastic band, after stretching to socialize, once they escape the energetic menagerie, they return to their original predetermined relaxed state at their heavenly haven. As Elaine N. Aron, Ph.D. wrote in her remarkable bestselling book, *The Highly Sensitive Person: How to Thrive When the World Overwhelms You;* "Our trait of sensitivity means we will also be cautious, inward, needing extra time alone. Because people without the trait (the majority) do not understand that, they see us as timid, shy, weak, or that greatest sin of all, unsociable. Fearing these labels, we try to be like others. But that leads to our becoming over-aroused and distressed. Then that gets us labelled neurotic or crazy, first by others and then by ourselves."

An introvert's ideal house party is often just a serene and sensitive conversation at home around a candle-lit table for four, or sharing a cup of herbal tea, a biscuit and a mutually rewarding chat with a close companion. Being introverted doesn't necessarily mean fearing people or being shy, though that may be possible. Nevertheless, many prefer the inner peace and tranquility of a quiet corner with a warm blanket and a cool book. The solitude of home – their energy source – provides valuable time for introspection, contemplation and self-improvement. Unfortunately, though, a fast-moving society caught up in an inexorable drive for perpetual growth and accumulation of stuff, typically rewards the daring and entertaining, and often fails to celebrate the gentle unsung thinkers toiling quietly in the background, without whom some of that growth might not have come about.

> *"I was looking for love in all the wrong places,*
> *looking for love in too many faces." Waylon Jennings*

If you're an extrovert, then you have a significant advantage in any sales-driven industry – natural and voracious social courage, charisma. Since you're often out there connecting with new people, lead generation may be a piece of cake. You may, however, have a powerful protective ego to assist. Introverts, on the other hand, sometimes with tender egos, must be careful to avoid being taken advantage of, misjudged or misunderstood. Extroverts must be cautious to avoid overpowering people, being overly gregarious, domineering and not listening. I've met many extroverts who are quite delightful, and others whose behaviour bordered on obnoxious; no – some were definitely obnoxious. But in hindsight, maybe their behaviour was unpleasant because they were actually fellow introverts who'd temporarily pasted on a false face.

I've also met introverts who were pathetically shy and withdrawn, the self-proclaimed victims of the world, who lacked the pluck to honestly and fearlessly express themselves. Shyness symbolizes low self-esteem and a lack of understanding and acceptance of one's introverted identity. They feel they just don't fit the mold of the generally accepted misperception of a stereotypical societal denizen. They don't love themselves enough.

Lacking the extroverted charisma to persuade people of the merits of taking a certain position, introverts will attempt to thoroughly understand their clients by asking questions and listening carefully to their answers. They'll speak softly from conviction of the heart. But speaking softly mustn't be misinterpreted as unsure or incompetent. On the contrary, it can easily be the exact opposite; one doesn't have to shout to be sure. But depending on the strength of that conviction or in other words, their level of self-confidence, they're sometimes easily hurt, disappointed, ignored or even completely miss opportunities for advancement.

"I'm an introvert at heart. And show business, even though
I've loved it so much, has always been hard for me." Roy Rogers

Introverts often possess unique powers of observation that are extremely useful during negotiation proceedings. In her book, Ms. Cain says that "the ability to negotiate is not inborn ... and it does not belong exclusively to the table-pounders of the world. Anyone can be a great negotiator ... and in fact, it often pays to be quiet and gracious, to listen more than talk, and to have an instinct for harmony rather than conflict. With this style, you can take aggressive positions without inflaming your counterpart's ego. And by listening, you can learn what's truly motivating the person you're negotiating with and come up with creative solutions that satisfy both parties." This is certainly appropriate during both offer and listing commission negotiations.

Introverts tend not to try to dominate negotiations, which can be crucial to a successful outcome. Forceful imposition of will is frequently met with an equal and opposite resisting force. With their superior power of concentration, combined with an innate ability to ask probing focused questions, they can often more easily understand opposing perspectives and thereby work steadily and methodically toward a mutual accord. Whereas extroverts can sway people by the sheer power of their charismatic personalities, introverts tend to express themselves in a calm compelling manner and support their logical positions with well-prepared arguments based on solid facts and statistics. Extroverts can be somewhat more assertive; not necessarily a bad thing, provided it's sensitively measured. And people can also be somewhere in the middle; ambiverts, a lesser known type, are fairly comfortable with and skilled in social interaction, but still relish re-fuelling alone time.

When the subject comes up in conversation, my clients can't seem to reconcile that, as an introvert, I enjoyed considerable success in sales and management. I did it by being adept at performing well for limited periods of time, with re-charging breaks. (In public school, I found recess draining and re-charged in the classroom.) In other words, I behaved genuinely according to my natural inclinations because I enjoyed the work. Because the inherent nature of our business is sporadic bursts of energy intermixed with intervals of quiet solitude between appointments, it was a perfect business for me.

Ms. Cain suggests that "introverts are capable of acting like extroverts for the sake of work they consider important, people they love, or anything they value highly." She describes this capability by referring to a relatively new field of psychology created almost solely by Professor Brian Little, former Harvard psychology lecturer and consummate introvert, called "Free Trait Theory". He posits that "we are born and culturally endowed with certain personality traits – introversion, for example – but we can and do act out of character in the service of core personal projects" which are the facets of life that excite us. Free traits allow you to pretend to be the opposite type, whether introvert or extrovert.

To identify your core personal projects and deduce a glimmer of where your heart may lay, Cain recommends that you think about what activities fascinated you as a child. What characteristic do you envy in others? Jealousy is ugly, but it's honest. Also, be aware of the parts of your work that attract you. For prospect generation, do you prefer social networking and door-knocking (extro) or impersonal mass mail, referral and farm area prospecting (intro)? What part of the business stimulates you favourably? What ignites your fire? Answer these questions, and you'll have a better idea of how to enhance your abilities, income and your joie de vivre. It's simple; do more of what you enjoy and less of what you don't.

A few years ago, during my incarnation as a regional manager for a multi-branch brokerage, I experienced dramatically contrasting environments between my two main offices. Both were staffed by mostly productive sales reps, but one was almost continuously chaotic with extreme energy demands. The guest chair in my office was usually occupied by an agent with a quandary, and after they took their leave, immediately filled by another. Once, one of my delightful secretaries jokingly affixed a "take a number" sticker on the door frame.

As an introvert, my private office in the quieter branch became my refuge, my "restorative niche", as Professor Little puts it in Cain's book. There, I recharged my batteries and sought the solace of solitude so I could quietly attend to the other essential elements of the job. But performing in the busy branch, day after day, month after month, burned me out. I enjoyed the job and most of the people, but because I had to regularly extend myself further than my Free Traits could handle, I quit before the job was the death of me. It's important to have a "Free Trait Agreement", not only with your romantic or business partner, but also with yourself. Limit those times when you act out of character, like an introvert behaving as an extrovert, especially when you neglect to have regular restorative niches. Emotional labour, the effort to control and change your emotions, is associated with stress, burnout and ill health.

To manifest a successful career, as an introvert, you mustn't feel compelled to embrace the ideals of extroversion – at least not for prolonged periods – without regular restorative breaks. Learn to feel comfortable in your own skin, to monitor your activities and feel confident in honestly expressing yourself. Remain true to your inherently quiet and thoughtful nature. Good ideas and sage advice are not synonymous with being able to talk a lot; sometimes people talk too much and say nothing. You may simply be a little choosier with words. And don't feel inferior. Without introversion, the world would have lacked luminaries such as Newton, Einstein, Yeats, Chopin, Orwell, Spielberg, Rowling, Buffet and Gandhi. Don't be afraid to live authentically no matter who you are and from which camp you hale.

Sadly, our culture often doesn't readily recognize people for the sensitivity and compassion often associated with introversion. Rather than those who cherish their quiet alone time, it's the bold, brash and often criminal public actions that command the biggest headlines and bank accounts. But I feel we're transitioning – at glacial speed – into a new era wherein compassion, cooperation and sensitivity are becoming more recognized as valuable societal contributions. Yes, more men are bravely facing their fear and realizing it's okay to cry. And more women are courageously accepting that it's fine to be nurturing in business, industry and politics. Compassion and empathy have their own rewards. Don't be afraid to embrace your genuine self. You're worth it.

> *"Where you are in consciousness has everything to do*
> *with what you see in experience."* Eric Butterworth

Unification of Opposites

> *"Many people who have practiced the Marriage of Spirit techniques*
> *have blossomed and developed highly successful careers because that was what*
> *they were seeking. However, their success is a success generated by a flow of light*
> *which comes from their centre of inner inspiration and fullness. It is not a success*
> *driven by outer goals and ambition, which come from a sense of inner emptiness,*
> *and which are seldom fulfilling or fully satisfying."*
> Leslie Temple-Thurston

We live in a materialistic and dualistic world, where opposites such as up/down, generosity/greed and compassion/indifference are the norm. They're endemic to human society. By their very nature, polar opposites cannot exist without their counterparts because they're directly relative to each other. And like the outside world, each of us possesses opposites within, associated as being part of both the light and the dark sides. An ancient traditional native tale tells of two wolves, one light and the other dark, that dwell within each of us. When asked by a small boy about which wolf would determine his life path, hence dominate, a tribal elder is said to have replied the one the boy feeds. The clear moral of the story is that you should nurture that side of you which you find most naturally attractive, and behave accordingly. Hopefully, Luke, you'll choose the light side. Consciously choose to be the good guy and make it a habit. Your programming will gradually change, you'll become that person and your life will be more rewarding for the world and hopefully – for you.

> *"What you get by achieving your goals is not as important as what you become by achieving your goals."* Henry David Thoreau

In her beautiful book, *The Marriage of Spirit; Enlightened Living in Today's World*, Leslie Temple-Thurston wrote that everyone experiences remarkable mystical experiences, but many are either unaware of or deny having them. They're afraid that those moments might threaten their existing and possibly fragile sense of reality. Humans are typically change-averse and prefer to maintain everything as it has always been. We're into what we perceive to be secure comfort zones and try to stay within them, often to our detriment. Temple-Thurston says that "a process of bringing together or unifying all the polar opposites inherent in this dualistic life brings us into the vast oneness of consciousness that is the true source of life." She believes that by "finding the fundamental unity of consciousness underlying all of life's dualities is enlightenment – our real state of consciousness." To experience enlightenment, we must integrate the "dualistic or polarized schisms in our personality." Then "we can know directly and palpably the unity which we truly are, beyond the limited personality." If you're attracted to the idea of finishing forgotten lessons, learning from them and releasing potentially destructive behavioural patterns and limiting beliefs, I highly recommend her book.

While plying your trade, know that you'll undoubtedly be faced with both wins and losses. You'll enjoy the rewards of referrals and happy, satisfied clients. And you'll experience rejection from others whose destined time to move has yet to arrive, at least with *your* assistance. Whether something seems good or bad, accept all experience as a normal part of life. Make those experiences emotionally neutral. Don't permit yourself to be hurt by failure. Know that another victory is on the horizon. Maintain your calm centre. And be open to sudden epiphanies to change direction by following your instinct, for it always speaks the truth.

To know who you truly are, be prepared to bravely take that first tentative step toward personal growth. It you don't, you'll definitely not arrive. But before you can do that, you must be aware – to know that you don't know. Hopefully, your curiosity is ignited to begin a personal exploration of the mysteries of this life of which we are all an integral part. Face your fear and get out there – and in there – to seek your answers.

"Out beyond ideas of wrongdoing and right doing,
there is a field. I will meet you there." Jalal ad-Din Rumi

Analysis Paralysis

"You must do the thing you think you cannot do." Eleanor Roosevelt

Whatever your personality type, you may occasionally feel a lack of professional confidence, especially if your career is in its infancy or you're in what you hope is a *temporary* slump. Your biggest obstacle to success, however, may be your social phobia, especially if you're introverted. If you find yourself unable to move forward, it's probably the fear of failure that's blocking progress, or you're going about business in a manner unsuitable to your genuine self. You may be trying to be somebody you're not. Nevertheless, it boils down to that same old ingrained fear of being judged deficient, of being rejected.

The best way to elevate your mood and/or productivity is by taking imperfect action rather than no action. Just the mere act of doing something will likely help you feel better and generate an endorphin release. Positive energy can snowball. From a spiritual perspective, I feel we're perfect beings. But while occupying our current corporeal bodies with their lamentably powerful egos, we're far from perfect. So, don't try to be.

"The possibilities are numerous once we decide to act and not react."
George Bernard Shaw

No doubt you've heard the cliché that too much analysis can lead to paralysis. Well, it's true. Doing nothing because you're not an expert, because you've never done it before, won't translate into a satisfying career – or life. We learn far more from our failures than from our victories. (As you now know, I speak from personal experience.) To illustrate this principle, take the popular story about Thomas Edison. While enduring endless attempts to invent the electric light bulb, he was once asked by an admirer how he coped with his endless failures. He apparently replied that he didn't consider them failures as such, but as a string of successful ways the bulb wouldn't work. It's all about perspective; the half full or half empty glass metaphor. He was true to himself and never lost his vision or his faith. (By the way, with all that devoted solitary lab work, he must have been an introvert.)

"If you wait to do everything until you're sure it's right, you'll probably never do much of anything." Win Borden

Nothing ventured, nothing gained. Once you accept this idea, you'll be propelled into action. Just perform to the best of your ability. All you can do is the best you can. Try to avoid mistakes, but to progress, be prepared to make them. Anyone who has never made a mistake has never tried, never risked anything. And they'll probably die unfulfilled. As I oft say, the biggest risk in life is not taking any. Get busy making some mistakes. At some point, maybe after a few failures, the odds will favour you with a victory and another and another. By taking action, through trial and error, you'll learn who you are, what you're good at and what works best for you.

"No man ever achieved worth-while success who did not, at one time or other, find himself with at least one foot hanging well over the brink of failure." Napoleon Hill

PIP

"This above all: to thine own self be true, and it must follow, as the night the day, thou canst not then be false to any man." Hamlet – William Shakespeare

Permitting yourself to be defined by and living in accordance with the expectations of others from your past, present or both, as opposed to living authentically and in the moment, limits your ability to fully realize the joyful life of abundance you were meant to enjoy. In simpler terms, to be happy and live a fruitful, low-stress life, don't try to be somebody you're not. People generally feel more comfortable with someone who is naturally relaxed and self-assured. They can often sense a façade, which can be interpreted as insecurity or untrustworthiness. Such a self-imposed veneer only emphasizes separation and precludes the possibility of establishing strong interpersonal connections, making relationships superficial at best. Living a false life is like existing in a virtual "open-concept" office cubicle; together but divided, which means no real trust.

To enjoy a rewarding sales career and a happy, contented life, you must know your product. Since you're in a service business, that product isn't property; it's people. Thus, it's helpful to understand what makes them tick and how to successfully communicate your authentic identity. Know who you are and just as critically – love who you are. How can you love what you don't truly know? Knowing yourself as the spiritual being that's typically subjugated by a programmed personality – a public persona – will help you move from a place of fear of judgement to one of increased self-confidence, self-love and the lowering of "protective" barriers. You'll live a truly open-concept lifestyle. The slow but sure implementation of this knowledge into your daily life will organically attract more positive life-loving people into your sphere – both personally and professionally.

I recently had a delightful former client contact me to help with a home transition. During our first consultation in nearly three decades, the subject arose about why he'd called me and no other agents. Aside from the fact that I called periodically to say hello and faithfully sent a calendar every year, he said that he trusted me. He claimed he didn't really know why; he just did. Instinctively, he knew I cared and was worthy of his trust.

People are drawn to positive, confident people like bees to blossoms, like the morning sun to the darkness of night, like ducks to water, like flies to … okay, you get the idea. Be the business person you're genuinely capable of being. Formal is usually associated with the artificial ego, whereas casual and candid is usually interpreted as genuine and natural. Relax and be yourself. If you faithfully and fearlessly match your business practice to the real you – your true identity – you'll be better equipped to contribute more effectively to your client's lives. As I said, you're not in the business of sticks and bricks, but of people. It's *all* about human relationships. People will feel increasingly compelled to do business with you – again and again – and to recommend your services, not because you're a top-producing, number one, award-winning braggart clone who never sleeps, but because you honestly care. You'll become their trust-worthy friend in the business to whom they'll habitually turn in confidence.

> *"Without deep reflection, one knows from daily life*
> *that one exists for other people."* Albert Einstein

To help you learn about yourself, spend some time now and again in serious contemplation and when ready, prepare a Personal Identity

Proclamation. It could take hours, days or months, probably longer. But hey – you've got the rest of your human life. It begins with self-awareness. Who are you? Why do you do what you do? What inspires you? What excites you? What brings you joy? Why are you here? Think about it. Feel about it. Massage it in quiet solitude. Then write it out, returning to edit a work in progress. As you examine your inner self, your self-awareness will gradually increase as though you were slowly turning up a dimmer switch. And your PIP will evolve along with you.

Do your best to align your business and personal goals with your PIP. If you're an introvert, attempting to create a successful practice by pretending to be a boisterous business-first, team-building socialiser running on adrenalin highs will burn you out in no time. Try focusing on increasing your conversion rate – prospect to client – of the few, rather than diluting your efforts with the many. Conversely, an extrovert could be bored to tears without the perpetually frantic high-octane lifestyle involved with trying to connect with everybody. Be the real McCoy. Be genuine and the Universe will bless you with happiness – along with an ever-increasing awareness of Oneness – and an ideal business practice. It's all up to you. Be conscious.

> *"A person experiences life as something separated from the rest, a kind of optical delusion of consciousness. Our task must be to free ourselves from this self-imposed prison, and through compassion, to find the reality of Oneness."* Albert Einstein

Chapter Thirty-One

Happy Faces

"I, not events, have the power to make me happy or unhappy today.
I can choose which it shall be. Yesterday is dead, tomorrow hasn't arrived yet.
I have just one day, today, and I'm going to be happy in it."
Groucho Marx

Crappy to Happy

"Every time you smile at someone, it is an action of love,
a gift to that person, a beautiful thing." Mother Teresa of Calcutta

Several years ago, while strolling through our neighbourhood, my wife and I had impulsively begun to skip along the sidewalk, hand in hand. I realize it's rare for adults to partake in such a childish activity, but we did it anyway. I guess our inner kids were alive and having fun in the moment. During this playful interlude, we couldn't help but notice the face of a woman in an approaching car that, upon seeing us, broke into a big toothy smile. We laughed. She beamed. Because *like* energy attracts and stimulates *like* energy, during that intimate instant, our happiness had a sudden, maybe momentary impact. Our energies attracted, aligned and mutually resonated in a blissful exchange of utter joy.

The opposite holds true as well. If you're feeling angry, worried or anxious (all fear-based), you'll naturally attract people feeling similar negative energy. If you were to walk into an angry crowd while in a neutral or positive state of mind, unless you were equipped to deflect it, you'd be infected and share their anger or fearfully flee. Instead of merrily skipping along, if my wife and I had been immersed in a heated argument, would that driver have reacted negatively? If she didn't ignore us completely, she probably would have felt some derivative of fear – sadness, distress or disappointment – and quickly passed us by to avoid being contaminated by our polluting vibes. Since misery loves company, though, if you're feeling miserable, at least you'll not be miserable alone. (There's only one letter difference between "miser" and "misery" and it's a "Y". So, *why* be miserly?)

"If misery loves company, misery has company enough." Henry David Thoreau

Shedding sympathetic tears with a friend during the telling of a forlorn tale represents an exchange of loving, compassionate energy. Same thing if a companion spontaneously bursts into laughter about something they alone find hilarious. Even though there's no apparent reason for their eruption, you smile or laugh whilst wondering what's so funny. These are but a couple of examples of attracting and generating positive energy. It's the principle behind laugh tracks on dumb television sitcoms. Confident in their comic scripts and performances, the older and arguably better ones were often filmed before live audiences with unprompted bona fide hilarity. Theory has it that even canned laughter will make something that isn't very funny *seem* humourous. Laughter is contagious, like yawns. (It's also good medicine.)

Though *acting* happy can have a similar effect, feeling it inside is obviously best. If you're a poor actor, as I've said, people might sense a lack of authenticity and respond accordingly to your insincerity by not trusting you. Smiling eyes and happy hearts count for more. So, project the real deal.

"Understanding of our fellow human beings...becomes fruitful only when it is sustained by sympathetic feelings in joy and sorrow." Albert Einstein

According to Eckhart Tolle in his wildly popular book, *A New Earth: Awakening to Your Life's Purpose*, there are numerous common subtle forms of negativity. They include impatience, irritation and nervousness that "constitute the background unhappiness that is many people's predominant inner state. You need to be extremely alert and absolutely present to be able to detect them. Whenever you do, it is a moment of awakening, of disidentification from the mind."

If you can be aware of your emotional state, the feelings with which you may have self-identified for a very long time – perhaps a lifetime – if you can virtually step outside that state and objectively witness those feelings as a dispassionate observer, you can begin to alter your state. Underlying those feelings, Tolle says, "are certain unconsciously held beliefs, that is to say, thoughts. You think these thoughts in the same way that you dream your dreams when you are asleep. In other words, you don't know you are thinking those thoughts, just as the dreamer doesn't know he is dreaming."

When you're consciously thinking or deliberately experiencing a thought during a *lucid* dream, however, you're actually aware that you're dreaming.

During a particularly unpleasant dream, to escape a monster's craven embrace, have you ever attempted to wake up? Following the same principle, you can become conscious of a thought or belief during a wakened state and alter or break out of it. For example, if you find yourself worrying about money, you can consciously realize that worrying is not a *present* thought, but a *future* one. You can evade it by bringing yourself into the present moment and expressing gratitude for all the beautiful blessings in your life. You'll then stop worrying and automatically emit positive energy, and attract more of the same in return. Isn't happy better than crappy? If conscious enough, you can deliberately choose to change.

> *"Be miserable or motivate yourself. Whatever*
> *has to be done, it's always your choice." Wayne Dyer*

End of Ego

> *"If you don't change your beliefs, your life will be like this forever.*
> *Is that good news?" William Somerset Maugham*

Tolle believes that many people suffer from conscious or subconscious feelings of discontent or resentment which contribute to their chronic unhappiness (and chronic illness) or feelings of lack of peace. You may have somehow fooled yourself (or been duped) into believing that before you can be happy, you must experience a specific life event. Maybe you're awaiting the arrival of the proverbial champion on a white steed to rescue you from your prison tower of unconsciously self-inflicted distress. Or you tell yourself you'll be happy after you've generated a certain amount of commission, bought a new car, discharged your onerous credit card debt, met the love of your life or shed unwanted body fat. In the meantime, you unconsciously choose to be impatient, envious, worried or resentful. That's called conditional happiness. It's not unlike conditional love; you'll continue to love someone as long as their behaviour doesn't change. Or you'll love someone when they shape up to your preconceived notion of how they should behave.

Have you ever looked forward to a music concert? You were excited by the prospect of attending, thereby bringing the anticipated pleasure (positive energy) from the future into the present. You may have said you can't wait, that you wish it was tomorrow (don't wish your life away). This might be a good feeling, provided you're not impatient. You can also bring worry (negative energy) about a future responsibility into the present. Maybe you're fretting about being short of funds for the next mortgage payment, or if introverted, feeling anxious about an upcoming social event. Pleasure good – worry bad. You can also bring pleasure or regret from the past into the present. You enjoyed a yummy chocolate donut, but now regret it and imagine an ugly ball of fat heading for your hips. Or you had fun on a date and just recalling it brings a surge of warmth. Pleasure good – regret bad.

Maybe something is happening in your life right now, such as an acrimonious divorce or a debilitating disease that you believe is denying you peace and happiness. Or it could be something that's already occurred and you're still harbouring anger, remorse or resentment. You might be stuck in blame – of someone or yourself – and feel unhappy as a result. Tolle says that these are all "assumptions, unexamined thoughts that are confused with reality. They are stories the ego creates to convince you that you cannot be at peace now or cannot be fully yourself now... Peace, after all, is the end of the ego." By being consciously aware of your thoughts, you can alter them, and your actions, to achieve and maintain a happy life. Thoughts can easily be changed; it's becoming peacefully aware that's the more challenging part of the equation.

> *"You are the embodiment of the information you choose*
> *to accept and act upon. To change your circumstances,*
> *you need to change your thinking and subsequent actions." Adlin Sinclair*

Dancer and the Dance

Deliberately making peace with the present moment because it's "the field on which the game of life happens," Tolle suggests is the best way to be at peace now. "It cannot happen anywhere else." New edge thinkers share the belief that the secret to the art of living, of all success and happiness, is to be one with life – with the Now. Tolle says "that you then realize that you don't live your life, but life lives you. Life is the dancer, and you are the dance." Ask yourself if there's any negativity within you in this present moment. Be aware of your current thoughts and emotions, including those subtle droning ones that seem to run continuously in the background like white sound, and those that seem to justify or explain, but really may be the root cause of those negative feelings. If you can become aware of those egoic thoughts and feelings, you can disidentify with them or at least distance yourself from them. Tolle expresses the result succinctly when he says that "before you were the thoughts, emotions, and reactions; now you are the awareness, the conscious Presence that witnesses those states." Once accomplished, you'll be free of the ego or more realistically, free of its negative impact.

To attain this level of freedom, you must shift from believing you *are* your thoughts and emotions to believing you *are not* them. You are the consciousness that is aware of them. When you accept this, Tolle says that "an intelligence far greater that your ego's cleverness begins to operate in your life. Emotions and even thoughts become depersonalized through awareness. ... Your entire personal history, which is ultimately no more than a story, a bundle of thoughts and emotions, becomes of secondary importance and no longer occupies the forefront of your consciousness. It no longer forms the basis for your sense of identity. You are the light of Presence, the awareness that is prior to and deeper than any thoughts and emotions."

When you have a negative thought, calmly step outside of it, and as the silent conscious witness, objectively observe its unfolding. You can still have a bad thought, but don't allow yourself to *feel* badly as a result of having it. If somebody accuses you of being stupid, for example, realize that that is *their* thought – not *yours*. It's their judgement. You mustn't allow their thought or your subsequent thinking to trigger distress in you because it's just a thought – and not even yours. You won't ever feel guilt, for instance, unless you allow someone else's thought – present or past – to come into your conscious moment.

> *"There's no problem so awful that you can't add some guilt*
> *to it and make it even worse!" Bill Watterson*

When you eat ice cream, you may feel positive pleasure or negative guilt. But you're not the ice cream, nor are you the feeling you experience as a result of eating it. Step outside of your thought, whatever it happens to be, and consciously choose how to feel. Unless you have masochistic tendencies, perhaps you'd prefer to permit the pleasurable feeling to percolate to the surface and block the guilt. Feeling guilty is usually a reaction to somebody else's programming.

If you can appreciate that the thought is not you, that you are the sentient being currently having that thought and associated feeling in the moment, you've begun the journey to genuine freedom. Once adept at this, you'll be more able to control your thinking, reduce your chronic negative thoughts and associated emotions such as anger, impatience and regret, and maybe heal a chronic disease. Replace them with positive thoughts and feelings such as love, gratitude, happiness and a delightful radiant wellness. You already have this skill and all this knowledge, but have forgotten you know it. It's time to remember who you are and the power you possess.

> *"Right now I'm having amnesia and déjà vu at the same time.*
> *I think I may have forgotten this before." Stephen Wright*

The Great Pretender

*"Sometimes your joy is the source of your smile, but sometimes
your smile can be the source of your joy." Thich Nhat Hanh*

There's something to be said for acting happy, even if you're not truly feeling it. Someone once told me that by changing my physiology, I can alter my psychology; the phrase stuck with me. When you're feeling low, you may be oblivious to your pessimistic physical posture. To withdraw from the world, to figuratively lick your emotional wounds, you may have a tendency to shrink your stance, to slouch and hang your head. When becoming aware of such a bodily transformation, by consciously standing straight and tall with shoulders back and chin up, you may indeed be able to make yourself feel better. With chest out and head high, feeling glum is difficult. Try it.

Scientists working in the field of neuroplasticity have recently uncovered compelling evidence that when thinking positive thoughts, your brain actually develops new neural pathways to support those happy thoughts. Those new pathways facilitate a general increase in optimistic thoughts and incidents throughout your life. It's heady stuff (pun intended). Thus, by pretending to be happy, you may actually succeed in elevating your sullen mood. Remember my story about skipping? I dare you to do it next time you're feeling blue. If for no other reason than the healthy effect of the physical exertion, the exercise may trick your body into generating an endorphin rush – the happy "drug". If you allow it, silly can be fun.

"Against the assault of laughter, nothing can stand." Mark Twain

Here's a little more science for you. Endorphins are small protein molecules produced by cells in your body and particularly in the central nervous system. Their primary role is to relieve common pain by working with analgesia-producing sedative receptors located in your brain, spinal cord and other nerve endings. Endorphins have also been shown to control cravings for such things as chocolate and other potentially addictive substances (the fun stuff). In addition, they can control feelings of stress and frustration, the production and regulation of sex and growth hormones and help reduce the symptoms of eating disorders. Since they're produced naturally by the body, endorphins are arguably the best (legal) way to achieve a natural high. Endorphin release is credited with the delightful feelings of post-coital bliss, and also with such activities as ribald laughter, meditation, acupuncture, massage, deep breathing, consuming spicy food, spa treatments and even hiking in a lush forest. Infant laughter and funny flicks can also have the same effect. These useful endogenous opioid peptides are basically good for your health. Thus, it's smart to frequently indulge. Laugh long and often. Make love regularly and rejoice in the momentous pleasure.

"Most folks are as happy as they make up their minds to be."
Abraham Lincoln

Resolution Road

Years ago, while operating my own brokerage, through the glass wall of my private office, I'd observe my agents as they entered the foyer. If someone sullenly shuffled in, I'd immediately invite them into my office to talk, not only about their business challenges, but more importantly, their feelings. If business trouble, we'd usually arrive at some viable solutions and they'd leave armed with ideas, and more importantly, feeling better. However, if they were feeling despondent, but unsure why, I'd get into a bit of counselling; not necessarily in any ill-conceived attempt to permanently fix their emotional wounds, but to hopefully help identify some root causes of their morose mood. Just like I may now be introducing you, dear reader, to new concepts, I'd do my best to start my agent on the road to resolution.

If they were feeling, say, regret or guilt, I'd explain that their thoughts were in the past. If they were worried, fretful or feeling anxious, they were suffering from future thought. I'd encourage them to have no regrets about things past since they couldn't be changed and could only adversely affect their present and possible future. History is like a cancelled cheque with no further value. We can only learn from our past mistakes (or victories) and move on. And the future? It's like a post-dated cheque with no current value – just potential – over which they also exert no control. It's been posited that we each have multiple optional destinies and that we individually determine which one manifests into our conscious reality. To some degree, our future is determined by the choices we make in the present – the Now. Look at your current challenges from a fresh perspective and try a different approach. Slip on a new hat. You might make a mistake, but usually, you have nothing to lose by trying out a new idea.

"Anyone who has never made a mistake has never tried anything new."
Albert Einstein

If I was unable to help alleviate their despondency, I'd summarily kick them out of the office. But accompanying my metaphoric boot would be the admonishment that by forcing themselves to work and speaking to prospects while in a negative state, they'd probably not only exacerbate their bad disposition, but also aggravate their business slump. What they really needed was to recharge their batteries. My advice? Go have some fun. Do something joyful; golf, bike, hike or sit in the park and read a good novel or self-help book (especially if introverted). Or visit someone who'd appreciate their company, someone with whom they'd shared a good feeling in the past (extrovert alert). Go commune with a loved one. Get hugged! Feel the love! Do something to stimulate positive thoughts and feelings and maybe a nice endorphin rush.

> *"I've learned that people will forget what you said, people will forget what you did, but people will never forget how you made them feel."* Maya Angelou

If they refused to heed my advice to take time off for personal healing, I'd recommend they contact a former client with whom they'd enjoyed a warm, successful relationship. After a brief chat, that client's positive energy would wash over them and help them feel better about life. Since thoughts are powerful, maybe merely thinking about that wonderful experience might rejuvenate their energy and self-confidence.

The network marketing industry is reputed to share our industry's high attrition rate. In that business, it's really easy to be depressed when you realize that your enthusiastic, but misinterpreted actions have alienated a friend. To boost a marketer's low mood, it's popular to call *up* when feeling *down* and to call *down* when *up*. It refers to the practice, when feeling low, of calling someone in their up-line, particularly the person responsible for sponsoring them into the company, with the hope that their sponsor can lift their spirits. The reverse would be a sponsor, while in high spirits, calling their down-line people to offer encouragement and support. It can be quite effective. I used to do the same thing with my agents, if I felt they needed some cheer, by surprising them with a mini-visit in their private office. After I donated some positive energy, they were usually smiling with a credit balance in their energy account. Sometimes, all it takes is a simple positive thought. And enough of these can lead to the creation of a belief.

> *"Your beliefs become your thoughts, your thoughts become your words, your words become your actions, your actions become your habits, your habits become your values and your values become your destiny."*
> Mahatma Gandhi

Chapter Thirty-Two

Believing is Seeing

"One life is all we have and we live it as we believe in living it. But to sacrifice what you are and to live without belief, that is a fate more terrible than dying."
Joan of Arc

Possibilities

"The happiness of your life depends upon the quality of your thoughts: therefore guard accordingly and take care that you entertain no notion unsuitable to virtue and reasonable nature." Marcus Aurelius Antoninus

Early in my career, I never actually thought much about this esoteric stuff. With the passage of time, though, it gradually began to dawn on me that throughout my adult life, I'd been instinctively cultivating success habits. With the power of hindsight, I realized I'd been on a life-long growth curve, sometimes at glacial velocity and occasionally, a sudden rapid and exponentially steep one. Due to a life-long voracious appetite for interesting books written by courageous independent thinkers, I've been serendipitously introduced to all sorts of fascinating philosophies, theories and techniques on subjects as diverse as business psychology, human behaviour, communication, spirituality, quantum physics, economics, politics and wellness. Without any doubt, the modest knowledge I've gleaned from the works of these sages played a big part in my personal growth and hence, the viability of my business practice. Nevertheless, I've enjoyed a great long career for a single underlying reason.

With the exception of one major but relatively short-lived setback, which still provided enough for a reasonable, though more humble lifestyle, I've lived fairly well. Why have I prospered? I *believed* in limitless possibilities, that there would always be sufficient available resources to support a comfortable lifestyle. Do I still occasionally wrestle with the ghosts of limiting beliefs? Yes, of course, for it's an unavoidable part of the human condition. But at my core,

I've always *expected* to have enough. When I sought new business, I *always* found it. My phone rang when I *expected* it. Whatever belief I hold firmly in mind, reinforced with positive thoughts and emotions, manifests into my everyday reality. That's the way it's been for me, and it can be for you too.

Whatever Newtonian thinker coined the expression "seeing is believing" had it backwards. From a more contemporary quantum physics perspective, it's actually "believing is seeing". Belief is exceptionally powerful, more than you ever probably imagined. It determines, in every respect, how you live your life. I'm sure you've heard the old truism that whatever you believe, you achieve. Well, it's absolutely true. If you believe in nothing, you'll generally achieve exactly that – nothing – because a belief in nothing is still a belief. If you believe you lack the talent to be a top producer, any noteworthy business accomplishment will almost certainly elude you, along with any accumulation of significant wealth. If you sincerely believe you're incapable of attaining the pinnacle of success, finding true love or whatever you feel is missing from your life, that's exactly what is destined for you. But here's the good news; because of the universally unlimited possibilities available to *everyone*, your presumed destiny can be changed.

> "Man is made by his belief. As he believes, so he is."
> Johann Wolfgang von Goethe

Limiting Beliefs

> "None are so hopelessly enslaved as those who falsely believe they are free."
> Johann Wolfgang von Goethe

In this dualistic world, you're voluntarily and involuntarily conditioned by authority figures with both light and dark energy – love and fear – the fundamental motivations for *everything* you do, how you behave and how successful you become. Virtually everything manifested in your life is the result of choices based on patterning established in response to cultural mandates and familial requirements embedded during your upbringing. To feel you belong, not only to a blood family but also to a cultural one, that you're part of the herd, you instinctively follow lessons learned consciously and unconsciously.

At an early age, you're conditioned to believe what's real and what's not, what you should or shouldn't be, say or do. You're taught what to think and feel about yourself and others, about your body, intelligence, spirituality, religion, class, rules, laws and moral standards. You're programmed to mind your manners, be a good kid, toe the line, stand up straight, go to bed, play by the rules, respect your elders, get an education, win at all costs, follow doctor's orders, line up, save money and eat your vegetables. Sometimes, fearful, toxic and disempowering beliefs, such as hatred, anger or racial, religious and sexual discrimination are entrenched in your psyche. You're indoctrinated to live by the clock, crawl to work through rush-hour traffic to collect a paltry man-made currency to pay artificial debts, obey synthetic statutes of the land and view trivial television with subliminal marketing. After idling through the donut drive-thru and polluting the outer environment, you ingest toxic "Frankenfoods" and pollute your inner environment. Such is life for countless millions.

For being good, you're permitted by the "elected" and (self) appointed establishment to maintain your liberty and relative decreasing privacy, and at the same time, deprived of individual inalienable rights for what is referred to as the common good. Most people normally obey the laws of the land and follow the behavioural rules of civilization, family traditions, cultural customs or religious doctrine out of fear of being punished – here or hereafter – for non-compliance. For better or worse, you choose to live by standards imposed by a societal system of reward and punishment.

> *"People usually think according to their inclinations, speak according to their learning and ingrained opinions, but generally act according to custom."*
> Francis Bacon

It's customary to accept cultural conditioning since the alternative is either a solitary hermetic life of self-imposed incarceration, one of penurious denial and deprivation or of involuntary internment. Of course, in our competitive world of surplus and scarcity, supply and demand, the potential undesirable alternative is lawlessness and violence. So, we blindly accept selfish, inept political and economic governance, a monstrously manipulated mainstream media "entertainment" industry and a strictly, but subtly regimented education system deliberately designed to create a compliant workforce of "good citizens". Some would argue, and not completely without merit, in favour of anarchy and the demise of our present dysfunctional, enslaving and self-perpetuating order. Many feel that today's various systems of government do not honestly serve as mandated, but only to preserve the status quo and the ever revolving cast of questionable carbon copy characters in multi-coloured coats.

But here's the thing; the prime difference between today's ambitious, but indentured workers and the downtrodden of earlier centuries is that the old world workers *knew* they were slaves. And think about this; humans are the only species of life on our planet that must *pay* to live here. Is there something fundamentally wrong with this?

To maintain a cohesive social collective, to some extent, compliance is necessary. But to be happy and self-fulfilled, we each must filter out the destructive, untrue and hurtful propaganda. The alignment of our personal core beliefs with such unnecessary negative mass brainwashing, such as rhetorical political doctrine, barking religious dogma and various limiting beliefs passed down through the system, is responsible for most of the misfortune experienced by the vast majority of the world's unthinking populace.

"Some slaves are scoured to their work by whips,
others by their restlessness and ambition." John Ruskin

A Child Learns

"We are shaped by our thoughts; we become what we think. When
the mind is pure, joy follows like a show that never leaves." Buddha

The Jesuits, the renowned 16th century Catholic "schoolmasters of Europe", claimed that if a parent gave them their boy until the age of seven, the priests would show them the man because they'd "form" the child's beliefs during his "formative" years. Nowadays, nothing has changed. We still live in accordance with subconscious programming, otherwise known as early childhood conditioning. Due to prolonged exposure to the powerful explicit and subliminal influence of parents, siblings, friends, teachers, coaches, political and religious leaders, implanted beliefs continue to develop, solidify and significantly affect our adult life choices, as well as those of society at large, long after the cessation of direct supervisory input.

Dr. Bruce Lipton, Ph.D., is a noted cellular biologist, internationally recognized leader in bridging science and spirit and a former professor at the University of Wisconsin's School of Medicine. He performed pioneering studies at Stanford University and co-authored a book with Steve Bhaerman, author, humorist and political and cultural commentator, entitled *Spontaneous Evolution*. In this entertainingly informative book, he wrote: "Is our presumed powerlessness and frailty a true reflection of human abilities? Advances in biology and physics offer an amazing alternative – one that suggests our sense of disempowerment is the result of learned limitations." There's that limiting belief concept again.

He goes on to say that "our first programmed perceptions are acquired through inheritance. Our genomes contain behavioural programs that provide fundamental reflex behaviours referred to as instincts. ... The second source of life-controlling perceptions comes from experiential memories downloaded into the subconscious mind. These powerful learned perceptions represent the contribution from nurture. Among the earliest perceptions of life to be downloaded into the subconscious mind were our mother's emotional patterns while we were in the womb. ... By the time the baby is born, emotional information downloaded from the mother's experiences has already shaped half of that individual's personality! ... However, the most influential perceptual programming of the subconscious mind occurs from birth through age six. ... the child's sensory systems are fully engaged, downloading massive amounts of information about the world and how it works."

*"Basically the school system sets you up with what it wants
to set you up with. They're really good at it. I think they're too good.
Problem is, what they're doing is conditioning kids to merely
accept the culture at hand. But the rebels won't accept it." Jack Bowman*

The field of psychology affirms that we live our lives based in part on programming and inherited beliefs. Dr. Carl Gustav Jung, the famous psychologist, postulated that the psyche consists of three parts: ego, personal unconscious and collective unconscious. Whereas the ego represents the conscious mind, he believed that the personal unconscious mind contains our personal memories, including suppressed ones. The collective unconscious, on the other hand, is a unique part of the psyche that serves as a form of psychological inheritance, and contains all the knowledge and experiences we share collectively as an Earth (maybe Universal) species. Many refer to it as Source or more commonly, God. It's like the "all-knowing" Internet that we can tap into anytime. If the Internet was self-aware, it might be the perfect metaphor, but thankfully, it hasn't evolved to that point ... yet.

Dr. Jung believed that archetypes, a term he coined, exist within the collective unconscious and that they're innate, universal and hereditary. Archetypes are instinctual, not learned, and function to organize how we interact with others and experience life events. He proposed that consciousness functions not only to recognize and assimilate the external world through our 3-dimensional five senses, but also to manifest our world's visible reality from the collective unconscious that dwells within each of us.

Have you ever said you do something a certain way because that's how you've always done it? Or you can't do something because it isn't you, or too frightened or intimidated to try something new? Can you logically explain why you believe or behave this way? My mother, bless her heart, always warned me to avoid running because I'd fall. So, even though I was always relatively able-bodied, for fear of being hurt, physical sports were anathema to me. Of course, it wasn't true, but if someone hears and/or experiences something often enough, for them, it becomes the truth. And later experiences only strengthened this conviction. While participating in a game of high school touch football, my ribcage and the rising heel of another player collided with a crack. Since it was my rib and not his heel, I still limit myself to being a team sport spectator.

Beliefs are the direct result of conditioning, and almost always not of your own choosing. For instance, as a youth, if your friendship overtures were regularly rebuffed, due to a subconscious fear of rejection, you might now be hesitant about initiating romantic or friendly relationships. Or if continually denied the "privilege" of hanging with the cool kids at school, because of a resultant deep sense of unworthiness, you may have stopped trying to fit in and still embrace that attitude to this day. Conditioning is usually responsible for the relentless voice in your head that serves as a constant reminder that you're incapable or unlovable or some other daft preconception. It makes you into a wounded "Doubting Thomas".

In his informative book, *the untethered soul; the journey beyond yourself*, Michael A. Singer opines that the voice in your head is not you. You know that conditioned "should" voice that nags you to do or not do something. It's also the unremitting mind chatter while performing automatic tasks. It's the continuous narration of self-talk that keeps you awake at night. Sometimes, you have complete conversations with yourself, even taking both sides of an argument. However, that incessant voice is nothing but a collection of random unexpressed thoughts – and is not you. You're the objective and perpetually silent awareness that *hears* the voice.

You've no doubt heard stories of (or personally experienced) a parent routinely demeaning their child as a lazy good-for-nothing, labelling them a layabout who'll never amount to anything. Guess what? Such prophesies often prove true because criticized, abused or neglected kids tend to make life decisions congruent with their parent's lowly expectations and create lives in alignment with such conditioning. Because their parents expected little of them, and failed to encourage or believe in them (probably because the parents didn't love and respect *themselves*), the kids fail to believe in themselves, even if they overtly possess a God-given talent. How could they be self-confident when the people who represent the centre of their Universe never consistently demonstrated any faith in them? The voice in their head is usually discouraging and defeatist.

There are exceptions, though. To earn parental approval, an emotionally driven adult off-spring can indeed achieve financial success, but often at the price of a life devoid of genuine love and joy. In exchange for a shallow life based on the illusory, sometimes misinterpreted goal of pleasing a living or deceased parent, they sacrifice an authentic life built around their true personal values. They become fixated on the grand prize and fail to appreciate the interesting diversity of the people and the richness of the ride.

To enjoy a long and fruitful career, if you believe it's right to *love* money and *use* people, in the interest of all humanity, please shift to the opposite paradigm – *use* money and *love* people – or find an alternate career that minimizes public interaction. Money is merely a means to an end. Unless you suffer from the miserly affliction of plutolatry, the excessive devotion to wealth, you don't actually love money anyway. You value it for what it can bring your family – security, lifestyle, toys or simply the chance to follow your bliss. Money is merely an unlovable tool, an artificial invention with a built-in depreciating exchange value.

Behind the malady of Money Madness lurks the shadow of a fear-driven society, one based on the fearful belief of perpetual scarcity, of never having enough. As a child, you may have been taught that money was the root of all evil or that it doesn't grow on trees or that you can't simultaneously be wealthy *and* spiritual or even be happy *without* money. Perhaps having survived the Great Depression, your parents learned to do without. Maybe they were life-long welfare recipients or never succeeded in breaking out of their low-paying, no-collar jobs. They may have lived a self-limiting life because they felt there was no point in even thinking beyond their station, and accepted their destined existence, their fated life. They may have felt that if it was good enough for *their* elders, it was good enough for them – and good enough for you too.

> *"Men often become what they believe themselves to be. If I believe I cannot do something, it makes me incapable of doing it. But when I believe I can, then I acquire the ability to do it even if I didn't have it in the beginning."*
> Mahatma Gandhi

Numerous long-term studies have concluded that the work and life decisions of the progeny of successive familial generations are significantly affected by the income and work ethic of their childhood households. It's the age-old controversy of nature verses nurture. Many forward thinkers now believe that *both* have significant influence on a child's mind, thus their life-long behaviour. For example, if the parents were chronic welfare recipients, the odds were high that their brood would inherit and accept their weak work ethic and defeatist attitude. Conversely, if the parents had successful business lives, their children learned the social, emotional and financial benefits of work and would normally reject any thoughts of welfare participation. Also, it's been said that alcoholic parents tend to raise children prone to alcoholism, smokers rear smoking kids and abusive parents unfortunately often pass along that trait. We're programmed by nurture – or the lack of it – as well as nature.

Stories abound about major lottery winners going broke after a few short years. I suggest this happens because they fail to think differently, to think bigger, as independent, self-made wealthy people usually think. And inheritors of great wealth, suffering the same fate, easily squander an unearned fortune. They fail to morph into the people they must be to sustain a life of abundance. Since they're not the actual wealth creators, they continue to think as they always have – unworthy. They luck out until their luck – and winnings – run out. The Universe aligns with their limiting beliefs – their lowly sense of self-worth – and strips them of those unearned riches.

> *"Your fortune is not something to find but to unfold."*
> Eric Butterworth

Parents have *gargantuan* control over the quality of life their kids are destined to live as adults. Please don't misinterpret; your mother and/or father probably did the best they could with the belief tools in their own mind-skill toolboxes. However, unless parents recognize and discard their damaging inherited beliefs and consistently implement a more progressive, enlightened parenting methodology, most are simply ill-equipped to raise their kids any differently than how they were raised by *their* parents. It's a multi-generational thing. So, forgive them and move on.

Nevertheless, due to prolonged exposure to such multi-generational coupon-shopping habits, your sponge-like mind naturally absorbed that doctrine into your subconscious as being *The Truth*. And no matter your endeavour, you may have unwittingly carried, nurtured and reinforced such habits throughout your lifetime by manifesting the same pessimistic attitude. Since you make major and minor choices based on your belief system – both consciously and unconsciously – unless you become aware of and replace negative thoughts and life-long limiting beliefs of scarcity with positive thoughts of abundance, your own train to Victoryville may be doomed to never depart from the same station that so constrained your parents.

> *"Your circumstances may be uncongenial, but they shall not remain*
> *so if you only perceive an ideal and strive to reach it. You cannot travel*
> *within and stand still without. Let a person radically alter his thoughts*
> *and he will be astonished at the rapid transformation it will effect*
> *in the material conditions of his life." James Allen*

Having said all this, not all conditioning is bad. Indeed, it's debatable that much of it contributes toward a sustainable social order. In addition to gems such as "wherever ye may be, let your wind blow free", my mother taught me high standards of morality and integrity. I still hear her voice in my head reminding me that sticks and stones may break your bones, but names will never hurt you. This old phrase was probably drummed into *her* head by her traditional Scottish parents. My father taught me that if a job is worth doing, it's worth doing well. Now, those are clearly exemplary examples of positive conditioning (except maybe about the free wind). As an adult, when I undertake a project, I always do my very best. Also, it's pretty tough to hurt me by hurling invective, though some no doubt have tried. Nevertheless, good or not good, the conditioning and resulting belief is not who you truly are.

To help you identify limitations that may dwell in your subconscious mind, take some time to remember your childhood family environment (and ponder how you're raising your own kids). How do you recollect being raised by your parents? Do any of their prominent beliefs come to mind? Think about the following statements and whether or not they apply to you – then and now:

"When I was a boy of 14, my father was so ignorant I could hardly stand to have the old man around. But when I got to be 21, I was astonished at how much the old man had learned in 7 years." Mark Twain

➢ If a child lives with criticism, he learns to condemn himself and others
➢ If she lives with hostility, she believes she must fight and struggle in life
➢ If he's ridiculed, he develops low self-esteem and becomes shy and insecure
➢ If she lives in fear, she becomes apprehensive, avoids risk and develops a victim mentality
➢ If he lives with shame, he learns to feel guilty about himself
➢ If she's taught tolerance, she learns patience
➢ If he's encouraged, he develops high self-esteem and self-confidence
➢ If she lives in an atmosphere of love and acceptance, she learns to love, to be non-judgemental and that she is lovable
➢ If he's respected and recognized as an individual and permitted to make his own life choices, he learns self-respect and to appreciate the importance of life goals
➢ If she lives with integrity, she learns the importance of truth
➢ If he lives with fairness, he learns justice
➢ If she lives in a happy home, she learns faith in herself and others
➢ If he lives with friendliness and love, he accepts the world as a good place to love and be loved and most importantly, that he is lovable

"When making your choice in life, do not neglect to live."
Samuel Johnson

Whether you enjoyed the many tangible benefits of a wealthy or middle-class lifestyle or subsisted in an environment of abject poverty, provided you were raised in a loving, respectful atmosphere, you possess the power to live a life of abundance. In all probability, though, you were still conditioned with at least some limiting beliefs. As a mathematical problem must first be defined before a solution can be found, before you can dispel a limiting belief about yourself or the world, you must first understand how it may adversely affect your life. If you can identify with any of the above classic circumstances, you've taken the first critical step to reprogramming your program.

Insanity has been succinctly defined as doing something the same way repeatedly and expecting different results. By extension, if you've been systematically practicing real estate with the same tired attitude and employing the same old methods, but without the success you desire, by this definition, you may be nuts. To advance, you must think, feel and do things differently. Unless a miracle occurs, to improve productivity, you need a new attitude and/or business methodology, and critically – become aware of and jettison any limiting beliefs. Otherwise, logically, you'll continue to generate the same mediocre results. Garbage in – garbage out.

A great litmus test to determine if you're actually living a life based on your own intrinsic values and not self-sabotaging beliefs is to ask yourself if you're happy *most* of the time. If not, you're probably living in accordance with someone else's creed. If you innately feel your lifestyle doesn't suit your instinctual purpose, if you don't feel excited every day, to bring more happiness into your existence, to free yourself from the disempowering confines of your cocoon and undergo a metamorphosis from caterpillar to butterfly, you have to recondition your conditioning. A leopard can't change its spots, you say? Well, this may be true, but because everyone possesses an instinctive need to excel, to be happy, you *can* alter your beliefs.

> *"Believe that life is worth living and your belief will help create the fact."*
> William James

Self-Actualization

> *"Whatever your mind can conceive and can believe, it can achieve."*
> Napoleon Hill

Abraham Maslow, a prominent American psychologist during his lifetime, is reputed for introducing the Theory of the Hierarchy of Needs. His theory was predicated on the fulfillment of innate human needs in priority and culminating in self-actualization. He spoke of needs based on deficiency and growth. As mentioned earlier, needs which result from a perceived deficiency spring from a place of fear – and initiate a move *away* from scarcity. On the other hand, a need for growth originates from a place of love – and creates a move *toward* abundance. Someone functioning in the first camp and another in the second may outwardly appear to be equally successful. However, the fearful person is in a state of personal disharmony, whereas the second is living in harmony with their intrinsic values.

Maslow emphasized the importance of focusing on the positive qualities in people. As a humanistic psychologist, he believed that everybody has a powerful innate desire to realize their full potential, to achieve a level of self-actualization – to be happy. He thought that each person possesses the potential to enjoy peak experiences, high points when they live in harmony with themselves and their surroundings. He defined these experiences as profound moments of love, understanding and happiness, when one feels more whole, alive, self-sufficient and more aware of truth, justice and harmony. He considered these experiences or states of flow to be the manifestation of evidence of the self-realization of one's potential.

He suggested that self-actualized people deeply accept themselves and others, along with the world in general, and enjoy more peak daily experiences than those less self-actualized. He also believed that *how* essential needs are fulfilled is just as important as their ultimate fulfillment. An essential component of self-actualization, he theorized, is the way by which one achieves cooperative social fulfillment or establishes meaningful relationships. If vital needs find selfish and competitive fulfillment, one acquires negative emotions and fewer congenial relationships. In other words, success at somebody else's expense won't win any loving friends or cooperative, trusting clients. Selfless beats selfish every time.

His views confirm my belief that to be truly happy, you must be aware of and live according to your own personal values and not those imposed on you by others. When you experience an epiphany, follow and learn from it since that's your higher self speaking. To experience frequent and regular moments of bliss – self-actualization – be genuine and loving. If you're truly happy doing what you do, opportunities for growth and advancement will "magically" appear. And by default, you'll continue to attract more of the same positive energy, people and success into all areas of your life.

> *"Follow your bliss and doors will open for you that you never knew existed. Follow your bliss and the Universe will open doors for you where there were only walls." Joseph Campbell*

Involution to Evolution

"As I have come to understand myself and my fellow humans better, it has become clear that the vast majority of our decisions are based on the beliefs we hold, not the information we possess. And by 'beliefs', I mean little stories, the individual narratives that combine into our larger selves, shaping and driving our daily decisions with many times the force of simple data. So, the first order of business is identifying which beliefs, which narratives, we are running. And then we need to figure out how to go about either modifying or replacing them if/as necessary." Chris Martenson, PhD, MBA

By accepting that your limiting beliefs were inherited, you can come to terms with the fact that many of your life choices and current world perceptions were and may not be genuinely your own. Even though you think you made crucial life decisions with full awareness, those choices may have been based on fearful habitual thinking. While *conscious* fear can contribute to physical survival by way of the fight or flight instinct, *subconscious* fear can generate irrational choices based on untruths because fear programming can distort instinctive perceptions.

If you're dissatisfied with your life, your task is to determine who's running the show. To harness the unique innate power to think and believe anew under your own steam, dig to the root cause of your dissatisfaction. A red flag that you're not the boss of you, that when presented with a choice, you're relying on cushy conditioning, is the use of the word "should". Do you think about what you *should* be, *should* have or *should* want? That powerful harping voice saying you should or shouldn't do something is that of a former or current authority figure telling you how *they* believe you *should* be living your life and about the decisions you *should* be making to measure up to *their* standards. Try superimposing that person's voice onto your mind-chatter. Then, respectfully tell it to shut up, that you'll make your own independent decision. Then, before making a critical decision, calmly ask yourself a few questions.

Why are you considering such an action? Does the probable result mesh with *your* true values? Does it *feel* right to you? Would acting or reacting in your usual manner serve your desired overall life picture? Would such a choice truly contribute to what you want in the long term? Consider alternatives, even if they seem somewhat uncomfortable. After all, you're contemplating leaving your comfort zone. After serious consideration, go ahead and make the decision. If you choose to *consciously* respond instead of *unconsciously* react, you might choose a different path, and that's where growth happens. As cows follow the same path back to the barn every night, the more you walk that new path, the easier it gets – with fewer obstacles. A natural good habit will develop.

In his channelled book, *I AM THE WORD, A Guide to the Consciousness of Man's Self in a Transitioning Time*, Paul Selig wrote that when you think, *you* created that thought based on your history or "the creation of the past. You have a thought in the past, it creates something for you, it becomes part of your world, and then that becomes the basis of future thinking." Because your thought manifested a certain result for you – good or bad – it's based on that result that you'll have a future thought and resulting experience. Hence, "you're always building a bridge towards the next phase of your life, to the next action of your life." So, choose your bridges (thoughts) carefully, for if you choose to regularly rely on thinking that emerged from a limiting belief, "you continue to get what you said you didn't want because you are still producing the same energy system in frequency that will attract to you those very things that are giving you trouble." To avoid such trouble, just as you upgrade a computer program, choose your thoughts consciously and overwrite your subconscious mind "software" with your own programming based on beliefs birthed from learning and experimenting.

> "Only as high as I reach can I grow, only as far as I seek can I go, only as deep as I look can I see, only as much as I dream can I be." Karen Ravn

If success remains elusive, it's often because you don't believe you're worthy and have fallen back onto limiting beliefs. Maybe you were told you're not as talented, smart, assertive or physically attractive as somebody who seems to have the world by the tail. Or you think you can't do something because you've never done it before or have always been that way, or if you tried, you'd probably fail anyway. Consequently, why bother trying? Every time you diminish yourself by feeling unworthy or inferior, you're not only reinforcing existing negative programming and holding yourself back, you're also lowering your vibrational frequency into darkness, thereby subjecting yourself to external fear-based control.

Discard all fearful thoughts about what you don't have and don't want. Shift your attention away from thoughts of scarcity toward loving thoughts of infinite abundance, wellness, gratitude and happiness. And fuel them with positive emotion. Since the desire to excel, to be happy and attain full potential, is an innate human characteristic, your actions will intuitively feel right. With your improved attitude and radiating positive aura, you'll serendipitously be presented with opportunities, acquire the necessary tools and skills and take the steps required to manifest your goals into your reality. Imagine all green traffic lights on your route through life. Don't *expect* obstacles, but when they appear, look for the opportunity to learn from them. Believe an open parking space at a busy plaza awaits your arrival. (This happens for me a lot.) Expect it. Begin by thinking the thought and then another and another. A series of small steps can lead to big changes and bigger results.

In another of Dr. Lipton's books, *THE HONEYMOON EFFECT – the science of creating heaven on earth*, he describes a series of steps for reprogramming your subconscious mind, the first of which is to "be conscious of what you ask for because you're going to get it." The next step is to review your subconscious programming. Ask yourself if your subconscious beliefs support or contradict your conscious desires? Then start reprogramming using a combination of various methods such as mindfulness or habit (as discussed), hypnosis, subliminal recordings and a deeper level of communication with others. According to Dr. Lipton, with patience, perseverance and practice, it can be done. I can most assuredly say that, over the years, by following such steps, I successfully transformed from a confirmed introvert with a quiet childhood into a confidently social ambivert with a great referral business. With consistent effort, you can recondition your condition. But remember; it isn't a magic bullet. As dieting to lose weight isn't a short-term effort, paraphrasing Dr. Lipton, evolution is not a destination, but an everyday practice.

> *"The world we see that seems so insane is the result of a belief*
> *system that is not working. To perceive the world differently, we must*
> *be willing to change our belief system, let the past slip away, expand*
> *our sense of now and dissolve the fear in our minds." William James*

You can begin to reprogram your programming only while in the present moment where happiness and contentedness await you. Not only is it virtually impossible to feel genuine joy and gratitude without being present, you're brought automatically into the present moment when you do something enjoyable. It works both ways. You can't make a choice for the past, nor can you choose a specific future. All you can do is choose today, which of course will affect your tomorrow. Behave in a manner that reflects who you want to be – not who you were. You're not your bank account or your dented car. Past accomplishments represent who you *were*. For a better future, make insightful life and business choices based on who you now consciously choose to be.

A good place to begin to search for advancement tools is outside of you, but growth is unquestionably an inside job. After you've been introduced to a novel idea, incorporate that new-found knowledge into your professional and interpersonal tool kit. Once you start looking inside – involution – and grow, your results on the outside – evolution – will manifest. Such introspection will inspire you to take different action to achieve different results. And those results will become the catalyst for newer and even greater goals, with one idea building onto its predecessor like a pyramid. After determining those loftier objectives and setting a solid intention to achieve them, you'll grow personally to fit those bigger shoes. Involution continues since it's a repeating cycle, if you allow it. *Be* the success you seek and assume full responsibility for everything that happens – or doesn't happen – in your life. You think, you feel, you act.

Determine your own programming. Within loving and mutually respectful reason, you decide how to live your life. If you can do this – with gusto – then your life on this planet will be lovingly abundant and emotionally fulfilling. You possess the power to heal yourself of limiting beliefs and to contribute toward the restoration of the health of our Earth. But to do so, you must passionately *believe* – at your core – that you can do it. Feel the ingrained resistance, overcome the inertia to change and then consciously move forward. Learn how to manifest the reality you want instead of the reality that the "powers-that-were" designed for you. Be the person you want to be. As is virtually everything in life, it's a personal choice. Remember that your will is far more powerful than the inner directing voice of habitual thinking. If you can find that silence between your thoughts – the real you – you can begin the odyssey of self-discovery and spiritual awakening to true happiness and live an authentic, more peaceful life by your own rules.

Teaching by Trial

You're not here in this incarnation to tread water, to live one day to the next like an automaton while earning money and accumulating assets. Rather, life is about personal growth – the supreme reason for our very existence. At precisely the right moments, you'll be serendipitously challenged with apparent trials. Everything that has happened to you, all the trials and tribulations, every victory and misfortune, every relationship won or lost, has been your teacher if you chose to see it that way. Your higher self, your soul, your subconscious mind, will continue to manifest such events or people with the aim of keeping you on track to achieve a higher goal of which you may be unaware. And these growth opportunities will continue in some form until you either learn the lesson or your body dies.

Thus, when something happens to you that in the moment, seems catastrophic, do your best to resist habitually reacting from conditioned fear. Since we learn more from our losses than from our victories, try observing it from a different perspective. What may have seemed a misfortune, might miraculously transform into a golden opportunity to change your life and propel you from your old conditioned comfort zone. A *conscious* recognition of such an event as a chance to grow will help allay your fears, and allow you to deal with it from a place of action, wisdom and knowing.

Conscious or unconscious fear can be a significant and familiar part of your personal comfort zone. You may feel a sense of entitlement to it and be reluctant to relinquish it. Better the devil you know than the devil you don't. Hogwash! Fear can manifest in several forms, including but certainly not limited to anxiety, anger, depression, shame, guilt, arrogance, envy, jealousy, greed and sloth. Fearful negative emotions as constant companions can also easily cause chronic ill-health, not to mention a life devoid of love and happiness. You can hang onto your fears for any reason. However, to escape them, you must first become conscious of them.

When you accept that you're a co-creator of your life, that you play a part in creating such trials, you cease being a victim. When you're no longer living as a victim and blaming somebody or something outside of you, you stop living in fear. And when you're no longer frightened, you can readily recognize a trial as a gift to alter a possibly long-held limiting belief and move toward living an authentic life. Therefore, when an opportunity for change in the guise of a trial arrives on your doorstep, welcome it as a fortuitous blessing. Pain is inevitable, but suffering is optional.

By opening your mind and stepping out of your egoic self, by becoming the impartial conscious witness of your personality (ego prefers you remain asleep), you begin to move away from implanted limiting beliefs which the ego uses as a defence against change. With the right program installed, and your ego sidelined, you can objectively and consciously learn from every experience. If you're completely present, with the arguable exception of violence perpetrated against you, there are no bad experiences. There's a lesson in everything that happens to you. If you're able to clear away the fog that clouds your ability to openly examine and understand the events that befall you and the choices you make, you'll be better equipped to resolve your personal challenges and install a new authentic program.

You might find such a transition difficult for awhile because you're in the process of change – of growth – and abandoning your comfort zone can be, well, uncomfortable. But this is a good thing. Being conscious of your reactive behaviour to certain stimulus is the first step to changing from a conditioned reactive or passive response to an active one. This will ultimately alter your subconscious beliefs, your thinking, which are typically the principle drivers of your behaviour. Actually, by being open-minded enough to read this book, as well as further explore the philosophies it expounds, you're becoming conscious of the human evolutionary changes already underway. Now, adjust your seat-backs to the vertical position, secure your seat-belts in anticipation of an interesting, but bumpy ride and enjoy the supersonic flight aboard Thoughtful Air.

"Sometimes people hold a core belief that is very strong.
When they are presented with evidence that works against that belief,
the new evidence cannot be accepted. It would create a feeling that is extremely
uncomfortable called cognitive dissonance. And because it is so important to
protect the core belief, they will rationalize, ignore and even deny anything
that doesn't fit in with the core belief." Frantz Fanon

Chapter Thirty-Three

Thoughts are Things

"When you change the way you look at things, the things you look at change."
Dr. Wayne Dyer

Speedy Thoughts

*"Nurture your mind with great thoughts, for you will never
go any higher than you think."* Benjamin Disraeli

It's been said that your conscious mind processes thought at about 40 bits per second. You might think that's speedy and it certainly is. But your subconscious mind – the real powerhouse – processes at 40 *million* bits per second! That's a million times faster! Variously referred to as instinct, intuition, gut feeling or higher self, your personal supercomputer automatically performs average daily activities without you having to deliberately think about them.

You routinely roll out of bed and habitually begin your morning ritual. (I do my best mind wandering and wondering in the shower.) Before crossing the street, you instinctively look both ways. If the guy in the car ahead unexpectedly brakes hard, do you consciously think to slam on the brakes too? No, because that would take too long. Unless you're a new driver with less than automatic response, or you're inebriated, you react in a nanosecond. Similarly, a large earth-moving machine operator can intuitively manage the sophisticated controls of his mechanical marvel without consciously thinking, minutely manipulating its limbs as an extension of his own.

That's your subconscious mind's reflexive, super-fast nature fulfilling its unremitting background responsibilities. It's like the operating system of your computer, instantaneously executing unseen functions without your direct input or control. If you do something repetitively and frequently enough, whether playing the piano or brushing your teeth, it becomes a habit stored in your mighty subconscious mind. Though a habit can be very powerful, be it constructive or destructive, it's nothing more than brain training. And as I continue to say, such training can be changed, either actively by you or passively by others.

Television service providers frequently run promotional campaigns wherein new subscribers are given a three month free service trial. Why three months? Because marketing experts have deduced that it takes at least that long to form a habit. Apparently, once customers are exposed to a service for awhile, it becomes part of their comfort zone and they won't bother cancelling the subscription. It's similar to the principle behind the devious methodology utilized by totalitarian tyrants like Adolph Hitler to alter the attitude of the citizenry; tell a particular lie often enough and people will believe it to be true.

"I have been impressed with the urgency of doing. Knowing is not enough; we must apply. Being willing is not enough; we must do." Leonardo da Vinci

Your reality is merely a reflection of your powerful subconscious beliefs, your habitual (sometimes life-long) thinking. Any thought you have – emotionally empowered – vibrates out into the Universe and returns into your material world. If you intend to change something in your life, you must first develop a new habit. If you want a dream real estate practice or romantic relationship, you must continuously think and behave as if you already have it. Entertain no doubts whatsoever. Repeat, repeat and repeat the thoughts and behaviour until you completely believe. When you assume complete responsibility for your life, whether it's the one you have or the one you want, only then will you possess the power to change it. Actively control your thoughts, and you'll begin to instinctively take different actions. Retrain your brain, and when you succeed, your belief will be reinforced.

There's a war-time story about Winston Churchill ordering one of his senior officers to conquer a particular town in enemy territory. The general hesitantly replied that he'd do his best. Finding his reply unacceptable, the controversial war-time prime minister emphasized that capturing the town was critical to the war effort. The general said he'd try. Churchill very patiently explained that by just *trying*, the general was preparing himself for failure, and failure was not an option. Finally committing, the general didn't just try or make his best effort; he succeeded. And no doubt, the general's victory reinforced his confidence in his own military prowess. He altered his belief.

Most people create unwittingly by default because they're unaware of the power of their subconscious thinking. They assume no responsibility for what occurs in their lives, be it good, bad or indifferent. They believe it's all about luck, about being at the right place at the right time. You can continue to ignore the Universal Law of Attraction (see the next chapter) and accept whatever happens, blame and remain a victim, an unconscious attractor, or move to a higher level of awareness, begin to consciously conquer your personal fears and experience your own victories. Don't just try your hand at the real estate business or do your best to be a top producer. Make the commitment to be great and develop constructive habits by retraining your brain. To create your own desired circumstances, think optimistically and take positive assertive action. Believe in yourself. Apply your skills and make it happen. It's always your *choice*.

> *"People are always blaming their circumstances for what they are.*
> *I don't believe in circumstances. The people who get on in this world*
> *are the people who get up and look for the circumstances they want*
> *and if they can't find them, make them." George Bernard Shaw*

You Think

> *"All that we are is the result of what we have thought.*
> *The mind is everything. What we think we become." Buddha*

As a young man in the late spring of 1974, with tremendous excitement, I eagerly embarked on my real estate career. Unfortunately, the timing occurred contemporaneous with a market correction. But as fate would have it, this was just another in a series of major life trials that would befall me. But all was not nearly as bad as it seemed at the time.

My wife and I already had a beautiful young daughter, Melanie Dawn. We had also recently undertaken our first foray into home ownership, complete with two mortgages and a bank loan for the down payment. We owned two cars with corresponding loans and were expecting another child to soon make her Earthly debut. Maybe to compound our stress, as it happened, the day our second child chose to inhale her first breath coincided with the day we closed the deal on the house. Moving day took on an entirely different complexion. Tongue firmly planted in cheek, of course, I accused my wife of going to extraordinary lengths to avoid helping to move our meagre possessions into our new home. While grunting and sweating unloading the rental truck, my wife was at the hospital, well, grunting and sweating unloading our delightful little Joanna Lee.

As a brand new agent with essentially no savings and, in the very early days, minimal commission income, to eat, fuel the cars and make monthly debt payments, we were regrettably unable to pay off our credit cards each month. Sound familiar? That was definitely deficit-living. We took a risk – a biggie. Some called us brave and others probably foolish, but I deeply believed my business would flourish; I felt it in my bones. I refused to listen to the naysayers and ignored those harping "should" voices in my head. I just knew I'd make it like I knew the sun would rise in the morning. If nothing else, I'd prove the naysayers wrong. I felt I was a good person and knew I cared about people. If I worked hard and smart enough and applied the skills I'd acquired during my brief but successful incarnation as a store manager and salesman in the men's haberdashery industry, and no less importantly – was honest and genuine – I'd thrive in my exciting new endeavour. How did I know this? I truly believed I was a top producer. Thus, it was relatively easy for me to behave like one; I just acted naturally. And I don't mean with a super-ego like some of the larger-than-life colleagues I've befriended along the way.

"All that we are is the result of what we have thought. If a man speaks or acts
with an evil thought, pain follows him. If a man speaks or acts with a pure
thought, happiness follows him like a shadow that never leaves him." Buddha

My philosophy was to talk the talk and walk the walk. I read, listened, researched and attended every available seminar (which weren't compulsory or as common in those days – no Internet) to be thoroughly equipped to address customer concerns. And I made mistakes. But I learned from them; a house didn't have to fall on me twice. I availed myself of the appropriate tools. Knowledge and information, bolstered by my sincerity, youthful energy and abundant charm (smile) were obvious tools in my toolbox. If I couldn't answer a question, I'd freely admit it and get an answer. I didn't allow my ego to get me into trouble. My clients knew I wasn't a know-it-all. I was honest, authentic – and having fun. And in the process, I did whatever I could to make their transition as pleasurable as possible.

Simply said (and without exercising the conscious intent of which I'm now aware), I conducted myself according to what I then perceived to be the real me – in alignment with my beliefs. It's much easier to behave authentically than act a part since the former consumes considerably less energy. Plus if you're always natural, there's no risk of being caught out of character. As the old adage goes – honesty is always the best policy. And as a new pair of slippers become increasingly comfortable as they age, I grew progressively more comfortable in my own skin.

"Three things cannot be long hidden: the sun, the moon and the truth." Buddha

My business thrived in direct proportion to the growth of my competence and confidence. During the first couple of years, I rocketed to the upper tier of top 10 agents with a major independent multi-branch brokerage of over

350 agents. Aside from a strong belief and great time-management skills, I succeeded by having fun (and until I hired a live-in nanny, a long list of baby-sitters). Thankfully, I quickly and easily gained the trust of nearly everyone who crossed my professional path. They knew they could trust me. I was the real deal. Gratefully, a growing number of people considered me their friend in the business. And four decades later, many still do.

I worked long hours to achieve financial success and was making serious money. Sadly, though, since I hadn't yet been introduced to the brilliant concept of harmony, naked ambition cost me my marriage. As I said, my life has had many roses, but also a fair number of thorns. However, the amicable divorce agreement blessed me with full custody of our two daughters whom I chose to raise solo for several years. That challenge was just as gargantuan as building a real estate practice, but I did it joyfully. Many valuable life lessons with my two little ones were exchanged, and wonderful memories made during those early years so long ago.

For people to believe in you, you must believe in yourself – and by all means, hold truthful non-limiting beliefs. Once accomplished, you can sell anything because you're actually selling your authentic self and not a guarded egoic phoney-baloney. To quote Beatle, Ringo Starr; "All you gotta do is ... act naturally."

"You have to believe in yourself, that's the secret. Even when I was in the orphanage, when I was roaming the street trying to find enough to eat, even then, I thought of myself as the greatest actor in the world." Charlie Chaplin

If you like the idea of altering your beliefs and maintaining an optimistic attitude, don't expose yourself to mainstream media news. The distinguished news anchor usually opens the show with a "good evening" and then proceeds to tell you exactly why it *isn't*. Rarely is the news elevating, whether broadcast or printed, unless you consider announcements of murders, fires, riots, atrocities, disasters, political or military shenanigans and how bad the economy is doing as positive. Plus it's highly manipulative. To control the masses, the mainstream media does their best to keep everyone in a constant state of fear. God knows how many times Buffalo, NY burned as reported by Irv Weinstein on *Eyewitness News*.

Actually, the same goes for the current and seemingly endless supply of mind-numbing reality, crime, hospital and lawyer shows on network television that serve as Weapons of Mass Distraction (WMD). They all depend on dumb competitions, confrontation, family dysfunction, conflict, acrimony, personal misfortune or violent victimization. It couldn't get more negative.

You wouldn't desire something if, at a subconscious level, you didn't truly believe you were capable of achieving it. If you fail to fulfill that desire, you lacked sufficient faith in yourself, failed to put your heart into the effort, failed to modify your habitual subconscious thinking and quit early. And while we're on the heart; don't fear relying on it for a decision since your heart represents instinct. According to Dr. Lipton, we all have neural cells and cellular memory throughout our bodies. And after your brain, your heart is the largest repository of such cells. Thus, when you make a heart-felt decision, you're actually still thinking. Believe in yourself and your goals will manifest into your reality. Don't quit. Keep the faith – in yourself – and you will evolve.

> *"Most people give up just when they're about to achieve success.*
> *They quit on the one yard line. They give up at the last minute*
> *of the game one foot from a winning touchdown." Ross Perot*

They Think

> *"Risk! Risk anything! Care no more for the opinions of others, for those voices.*
> *Do the hardest thing on earth for you. Act for yourself. Face the truth."*
> *Katherine Mansfield*

According to Jim Self, international speaker, author and American presidential advisor, thoughts are electrical and emotions are magnetic. He purports to believe that experiencing heavy, powerful emotions such as anger or worry will magnetically attract other negative energy into your life. If you're happy and full of humour, which are light energies, then similar light energies will be drawn to you. To maintain a positive outlook, to remain in the present and refrain from projecting yourself into the past or future due to programmed limiting beliefs, Self suggests you create a ring-road, an imaginary bubble around yourself. It doesn't separate you from the world, but provides a semi-permeable boundary for your identity through which nobody's negative energy can pass. (Remember the concept of membranes dividing your concentric trust circles?) It's analogous to polarized sunglasses or a camera lens that block certain types of undesirable light such as glare from a shiny surface. Refuse to be infected by anyone's foul mood or accept their destructive issues as your own. Remain authentic and unaffected by their critical judgement. No one can insult you unless you give them permission. What other people think of you is none of *your* business.

> *"No one can make you feel inferior without your consent." Eleanor Roosevelt*

By all means, interact with your friends, family and clients. To remain true to yourself, though, resist reacting to their spoken or implied judgements since those comments are not you. Don't make their issue your own because in reality, it's *their* issue that they're attempting to project onto you in a misguided attempt to make *them* feel better. If they can successfully bring you down or convince you they're right, they'll feel better about themselves. *Your* identity is who *you* truly are. Resist being defined by others. To live a blessed life, you must be authentically yourself and reject the usually convivial efforts made to program you. It's okay to listen and learn through your protective energetic membrane, but follow your own authentic thoughts and inclinations.

Too many people concern themselves with how they're perceived by others. This process begins early in life with our highly judgemental education system built on the premise of grades, competitiveness and comparison and reinforced by reward and punishment. Kids live in constant fear of being judged deficient, failing, not measuring up, of being outcast. And sadly, they often deny their authentic selves in the process, even to the point of wearing silly, impractical "uniform" fashion clothing. They feel they must fit into the homogenized system, yet still be accepted by their peers, or be labelled misfits or losers.

They're sometimes openly or covertly coerced into following in their parent's footsteps. Ironically, they fear being disliked, disrespected, disinherited or damned. Due to this early programming, unfortunately, such behaviour has become quite common. Often, the only way kids can win the love and respect they crave is to submit to peer pressure or conform to their parental, school or religious teacher's expectations, even though such behaviour might contradict their very essence. In my view, that's conditional love. It's no wonder there's a shortage of self-respecting and self-loving adults in the world. Live a genuine life and you'll attract others doing the same. Be the greatest person you can possibly be – by your own thoughtful definition.

"We are shaped by our thoughts; we become what we think.
When the mind is pure, joy follows like a show that never leaves." Buddha

So Within - So Without

As a devoted single father of two very young children, I naturally wanted to spend as much time as possible with them. For those two reasons, it was my habit to book evening appointments to begin after they'd gone to bed with a story, kiss and a squeeze, and one of many punctual babysitters had arrived. Since Sunday was a sacrosanct family day, my policy was to refuse work on that day. The summer months and winter holiday season were also designated top priority family and personal periods. You might question this wisdom, but my earnings for the remainder of the year were more than sufficient for our needs. They were *enough*. For me, it was all about priorities; my family and personal life came first. For me, being a "gazillionaire" wasn't important. Anyway, how much money can someone spend?

During these breaks, thankfully, few prospects called me. And so, my wishes were made manifest; I literally got what I wished for. The phone refused to ring – by design. Of course, there was always somebody needing service during these down times, but it was rare, and I was usually able to postpone until I returned to work. After the long weekend in September, my phone would once again begin to ring. Why? Because I *expected* it. I intended to return to active duty after my kids were back to school. That's the way I wanted to do business and beyond a shadow of a doubt, I believed it would happen just like that. And throughout my career, it did.

"He who is plenteously provided for from within needs but little from without."
Johann von Goethe

A few years ago, after I resigned my position as regional branch manager for a large multi-branch franchised brokerage, I returned to sales with a brand new brand. With no formal media advertising, aside from a network mailer, my phone began to ring almost immediately and I became one of the bigger producers in the company. Luck? Nope. I believe we generate our own luck by creating the circumstances in which "lucky" things happen. I manifested it into my reality. Indubitably, I believed it into existence. My thoughts – hence my beliefs – and resulting action, powered by emotion, became my reality.

If you believe in yourself, others will believe in you too. You'll be an irresistible business magnet. So within – so without. The Universe will provide whatever you believe is possible, whatever you need to live the life you feel you *deserve*. It will provide you with enough to reach your goals. Thoughts are energy. Things are energy. Reality is energy. And your thoughts become your reality. All you need is faith in yourself as a successful agent who lives a life of love and abundance. Now, here's some more science.

"There is no such thing as a lack of faith. We all have plenty of faith; it's
just that we have faith in the wrong things. We have faith in what can't be
done rather than what can be done. We have faith in lack rather than abundance,
but there is no lack of faith. Faith is a law." Eric Butterworth

Thought Power

"It is a fact that you project what you are." Norman Vincent Peale

Using the technologies of micro-cluster water and magnetic resonance analysis, Dr. Masaru Emoto, researcher, doctor of alternative medicine and chief of the Hado Institute in Tokyo, Japan, regularly demonstrates highly compelling effects of human consciousness on physical reality. His discovery of the effect on water, referred to as Hado, is described in his 1999 book *The Message from Water* as "the intrinsic vibration pattern at the atomic level in all matter, the smallest unit of energy. Its basis is the energy of human consciousness". According to *Wikipedia*, millions of copies of his book in multiple languages have sold around the globe. His theory became even more popular with the release of the widely-viewed movie mentioned earlier, *What The Bleep Do We Know*.

While performing a series of experiments with water and ice crystals, he theorized that our thoughts and feelings affect our physical reality. After gathering samples of different types of water from around the world, he began a detailed study of the resulting frozen crystals. Water from heavily polluted rivers refused to crystallize, whereas natural clear spring water produces beautiful, perfectly-shaped crystalline structures; not too surprising. However, to his amazement, he discovered that the crystallization process of the water molecules reflected his own personal mood!

During his experiments using regular tap water, Dr. Emoto projected, verbally and with written labels, into each sample before freezing, various intentions with thoughts and emotions such as love, God, hate and devil. The water reacted to both verbal and written projections. The negative produced chaotically configured crystals or none, and the positive produced beautiful, highly organized symmetrical crystals. After testing projections of various categories of music (which of course, is all about sound waves and vibration), he was not surprised to learn that classical pieces produced beautiful crystals and aggressive acid rock the opposite. He concluded that since all phenomena consist basically of resonating energy, by altering the vibration of that energy, material substances can be significantly altered.

If we want to clean polluted water, we can do so by using the power of positive intention to change its internal vibration. Prior to proving his Hado cleansing rituals around the world, he demonstrated the effect in July 1999 when he gathered 350 people around Japan's highly polluted Lake Biwa. During that miraculous event, after he took a sample of the water, he asked everyone to project positive intentions into the malodorous water. A second sample afterward showed a dramatic improvement in crystal structure.

A month later, a newspaper article in the influential newspaper, *Kyoto Shinburn*, stated "the spread of the water algae had improved and that the foul stench had disappeared". A rapid understanding of Hado quickly spread throughout Japan and the term, Hado, has been adopted into that country's daily lexicon.

If you consider the possible effects of thought and emotion on your body, his revolutionary highly magnified photography of water crystals becomes quite profound. Think about it. If thoughts can have such a substantial effect on water, imagine for a moment how your thoughts affect your own body – which is up to 80 percent water! Emoto submits the phenomenon as proof that thoughts and feelings, such as gratitude, love, fear, worry and greed, affect our physical reality. He concludes that written or spoken words and music change water's expression. (To learn more, visit http://masaru-emoto.net/.)

> *"You create your own universe as you go along."*
> Winston Churchill

Here's more science. During the summer of 1993, a highly controlled experiment was performed in Washington, DC by John S. Hagelin, Director of the *Institute of Science, Technology and Public Policy* in Fairfield, Iowa. It was a landmark project organized as a scientific experiment to test the hypothesis that a reduction in social stress could correspondingly reduce urban crime. Hagelin said that over 40 research studies testing this hypothesis had been previously performed and published in leading peer-reviewed journals. A 27-member independent scientific review board was appointed to monitor and evaluate the experiment.

A group of 400,000 people met to collectively meditate and focus on positive, healing, peaceful thoughts with the specific intention of reducing violent crime in that city by believing and thinking it to be so. For control purposes, current and historical data gathered from the FBI and local police, weather conditions including temperature, precipitation, humidity and daylight hours, and changes in police crime reduction activity during the study period, were all factored into the experiment. In the final analysis, during the study period, a 25 percent maximum decrease was measured in the rate of violent crime. This was yet another successful demonstration of the power of collective thoughts to affect reality.

> *"Happiness is when what you think, what you say*
> *and what you do are in harmony."* Mahatma Gandhi

Attention to Intention

"Action is a great restorer and builder of confidence. Inaction is not only the result, but the cause of fear. Perhaps the action you take will be successful; perhaps different action or adjustments will have to follow. But any action is better than no action at all."
Norman Vincent Peale

Is productivity directly related to how hard or smart you work and how many prospecting hours you invest? Or is it relative to the skills you possess and the quality of your service? Well, all of these are certainly success factors, but there's far more involved.

Let's say a rookie in your office is excelling, in spite of their not working long hours or, in your humble opinion, by being the brightest bulb in the pack. No matter what you do, you don't seem able to even match their production. And even though you feel you're ten times more skilled and experienced, you're not earning ten times their income. What's their secret?

While you're stuck at the roadside in a rut of frustration, fear, envy, resentment or blame, thinking how bad things are, they're accelerating down the paved road to success – and they make it look easy. While you're thinking and acting from a position of scarcity and wondering what you're doing wrong, they're thinking life is grand. Nobody told them they couldn't win. So, they keep going until a trusted authority tells them they're doing it wrong – and crucially, they *choose* to believe them. Until that happens, they'll keep the productive service pedal to the metal.

They (probably naively) focus their *attention* on the *intention* to succeed and as a result, think, feel and act quite differently than you do. Skill and talent, though important, take second seat to attitude, positive emotions and optimistic thoughts. What that rookie lacks in skill, they more than compensate for in desire, determination, attitude, belief and a positive commitment to be outstanding in their field. Because they *intend* to be successful, doors open, and when one closes, a window of opportunity magically appears. Intention creates both opportunities and capabilities.

Experience is fantastic, but you'll accomplish much more in life with qualities such as determination, focus, trust, compassion, integrity, patience, enthusiasm, confidence, perseverance, kindness and unswerving intention. Consistent and strategic thinking can have significant impact on your business practice and your personal life. Energy flows where attention goes. Success is the result of thinking the thoughts, taking the action and intending to provide competent and honest service.

*"Wealth, like happiness, is never attained when sought directly.
It comes as a by-product of providing a useful service."* Henry Ford

If two waves of water converge, they resonate with each other and effectively double in size and power. Conversely, if they're travelling in opposite directions, they tend to cancel each other out. Since thoughts are energy, which also travels in waves, by the same laws of physics, if your thoughts are not in harmony with your actions or conflict with other thoughts, they'll cancel out each other. The result? Nothing. Thus, if you're thinking, feeling and behaving as a highly successful agent, but in the next moment, worrying about your credit card statement, the second thought cancels the first and you end up with nothing. If you've set a hefty income goal and in the next breath, you're complaining about being broke, you'll continue to be broke. Stop it! This isn't just faith or belief; it's science.

You are who you *think* you are. You practice real estate (or anything for that matter) in a manner that matches your belief system. Think you're a struggling agent? You're right. Think you're a great agent? You're right again. Think your clients trust you? They do. Think you deserve their loyalty? Yup. It happens. How you think, you create. Whatever you believe, you achieve. So, don't quit; just change your thoughts, and be consistent.

"It's always too early to quit." Norman Vincent Peale

To attract business, or virtually anything you wish to have or be in your life, set an intention to achieve it. Move from a place of fear and resentment to one of love and gratitude. Then focus your *attention* on that *intention*. Think about it. Feel the feeling as if you already have it and you'll be inspired to act. Make a personal commitment to yourself, not to have the money, accolades and toys normally associated with wealth, but to *be* that successful person. Learn and grow to be worthy of achieving and sustaining that lifestyle. If you occasionally meet with misfortune, such as losing a client, you'll not be devastated. As that person with new habits and a powerful belief in yourself, you'll continue to manifest even more business. If you fail, it's because you weren't having fun and quit early. Or you didn't believe you could do it in the first place. It's not complicated. By adopting a joyful attitude, by believing that your life is an adventure and that in the bigger picture, stuff doesn't really matter, you'll never work a day in your life. Have fun!

"The secret of success is to make your vocation your vacation."
Mark Twain

Matter Doesn't Matter

"Be who you are and say what you feel because those
who mind don't matter and those who matter don't mind." Dr. Seuss

In his inspirational book, *I AM THE WORD*, writer and medium, Paul Selig, discusses self-realization, including the "emotional boulders – residues of pain, fear or anger – that block our true nature." He offers advice on how to "strip away layers of apprehension, doubt and self-suffocating habits" and to "feel and live as the authentic men and women we were born to be." I gleaned a few of the following concepts from its pages.

Think about this; nobody really owns anything. You don't own your home, car or the cash in your jeans. Aside from the fact that the entire concept of asset ownership is man-made, all property is transitory. It doesn't last. Even the old axiom that land is the only thing that lasts is untrue because eventually, in a zillion years or so, Earth will be extinguished in a sulphuric flash when our sun meets its inevitable supernova destiny. When your body is dead and buried, what you believe you now own will *belong* to somebody else or cease to exist. Will your beautiful luxury automobile be around in a hundred years? It'll probably be part of somebody's toaster. What about the lovely house in which you place much pride? The way they're built these days, I don't see it lasting long either. Your spiffy new smart phone? Nope. Designed obsolescence is a relatively recent innovation of consumerism and average product life span is rapidly dwindling. So, enjoy your toys now, but don't be too attached to them.

You don't have a life partner, but you may be living with such an illusion in this virtual reality matrix we call human life. Will they be with you in 50 years or even five? Hey – no guarantees. Until death do you part doesn't have quite the same ring anymore. You're just borrowing this stuff and temporarily encountering these fleeting relationships. To attach personal security or happiness to a belief system based on transitory matter or relationships instead of your own consciousness – which accompanies you into infinity – is like anchoring your personal safety or joy to a block of ice in the Amazon basin during the rainy season.

"We cannot conceive of matter being formed of nothing, since things require a
seed to start from. Therefore, there is not anything which returns to nothing,
but all things return dissolved into their elements." William Shakespeare

If you lose your home, spouse or wealth to which you had confidently attached your personal security, sense of self-worth or identity, you're inviting a traumatic trial from which you'll likely experience great pain *and* suffering. (As you now know, I speak from personal experience.) If you accept that they're not truly part of who you are and do not define you, if you experience such a potentially devastating loss, that loss transforms from one of suffering from a fractured belief into a learning experience. Approached consciously without fear, they become opportunities for growth.

Losing of a job could engender years of self-loathing, depression, unemployment and dependency. Or it could be viewed as a glorious opportunity to start an exciting new career, a chance to finally do something for which you possess great passion and talent. Maybe it's a business you never had the time or the nerve to pursue. The dissolution of a marriage could be viewed as a bitter, vengeful and acrimonious episode, or because you'd been controlled, discouraged or eclipsed by your partner, as an ideal chance to realize a whole new aspect of yourself. With a more optimistic outlook, the added bonus could be the prospect of maintaining an affable relationship with your former spouse – a wonderful benefit, not only for yourselves, but for shared children.

Change can hold great promise. Don't run from it. Embrace it. Be bold. Comfort zones, habitual by nature, aren't always constructive. On the contrary, they can be non-productive and occasionally, downright destructive.

> *"Don't be afraid to expand yourself, to step out of your comfort zone. That's where the joy and the adventure lie." Herbie Hancock*

Mediocrity to Magnificence

> *"Whatever course you decide upon, there is always someone to tell you that you are wrong. There are always difficulties arising which tempt you to believe that your critics are right. To map out a course of action and follow it to an end requires courage." Ralph Waldo Emerson*

According to Michael Roads, international speaker, teacher and author of 14 books in 16 languages on organic farming, spirituality, metaphysics, emotional balance and unconditional love, the average human has about 60,000 full or partial thoughts daily. And 80 percent of those thoughts are negative from yesterday, yesteryear or previous incarnations.

Many people focus on lack. They think about what they don't have and what they want, but can't afford. They have plenty of dreams, but no definable goals. More importantly, they feel little gratitude for the blessings they already have. Living such an unconscious life is a measly pantomime of a truly authentic life of love and abundance. Those who focus their attention to the intention of scarcity usually fear ridicule, and to gain acceptance, *pretend* to live authentically, thereby living a diminished life. But to present that false façade of success, they're often deeply and stressfully in debt. It takes considerable courage to be genuine. To do so, you must face your fear of judgement. Success can manifest with a shift in consciousness, from scarcity to abundance. Think about what you have, not what you don't. Feel rich in every respect and as a reward, you'll be happier.

> *"Feeling gratitude and not expressing it is like*
> *wrapping a present and not giving it."* William Arthur Ward

To produce durable fundamental changes in your life, to live in accordance with your own personal philosophies and not those involuntarily installed in your subconscious hard-drive, involves the following three steps:

Firstly, determine your intentions, hence, your purpose and direction, both personally and professionally. If you don't know where you want to go, paraphrasing the *Cheshire Cat* from *Alice in Wonderland*, that's exactly where you'll end up – lost, confused and aimlessly meandering through life as a victim. Who are you? What do you want to accomplish? How do you prefer to live? What makes your heart race? Your written intentions will start things moving and changing in your subconscious mind.

Secondly, those intentions must be reflected in your personal reality. Your daily conscious choices must be congruent and resonate with your declared specific and overall written intentions. Make your choices – not while regretting yesterday or worrying about tomorrow – but while you're in the moment. When you make potentially life-changing decisions, be aware and completely present. Think with your heart.

Thirdly, practice. The more you follow the same path, the more easily you'll be able to see and follow it. Just like a timeworn forest trail, your chosen path will eventually become a comfortable daily habit, an integral part of your natural routine. You'll develop new neural pathways to support your committed intentions. Remember the example of learning to drive a car; unconsciously incompetent to unconsciously competent? Have faith in yourself and your choices. Trust your instincts. With devotion and perseverance, the transition from mediocrity to magnificence will be smooth and relatively effortless. There may be potholes; don't expect them, just steer around them. It may be a case of two steps forward and one back, but with persistence and patience, you'll eventually reach your destination. And when you finally arrive, you'll happily wonder why it took so long.

Since life is more about a happy journey than an obsessed destination, feel the joy of the journey. To be jubilant as well as effective, your regular on-going behavioural choices in the outer world must be consistently congruent with your inner world's emotional well-being. For this to manifest, to personally evolve, know who you are and behave genuinely. Life choices must *feel* right. And change isn't a part-time endeavour. Unswerving full-time effort, combined with an awareness of all the blessings in your life, will make for a shorter path to lasting change. If you're always *aware* of your thoughts and make *conscious* choices, the sun will shine upon you and the road afore you will warmly rise up to greet you.

> *"The more you praise and celebrate your life, the more there is in life to celebrate. Be thankful for what you have; you'll end up having more. If you concentrate on what you don't have, you will never, ever have enough."*
> Oprah Winfrey

Chapter Thirty-Four

Evolutionary Changes

"The greatest discovery of my generation is that human beings can alter their lives by altering their attitudes of mind." William James

Convergence of Faiths

"No matter where you go, there you are." Confucius

After an arduous and controversial mountain ascent to the summit, an exhausted scientist is greeted by a gently reposing mystic who calmly asks; "What took you so long?"

We now live in miraculous times. Until recently, science and spirituality have been in opposite corners, each vying (not always peacefully) for the prominent position of Holders of the Truth. But over the past few decades, highly compelling anecdotal and scientific evidence from on-going research by quantum physicists, chaos theorists, epigeneticists and biologists – the mystics of the 21st century – has been suggesting what theologians have been preaching for millennia, that we're eternal spiritual beings having a series of relatively brief human experiences. Many great minds now believe that everything physical in our material world originates and manifests from the non-physical spiritual realm. It appears to be increasingly evident that the death of our corporeal bodies is not the end – merely a change in lifestyle.

Quantum science tells us we're all part of a massive, omnipresent and omniscient energy field. This singularity is variously referred to as the Field, Source, Universe, Oneness, Quantum Hologram, Zero Point Field and Divine Matrix or more religiously as God and Allah. From this Oneness, all form is created – and the possibilities are limitless. You've also no doubt heard the expression "intelligent design". It's been hypothesized that our extremely complex 3-dimensional reality couldn't possibly have evolved naturally, as Darwin professed, from a single-cell entity, but was meticulously created by a conscious intelligence, powerful and knowledgeable beyond the limits of human imagination. Do you see how it all fits together?

"The God who existed before any religion, counts on you to make the oneness of the human family known and celebrated." Desmond Tutu

Do you ever wonder about the source of your original creative ideas? Do you think they just pop into your brain from the ether? Well, I suppose one could argue that that's exactly what happens. Experts suggest that each of us possess the innate ability to voluntarily and involuntarily tap into the infinitely intelligent Field, or as Dr. Jung called it, the Collective Super-Consciousness. However, the vast majority of the populace lack the requisite belief or even the awareness of the existence of this interconnection of our individual subconscious minds and fail to deliberately exercise their psychic muscle. In an attempt to attain this legendary Nirvana, some people meditate or pray, whilst others unwittingly have sporadic epiphanies (or peak experiences as posited by Maslow) generated from the depths of their subconscious minds (imagination). And a fortunate few, blessed with the awareness of this innate psychic ability, connect at will.

It's also been suggested that since infinite knowledge – everything that has been, is currently and will ever be known – already exists in the Oneness, awaiting conscious selective manifestation, there are no new ideas. People around the world suddenly, sometimes simultaneously, get bright and seemingly novel ideas. A popular example of such inspiration is the classic controversy surrounding the invention of the telephone. Though Alexander Graham Bell is widely credited with its creation, many others from the same era have also claimed the glory. Could Bell and Guglielmo Marconi have "thought" of the idea simultaneously? I think so. Have you ever been thinking of someone and in the next moment, they phone or appear at your door? These "coincidences" demonstrate the spiritual connection – the original wireless network to which we're all constantly interconnected.

Beliefs are gradually changing for the better. After a pathetically long and tumultuous slumber, more and more people are awakening and beginning to remember who they are. My sincere hope, though, is that these fundamental evolutionary changes will help our species in time to rejoice in our Earthly differences and bring all the diverse separate global cultures together in peace, harmony and love. Maybe our currently failing competitive capitalistic "democracies" that depend on the fearful concept of supply, demand, surplus and scarcity, and the communist and fascist totalitarian regimes dependant on the blatantly corrupt exercise of power, will transform into cooperative, compassionate social democracies based on interconnectedness and sharing of the abundance. After all, we're all living together on this tiny blue ball whizzing around in space. Why not feel the unity, the love? There's enough for everyone. The trick is to recognize it before our species is recategorized from endangered to extinct.

"It's difficult to believe in yourself because the idea of self is an artificial construction. You are, in fact, part of the glorious oneness of the universe. Everything beautiful in the world is within you." Russell Brand

The Illusion of Separateness

"The fundamental delusion of humanity is to suppose that I am here and you are out there." Yasutani Roshi

It's common knowledge that everything in our Universe ("Multiverse", according to theory), such as our bodies, minds, thought, air, earth, fire, water, frogs, ice cream, plants and light, is composed of the same basic ingredient – energy. Even what was formerly believed to be the vacuum of space is now thought to be dark energy. If you were to deconstruct all Universal matter into its basic components, you'd discover a very complex world of particles, atoms, molecules and compounds. Protons, neutrons and electrons variously combine to form a multiplicity of atoms which unite into molecules which thence materialize to form all inanimate (rocks, water) and animate (plants, animals) objects. (Technically, at a microscopic level, even inanimate material is perpetually animated.) Everything we sense – and don't sense – in our fundamental 3-dimensional reality is built from the same basic building blocks.

The composition and density of molecules determine the form of the matter. For example, gas molecules are very loosely combined, which allows easy circulation without colliding with other matter. The molecular consistency of liquid is somewhat more compact, causing the particles to flow together like a school of fish or a flock of birds (natural visual demonstration of collective consciousness). But neither can penetrate more dense inflexible matter such as rock, except under extreme heat when rock becomes liquid magma. The molecular structure of, let's call them soft solids such as human flesh, is still fairly compact, which restricts any significant molecular movement. This means (as far as we know) we can't walk through walls, fly unassisted or shape-shift. Sounds like energy to me! We're not separate as our egos, governments, the medical establishment, the military-industrial complex and many religious leaders would have us believe, but all one with each other in the Universe – and undoubtedly beyond. Leaders in the field continue to affirm that we're all tiny integral slivers of the eternal interconnectedness that is everything everywhere.

"I should say: the overall number of minds is just one." Erwin Schrödinger

In our perceived reality, what differentiates each piece of matter is its individual vibrational frequency. A rock vibrates slower than water, our bodies or light. Just like sound is created as vibration, our thoughts and emotions also vibrate at various frequencies. Spiritual leaders teach, for example, that love has a much higher vibration than fear. Everything is vibrating together in a gigantic cosmic ocean. Just as a droplet of water is part of an ocean, you're a vibrating field of energy functioning within a larger ocean of energy. But you're not only a droplet of water in the infinite energetic sea; you're also the sea.

The celebrated scientist, Albert Einstein, famously resolved that energy can be neither created nor destroyed – only transformed into another form of energy. For example, the carbon energy stored in wood, when burned, is converted into heat and light energy. The air molecules you're currently breathing have never been and never will be destroyed; only converted by another organism upon your exhalation. At some point, those air molecules you just *inhaled* were *exhaled* by another body, and not just yesterday, but millions of years ago. It's the same energy. The apparent passage of time is irrelevant. Amazingly, you're connected to some Neanderthal man or great dinosaur that walked the Earth eons ago. You're also breathing oxygen exhaled by the lawn and shrubs and bees in your flower garden.

If you accept that you and the Field are one and the same, then it logically follows that you already have everything you want, but may not yet consciously realize it. Because of your thoughts and limiting belief system, your wishes may not have yet manifested into your life. It's up to you to take the steps necessary to consciously attract what you want into your physical reality. But you must first think the appropriate thoughts.

"When one tugs at a single thing in nature,
he finds it attached to the rest of the world." John Muir

The Universe is Us

"Imagination is everything. It is the preview of life's coming attractions."
Albert Einstein

Current evolutionary thinking is that our general reality is manifested from the collective thoughts of all humanity – the Super-Consciousness. And according to main-stream media news reports, this reality is rife with anger, greed and hatred, all fearful emotions, which violently and selfishly divide us. I suggest, though, that it's the paranoid, narcissistic few that cause most, if not all our worldly grief, and that nearly all mankind would prefer to live in peace and harmony. However, according to the deluge of information available from the less strategically biased Internet community, a global warming is causing a growing tide of love, peace, generosity, compassion and selflessness to rise around the world.

Look at what's happening these days; crowds of conscientious, courageous protesting citizens are marching the streets, placards in hand, bravely facing the authorities to voice their objections to the established dystopian order while government and corporate-paid minions attempt to disrupt their progress. Such messages spread throughout the country, polarizing virtually everyone. If you were suddenly thrust into such a troubled spot, you might unwittingly be infected by that fear, even though you didn't thoroughly understand the possibly centuries-old history underlying it.

Have you ever wandered into an expansive room of people, maybe a union meeting, and immediately sensed the communal mood? The atmosphere, the combined energy of the crowd, hostile and angry, for example, could easily generate a similar negative emotion in you, and you'd likely want to head for the hills. On the other hand, amble into a joyful celebration like a wedding and see what happens; you're instantly uplifted. Now, envision the world's 7 billion people in that same room (I know – big crowd, but imagine the conversation and exotic food potential). As a group, their thoughts and feelings create a general mood that would affect you individually on a conscious and/or subconscious level.

As Dr. Jung proposed, you can and do connect with the larger collective consciousness to send and receive thoughts. You may be unaware of the process, but you can instinctively pick up on the mood. And moods result from thoughts. Have you ever felt someone watching you from across the room and suddenly turn and lock eyes? Their thought about you traversed the ether into your auric field and attracted your attention. Or have you ever experienced an epiphany – a "eureka" moment? That thought resulted from your connection to The Field. At some level of consciousness, you attracted it. You are in the Universe and the Universe is in you.

"As within – so without; as above – so below."
Ancient Egyptian Axiom of Hermes

The Law of Attraction

We all possess the innate ability to control our lucid dreams, to create multiple versions and outcomes and by forcing ourselves awake, escape a nightmare. Now, imagine being able to awaken from the day-dream (or "daymare") that is commonly believed – maybe incorrectly – to be the conscious state of everyday life.

Philosopher scientists have hypothesized that sleeping dreams are the true reality and the awakened state is actually the dream. How's that for turning things upside down? They further suggest that when your body is awake and consciously imagining, you're actually connecting to the Field in a state of wonderment, with the power to telepathically exchange thoughts with someone or instantly and vividly travel anywhere you can envision. Not unlike speaking on the phone or transmitting a wireless video message, you can technically send *your* thought energy across the planet or beyond. Visualize, for a moment, the meteor-peppered surface of the moon or a magnificent multi-coloured galaxy spiralling timelessly in the vast expanse of space. Or think about a friend on the other side of the world. Are you actually here, there or in both places contemporaneously? Since they're *your* thoughts, are you not energetically teleporting your essence to those faraway places?

You must admit that it's interesting to ruminate about such possibilities. Actually, with recent advances by independent thinkers in the field of quantum physics, such musing may be moving from the realm of pure conjecture into everyday reality. In the near future, such critical thinking may spread around the globe like wildfire. But for now, let me bring you back to Terra Firma.

"The ancestor of every action is a thought." Ralph Waldo Emerson

Unbeknownst to them, many people don't actually think independently or critically. Instead, they basically run on automatic and rely heavily – almost exclusively – on their programmed subconscious mind. Their habitual thinking influences most, if not all their daily decisions. They blindly believe newspapers and radio and television broadcasts. It's in the news, so it must be true. Rubbish! They entrust their doctor and government with the ethical responsibility to take good care of them. Frightening! They habitually go about each day without looking around, and methodically place one foot in front of the other in a relentless route to retirement and inevitable earthly demise. The whole idea of questioning anything – seeking their own answers – doesn't even occur to them. Remember *The Matrix* movie trilogy that spawned the pop culture symbol of the choice between embracing the sometimes painful truth of reality and the blissful ignorance of illusion? It serves as a great metaphor for our current increasingly dystopian world.

Many people have opted to forgo the red pill and instead, swallow the mind-numbing blue one.

If you're new to the concept of conscious thinking, the idea that your thoughts create your reality might seem a pretty weird new-age red pill notion promulgated by the multi-billion dollar self-help industry. (It's a huge industry due to an exponentially growing number of people questioning traditional thought.) However, it's actually "new-edge" science that's been sharpening for a long time. Since such thinking isn't widely exposed through the mainstream media – a system controlled by those who prefer we remain docile – you probably haven't heard much about it. Well, conscious thinking is a prerequisite for implementing The Law of Attraction.

"A man is but the product of his thoughts; what he thinks, he becomes."
Mahatma Gandhi

This most fundamental of all universal laws basically states that like vibrations attract each other, whereas dissimilar ones repel. It explains why we tend not to physically merge with the ground since our bodies and the ground vibrate at different frequencies. Your thoughts, a form of energy, eventually manifest as physical matter into your world and contribute to your wealth, health and relationships – virtually everything – or the lack of same. Like it or not, both your conscious and unconscious thoughts determine who you are and the life you live in our tangible world.

There has certainly been a lot controversy surrounding this law over the past few years. After it was popularized by Rhonda Byrne in her bestselling book and film, *The Secret*, many naively believed all they had to do was think the thoughts and poof – a genie would magically appear to grant their wishes. Surprise – it doesn't work that way. (I'm glad, though, that she was able to stir many in the right direction.) Nevertheless, you'll never attract consistent abundance with fearful, low-vibration thoughts of scarcity. By thinking optimistically and *feeling* higher-vibration upbeat emotions, you'll become more cheerfully confident. As a consequence of an improved attitude, the actions you'll naturally undertake will raise your vibrational frequency even further, thus transforming you into a high-frequency energy magnet. Your self-assured attitude will undoubtedly synergistically infect others around you, be they clients, family or whomever. Doesn't it make sense that someone consistently optimistic is more likely to lead a happier, healthier and more materially successful life?

"Remember happiness doesn't depend upon who you are
or what you have; it depends solely on what you think." Dale Carnegie

I touched on a similar example in an earlier chapter, but to illustrate this fundamental law, let me allude to it again. While out strolling, have you ever encountered someone shuffling dolefully along with head hung low on droopy shoulders? Or maybe they were angry? Were you compelled to smile and say hello? Unless you're a Mother Theresa clone, I doubt it. If you greeted them, they probably ignored or glared at you. You may have felt they were depressed, drugged or mentally ill – perhaps all three. To avoid possible danger or energetic contamination, you probably gave them a wide berth. Or if you were in the same negative state, you may have been drawn to share your anger or compare complaints. Or perchance, while *you* were in a fowl mood, you crossed paths with a happy stroller and steered clear again. You may have felt envy, or blamed them for some imagined contribution to your disastrous disposition. How dare they be happy when you're miserable?

On the other hand, what if that chance encounter involved someone whose mood matched your upbeat frame of mind? I'd wager you greeted them with twinkling eyes and a proverbial tip of the hat. Your shared positive energy connected and created an immediate relationship, however brief.

How about a quantifiable example? Take two identical tuning forks; strike one and hold it close to but not touching the other. The second fork will begin to vibrate in harmony with the sound energy emitted by the first fork. Now try the same test with two forks of different frequencies; the second will not react. Since thoughts are also energy, if you think negative thoughts, which vibrate at a lower frequency than positive thoughts, you'll attract negative energy into your life. It's not complicated. Smile and the world smiles with you. Cry and you'll only attract other criers, or cry alone.

Chronically depressed or angry people don't usually experience great victories. They typically live quiet lives of unspoken desperation, loss, frustration and lonely solitude. To bring greatness into your reality, you must consciously raise your vibration into harmony with whatever matter you desire to manifest. According to the Law of Attraction, a thought with serious intent, free of limiting beliefs and fuelled by affirming positive emotion, can contribute toward dynamic constructive change. But your emotion should be sincere. If you pretend to be positive while silently worrying, the lower vibration energy will repel any potential reward, like a water wave cancelling out its opposite.

Having said this, to develop those new neural pathways described earlier, you could fake it. Eventually, your artificially buoyant behaviour may cause you to feel sincerely optimistic and bring the good stuff into your life. But it may take longer, so be patient. By the way, if you're feeling cynical about this law, you're already in a negative place. Thus, any effort is doomed. As Yoda from the *Star Wars Trilogy* would say, believe you must.

If you tell yourself you're broke, that's a story that limits you and may prevent you from taking the necessary action to rectify the situation. It may indeed be a fact, but you must realize that having little money is not you – it's your situation. Entertaining fearful thoughts about your situation will generate destructive negative emotions and a lower vibrational energy frequency. If you're able to objectively witness the link between your thoughts, emotions and the subsequent actions, then choose your thoughts, carefully and consciously, to generate the positive emotions and resulting constructive attitude necessary to actively attract more abundance into your life.

Whether or not you're aware of the Law of Attraction, it's operating in your life as you read this page. It's perpetually activated. One way or another, you get what you think about. Even if you don't believe, you attract whatever occurs in your life. Thus, it happens either by conscious intention or by unconscious default. If your vessel consists primarily of low-energy thoughts and feelings, you'll never consistently attract positive high-energy results.

> *"By choosing your thoughts and by selecting which emotional currents*
> *you will release and which you will reinforce, you determine the*
> *quality of your Light. You determine the effects that you will have*
> *upon others and the nature of the experiences of your life."*
> *Gary Zukav*

Now, what can you do today to change your vessel's energy? Begin by making a list of everything you don't want, don't have and don't like about your life. Take your time. It should be fairly easy since we all know what we dislike. I *don't* own a home; I *never* have enough money; my clients *don't* trust me; I *don't* want to be poor, fat or alone; I *hate* my car; I have *no* control over my life; I *don't* like being a low-producer. (Note the use of all *negative* words in my sample abhorrences. A negative word (thought/energy) repels positive results. Whether you can or can't do something, you're right.

Then using the Universal Law of Polarity (everything in existence has its polar opposite), beside each of these points, jot down the exact opposite as if you already possess it. I *love* my own home; I *always have* enough money; my clients *trust* me; I *am* financially secure; I *love* my perfect weight of whatever; I *am* grateful for my delightful romantic relationship; I *love* my luxury car; I *am* relaxed and in control of my life; I *appreciate* being a happy top producer. By replacing lower frequency fearful thoughts/words with frequently affirmed higher vibrational loving thoughts/words, you'll be inspired to take more confident, assertive action. And the Universe will "hear" and manifest your beliefs into your life. You'll not only attract events and people whose vibrational energy is simpatico with yours, you'll also co-create a better global reality by way of your positive individual contribution to the Collective Super-Consciousness.

"Everything is energy and that's all there is to it. Match the frequency of the reality you want and you cannot help but get that reality. It can be no other way. This is not philosophy. This is physics." Albert Einstein

Down the Rabbit Hole

"Reality is merely an illusion, albeit a very persistent one." Albert Einstein

Due to continuing advances in science, fantasy often becomes fact. It seems that if mankind can think it – and a critical number of people want it – we can create it. Microwave ovens, holograms, space travel, instantaneous international wireless video communication and 3-dimensional printers, once considered impossible, are now part of our everyday reality. Do you remember the virtual reality "holodeck" from Gene Rodenberry's popular *Star Trek ; The Next Generation* TV series? It was a completely and very convincing computer-generated virtual reality. Well, the world in which we live could be thought of as similar to that incredible manifestation of a writer's vivid imagination. And your individual mind is an integral component of the super-computer that generates it. It appears that we co-create this world-wide hologram we call reality. Since there's plenty of science to support this claim, even though you may think the idea ludicrous, try to maintain an open mind.

Numerous studies by quantum physicists have *indisputably* proven that the mind of the observer influences the outcome of scientific experiments. In the now classic documentary flick, *What the Bleep Do We Know* and its extended version *Down the Rabbit Hole* starring film actress Marlee Matlin, numerous renowned scientific and spiritual luminaries opine on this startling reality. It appears unequivocal that we're not simply passive observers of our reality, but unconscious active participants in its creation. As Bruce Lipton, PhD said, "While almost everyone thinks that the physical world we observe is real, quantum physicists have verified as fact that the world we observe is not real." And this isn't recent news. "Astrophysicists Sir Arthur Eddington and Sir James Jeans recognized this immediately when physicists adopted the principles of quantum mechanics in 1925."

Dr. Lipton goes on to say, "Quantum physics has absolutely verified that information processed by our minds influences the shape of the world in which we live." He continues, "... leaders in the field, such as *John Hopkins University* physicist Richard Conn Henry, are addressing the misperceptions about the perceived primacy of the material world. Henry offered an elegantly simple definition on the true nature of the Universe, 'The Universe is nonmaterial – it is mental and spiritual. Live and enjoy.'" According to Dr. Lipton and many of his peers, our minds actively co-create the world, just as the on-board computer of the fictional USS Enterprise fabricates the holodeck. By altering your beliefs, you can indeed affect your reality, and together with the Field, the wider world. Your *conscious* choices, your thoughts, determine what happens – or doesn't – in your life.

> *"Life does not consist mainly or even largely of facts*
> *and happenings. It consists mainly of the storm of thought*
> *that is forever flowing through one's head." Mark Twain*

Choice Points

> *"The greatest weapon against stress is our ability*
> *to choose one thought over another." William James*

Every moment of every day, you make mini-decisions that determine your near and far future. Most are mundane, such as when to get up in the morning, what to eat for breakfast and when to go to work. You choose who to call, what to say and at what moment you step off a curb into a busy intersection. You make career and romantic choices, whether to exercise or from whom you seek wellness advice. Your life is full of choices, major and minor, conscious and unconscious. And a really big one is whether to abide by programmed limiting beliefs.

Even if you behave passively, *you* are choosing such behaviour. Whether you act, refuse to act or how you react, you *always* have the power to choose. With a gun to their head, someone is ordered to do something that their conscience wouldn't normally permit them to do. Or consider the infamous concentration camp guards during the Holocaust who feebly defended their heinous acts by saying they were just following orders. You might think that under such severe circumstances, they really would have no choice but to comply. Nevertheless, they still do; they could refuse to cooperate and of course, suffer the consequences. There's always a choice.

Unfortunately, the general emphasis of our institutional education is more learning by rote than creative independent critical thinking. While confined in this abysmal regimented system, kids are methodically indoctrinated to believe they have limited personal control over their lives, that life is accidental and all about luck. Yes, students can later select courses of study from various predetermined curricula which may lead to diverse career choices. But once stuck on a prescribed track, they fall into line.

Many adults exist to varying degrees in a constant competitive state of fear, want and debt, which eventually manifests as chronic low-grade anger, hate, frustration, worry, envy, greed, regret, disease, defeatism and/or the ever-popular, victim mentality. Instead of active, they lead inactive or reactionary lives. Worker drones usually accept their lot in life, and assign blame elsewhere for their general malaise. By choosing to swallow the blue pill, they surrender – consciously or unconsciously – to their "predestined" roles, completely unaware of the innate human power of free will to choose their own destiny.

> *"Thought is the blossom; language the bud; action the fruit behind it."*
> *Ralph Waldo Emerson*

Have you ever heard someone ask, "Why does this always happen to me?" or "Why can't I get ahead?" What about the labels "accident-prone" and "loser"? How about the common complaints that nobody loves me or I can't do that? Such stereotypical limiting beliefs exist because the system convinces people to surrender to their perceived fearful fate. And worse, they choose to regularly affirm such thoughts and of course, get what they expect. However, every seemingly minor choice is potentially more important than you may realize.

Have you ever been involved in an automobile collision, maybe on the way to the office? If you had chosen to leave home a bit later than usual that "fateful" morning, thereby avoiding a particular intersection at the precise moment when a distracted driver chose to run the red light, your future would certainly have been different, if you even had one. You could have allowed your tardiness to stress you out, and sped through traffic to meet that destiny. Or you could have chosen to enjoy the drive by calmly accepting that everything is as it should be, and missed that momentous moment. A series of micro-decisions, such as snoozing an extra 10 minutes or having a rare second cup of coffee, can indeed steer your life path. The causal compounding effects of an arbitrary last minute choice could mean missing an obstacle – or hitting one – and manifesting a completely different future.

In spite of the indoctrination imposed on you during your traditional upbringing and formal education, every decision, every thought, is important. What I'm saying is that you should do your best to make *conscious* choices – and peacefully accept the results as a natural consequence of those decisions. And importantly, learn from the experience. When you're conscious, that is to say present, you make decisions, neither from fear nor from an egoic need for recognition and approval. Thus, your choices become congruent with your own genuine value system.

We manifest all the necessary life occurrences, be they delightful or disastrous, to learn certain lessons while occupying these bodies. And based on those experiences, a continuing series of "choice points" on our individual time line during our "awakened" lives provide us with the opportunity to make seemingly insignificant daily decisions. However, these choices collectively create a general life direction for each of us and our greater world. Because we possess the power of free will, we each have optional paths – with relatively unlimited possibilities – which lead to different destinies. By way of our daily macro and micro-decisions, we alone possess the power to select which path we take to which future. And like a series of traffic lights, one ostensibly simple choice to run a yellow light or work an extra hour can affect the next moment and the next. Each decision leads to multiple options for future choices, which by the principle of compounding, lead to even more.

Remember Mark Twain's delightful characters, *Huckleberry Finn* and *Tom Sawyer,* as they rafted care-free down the Mississippi River on a sunny summer day. Depending on their choice whether to consciously steer the raft or unconsciously allow the current to carry them wherever, their voyage could have any number of exciting misadventures at a variety of unpredictable destinations along the way to the river delta. So, if life throws you an unexpected curve, taking you in a slightly and perhaps frighteningly different direction, don't get upset. You're there by choice. Accept that you're exactly where and when and doing precisely what you're supposed to be doing. Go with the flow, but with your hand on the helm.

The concept is well described in the Choice Point Movement, which produced an inspiring movie by the same name featuring world leading visionaries such as Sir Richard Branson, Archbishop Desmond Tutu, Gregg Braden and Barbara Marx Hubbard. (www.choicepointmovie.com.) Now, don't brush these ideas off as being too "out there". Make the personal choice to take a moment and really think deeply about this material. To accomplish more in your life, you mustn't fear entering deeper water.

To break free of the mental prison of your educational programming, to steer your own boat down the river of life, to seek the benefits of the Law of Attraction, the key is to first become aware of the problem – negative thoughts and lack of consciousness – and release the anchor of conditioned limiting beliefs that is responsible for braking your progress. Then, consciously choose to learn how to purely and clearly focus your thoughts. It may be difficult at first, but with serious intention and regular persistent practice, it will gradually become easier. Thoughts – intentions – are critical, but it's the accompanying emotion, underscored by belief, that will power your boat toward the successful manifestation of your thoughts and dreams in this tumultuous sea of life.

Brake Failure

"The best years of your life are the ones in which you decide your problems are your own. You do not blame them on your mother, the ecology, or the president. You realize that you control your own destiny." Albert Ellis

Let's say you possess or are prepared to learn and develop the necessary skills to be a successful agent. However, deep in your subconscious, you hold the limiting belief that wealth doesn't come easy, that you don't deserve to be rich or you're not a good sales person. Perhaps you worry about whether you could efficiently manage significant wealth. Or with a fancy new home or luxury car, you'd feel guilty, shameful or fearful that others might judge you harshly. Maybe you're broke and blame and complain to anyone who'll listen.

Blame is a symptom of unconsciousness. Someone who blames others for their own misfortune is unaware that their own thoughts – and resulting action or inaction – are attracting that misfortune. If your real estate practice is not doing well, you may have a tendency to blame the economy, the local market, a lack of contacts, the weather or your brokerage's perceived deficiencies. You might even blame your spouse for being unsupportive, or your old clunker car for projecting an unsuccessful image. When you blame, your ego can be quite creative.

But how do you explain the apparent success of other agents in the same marketplace? A better car? I don't think so. Our industry's movers and shakers don't blame or complain. In spite of the economy, these dynamos ignore bad news or turn it to their advantage. They make conscious choices and confidently adapt, and do what others neglect to do, perhaps because nobody told them it couldn't be done. By blaming your adversity on something external, you're refusing to accept responsibility for the thoughts that are manifesting an undesirable reality. Blaming protects your ego, but makes a hapless victim of you.

Nothing happens to you by mistake – absolutely nothing. Aware or not, you either choose to allow events to happen, or to stop them, choose to resist. If your life isn't how you want it, it's because you're either not attracting what you want or you're resisting, hence attracting something you *think* you don't want.

Have you ever witnessed someone driving along the highway with their brake lights on? It's obvious they're oblivious (under subconscious control) that their foot is resting on the brake pedal (limiting belief). If they unconsciously depress the pedal harder (affirm a powerful unconscious limiting belief), they never actually arrive at their destination (goal). If they grow frustrated with the lack of progress, they may choose to stop (quit) and accept where they are as an adequate destination (compromise goal), saying with a sigh that they didn't think they could make it. Thus, their ego was proven right.

Limiting beliefs can evolve into lame excuses for failure and shift you into a state of resistance. Your proverbial foot (limiting belief) moves onto the vibrational progress brake pedal and success continuously eludes you, maybe forever. Your perceived failure to succeed will feed on its own compounding negative energy, like a snake swallowing its tail, until you reach the point of exhaustion, compromise and defeat. The solution? Don't blame. Accept conscious responsibility for your life and business. Keep your goals in sight, maintain your ability to achieve them and enjoy the ride – with no foot resting on your limiting belief brake pedal.

> *"All blame is a waste of time. No matter how much fault you find with another and regardless of how much you blame him, it will not change you. The only thing blame does is to keep the focus off you when you are looking for external reasons to explain your unhappiness or frustration. You may succeed in making another feel guilty about something by blaming him, but you won't succeed in changing whatever it is about you that is making you unhappy." Wayne Dyer*

Many people are victims and don't know it. I call it sabotage camouflage. They unwittingly sabotage their own lives to remain in their familiar victimhood. Have you ever met someone desperately anxious for love? Deep down, they feel unworthy and fear being old, wrinkled and alone. But ironically, their low-vibration fear manifests as an anxious, clinging neediness, a possessive jealousy or a controlling personality that drives away suitable suitors. It's the same thing with low producing agents who have grown comfortably accustomed to a lifestyle of scarcity and *expect* it to continue. Familiarity is like a drug addiction; for better or for worse, they're drawn to it. So, they consciously or unconsciously persist with the same business methods, living by the same philosophies and generating the same mediocre results. They're emotionally invested into being – and expect to remain – sub-average sales people.

There's an old adage that if you go looking for trouble, it'll find you. When you're troubled about having no business, that's exactly what you'll get – no business – because your thoughts of failure are actively involved in sabotaging your efforts. Instead of controlling your thoughts and developing good habits, seeking new tools, enhancing your skills or trying something different to change your results, you make excuses and accept a lacklustre career – or quit. Failure is an easy way to escape frustration. And of course, you shirk personal responsibility for failure by blaming something external. Why? Because in the short term, you'll feel better. It wasn't your fault, right? You're not to blame. With the odds stacked against you, you couldn't help but fail. Balderdash!

> *"Failure is simply the opportunity to begin again, this time more intelligently."*
> Henry Ford

If you want your ideal life, consciously choose your thoughts and feelings – thus your vibration – to harmonize and align with what you wish to manifest. You must break free from negative thoughts and programmed limiting beliefs. Consider obstacles as strength-building challenges, as opportunities to learn, and see past them. When it comes to the more significant life decisions, be aware. Make your choices based on your authentic values and not those of your programmed limiting fears.

According to the Law of Attraction, if you focus on scarceness, you'll live a life of lack. On the contrary, if your energy is positive, your life will be one of abundance. It's that straight forward. If you're an optimistic, enthusiastic person who enjoys life and loves people, chances are you already live in relative abundance. However, if you're a fearful, pessimistic miser who worries about not having enough, regrets past choices, regularly checks their bank balance or believes their clients will be disloyal, guess what? That's probably your life in every respect. If you consciously work hard to *not* be poor, in other words, *away* from poverty and scarcity instead of *toward* wealth and abundance, your plane to the land of enrichment is not likely to leave the tarmac.

> *"Your complaints, your drama, your victim mentality, your whining, your blaming and all of your excuses have never gotten you even a single step closer to your goals or dreams. Let go of your nonsense. Let go of the delusion that you deserve better and go earn it! Today is a new day!"*
> Steve Maraboli

Chapter Thirty-Five

Awareness

"Gratitude unlocks the fullness of life. It turns what we have into enough and more. It turns denial into acceptance, chaos to order, confusion to clarity. It can turn a meal into a feast, a house into a home, a stranger into a friend. Gratitude makes sense of our past, brings peace for today and creates a vision for tomorrow." Melody Beattie

Reflections

"When I first open my eyes upon the morning meadows and look out upon the beautiful world, I thank God I am alive." Ralph Waldo Emerson

When I was a small boy, on a sunny summer day, I'd often head for the wild fields behind our home to rove silently and alone amongst the gently swaying long grasses, delightful daisies and regal Queen Anne's Lace. I recall standing eye to bloom with these majestic wildflowers. Wordlessly, I'd wonder on the delicate beauty of the creamy bunches of dainty petals that encircled a diminutive dash of orange. Sometimes, I'd see two such colourful dots, only to realize the second tiny splash of colour was a lollygagging lady bug basking in the summer sun. In a tranquil state of enchantment, I'd collapse amongst nature's undulating bounty and gaze skyward to watch our frolicking feathered friends darting about against an artist's pallet of malleable white clouds inching across an azure blue sky. I relished those rich timeless childhood moments of awareness, and at any given opportunity, seek them out still.

It's easier to appreciate the world's bounty when walking, biking or paddling than when hustling along a hectic highway encapsulated within a wheeled cocoon. If you're conscious, present and all your senses are functioning, you can feel the sun's golden warmth, smell the distinctive fragrance of fresh mown grass or the delicious scent of wildflowers, and hear delightful birdsong or the enchanting lap of the water against the hull of your canoe. In colder climes, awareness permits you to feel the crisp bite of winter, the satisfying crunch of crystalline snow underfoot or the gentle overhead rattle of snow-covered spruce branches. If you're aware, all the visual, audio and olfactory spendour of our beautiful Mother Earth lovingly encircle and embrace you.

"Let us not look back in anger nor forward in fear, but around in awareness."
James Thurber

Aside from the luxuriant music from your audio system or the whisper of slipstreaming wind, all you may notice while driving is the intermittent flashes of the utility poles and other cars chaotically scurrying to who knows where. But at least you have those if you're present and not thinking about some past or future event that can neither be changed nor assured to occur. If you make a point of being more aware of your surroundings, including the people, other animals and life happenings, from the tiniest details to the grand illusion of the incarnated matrix, then you can truly live a happy and contented life of love and gratitude.

"Wake at dawn with a winged heart and give thanks for another day of loving."
Kahlil Gibran

We are blessed with the awareness provided by our five senses, and a small number of people enjoy the abnormal benefits of a sixth. To maximize the advantages of your senses, bring as much as you possibly can into your conscious awareness. Smell the fragrance of the air and plants. Hear the trees in the breeze. Listen to the sounds of life and to the silence between the sounds. Pause often on your path. Don't just eat to fill your belly – relish your food with zest as did author Elizabeth Gilbert in Italy in her now classic memoir, *Eat Pray Love.* Savour the flavour and feel the nourishment healing your temple. Truly appreciate the bounty available in this precise moment. Instead of awaiting a future occasion, which you hope will bring you happiness, see and be grateful for the beauty all around you and be happy in the Now. Human life consists of a limited series of precious moments, so be completely present and be thankful for each one of them, for they're irreplaceable. Yesterday is gone and never to return. If we had arrived in this incarnation with an operations manual, it would have plainly proclaimed that we should live simply and enjoy the ride.

The natural human state of peace and happiness may be found more readily if you choose to avoid hiding behind an artificial ego. Ego, the conditioned individual mental sphere of the "little mind", as described by Zen Master Shunryu Suzuki, is where fear is manifested. Instead, be in the "big mind", the Field, by being vulnerable with others, since that's the place where love may be found. Touch everything with loving compassion and respect. Be grateful for all your blessings. Be aware of and appreciate the diverse and sensually rich mystery that is life. By living thoughtfully in this manner – with consciousness – you can truly live a wonderful experiential life, and when your time arrives, pass away with no regrets. For now, just be.

"I would maintain that thanks are the highest form of thought, and that gratitude is happiness doubled by wonder." G. K. Chesterton

Consciousness

"The ultimate value of life depends upon awareness and the power of contemplation rather than upon mere survival." Aristotle

For centuries, consciousness has been viewed with skepticism by the mechanistic mainstream scientific community. But in recent decades, the subject has become a major field of study. Philosophers, past and present, have and continue to struggle to understand the nature of consciousness and clearly define its essential properties. Questions continue to be asked whether it will ever be explained mechanistically, if non-human consciousness exists and how it can be recognized. Consciousness has been defined as the quality or state of awareness of an external object or of oneself, that is to say self-awareness. The terms sentience, subjectivity, wakefulness and the ability to experience or feel have also been associated with the concept. Nevertheless, leading edge philosophers and quantum physicists believe there to be a broadly shared underlying intuition about it. There are four distinct levels.

The first is unconscious unconsciousness. Sadly, most people never escape this stage and remain asleep, oblivious to the fact that they're sleep-walking though life. Usually the result of programmed limiting beliefs, they're essentially unthinking drones – lost in the land of separateness – and unknowingly continue to attract negative energy into their lives. They blame external events for their humdrum or calamitous lives, and assume zero responsibility for things that happen or don't happen to them. For solutions, including health and wellness, they're almost totally externally dependent. They fail to recognize apparent catastrophes as opportunities for growth and remain society's self-proclaimed victims.

The second level is conscious unconsciousness. Someone in this stage is, to some extent, aware of their negative thoughts and the possible consequences of having them. Gradually opening their eyes from slumber, they begin to realize that not everything is as it seems. It's like awakening from a lucid dream wherein they were aware they were dreaming and choose to rouse themselves to question their reality. They begin to understand the importance of assuming responsibility for both the constructive and destructive patterns affecting their life. Whereas it's exceedingly difficult to break free of the first level, the second is less challenging. With budding consciousness and growing gratitude, I sense a growing number of people escaping this level to create lasting change.

> *"If you want to feel rich, just count the things you have that money can't buy."*
> Old Proverb

In the third level of conscious consciousness, someone can deliberately choose to focus pure positive thought on a goal and move from a place of resistance to one of allowing something to enter or exit their life. They're aware they've been resisting and go about changing their attitude. For example, they deliberately intend an empty parking space to be awaiting their arrival, allow it to manifest into their reality and silently express their gratitude as they knowingly slip into it. They know that they know and don't know, and set about seeking answers to the latter.

The fourth and final level is unconscious consciousness. When someone arrives at this elevated level, life is simpler. They're *unaware* that they're aware. They don't know that they know; they just instinctively do, and are truly connected to Source. Success becomes automatic. They completely believe and never harbour any doubt, intuitively understand the power of their thoughts and as a matter of course, create a blissful life. Others may think they're just lucky. Maybe they are because they've spiritually evolved. Without realizing how or why, good things inexplicably happen to them. They instinctively think and feel grateful for their prosperity.

> *"Prosperity is a way of living and thinking, and not just money or things.*
> *Poverty is a way of living and thinking, and not just a lack of money or things."*
> Eric Butterworth

Fish in Water

A small boy calmly approached his father who was relaxing on a lake-side bench. Clutched gently in the boy's small hand was a tiny fish. He held up his prize and proudly reported, "Look what I found, father." As the man looked at the fish, he initially thought that its spirit had passed on. But then he noticed subtle signs of life, a slight quiver in its mouth and gill area.

"It seems to be alive, John, but barely so. Shall we try to save its life?" After the briefest of moments, the boy responded, "That's a good idea." Together, they carried the little fish to the water's edge, where the boy lovingly lowered it into the shallow water. However, there was meagre movement from the little creature.

"Maybe it needs more help," said the father. As he gently grasped it by the tip of its dorsal fin, he unhurriedly moved the fish through the water in a figure eight. At the same time, he began to patiently explain to his son that as people need oxygen from the air to breathe, fish need oxygen from water. People inhale air through their noses and mouths so their lungs can absorb life-giving oxygen, while fish must take in water past their gills to do the same. After several minutes of mellow ministration, the little fish slowly began to display subtle signs of life, weak at first, then gradually more pronounced. As the man finally released his tender grip, the tiny fish, no doubt exhausted by its brush with death, began to move away.

"We did it, John. It lives! You and I saved it from drowning." The boy beamed with delight. But a moment later, a puzzled look appeared on his face.

"Why was it drowning, father? I thought someone had to be *under* water to drown."

The man replied, "Somehow, something forced it from the water into the air where it could no longer breathe. And just as we cannot breathe under water and would drown, the fish couldn't breathe in the air. So, it could be said that it was drowning in air. But the fish probably didn't realize that he must return to the water to survive because he's unaware of water. He likely has no concept of it, or even of air, for that matter. He may indeed not even be self-aware as people are. If we were able to ask the little fish what he thinks about the water, if he could speak, he would probably ask, 'What is water?' He wouldn't realize that he lives in water, that it's critical for his survival." John listened to his father with wonder in his eyes. "Because we humans are conscious, at least to an infinitesimally small degree, and sometimes we must be reminded, we're aware of the difference between air and water, that we need air to breathe and that we'd effectively drown if deprived of it. The fish was drowning in air, but probably didn't understand what was happening to it or how to remedy its catastrophic situation."

"I think I understand, father." And another small light was ignited along the long and winding road to enlightenment.

As the little fish is unaware – or unconsciously unconscious – of the existence of the water, without which it would perish, most humans are also generally unconscious of their need for clean air. As they go about their day, it's safe to say that most people don't even think about air and take it totally for granted. They're as unconscious of their environment as the little fish is of its watery home. But unlike the fish which is unable to develop awareness or do anything about its environment, humankind can – if we choose to awaken in time.

People are generally unaware of not only their body's dependency for survival on our beloved Earthly environment, but also about whom they truly are – an integral and participating component of the divine matrix. As the fish is not self-aware, so is the vast majority of humankind to the truth. Just as the fish is oblivious to water, humans are also generally oblivious to the greater field of energy that surrounds and is us and everything in the Universe. And worse, most are unaware of their unawareness. Simply put, they don't know that they don't know; they're unconsciously unconscious. Nevertheless, each of us can awaken – if we so choose. All it takes is a spark of curiosity.

It's been said that man cannot find God. This may be true because, in a timeless quest, our species unconsciously looks outside for God. They look outward for solutions and for self-identification instead of inward – and actually fail to see at all. Unfortunately, many people subscribe – as they have been generationally conditioned – to the concepts of competition and separateness, that their God is the one true God. Their limiting belief systems of fear, judgement, prejudice and discrimination blind them to Source, which is all around and in all of us everywhere.

"The one thing that a fish can never find is water, and the one thing that man can never find is God." Eric Butterworth

Chapter Thirty-Six

Relief in Belief

"Men often become what they believe themselves to be. If I believe I cannot do something, it makes me incapable of doing it. But when I believe I can, then I acquire the ability to do it even if I didn't have it in the beginning."
Mahatma Gandhi

A Paradigm Shift

"Destiny is no matter of chance; it is a matter of choice. It is not a thing to be waited for; it is a thing to be achieved." William Jennings Bryan

Not long ago, anyone who believed space flight possible was considered at best, to be highly imaginative or at worse, a delusional lunatic and ostracized from mainstream society. Mankind believed our Earth to be flat and that anyone insane enough to sail to the distant horizon would meet a horrible demise in the gaping jaws of a giant sea monster or tumble to a tragic death off the edge of the world. If man was meant to fly, God would have given him wings. Speak with someone on the other side of the planet via wireless radio? Pure fantasy. Run a mile in under four minutes? It's never been done because it's not humanly possible; nobody told Roger Bannister he couldn't do it. Heat food with microwaves? What a whimsical idea. The Earth revolves around the sun? Poppycock! I'm going to send you to the moon; oh, wait – Neil Armstrong's boot-print is already there. Computers that will do sophisticated mathematical calculations in nanoseconds? Get real. Map the human genome system? What's a genome? Accelerate particles to the speed of light? Are you off your meds?

Examples abound of what were once considered impossible achievements, but are now commonplace. I believe that virtually anything is possible. If someone can imagine it, then it's possible. Untold records continue to be broken. Scientific and technological discoveries continue to manifest. Miracles continue to occur. Why? Because beliefs continue to evolve.

My point is that the general perception of truth – belief – unquestionably changes and will continue to do so. While journeying toward the ultimate Universal Truth, today's accepted truth may be different from tomorrow's. Any limiting beliefs you possess, such as those that prevent you from being a top producer, meeting the love of your life, being in a perfect state of physical or emotional wellness or enjoying unending bliss and contentment, can change anytime. It's all a matter of choice, intention and attention and employing the power of thought. First, though, you must choose to change.

Few people believed that a flying human was possible or that the world was a sphere. And many people still don't believe that we're energetically interconnected spiritual beings having a physical experience. However, in spite of the naysayers, a small minority regularly choose to ignore current mainstream beliefs and resistant "laws" of science by breaking free from their programmed beliefs. They follow their own imaginations – their own beliefs – to forge ahead, often in the face of ridicule and persecution, to bring their beliefs into reality. And behold – a miracle! I'm sure you've heard the expression of a new idea first being ignored, then ridiculed until it's found to be self-evident. Well, what I'm suggesting here is no different.

What do you believe about yourself? Do you feel you're smart enough to succeed? Are you happy? You may be an unhappy low producer and believe that without divine intervention, that's where you're destined to remain for the remainder of your days. You may continue to live alone while perpetually pining for romance, but lack the self-love necessary to achieve and maintain a successful relationship. Remember that such feelings relate to your life situation, and are not you. If you wish to improve your life and your career, you must change that belief by first making a conscious choice and a serious commitment to change your situation. Have faith in miracles, for they occur regularly. You possess the innate power to jettison self-limiting beliefs and dismiss all thoughts of personal change being impossible. By deliberate conscious choice, your life-long frame of reference can undergo a paradigm shift. Believe that change is not only possible, but that it has happened already, and the Universe will catch up.

As you begin the process of changing your personality and altering your life, when you stop acting and begin to behave in a manner more congruent with your genuine self, others may ignore you. Some may criticize or not even recognize you because you're different, and no longer feel comfortable around you. They may not relate with you anymore and *blame* your metamorphosis on some emotional issue. That's okay because their perception of your "problem" demonstrates your progressive metamorphosis from caterpillar to butterfly, while they remain stuck in their old conservative no-growth paradigm. As you develop, because you're no longer in sync with them, you may lose friends. The "new" you will attract new dynamic thinkers who share your beliefs, and who offer support and encouragement to continue on your path of spiritual growth. So, fear not. Be who you genuinely choose to be and you'll attract your heart's desire, whether it's business, adventure, love or anything you can dream.

> *"You laugh at me because I'm different. I laugh at you*
> *because you're all the same." Abdullah Ahmad*

Wander in Wonder

> *"If you're really listening, if you're awake to the poignant beauty of the world,*
> *your heart breaks regularly. In fact, your heart is made to break; its purpose*
> *is to burst open again and again so that it can hold ever more wonders."*
> *Andrew Harvey*

Wonder is wonderful. When you wonder, your identity changes because you move into and become engaged in a practical relationship with the subject of your wonderment. Your imagination soars, thereby raising your energy frequency. Albert Einstein said that imagination is more important than knowledge. Well, without the power to imagine, there'd be no significant knowledge. All progress begins with a critical and independent thinker freely imagining something previously unimaginable, having a thought about something considered impossible at the time. They wondered.

Neil Kramer, in his insightful book, *The Unfoldment,* expressed almost poetically how imagination is related to reality; "The greatest achievements from the greatest men and women are often feats of the imagination. Acts of ingeniousness always arise from the subtle but miraculous crucible of the inner realm. Throw in a healthy dose of tenacity and application, and that quiet spark of potential transmutes into a spectacular blaze of materialism. Imagination is the beginning of reality. It is the holographic engine for creating certain energy configurations that we call *form*. With the proper concentration of will, intent, spirit and discipline, those forms can achieve a level of consistency that may convey them from the inside to the outside, should we so wish. The dream of consciousness shifts its density and becomes an actual thing, a thing we can witness and experience. The more coherent and solid it is, the stronger its manifestation in consensus reality and the more people can share in it."

When you have a peaceful moment, slip gently into wonder and imagine living a happy and contented lifestyle with a steady stream of smiling, trusting loyal clients. Imagine driving your shiny luxury automobile into the garage of your beautiful home on a shady street after gratefully depositing several large commission cheques into your ever-expanding credit union account. With consistency, your spirits will climb since it's tough to witness a miracle without being emotionally engaged with it. It becomes you.

The Universe doesn't differentiate between real or imagined. When you begin to consistently feel good, your restrictive limiting beliefs will begin to relax and with persistence, eventually dissipate. Your doubts will dissolve and you'll transition into a place where "lucky" things happen. And once there, you'll embrace a fresh and exciting reality paradigm plump with possibilities.

"It is a great piece of skill to know how to guide
your luck even while waiting for it." Baltasar Gracian

WOW in NOW

"The noblest pleasure is the joy of understanding." Leonardo da Vinci

Be in the Now. This is popular advice these days from numerous philosophical luminaries, one of whom is Tim Freke. Philosopher, scholar, free-thinker and internationally respected authority on world spirituality, his books embrace both science and spirituality. In *The Mystery Experience: A Revolutionary Approach to Spiritual Awakening*, he describes an exhilarating journey for adventurers into the mystery experience of life. What is the now? How long is the now? What is a moment? What actually is life? Can you define it? Freke reminds us to wonder and become "deep awake", to know the "deep self" and feel the "deep love", to celebrate life and to learn to think "paralogically" beyond the limits of normal logic, to think critically outside the box of conventional wisdom.

He posits that if you're not curious about life, you're already half dead, asleep. To be curious is to wonder about the mysteries of life. While in the state of wonderment, you'll not be worried, stressed or feel some other negative energy. When wondering, you're on the road to awakening, to consciousness. When asked to describe awakening, Freke says it's like trying to describe a beautiful sunset to someone who has been blind since birth. Try to describe the colour red to a friend. What would you say? Well, it's like the colour of blood; you compare it to something known. If I say I'm feeling happy, you understand since you've also experienced it. So, I don't have to describe it. Communication and understanding is often defined by comparison to previous experience. But when someone begins to awaken, they'll just know.

"Find ecstasy in life; the mere sense of living is joy enough." Emily Dickinson

Freke believes that "the WOW is not just some passing peak experience or ultimately irrelevant high. Spiritual awakening affects how we think, feel and act. It gives rise to a new way of living our everyday lives." He goes on to say that "if we never dare to examine life, we subsist in a semi-conscious stupor." I share his belief; to live and love life more fully, we must begin to awaken, to become aware of the wonderment that is us and everything around us, to question everything. If you can become present, without regretting the past or worrying about the future, you can experience joy. And as I continue to emphasize, an effective way to be present is to regularly feel and express gratitude for all the miracles already in your life.

It's kind of a catch-22; if you express heart-felt gratitude for all your blessings, be they large or small, you'll be in wonder. If you pause to be in wonder, you'll instinctively appreciate everything wonderful in your life. As I've said, it's impossible to feel happiness and joy if you're not completely in the present moment. Freke suggests that "if you wonder deeply enough, you'll start to awaken. You'll become conscious of the breathtaking mystery of existence and the mystery experience will spontaneously arise." Begin by truly seeing and appreciating yourself and everything around you, including the exquisite details and loveliness that is life.

"After forty years intensely exploring the philosophy and practice of spiritual awakening", Freke's books are "refreshingly down-to-earth, profoundly funny and uncompromisingly authentic" and make "the awakened state available to all." If you're interested in learning more, I highly recommend the works by this knowledgeable and entertaining self-proclaimed stand-up philosopher. But know this; all we truly have is Now. Believe it.

"Once we believe in ourselves, we can risk curiosity, wonder, spontaneous delight, or any experience that reveals the human spirit." E. E. Cummings

Coincidence or Serendipity?

"As we express our gratitude, we must never forget that the highest appreciation is not to utter words, but to live by them." John F. Kennedy

A gradual awakening is occurring in our world. A whisper of change is rising into a more voluminous, yet velvety voice of progress in human evolution. It's far from reaching a crescendo, but tune in to the higher frequency wave of awakening. To evolve, you must be prepared to change, to grow, for the terms are synonymous. Be open to it. Accept life as it happens because there are no coincidences. Everything that happens to you has a purpose – absolutely everything. Whether an experience seems fortunate or catastrophic, surrender to it. Learn and advance at every gifted opportunity. Think deeply and critically.

Your life is like a stream, ever in motion. By struggling against the current, you'll exhaust yourself while drifting inevitably to your destiny. Unfortunately, though, you'll be facing the wrong direction and not see what's coming, nor will you enjoy the ride. Embrace life, not with your eyes wide shut, but wide open. Go with the flow because there's nothing you want or need upstream. Upstream is yesterday. It's old news. That's where the water came from. Enjoy the freshness of the ride and the fabulous view on the way to the ocean.

I cannot over-emphasize that life is a multitude of choices. And your many *conscious* choices determine which path you follow and how your life unfolds. When you awaken tomorrow, begin to choose, not based on fear, but on love of self and the world at large. Be inner quiet for a moment and listen. Just sit for a few moments. Don't automatically leap into habitual thinking about the new day. Feel your environment. Just be; you're a human *being* – not a human *doing*.

Hug yourself because you're the most important person in the world. Love, respect and trust yourself and everyone around you throughout your day because you're connected to everyone and everything everywhere. Refrain from judging others because you're only judging yourself. Choose to have a good day and to do what you can to help others enjoy their day too. Express gratitude for all your blessings, most of which money can't buy. Be grateful for your ability to open your eyes to see, to rise from a warm bed and stand on two feet, to feel the comfortable carpet as you walk to the bathroom to cleanse yourself in a warm shower. Be thankful for your comfortable clothes and nutritious food. Be grateful for the abundance in your life.

With this attitude, you will indeed enjoy a wonderful life – today, tomorrow and the day after. Your positive energy will attract like energy. Your real estate practice will flourish. Imagine love all around you. Realize that imagination creates your entire physical life in a world that is unmistakably a grand illusion. Michael Roads expressed it well when he said that you're not your body, but a "magnificent metaphysical multi-dimensional being of love and light". And remember that energy flows where attention goes. Consciously choose unconditional love, for it's all anyone really needs.

"I laugh, I love, I hope, I try, I hurt, I need, I fear, I cry. And I know you do the same things too. So we're really not that different, me and you." Colin Raye

The Greatest Lie Ever Told

"The ego creates separation, and separation creates suffering.
The ego is therefore clearly pathological." Eckhart Tolle

Eckhart Tolle wrote a wonderfully simple passage in his book, *A New Earth; Awakening to Your Life's Purpose.* He said that people often seem to be happy, but are not. When asked how they're doing, with a smiling façade, the customary response is "I'm fine" or "I'm great" or "no complaints" or "if I were any happier, I'd be locked up". They may habitually respond by asking the same question in return and receive a similar programmed response. It's arguably the greatest lie told every day around the world. It has become an accepted but hollow societal greeting without sincere meaning.

By participating in this traditional ritual, you're playing a conditioned ego role because you're expected to. Regrettably, that's how society generally functions. We each follow a prescribed script and play our part. To gain acceptance and hopefully win love and respect, we sometimes repress our true feelings and beliefs. However, winning warmth requires the opposite behaviour; only with honesty will there be truth in a relationship.

Tolle says that depression is common when unhappiness is hidden "behind a smiling exterior and brilliant white teeth". He suggests that "if there is unhappiness in you, first you need to acknowledge that it is there. But don't say, 'I'm unhappy.' Unhappiness has nothing to do with who you are." Recognize that there may be unhappiness *in* you – and make up your mind to investigate. He says that "action may be required to change the situation or remove yourself from it." Your unhappiness is never your situation, but the result of your thoughts and reaction to that situation. Aside from a painful physical assault, no one can hurt you or make you unhappy unless you permit them. Retain your power. Make yourself consciously aware of your thoughts and "separate them from the situation, which is always neutral". Be in the Now.

"There is no cure for birth and death, save to enjoy the interval."
George Santayana

Plain Living and High Thinking

"Participate joyfully in the sorrows of the world. We cannot cure the
world of sorrows, but we can choose to live in joy."
Joseph Campbell

What really matters? How somebody spoke to you yesterday or last year or what happened to you recently or when you were a child? I don't think so. With the considerable misfortune I've experienced in my life, if I made it matter to me, I'd be a basket-case. Imagine you have only 127 minutes left to live. Now, consider your life to date. What truly mattered?

How important was the erratic driver that cut you off this morning? How critical to your general happiness were those occasions when a client, spouse or colleague betrayed your trust? How significant today is that derogatory remark made to you ten years ago? Does it really matter that your favourite sports team hasn't won the championship for two decades, or that your lawn is perpetually filled with dandelions? How critical is it to your life today that you were jilted by a lover years ago or that your mother never said she loves you? Why continue to hear your father's harsh judgements about not being good enough? What's the real difference which political party wins the next election? Does it truly matter that you lost a listing or a prospective new client last week?

> *"More important than learning how to recall things is finding ways*
> *to forget things that are cluttering the mind." Eric Butterworth*

Past events can only affect you in the present if you permit them. Free yourself and your thoughts from the beliefs programmed in your subconscious and firmly state your intent to be present, for now is all that truly matters. You don't have the past anymore – only the memories of it – along with current interpretations of those memories. Nor obviously do you have the future. All you truly have is Now. Become more heart-centred instead of brain-centred. Clear your mind of all the clutter than doesn't really matter because it's just junk. Follow your intuitive knowing and synchronistic occurrences will manifest.

What really matters is how much you love and have been loved, how much joy and happiness you give and receive. How many hearts do you help dance with delight? How many people do you happily serve? Are you living a kind life? What is most important; how much money you make or how many smiles you elicit? Feel more and think less. Avoid low-vibrational energy diversions such as negative people seeking power over you. Skip unimportant events. Don't make mountains out of mole hills. Just see them in your rear-view mirror and enjoy the journey. Refuse to live in fear.

> *"You shall have joy or you shall have power, said God;*
> *you shall not have both." Ralph Waldo Emerson*

In Dr. Richard Carlson's wonderful book, *Don't Sweat the Small Stuff ... and it's all small stuff,* he suggests that you refuse to allow life's little things from driving you crazy. To be happy in the midst of a harried and stressful life, you must maintain an oasis of calm. Put things into perspective by thinking of your problems as potential lessons, by remembering that you'll not likely accomplish everything before you pass. Focus on doing things one at a time. Live in the present moment and learn to trust your intuition. Live each day as if it might be your last. Dance like nobody is watching and sing like no one is listening. Laugh long and often.

> *"Happiness often sneaks in through a door you didn't know you had left open."*
> John Barrymore

Tolle recommends that you not seek happiness, for if you do, "you won't find it because seeking is the antithesis of happiness. Happiness is ever elusive, but freedom from unhappiness is attainable now by facing what is, rather than making up stories about it. Unhappiness covers up your natural state of well-being and inner peace, the source of true happiness." Live in gratitude, away from unhappiness, by being in a state of peace and acceptance. That's where you'll find happiness. Stop striving to be happy and you'll increase the odds of organically attaining that blissful state.

World-renowned and esteemed independent thinker, Henry David Thoreau, whose books have been translated into virtually every major language, believed that to be truly happy, one need only keep life simple and uncomplicated. To live a joyful life, he advised others to flee the false gods preaching the curse known as a "high standard of living", to embrace unpretentious ambitions and reject the common measurements of success, to scorn public opinion, ignore the personal judgements of others and to delight in the simple pleasures provided freely by Mother Earth. He believed that the secret to happiness may be found in "plain living and high thinking", while espousing an almost religious love of nature.

> *"Who is the happiest of men? He who values the merits of others,*
> *and in their pleasure takes joy, even as though t'were his own."*
> Johann Wolfgang von Goethe

Since work is pragmatically part of life, to be truly successful in any business, you must be authentically happy. And this requires that you be on a path to spiritual awakening, to think critically and independently and to remember who you are. It can be a long and sometimes lonely road, but there are other travelers and sign posts along the way to serve as guides, if you're aware enough to recognize them. Allow things to happen rather than try to make them happen. Instead of acting from fears based on programming and past experiences, think and act spontaneously. If you worry no more, shed regrets, avoid conflict and judgment of others – or yourself – you're well on your way to achieving true happiness. If you can smile for no apparent reason, feel grateful for the small moments between daily activities, enjoy warm, respectful connections with people, animals and nature and love without expecting in return, you're making beautiful blissful progress. And if you occasionally trip and fall on your life journey, as Julia Child famously said; "If you drop the lamb, just pick it up. Who's going to know?" Get back up and keep moving. It's okay to make mistakes.

The irony of this philosophy is that by simply enjoying each moment of your life, by being grateful for each blessing, by appreciating that you *always* have enough, the resulting positive attitude and personal happiness will trigger your business and your personal life to flourish. You'll become unsinkable. What you seize is what you get. So, seize the day and enjoy each and every moment as if it were your last.

"Joy increases as you give it and diminishes as you try to keep it for yourself. In giving it, you will accumulate a deposit of joy greater than you ever believed possible." Norman Vincent Peale

I Wish You Enough

I wish you enough sun to keep your attitude bright.
I wish you enough rain to appreciate the sun more.
I wish you enough happiness to keep your spirit alive.
I wish you enough pain so that the smallest joys in life appear much bigger.
I wish you enough gain to satisfy your wanting.
I wish you enough loss to appreciate all that you possess.
I wish you enough hellos to get you through the final good-bye.

Bob Perks

Quotation References

- **Abraham Lincoln** (1809–1865), former American President
- **Adlin Sinclair,** British-born businessman, speaker; bestseller The Answer
- **Albert Camus** (1913–1960), French Nobel Prize author, philosopher
- **Albert Einstein** (1879–1955), theoretical physicist
- **Albert Ellis,** M.A., Ph.D (1913–2007), American psychologist
- **Albert Schweitzer** (1875–1965), theologian, musician, philosopher, physician
- **Alice Koller,** writer, essayist, philosopher; *An Unknown Woman*
- **Alphonso Lingis** (1933), American philosopher
- **Amelia Earhart** (1897–1937), American aviation pioneer, author
- **Amy Cuddy,** American social psychologist, researcher, Harvard Professor
- **Andy Rooney** (1919–2011), American radio/TV writer; CBS News
- **Andy Warhol** (1928–1987), American renowned controversial artist
- **Anita DeFrantz** (1952), American Olympic rowing athlete
- **Anne Frank** (1929–1945), highly discussed Jewish Holocaust victim
- **Andrew Harvey** (1952), author, scholar, teacher; 30+ books
- **Andrew Jackson King** (1833–1923), lawman, lawyer, legislator, judge
- **Anthony J. D'Angelo,** author/editor
- **Anton Chekhov** (1860–1904), Russian physician, dramatist, author
- **Aristotle** (384–322 BC), Greek philosopher, polymath
- **Arthur Golden** (1956), American writer; bestselling Memoirs of a Geisha
- **Arthur Guiterman** (1871–1943), American writer
- **Ayn Rand** (1905-1982), novelist, philosopher, playwright; Atlas Shrugged
- **Baltasar Gracian** (1601–1658), Spanish Jesuit, writer, philosopher
- **Barbara Corcoran** (1949), American businesswoman, author, *Shark Tank*
- **Benjamin Disraeli** (1804–1881), British PM, literary figure
- **Ben Stein** (1944), American actor, writer, political/economic commentator
- **Benjamin Franklin** (1706–1790), author, political theorist, politician, scientist
- **Bill Nighy** (1949), English actor
- **Bill Watterson,** American cartoonist
- **Bo Bennett** (1972), American businessman, author, speaker
- **Bob Hope** (1903–2003), English-born American comedian, vaudevillian

- **Brian Tracy** (1944), motivational speaker, author
- **Brit Hume** (1943), American conservative political commentator, TV journalist
- **Buddha,** sage on whose teachings Buddhism was founded
- **Carl Gustav Jung** (1875–1961), Swiss psychotherapist, psychiatrist
- **Carl Sandburg** (1878–1967), American writer, poet, editor
- **Cary Grant** (1904–1986), debonair film, stage actor, Hollywood leading man
- **Charlie Chaplin** (1889–1977), English comic actor/filmmaker
- **Chris Martenson,** PhD, MBA, author/macro-economic trend forecaster
- **Colin Raye** (1959), American country music singer
- **Confucius** (551–479 BC), Chinese teacher, editor, politician, philosopher
- **Corrie Ten Boom** (1892–1983), Dutch Christian writer
- **Dale Carnegie** (1888–1955), American author
- **David Lloyd George** (1863-1945), first and only Welsh Prime Minister
- **David Guterson** (1956), American novelist, short story writer, poet, journalist
- **David Sarnoff** (1891–1971), American businessman, pioneer of US radio/TV
- **Dean Acheson** (1893–1971), American lawyer; former US SecState
- **Denis Waitley** (1933), American motivational speaker, author
- **Desmond Tutu** (1931), South African social rights activist
- **Diana Scharf Hunt,** The Tao of Time-Time Management for the Real World
- **Doug Larson** (1926), former columnist, newspaper editor
- **Dwight D. Eisenhower** (1890–1969), 34th US President
- **Eckhart Tolle,** author, spiritual teacher; A New Earth and others
- **Erwin Schrödinger** (1887–1961), Austrian Nobel winning physicist
- **Edward Young** (1681–1765), English poet
- **E.E. Cummings** (1894-1962), American poet
- **Eleanor Roosevelt** (1884–1962), former American First Lady
- **Emily Dickinson** (1830–1886), introverted, reclusive American poet
- **Epictetus** (55-135 AD), former slave; became Greek sage, Stoic philosopher
- **Eric Butterworth** (1916-2003), Canadian minister, *Spiritual Economics*
- **Erica Jong** (1942), American author, teacher
- **Ernest Hemingway** (1899-1961), American author, journalist
- **Fran Lebowitz** (1950), American author; sardonic social commentary
- **Francis Bacon** (1561-1626), English philosopher, scientist, orator, author
- **Frank Sinatra** (1915-1998), American actor, singer, filmmaker
- **Frank Tibolt** (1897-1989), writer/motivator/success trainer
- **Frantz Fanon** (1925-1961), French-Algerian psychiatrist, philosopher, writer
- **Friedrich Nietzsche** (1844-1900), German philologist, philosopher
- **Fulton J. Sheen** (1895-1979), American archbishop of the RC Church
- **G.K. Chesterton** (1874-1936), English writer
- **Gary Zukav** (1942), American spiritual author of 4 NY Times bestsellers
- **George Bernard Shaw** (1856-1950), Irish playwright, novelist, writer, socialist

- George Burns (1896-1996), American comedian
- George Dennison Prentice (1802-1870), former editor of Louisville Journal
- George R. Kirkpatrick (1867-1937), American anti-militarist writer, activist
- George MacDonald (1824-1905), Scottish author, poet, novelist
- George Santayana (1863-1952), philosopher, essayist, poet, novelist
- Gisele Bundchen (1980), Brazilian fashion model, actress, producer
- Groucho Marx (1890-1977) American comedian, film, TV star
- H. G Wells (1866-1946), English writer; Father of Science Fiction
- H. Stanley Judd (1936), American author, film producer; Yale Honors Grad
- Hannah More (1745-1833), English religious writer, poet, playwright
- Harold MacMillan (1894-1986), former Conservative UK PM
- Helen Gurley Brown (1922-2012), American author/publisher
- Helen Keller (1880-1968), American author, political activist, lecturer
- Henry David Thoreau (1817-1862), author, poet and philosopher
- Henry Ford (1863-1947), American industrialist
- Henry James (1843-1916), American writer
- Henry R. Luce (1898-1967), publisher of Time, Life, Sports Illustrated
- Henry Wadsworth Longfellow (1807-1882), American poet, educator
- Herbert Hoover (1874-1964), former American President
- Herbie Hancock (1940), American pianist, keyboardist, jazz band leader
- Jack Bowman (1875-1931), Canadian-born businessman, American hotelier
- Jalal ad-Din Rumi (1207-1273), Persian poet, jurist, theologian, Sufi mystic
- James Allen (1864-1912), British philosophical writer; self-help pioneer
- James Thurber (1894-1961), American author, cartoonist, celebrated wit
- Jean-Paul Sartre (1905-1980), French existentialist, philosopher, novelist
- Jef I Richards B.A., PhD, J.D., advertising/public policy, marketing
- Jiddu Krishnamurti (1895-1986), Indian writer, philosophy, spirituality
- Jim Rohn (1930-2009,) American entrepreneur, author
- Joan of Arc (?-1431), 15th century virgin saint, national French heroine
- Johann Wolfgang von Goethe (1749-1832), writer, artist, politician
- John Barrymore (John Sidney Blyth) (1882-1942), American actor
- John F Kennedy (1917-1963), JFK, 35th American President
- John Lennon (1940-1980), English musician, singer, songwriter; Beatles
- John Kenneth Galbraith (1908-2006), Canadian/American economist
- John Maynard Keynes (1883-1946), British economist
- John Muir (1838-1914), American founder of The Sierra Club
- John Ruskin (1819-1900), English prominent social thinker
- Jonathan Swift (1667-1745), Anglo-Irish cleric/satirist/essayist/poet
- Joseph Campbell (1904-1987), American mythologist, writer, lecturer
- Julian Barnes (1946), contemporary English writer; Man Booker Prize
- Kahlil Gibran (1883-1931), Lebanese American artist/poet/writer

- **Karen Ravn**, published writer; *Little Seeds of Wisdom*
- **Karl Barth** (1886-1968), Swiss Reformed theologian
- **Katherine Mansfield** (1888-1923), prominent modernist fiction writer
- **Kurt Vonnegut** (1922-2007), American writer, critical pacifist intellectual
- **Lao Tzu** (6th century BCE), Father of Taoism, philosopher of ancient China
- **Lena Horne** (1917-2010), African-American singer, actress
- **Leonardo da Vinci** (1452-1519), Italian Renaissance genius polymath
- **Leslie Temple-Thurston**, enlightenment teacher
- **Madeleine Albright** (1937), first woman US Secretary of State
- **Mahatma Gandhi** (1869-1948), preeminent leader of Indian nationalism
- **Marcus Tullius Cicero** (106-43 BC), Roman philosopher, political theorist
- **Marcus Aurelius Antoninus** (121-180 AD), Roman Emperor
- **Marianne Williamson**, spiritual teacher, lecturer, author
- **Maimonides** (1135-1204), influential Middle Ages scholar/physician
- **Margaret Mitchell** (1900-1949), American Pulitzer Prize author
- **Mark Twain** (1835-1910), American author, humorist
- **Mark Victor Hansen** (1948), American inspirational/motivational speaker
- **Martin Luther King Jr.** (1929-1968), American clergyman, activist
- **Martha Beck** (1962), American sociologist, therapist, life coach, author
- **Martina Navratilova** (1956), retired Czech-American tennis player
- **Marvin Gaye** (1939-1984), American singer-songwriter, musician
- **Mason Cooley** (1927-2002), American former professor emeritus
- **Maya Angelou** (1928), American author, 30 honorary doctoral degrees
- **Melody Beattie** (1948), author introduced term 'codependent'
- **Michael LeBoeuf**, American business author, speaker/consultant
- **Morgan Freeman** (1937), American actor, film director, narrator
- **Mother Teresa** (1910-1997), Albanian born, Indian RC Religious Sister
- **Napoleon Hill** (1883-1970), American author; Think and Grow Rich
- **Norman Vincent Peale** (1898-1993), author; The Power of Positive Thinking
- **Oprah Winfrey** (1954), American talk show host, actress, producer
- **Orison Swett Marden** (1850-1924), American spiritual author
- **Pablo Picasso** (1881-1973), Spanish painter, sculptor
- **Peter McWilliams** (1949-2000), American writer, cannabis activist
- **Paul Samuelson** (1915-2009), Father of Modern Economics
- **Peter Drucker** (1909-2005), American management consultant, author
- **Rabindranath Tagore** (1861-1941), Bengali; Nobel Prize in Literature
- **Ralph Marston**, professional football player
- **Ralph C. Smedley** (1878-1965), founder of Toastmasters International
- **Ralph Waldo Emerson** (1803-1882), American essayist, lecturer , poet
- **Ray Kroc** (1902-1984), American businessman, former CEO of McDonald's
- **Red Adair** (1915-2004), American innovator in oil well firefighting

- Richard Bach (1936), American writer
- Robert G. Allen (1948) MBA, Cdn/US multi-millionaire real estate author
- Robert Louis Stevenson (1850-1894), Scottish novelist, poet, essayist
- Robert McCloskey (1914-2003), award-winning American writer/illustrator
- Rodney Lovell (1961), Australian educator
- Rosalynn Carter (1927), former US First Lady
- Ross Perot (1930), American businessman
- Roy H. Williams (1958), American best-selling author, marketing consultant
- Roy Rogers (1911-1998), American singer, cowboy actor; 100+ movies
- Russell Brand (1975), English comedian, actor, author
- Ruth Stafford Peale (1906-2008), American writer, editor, speaker
- Sam Ewing (1949), baseball player; master's degree in Exercise Physiology
- Samuel Johnson (1709-1784), English writer, poet, essayist, moralist
- Sarah Ban Breathnach, New York Times Best Selling author, teacher
- Sir Archibald McIndoe (1900-1960), pioneering plastic surgeon
- Socrates (469-399 BC), classical Greek Athenian philosopher
- Sophocles (497/6-406/5 BC), most fêted playwright of Athens, Greece
- Stephen Covey (1932-2012), American educator, author, businessman
- Dr. Steve Maraboli, American behavioral scientist, author
- Steven Jobs (1955-2011), American entrepreneur, marketer, inventor
- Stephen Wright, American comedian
- Tacitus (AD 56-117), Roman Empire senator, historian
- Thich Nhat Hanh (1926), Vietnamese Zen Buddhist monk, teacher, author
- Thomas Edison (1847-1931), American, 4th most prolific inventor in history
- Thomas Huxley (1825-1895), English biologist known as 'Darwin's Bulldog'
- Thomas Leonard (1955-2003), American businessman; personal coaching
- W. Clement Stone (1902-2002), new-thought self-help author, philanthropist
- Walter Benjamin (1892-1940), German-Jewish Marxist philosopher
- Washington Allston (1779-1843), American painter, poet
- Washington Irving (1783-1859), American author, essayist, historian
- Waylon Jennings (1937-2002), American country singer, songwriter
- Wayne Dyer (1940), American self-help author, motivational speaker
- Will Rogers (1879-1935), American vaudeville actor, humorist
- Will Smith (1968), American TV/film actor, producer, rapper
- William Arthur Ward (1921-1994), writer of inspirational maxims
- William Cobbett (1763-1835), English farmer, journalist
- William James (1842-1910), American philosopher, psychologist
- William Jennings Bryan (1860-1925), American politician, pacifist
- William Ralph Inge (1860-1954), English author, Anglican priest
- William Shakespeare (1564-1616), English poet, playwright
- William Somerset Maugham (1874-1965), British playwright, novelist

- **William Wordsworth** (1770-1850), major English Romantic poet
- **Win Borden,** former state legislator, business executive, farmer-philosopher
- **Winston Churchill** (1874-1965), Nobel Prize in Literature, former UK PM
- **Woody Allen** (1935), American screenwriter, director, actor
- **Yasutani Roshi** (1885-973), founder of the Sanbo Kyodan Zen Buddhist

"Our deepest fear is not that we are inadequate. Our deepest fear is that we are powerful beyond measure. It is our Light, not our Darkness, that most frightens us." Marianne Williamson

"Man is the religious animal. He is the only religious animal. He is the only animal that has the True Religion – several of them. He is the only animal that loves his neighbour as himself and cuts his throat if his theology isn't straight. He has made a graveyard of the globe in trying his honest best to smooth his brother's path to happiness and heaven."
Mark Twain

Further Reading

This short list is certainly not intended to be an exhaustive one, for there are countless other wonderful books available, not only by these esteemed authors, but a multitude of others equally worthy of your time. However, these may be enough to get you started down a new, exciting, adventurous path toward self-discovery and personal growth. Enjoy!

- *The Unfoldment – The Organic Path to Clarity, Power and Transformation* by Neil Kramer; www.neilkramer.com; New Page Books, A division of The Career Press Inc.
- *Spontaneous Evolution – Our Positive Future (And a Way to Get There From Here)* by Bruce H. Lipton, Ph.D. and Steve Bhaerman, and *Biology of Belief - Unleashing the Power of Consciousness, Matter and Miracles*, and *The Honeymoon Effect – The Science of Creating Heaven on Earth* by Bruce H. Lipton, Ph.D.; Hay House www.brucelipton.com
- *A New Earth – Awakening to Your Life's Purpose* and *The Power of Now: A Guide to Spiritual Enlightenment* by Eckhart Tolle; Namaste Publishing, Penguin USA, Dutton www.eckharttolle.com
- *Nonviolent Communication – A Language of Life* by Marshall B. Rosenberg, Ph.D., 2003; PuddleDancer Press www.nonviolentcommunication.com
- *Think and Grow Rich* by Napoleon Hill; Jeremy P. Tarcher/Penguin
- *Don't Worry, Make Money – Spiritual and Practical Ways to Create Abundance and More in Your Life*, and *Don't Sweat the Small Stuff and it's all small stuff*, by Richard Carlson, Ph.D.; Hyperion
- *Think on These Things* by Krishna Amurti; Harper Perennial
- *Fractal Time* by Gregg Braden; Hay House Inc *www.greggbraden.com*
- *The Source Field Investigations – The Hidden Science and Lost Civilizations behind the 2012 Prophesies* by David Wilcock; Dutton www.divinecosmos.com
- *Sacred Contracts – Awakening Your Divine Potential* by Caroline Myss; Harmony Books www.myss.com
- *Out of the Blue – Delight Comes into Our Lives* by Mark Victor Hansen and Barbara Nichols with Patty Hansen; Harper Collins Publishers Ltd.

- *New Passages – Mapping Your Life Across Time* by Gail Sheehy; Random House of Canada
- *Change Your Thoughts – Change Your Life – Living the Wisdom of the Tao, 10 Secrets for Success and Inner Peace, Inspiration* and *Getting in the Gap – Making Conscious Contact with God Through Meditation* by Dr. Wayne W. Dyer; Hay House
- *Sage-ing While Age-ing* by Shirley MacLaine; Atria Books
- *Chicken Soup for the Soul – 101 Stories to Open the Heart and Rekindle the Spirit* by Jack Canfield and Mark Victor Hansen; Health Communications Inc
- *The Monk Who Sold His Ferrari* and *The Greatness Guide* by Robin Sharma; Harper Collins Publishers Ltd
- *The Heart of the Soul – Emotional Awareness* and *The Seat of the Soul* by Gary Zukav and Linda Francis; Simon & Schuster Source
- *The Art of Smart Thinking* by James Hardt, Ph.D.; Biocybernaut Press
- *How Long Is Now? – A Journey to Enlightenment … and Beyond* by Tim Freke; Hay House www.themysteryexperience.com
- *Revolution from Within – A Book of Self-Esteem* by Gloria Steinem; Little, Brown and company
- *Awaken the Giant Within* by Anthony Robbins; Summit Books
- *The untethered soul; the journey beyond yourself* by Michael A. Singer; New Harbinger *Publications and Noetic Books,* distributed in Canada by *Raincoast Books*
- *The Marriage of Spirit – Enlightened Living in Today's World* by Leslie Temple-Thurston with Brad Laughlin; Corelight Publishing www.corelight. org www.marriageofspirit.com
- *Quiet: The Power of Introverts in a World That Can't Stop Talking* by Susan Cain; Random House, Inc., New York www.thepowerofintroverts.com
- *The Universe Within – From Quantum to Cosmos* by Neil Turok; House of Anansi Press Inc
- *The Highly Sensitive Person: How to Thrive When the World Overwhelms You* by Elaine N. Aron, Ph.D.; Kensington Publishing/Carol Publishing Group and Broadway Books, New York
- *TRUE REFUGE – Finding Peace and Freedom in Your Own Awakened Heart* by Tara Brach, PH.D.; Random House, Inc., New York.
- *Map of Heaven – How Science, Religion, and Ordinary People Are Proving the Afterlife,* and *Proof of Heaven – A Scientist's Case for the Afterlife,* by Eben Alexander, MD; Simon & Schuster http://www.ebenalexander.com/
- *Morphic Resonance – The Nature of Formative Causation* by Rupert Sheldrake; Park Street Press http://www.sheldrake.org/
- *The Essential Rumi –* Translation by Coleman Barks http://www. colemanbarks.com/

*"Your time is limited, so don't waste it living someone else's life.
Don't be trapped by dogma, which is living with the results
of other people's thinking. Don't let the noise of other's opinions
drown out your own inner voice. And most important,
have the courage to follow your heart and intuition.
They somehow already know what you truly want to become.
Everything else is secondary." Steve Jobs*

About the Author

Ross Wilson's first inclination to write emerged at the tender age of 10 when he penned a little boy's adventure story. To him, it was exciting stuff. But it was a decade later before his skills were officially recognized when, while attending Sheridan College, he was awarded the Archdeacon W.P. Robertson Prize in English. Since then, he has contributed to magazines and Real Estate Monthly (REM), a national trade newspaper, and enjoyed a sojourn as a columnist with a small town newspaper.

After studying business at Ryerson and a stint in the new home industry, he entered the resale realty business. Forty years later, he can boast a career that encompassed a highly productive referral sales practice and extensive experience as a brokerage owner, manager, trainer and mentor.

It's been said that those who can't do, teach. During a tumultuous life mixed with both personal adversity and much reward, this quiet introvert did it. It's also been said that a writer should write what they know. As an ardent reader and life-long student in the field, he knows real estate. He currently lives a peaceful life – with occasional business travails to the city – in rural Ontario. He may be reached at www.realty-voice.com.